The Developing World
An Introduction

E. S. SIMPSON

Longman Scientific & Technical
Longman Group UK Limited,
Longman House, Burnt Mill, Harlow,
Essex CM20 2JE, England
and Associated Companies throughout the world.

Copublished in the United States with John Wiley & Sons, Inc.,
605 Third Avenue, New York, NY 10158

© Longman Group UK Limited 1987

First published 1987
Reprinted 1990, 1993

British Library Cataloguing in Publication Data

Simpson, E. S.
The developing world: an introduction.
1. Developing countries — Economic conditions
I. Title
330.9'172'4   HC59.7
ISBN 0-582-30092-4

Library of Congress Cataloging-in-Publication Data
Simpson, E. S. (Edward Sinclair), 1926-
The developing world.

Bibliography: p.
Includes index.
1. Developing countries. 2. Economic development.
I. Title.
HC59.7.S535   1987   330.9172'4
ISBN 0-470-20783-7 (USA only)

Longman
Scientific &
Technical

Copublished in the United States with
John Wiley & Sons, Inc., New York

Longman Scientific & Technical
Longman Group UK Limited
Longman House, Burnt Mill, Harlow
Essex CM20 2JE, England
and Associated Companies throughout the world

Copublished in the United States with John Wiley & Sons, Inc.,
605 Third Avenue, New York, NY 10158

First published 1987
Reprinted 1988, 1989

British Library Cataloguing in Publication Data

Simpson, E. S.
    The developing world: an introduction.

    1. Developing countries – Economic conditions
    I. Title
    330.9172'4   HC59.7
ISBN 0-582-30092-4

Library of Congress Cataloging-in-Publication Data
Simpson, E. S. (Edward Smethurst), 1926–
    The developing world.

    Bibliography: p.
    Includes index.
    I. Developing countries – Economic conditions.
I. Title.
HC59.7.S4666   1986   330.9172'4   85-23945
ISBN 0-470-20683-7 (USA only).

Set in Linotron 202 10/12 pt Palatino
Produced by Longman Singapore Publishers (Pte) Ltd.
Printed in Singapore

For Julia, Alison and Ruth Claire
who growing up in the Developing World came to know mankind is one

Contents

List of Figures

List of plates

(All photographs are by the author)

1 Children in China
2 Children in Fiji
3 Villagers on the Jos Plateau, Nigeria
4 A village in Malawi
5 An anti-filariasis poster, Fiji
6 A worm-clinic poster, Port Harcourt, Nigeria
7 Family-planning poster, China
8 Family-planning poster, Tonga
9 Forest clearing by burning, central Nigeria
10 A shifting-cultivation field, central Nigeria
11 Fulani cattle on the move, northern Nigeria
12 Fulani cattle grazing stubble
13 Cotton growing on a peasant farm, northern Nigeria
14 Groundnut pyramids, northern Nigeria
15 Irrigated vegetable crops, Kano close-settled zone, Nigeria
16 Terraced vegetable small holdings, Sri Lanka
17 Rice nursery-beds, China
18 Paddy fields, Sri Lanka
19 Coconut small holding, Vanua Levu, Fiji
20 Harvesting sugar cane, Viti Levu, Fiji
21 Tea estate, Malawi
22 Rubber plantation, Malaysia
23 Hand-spinning, northern Nigeria
24 Hand-loom weaving, northern Nigeria
25 Labour-intensive tin paddock, Jos Plateau, Nigeria
26 Capital-intensive tin mining, Jos Plateau, Nigeria
27 Mini hydro-electricity station, China
28 Gas-turbine electricity station, Nigeria
29 Rural brickworks, China
30 Rural fan-making factory, China
31 Rural tractor factory, female welder, China
32 Rural tractor factory, the finished product, China
33 The Jurong industrial estate, Singapore
34 Flatted factories, Hong Kong
35 The container terminal, Singapore

List of tables

Preface

This book attempts to introduce its readers to the issues of development in the Developing World. It is designed as a beginning rather than an end and it inevitably leaves much unsaid. It is hoped that its bibliography will enable the reader to explore still further the issues raised. In it I have eschewed the use of the first person yet it is a book born of a long acquaintance with countries in the Developing World and my perception of it is inevitably a product of my experience. My first contact came as a result of my serving in the British navy during the Second World War. As a very young man I arrived in Ceylon, now Sri Lanka, and experienced the beauty, and the poverty, of a developing country. I had been at a school accustomed to see some of its pupils enter the Colonial Service and work in one of the patches of pink spread across the atlases of the day. A colonial empire had seemed a natural disposition of power and influence. I was shaken out of this unthinking acceptance when a young Sinhalese soldier told me that he had wished the Japanese had been victorious since this would have shown that the British were not all-powerful.

The intervening years have seen the collapse of that power as the British and other empires have been dismantled and scores of new independent nations have come into being. My eyes were opened further when, as a university don, I was seconded to Nigeria to help in the establishment of a new university. A minor incident gave me another glimpse into the development process. On the Jos plateau driving with half a dozen students on a field survey we passed a line of women from the local tribe. All were naked apart from a few leaves. Suddenly one of the students, a sophisticated young woman studying at this new university we had implanted in Nigeria, cried out 'There's my grandmother!' She was one of the line. It brought home to me the enormity of the shock which indigenous cultures experience as the material manifestations of development thrust their way into the heart of traditional values. But Nigeria taught me much more as it revealed to me the pain and trauma which many nations have experienced in the process of development. It put to the test many development theories in the searing heat of reality as I was witness to the tragedies of massacre and civil war.

In all this and in my present endeavour I am indebted to many individuals; indeed it is impossible to list them all but some I must mention. I owe a great debt of gratitude to Robert Steel who guided my scholarly interests into the Developing World and placed before me a challenge I could not resist. He has given me unfailing encouragement and support and I cannot thank him sufficiently. Second is the debt I owe to my friend Andrew Learmonth whose profound intellect I have always admired and envied. Third I wish to acknowledge the influence of Sam Richardson, former District Commissioner turned scholar, who showed me that the practice of pragmatism does not involve the abandonment of principle. All have been colleagues at one time or other. Their influence and friendship is always with me.

It has been my good fortune and privilege to have worked in the Developing World with and for men who were of rare distinction. I have abiding memories of the qualities of leadership and the unfailing courtesy of the late Ratu Sir Edward Cakobau, whose ancestors had ceded Fiji to Britain, and of the Prime Minister of Fiji, Ratu Sir Kamisese Mara, whose qualities of statesmanship are an example to everyone. But many are the men who each in his own way has revealed to me the nuances of meaning which are an essential to any attempt to understand societies other than one's own. Among them I must mention Savenaca Siwatibau and Israeli Lasaqa, C. P. Lo, Chek Lam So, Chi-Keung Leung and Tze-Nang Chiu, Kingsley Ologe, Samson Odingo and Justice Mlia. And there are the memories which remain vivid and indelible of the kindness and hospitality I have found throughout the Developing World. In Malawi I have enjoyed it both at the hands of those in high authority and of the poorest of peasants. In China I have been invited into the homes of people poor but dignified who with ancient courtesy have bid me share their limited resources. In the South Pacific I have enjoyed that open hospitality which the Fijians and Tongans combine with a gracious ceremonial. All shared kindnesses which made us one.

In the preparation of this book my particular thanks must go to three people; to Mrs Olive Teasdale for her great skill in the preparation of the maps and diagrams which illustrate it and to Miss Yvonne Lambord and Mrs Eunice Tubman who saw the conversion of a tangled manuscript into a typescript.

Most of all my indebtedness is to my wife, Christine, whose intellectual curiosity has been a constant delight and stimulus to me and whose ability to relate to, and be accepted by, peoples and societies new to her has done much to make us and our children a part of those societies we have known throughout the Developing World.

Acknowledgements

We are grateful to the following for permission to reproduce copyright material:
Mrs J. E. Allan for fig based on fig 8 p 95 (W. Allan 1965); The American Geographical Society for extracts from (J. H. Chang 1968) Vol. 58 No. 2 July 1968; Bell & Hyman Ltd for an extract from p 31 (T. G. McGee 1971); Cambridge University Press for extracts from (W. W. Rostow 1956); Jonathan Cape Ltd for the Estate of Ellen Thorp for extracts from (E. Thorp 1956); Croom Helm Ltd for extracts from (Hunter et al 1976) and p. 32 from *Trade and Developing Countries* by K. Morton & P. Tulloch (1977); The Institute of British Geographers for an extract from (J. Gottmann 1983); International Bank for Reconstruction and Development for extracts from (H. Chenery 1979), (J. Cody, H. Hughes & D. Wall 1980), (J. Fei, C. H. Ranis & S. W. Y. Kuo 1979) and (World Bank Development Report 1983); International Bank for Reconstruction and Development and The John Hopkins University Press for an extract from (A. M. Kamarck 1976); the Editor, Journal of Developing Areas for fig 30 (H. C. Weinand 1973); author's agents for The National Trust for Places of Historic Interest or Natural Beauty & Macmillan London Ltd and Doubleday & Co Inc & The National Trust for an extract from the poem 'The Benefactors' by Rudyard Kipling, copyright 1921 from *Rudyard Kipling's Verse, Definitive Edition*; Longman Group Ltd for fig 22 from figs 7.3 & 7.4 (P. Todaro 1977); John Murray Publishers Ltd for an extract from the poem 'The Planster's Vision' by John Betjeman from *Collected Poems*; Pan Books Ltd for extracts from (W. Brandt 1980); The Society of Authors on behalf of the Bernard Shaw Estate for 'The golden rule is that there are no golden rules' by Bernard Shaw from *Maxims for Revolutionists*.

Acknowledgements

We are grateful to the following for permission to reproduce copyright material.

Part 1 Dimensions and issues

'Now, here, you see, it takes all the running you can do, to keep in the same place. If you want to get somewhere else, you must run at least twice as fast as that.'

Lewis Carroll
Through the Looking-Glass

1 Worlds within Worlds

Dos linages sólas hay en el mundo, como decia una abuela mia, que son el tenir y el no tenir

(There are only two families in the world, as a grandmother of mine used to say: the haves and the have nots)

Cervantes
Don Quixote: El Cabellero de la Trieste Figura

That the world is divided by levels of economic prosperity is well known. It is possible to postulate that this has always been so. It is equally reasonable to argue, however, that the contrasts have never been as great as those which now exist and which had begun to emerge in the eighteenth and nineteenth centuries. That great upsurge in productive capacity with its associated transformation of not only the means of production but also the whole organization of societies and their economies, that change we call the agrarian and industrial revolutions, profoundly distinguished its participant nations from those not directly involved. This distinction came to the eyes of merchants and missionaries who, both knowingly and unknowingly, spun a web of interconnections which tied the outer countries to the inner industrial nations. As empires grew, colonial territories enhanced both the resource base and the potential markets of the industrial economies of Europe. Whether it became colonial or not, the world that was not part of the economic transformation of the nineteenth century remained distinct. In terms of technological application and economic organization it was undeveloped and, in consequence, poorer in material terms. It was variously described as savage, primitive or backward by the newly-rich world. In so much as these descriptions implied less developed in culture, religion or political systems, they were the product of both ignorance and arrogance; ignorance of the richness of the cultures of pre-industrial civilizations and an arrogance in an under-estimation of them. Attitudes have changed; the nature of the imperial powers and the political status of the non-industrialized world have changed; the world of today is not that of 1885 or indeed 1945 and the terminology has likewise changed. What remains are the differences, differences of both a greater and lesser degree between the many independent sovereign nations which now constitute the world community. There are still two worlds and the difference turns upon comparative levels of wealth and poverty. Development is about transforming both economies and societies in ways which diminish this difference.

The terms used to describe the poorer world are several. The most common is Third World, an example of an adopted and misused label. Wolf-Phillips has attributed the first use of this term to Alfred Sauvry who, in 1952, referred to the *tiers monde* (Wolf-Phillips 1979). Sauvry was, however, using the term to mean a third force, a political force, in a world where the North Atlantic community represented the first force and the communist bloc of the Soviet Union, eastern Europe and China a second force. It was a distinction based upon ideological commitment rather than conditions of economic attainment. In the latter sense the inclusion of China would have been singularly inappropriate. This origin appears to have been forgotten and later, in the early 1960s, Third World came to mean countries less economically developed than those of the industrialized nations of North America, Europe and the Soviet Union and so the Third World came to incorporate China. The situation has been further complicated by the current usage of the terms North and South. To anyone with any degree of geographical fastidiousness they are terms which can only be regretted when India and China are allocated to the South and Australia and New Zealand to the North. The term appears as the title of the first report of the Independent Commission on International Development Issues chaired by Willy Brandt (Brandt 1980). Other terms such as undeveloped, under developed, least developed, less developed, have all appeared and been used by bodies such as the United Nations. Underlying all these labels is a perceived distinction of differences in poverty and wealth and a belief that there is a process called development during which the condition of poverty is replaced by one of comparative affluence. This book is concerned with examining the nature of this transformation and the attempts made to promote it. It is appropriate, therefore, that it addresses the issues of the Developing World.

Where is this Developing World? The American political scientist Bruce Russett has likened the search for an all-purpose region to that of the alchemist trying to find a universal solvent (Russett 1967). Is there indeed an all-purpose region which encapsulates the Developing World? In 1961 an Atlas of Economic Development edited by Norton Ginsburg was published (Ginsburg 1961). Based on an extensive assemblage of the data available in the mid-1950s it contains a large number of world maps which depict many of the dimensions of economic activities and the characteristics of populations. Each in turn, whether it be a depiction of population density, infant mortality, proportion of the labour force in manufacturing, the use of inanimate energy, per capita food intake, primary school enrolment, per capita income or the consumption of steel, sets out a world pattern. Conspicuous and not unexpected, is the continual emergence of a congruent area of poverty, ill-health, social deprivation and low productivity. It is the area intuitively recognized as the Third World or the

Developing World of this book. But not all the maps are coincident. Countries rank higher on some evaluations than others. It becomes clear that there is no sharp, defining edge to the Developing World.

Brian Berry has attempted to bring together these various measures in an integrated analysis (Berry 1960, 1961). Using an early form of direct factor analysis, Berry examines forty-three indices of economic development for ninety-five countries for which comparable data were available. He was able to show that underlying the forty-three indices were four basic patterns which could as effectively describe the similarities and differences as the forty-three. Two basic patterns, the technological and the demographic as he termed them, proved to be particularly efficient in resolving the many indices and he produced a graph based upon the 'second values' of these two patterns. Berry's analysis spanned the whole range of economic levels from nations such as the USA and West Germany, commonly thought of as examples of advanced industrial economies, to nations such as Afghanistan and Ethiopia recognised as poor and disadvantaged. This analysis revealed that there is no natural division of the countries of the world into distinct socio-economic strata. Instead there is a continuum of levels of development from the very poorest and underdeveloped countries to the richest and technologically most sophisticated. There is a continuous transition between levels of development. The Developing World is thus as much a concept as a place. It has a core but no boundaries. It has a beginning but no end. Wherever one draws a boundary it must be arbitrary and it must enclose a range of internal differences.

It is possible to identify a group of nations which occupy the lowest points in this chain of development. In 1971 the General Assembly of the

Table 1 The least developed countries 1981

Afghanistan	Haiti
Bangladesh	Lao
Benin	Lesotho
Bhutan	Malawi
Botswana	Maldives
Burundi	Mali
Cape Verde	Nepal
Central African Republic	Niger
Comoros	Rwanda
Chad	Samoa
Democratic Yemen	Somalia
Ethiopia	Sudan
Gambia	Tanzania
Guinea	Uganda
Guinea-Bissau	Upper Volta
	Yemen Arab Republic

Source: United Nations Organisation

United Nations drew up a list of twenty-four countries which presented the most difficult conditions. They were identified on the basis of three criteria, GDP per capita, share of manufacturing in GDP and the literacy rate. To this list were added other poor countries bringing the total to thirty-one by 1981. They have been described as LDCs, the least developed countries, and are listed alphabetically in Table 1. They represent the core of underdevelopment, the nations at the bottom of the ladder, standing in poverty.

While Berry's analysis demonstrated the international continuum of development it also revealed that the geographical distribution is, to a large extent, discreetly aggregated. The nations lowest on his technological-demographic scale were largely, though not exclusively, tropical. The countries of sub-Saharan Africa congregated in the lowest levels of the scale followed in turn at higher levels by those of North Africa, Asia, Central America, South America, the Soviet bloc and the nations of north-western Europe and North America. There was relatively little overlap between these continental groups of nations though in total they embraced the whole development spectrum without break. It is a distribution suggestive of a ladder of development up which nations can climb, though with some further to climb than others and some encountering particular difficulties. The Developing World is clearly not one single unit in terms of the difficulties it presents nor in the stages of development through which nations will have to pass. There are worlds within worlds.

It is not possible to make direct comparisons with Berry's ranking list because countries have amalgamated or sub-divided since the analysis was carried out. In Table 2, however, the bottom sixty-eight of the ninety-five countries examined by Berry are listed in order of their ranking from least developed to most developed on the basis of their second value scores on the basic technological pattern. Alongside them is listed their per capita Gross National Product category in the World Banks list for 1981 (World Bank 1983). Allowing for the obvious inadequacies of the average per capita data and the elapse of some twenty-five years, the coincidence in ranking is remarkable but there are outstanding discrepancies. Libya, the second lowest ranked country on Berry's scale, now stands high in the rank of GNP per capita because of its oil wealth. This too has placed Iran and Iraq in the upper middle GNP categories. India is high on Berry's measure while her present GNP per capita puts her among the poorest countries in the world. Sri Lanka presents a similar situation. Iceland has pulled herself out of a situation behind Colombia and Egypt to become one of the world's high GNP earners.

Per capita GNP would appear to be a useful indicator of development though it is essential to have additional information to aid in the assessment of its significance. It is mapped for the nations of the world in Fig. 1. Three other indices have been selected and mapped to demonstrate the issues which many developing countries face. One is the proportion of the workforce engaged in agriculture (Fig. 2). The second is the adequacy of food

Table 2 Countries ranked on Berry's technological scale (World Bank 1981 Gross National Product per capita classification)

Afghanistan	Low	Tunisia	Lower-middle
Libya	High income oil exporter	China	Low
Ethiopia	Low	Brit. Guiana	Lower-middle
Liberia	Lower-middle	Panama	Upper-middle
Fren. Equat. Africa	Low	Philippines	Lower-middle
Haiti	Low	Iraq	Upper-middle
S. Vietnam	Low	Surinam	Upper-middle
Angola	Lower-middle	El Salvador	Lower-middle
Mozambique	Low	Algeria	Upper-middle
Sierra Leone	Low	Ceylon	Low
Fren. West Africa	Low	Morocco	Lower-middle
Jordan	Lower-middle	Costa Rica	Lower-middle
Paraguay	Lower-middle	Peru	Lower-middle
Sudan	Low	India	Low
Madagascar	Low	Iceland	High income
Thailand	Lower-middle	Colombia	Lower-middle
Burma	Low	Taiwan	Upper-middle
Nigeria	Lower-middle	Turkey	Lower-middle
Honduras	Lower-middle	Egypt	Lower-middle
Nicaragua	Lower-middle	Greece	Upper-middle
Indonesia	Lower-middle	Lebanon	Upper-middle
Dominican R.	Lower-middle	Rhodesia & Nyasaland	Lower-middle
Iran	Upper-middle	Brazil	Upper-middle
Pakistan	Low	Rumania	Upper-middle
Bolivia	Lower-middle	Israel	Upper-middle
Brit. Borneo		Hong Kong	Upper-middle
Brit. East Africa	Low	Cuba	Lower-middle
Syria	Lower-middle	Portugal	Upper-middle
Belgian Congo	Low	Uruguay	Upper-middle
S. Korea	Upper-middle	Yugoslavia	Upper-middle
Ecuador	Lower-middle	Chile	Upper-middle
Ghana	Low	Venezuela	Upper-middle
Guatemala	Lower-middle	Argentina	Upper-middle
Cyprus	Upper-middle	Mexico	Upper-middle

supply as measured by the daily calorific intake of food as a percentage of the basic physiological requirement (Fig. 3). On this map have also been indicated those countries which were identified by the FAO in the mid-seventies as being characterised by malnutrition. The third map depicts infant mortality rates (Fig. 4). These maps reveal a world which is still largely agricultural and yet cannot adequately feed itself, a world in which a combination of conditions still bring unacceptable risks of death to the

GNP Per Capita 1981

Low Income Economies < US $ 400

Lower Middle-Income Economies US $ 401-1,630

Upper Middle-Income Economies US $ 1,631-5,670

High-Income Oil Exporters US $ 8,450-24,660

Industrial Market and East European Non-market Economies

n – No data

Source of data: World Bank 1983

Figure 1 Gross National Product per capita

Percentage of Labour Force Employed in Agriculture 1980

> 75

50—75

25—49

< 25

Equator

Source of data: World Bank 1983

n – No data

Figure 2 Employment in agriculture

9

Daily Per Capita Calorie Supply 1980
Percentage of Requirement

< 80

80–100

90–100

> 100   Source of data: World Bank 1983

n – No data

▼ Serious Malnutrition
Source of data: FAO 1977

Equator

Figure 3 Adequacy of diet and occurrence of severe malnutrition

Equator

Infant Mortality Rate 1981

> 150

100 – 149

50 – 99

20 – 49

< 20

n – No data

Source of data: World Bank 1983

Figure 4 Infant mortality per thousand

very young. They reveal a world in which the sum total of natural resources and efforts are insufficient to provide basic means of subsistence. Yet the Developing World extends beyond these nations and that it does so is reason for hope.

The transformation of nations from a state of poverty to one of improved well-being, from a condition of adequate but self-limiting subsistence to one of continuing and self-generating growth is the nature and purpose of development. It must first encompass the basic physiological needs but must also embrace those other dimensions which make life something to be savoured rather than endured. The awakened world of the second half of the twentieth century has become aware of these issues. The many new nations have tried to grapple with them. The practice has proved much more difficult than the preaching. It is these issues which this book attempts to address. In its first part it examines what might be called the dimensions of development and discusses the evolution of ideas and theories as to how development might best be managed. In the second part it examines the translation of ideas into practice in a series of case studies spanning the continents and ranging from the smallest to the largest of nations. Here the theories of development have come face to face with the difficulties and diversities of reality. It has been a salutary experience. The last thirty years have yielded pointers to the future and it is these which are considered in the final chapter.

2 The Dimension of People: Disease and Mortality

'We who live in temperate lands find it difficult to realize how baneful Nature can be to man or to understand that in unreclaimed regions water may swarm with dangerous germs, myriads of blood-sucking insects may inject deadly microbes into the human body, and the very soil may be harmful to the touch'

Pierre Gourou
The Tropical World 1953

Population is variously and contemporaneously regarded in a number of ways. It is viewed as a resource, a strength upon which political power can be based or as a factor of production. It is considered as a burden, something to be fed, clothed, educated, employed and to be characterized by particularly burdensome sections, the too young and the too old. It is also seen as that which creates, shapes, nurtures, and indeed is, the very civilisation which our varied societies demonstrate. If social and economic development is about anything it is about people and the issues of population underlie all thinking on social and economic development and come to the fore in the execution of any development plan. The relationships between the characteristics of population and the process of development are complex and subtle. It is this relationship and these characteristics which will be examined. Since they are not peculiar to the Developing World, it is possible to analyse the population dynamics of the present industrialized, highly productive, urbanized and wealthy nations from their pre-industrial period to the present in an attempt to identify causes and consequences which might illuminate the demographic status of the less developed countries of today.

The first eighty years of the eighteenth century were characterized in England and Wales by a very slow population growth at an average rate of 0.36 per cent per annum. In the last twenty years of the century expansion accelerated to over 1 per cent per annum. The increase in population was discernible to people of the time who offered explanations. Habakkuk argues that increases in the birth rate had an important part to play and that the contemporary opinion was that the population was increasing because couples were having more children largely because of greater economic opportunities or because of the increased economic security afforded by the

13

poor relief scheme known as the Speenhamland system (Habakkuk 1971). The contemporary who applied an analytical mind to the situation was, of course, Thomas Malthus whose *Essay on the Principle of Population* published in 1798 not only attempted to explain the English situation but put forward a model to illustrate the dynamics of populations which has attracted comment ever since. As his views have a bearing upon the relationship between population and economic activity and as they have been applied by some to the population situation in developing countries today, they merit consideration. He wrote thus:

> Impelled to the increase of his species by an equally powerful instinct, reason interrupts his career and asks him whether he may not bring beings into the world for whom he cannot provide the means of support. If he attend this natural suggestion, the restriction frequently produces vice. If he hears it not, the human race will be constantly endeavouring to increase beyond the subsistence. But as, by that law of our nature which makes food necessary to the life of man, population can never actually increase beyond the lowest nourishment capable of supporting it, a strong check on population, from the difficulty of acquiring food, must be constantly in operation. This difficulty must fall somewhere, and must necessarily be severely felt in one or other or the various forms of misery, or the fear of misery, by a large proportion of mankind.
>
> That population has this constant tendency to increase beyond the means of subsistence, and that it is kept to its necessary level by these causes, will sufficiently appear from a review of the different states of society in which man has existed
>
> (Malthus 1798).

Malthus then argues that in places where there are no food constraints on population increase, he examines eighteenth-century North America, a population could double itself in twenty five years and possibly in fifteen and could continue to increase in a geometric progression pointing out that 'A thousand millions are just as easily doubled every twenty-five years by the population as a thousand'. He continues:

> But the food to support the increase from the greater number will by no means be obtained with the same facility. Man is necessarily confined in room. When acre has been added to acre until all the fertile land is occupied, the yearly increase of food must depend upon the melioration of the land already in possession. This is a fund, which, from the nature of all sorts, instead of increasing, must be gradually diminishing, . . . It may be fairly pronounced, therefore, that considering the present average state of the earth, the means of subsistence under circumstances the most favourable to human industry, could not be made to increase faster than in an arithmetic ratio.

Malthus brings his two ratios together and draws his alternative conclusions on the condition of man. He was thus arguing that since food subsistence levels could never be increased quickly enough to match an unchecked population increase, the limits of subsistence production would keep down the population either in a direct way, by causing malnutrition and starvation leading to an increase in death rates and infant mortality rates, or in an indirect way by man, the thinking animal, restricting his fertility rates to levels which could be supported. Malthus considered later marriage and sexual abstinence as appropriate means by which this could be achieved. He argued that attempts to increase food production to raise standards of living and health was not an answer since the population would always continue to increase until it pressed against the levels of poverty which would check it by death. He saw the population of England increasing around him and postulated a contained system in which the population would be reduced and held in check at subsistence level.

Poverty is characteristic of many developing countries and is a major index of their condition. Malnutrition is common and starvation by no means unknown. Are they in the demographic strait-jacket of Malthusian containment? Are there other factors in the population equation? The population of England and Wales continued to expand unchecked for over a century after Malthus published his essay, never falling below an annual average growth rate of one per cent from 1781 to 1911 and reaching 1.8 per cent between 1811 and 1821. That same century or so was characterized by an unprecedented increase in production and a major transformation of the British economy. This evidence is one refutation of the Malthus thesis. A second comes from an earlier, pre-industrial period of English history thick in the fog of uncertain demographic data, the period from the twelfth to the sixteenth century.

Here the evidence so elegantly presented by John Hatcher not so much rejects the Malthusian cycle as modifies it and does so in a way significant for the understanding of the demographic situation in the Developing World (Hatcher 1977). The population of England appears to have risen from less than 2 million in 1086 at the time of the Domesday survey, to between 4 and 6.25 million by 1300 yet the evidence of the Poll Tax some seventy years later, puts the population in 1377 at between 2.75 and 3 million. This dramatic decline is associated with the bubonic plague, the Black Death, which swept the country in 1348 and caused the deaths of between 30 and 45 per cent of the population. The population level did not recover and on into the fifteenth century a slow decline took place. Thereafter the population increased slowly reaching the pre-plague levels by 1650, three centuries later. The evidence reveals that the Black Death was followed by many subsequent outbreaks of plague, that the agricultural wages of the small population increased, per capita output went up and landowners prospered. The land which went out of cultivation was the poorer land, the remaining population could produce more, earn and spend more, so that towns and merchants also benefited. The fall in population was associated with an increase in living standards. Why did not the population rise in a Malthusian fashion to press against the level of subsistence? The explanation seems to lie in the continuing incidence of plague and other diseases. Contemporary accounts comment upon the mortality among children and young adults with obvious demographic effects upon population replacement. In the sixteenth century the population did begin to increase and continued to do so as real wage levels fell but as, importantly, the recurrence of plague unrelated to living standards fell away. The Great Plague of 1665 struck London but was not country-wide and since 1667 bubonic plague has never reappeared.

Hatcher believes that levels of mortality in medieval England were not related simply to the success or failure of harvest even though crises in limited localities were frequent and malnutrition did influence death rates. On a national scale he believes that it was the occurrence of the epidemic and infectious diseases which swept the country and were unrelated to the state of the economy and levels of subsistence. He agrees that the Malthusian argument holds true in so much as better living standards in pre-industrial England did favour population growth while periods when they were low inhibited population growth, but claims that this is only part of a more complex picture. Infectious and epidemic diseases quite unrelated to economic circumstances superimposed their death rates on any Malthusian cycle. Mortality rates rather than fertility determined the population dynamics of pre-industrial England.

Three seemingly major considerations in the discussion of the sinuosities of demographic change thus appear; first the Malthusian element whereby population levels are contained by the finite and depletable resource base which sustains them, a relationship suggestive of concepts of over-population and under-population; second the question of the changing use, and hence significance, of the resource base which the evidence of nineteenth-century Britain suggests; third the role of diseases, distinguishing between those which appear unrelated to conditions of living and those which are. The role of diseases will be examined first.

OF FLIES, FLEAS, LICE AND MEN: THE ROLE OF DISEASE

A wide range of zootic diseases are endemic in the Developing World, some are peculiar to it and many are associated with its tropical climates while others it shares with the rest of mankind. Pierre Gourou writing in 1953 states 'In physical and mental activity and in the reproduction of his kind, man is restricted in the tropics by serious maladies whose existence is entirely due to hot, damp climate' (Gourou 1953).

It is not, of course, easy to assemble direct data on the incidence of diseases for many countries in the Developing World. Indirect evidence such as the rate of infant mortality give some indication though data of comprehensive coverage are of recent origin. In 1960 infant mortality rates averaged 165 per thousand in low income countries and 145 in the low middle income group compared with 30 in the industrialized nations while corresponding life expectancies at birth were 41, 46 and 70 years in the three groups (See Fig. 4 for 1981). Though the incidence of disease and illness is high in the Developing World it was undoubtedly much higher in the recent past.

European awareness and comment upon the unhealthiness of the tropical world was consequent upon mercantile and colonial contact with its peoples. Ellen Thorp in her account of the history of Nigeria writes of Lagos in the 1850s 'But nightly and daily from the interior of the island came an enemy far more deadly than the leopard, because it was unrecognised – the mosquito, which, breeding in the surrounding swamps, brought malaria and yellow fever' (Thorp 1956). Those who went down with malaria and survived their 'conditioning fever' were also inevitably stricken with dysentery due, though they did not know it, to polluted water.

The scene in Lagos was paralleled in the Niger delta which was the great focus in trade first in slaves and later in palm oil. The 'oil rivers', as they became known, took a great toll of the European seamen and traders. Of all the river ports, Bonny had the worst reputation with its endemic malaria, yellow fever and dysentery. In 1862 it is recorded that 162 out of 300 Europeans died in a yellow fever upsurgence. Trading companies from the 1860s until almost the end of the century moored old hulks of sailing vessels, no longer safe for sea passages, in the delta for use as trading depots or 'factories'. In the foul water of their bilges mosquitoes found ideal breeding grounds. The young clerks who came out from Liverpool and London to handle the trade in palm oil from the interior in exchange for flint-lock guns, Lancashire cottons and other manufactures, were soon stricken with malaria or yellow fever and many died before their 'tour' was up. Ellen Thorp quotes a job advertisement of the period: 'Wanted, young man, eighteen to twenty-five, as book-keeper in a West African factory. A few hours work a day, in pleasant surroundings, unlimited shooting and fishing, in a fine tropic scenery, with a boat at his disposal. Free quarters, salary to commence at £70, with chance of rapid promotion.' She comments that successful applicants were soon to discover that the final statement was true 'for his chances of promotion could be as rapid as those in the Navy in wartime. If he himself were not dead of malaria or drink at the end of a few months, a good many of his companions were sure to be, and the young assistant might easily see his Agent buried and find himself in charge of the factory . . .' (Thorp 1956). This notorious coast, which gave rise to the jingle 'The Bight of Benin, the Bight of Benin, where few come out though many go in', is but one example of the experience by Europeans of the disease-inflicted countries of the tropics. The area became known as the 'White man's grave'. What was not said was that it was also the grave of black men. The causes of these many diseases were unknown and in consequence neither prophylactic measures nor cures could be used to counteract them.

It is commonplace to refer to 'tropical diseases' yet while some thus classified are indigenous and specific to the climatic tropics many are diseases
which were once widespread and have been eliminated or strictly controlled
in the temperate and, significantly, the affluent and technically sophisticated
world. Many 'tropical diseases' are essentially diseases now restricted in
their endemicity to the Developing World and are as much diseases of levels
of development as of climate. For this reason it is useful to group the 'tropical diseases' into those which are related to the physical environment, those
to the social environment, and those which in their ubiquity appear unrelated to either, in order to explore the relationship between disease, population dynamics and development.

A range of widely occurring diseases is transmitted by insects. Since these
insects are controlled in their range by their environmental requirements so
too are the diseases they carry. Yellow fever, a viral disease with a high
mortality rate, is transmitted by the mosquito *Aedes aegypti* whose range is
confined to areas where temperatures do not drop below 15 °C to 20 °C. It
is a disease endemic in tropical central and south America and Africa. The
mosquito is found in other tropical areas but not the pathogen. Dengue
fever, a less serious disease though it can cause death, is also carried by
Aedes aegypti but the virus is only transmitted when the temperature exceeds
20 °C (Wisseman and Sweet 1961). The vectors of Filariasis, which obstruct
the lymphatics and can produce elephantiasis, are another group of mosquitoes, one of the chief in Africa being *Anopheles gambias* (Kessel 1961). The
disease can be crippling, cause blindness and, as in most parasitic diseases,
reduces both energy and resistance to infections. Flies other than mosquitoes transmit filarial diseases in their bite. The particularly distressing River
Blindness, onchocerciasis, is a fly-borne disease carried by various species
of *Simuliidae*. The fly's habitat is along fast-flowing well-aerated streams. The
disease occurs in the near-equatorial areas of Central and South America but
it is most widespread along the rivers of West and Central Africa and along
the Nile. Some 20 million are estimated to be affected with this fly-borne
blindness. Outside the tropics, low temperatures prevent the evolution of
the necessary life cycle of filaria and fly. Leishmaniasis, a protozoan infection transmitted in sand-fly bites and known variously as Kala-azar, Delhi
boil or Oriental sore, is again widespread in the tropics and is debilitating
rather than killing. In Africa, the several species of tsetse fly (*Glossina* spp.)
carry the disease trypanosomiasis which debilitates and eventually kills
humans. Importantly, species of the trypanosomes also infect cattle and
have significantly determined the distribution of cattle in Africa. In thus
influencing agricultural productivity and the availability of animal protein,
Nagana, the trypanosomiasis of cattle, has made a major impact upon health
and mortality in the continent. At high altitudes and desert conditions in
tropical Africa the several species of tsetse fly cannot exist but in the rain
forests and Guinea savanna zone it is widespread while in the drier savanna

areas its distribution is riverine. A form of trypanosomiasis transmitted by the bite of bed bugs and known as Chagas' disease is found in scattered localities throughout central and South America where the domestic rather than physical environment is its habitat control.

By far the most important insect-borne disease of the Developing World and the tropics is malaria transmitted in the bite of one of the many species of Anopheles mosquito. Their habitats are not confined to the tropics and some Anopheles species can and do exist in temperate areas. They are, however, sensitive to low temperatures and cold winter seasons both restrict their occurrence and facilitate their elimination. The mosquito can, of course, transmit the disease only if it has access to the causal plasmodia in the blood of the infected human beings. Where the two exist together the disease can flourish and be spread. The disease varies according to the plasmodium involved but all can cause death and fatality rates amongst infected children are particularly high. In the mid-1960s the World Health Organisation estimated that some 100 million persons suffered from malaria of whom one million would die each year. It has been suggested that endemic and epidemic malaria has played a major role in the population dynamics of the nations of the world, notably in the sub-tropical and tropical areas, over many centuries. These, then, are the major diseases of the Developing World which are transmitted by insects and are associated with their habitats.

A second group of diseases is more closely related to the habits of man, to eating, drinking, excreting, of how man lives and where he works, of his personal hygiene and sanitary provision. Since these are features of cultures, life styles and standards of living, they are very much related to levels of development and the development process, and characteristics of man, the social animal. The worms which commonly infect and are parasitic on man in many parts of the Developing World are such manifestation of insanitary conditions. Open latrines, inadequate sewage facilities, polluted water and too little water, are all associated with the infestation of hookworms, round, whip and Guinea worms. All these infestations, and they are commonly multiple, are debilitating, draining energy causing anaemia and generally weakening large percentages of the population. The killing bacterial diseases of cholera and typhoid are transmitted through water, milk, food, with flies assisting in insanitary and crowded conditions of living and eating. The dysenteries, both bacillary and amoebic, occupy a similar niche whilst infective hepatitis is essentially transferred by the faecal-oral route.

These diseases are widespread in the Developing World. Cholera is believed to have been confined to the Indian subcontinent for a long period of time but in a series of four pandemics in the nineteenth century spread throughout wide areas of the world. In the early twentieth century the imposition of quarantine measures has prevented the intrusion of pandemic cholera into the western hemisphere and Europe. Today cholera is particularly associated with India, Bangladesh and Celebes in Indonesia where it can be considered endemic. It is not an environmentally specific disease but as Jacque May puts it 'it is a consequence of unwashed hands' (May 1958). The typhoid and paratyphoid salmonelloses diseases, classic examples of water-borne diseases, while occurring world-wide are very much associated with inadequacies in clean water supplies, insanitary living conditions and unhygienic food handling. As these situations are more prevalent in poor countries they are diseases of both town and country in Developing World. Bilharzia, or schistosomiasis, is at once both a disease of insanitary conditions and of subtropical and tropical areas. The pathogen, the schistosome, requires both man and freshwater snail as alternate hosts at stages in its complex life cycle. Man is infected by drinking, washing in or working in, water containing the cercariae stage of the life cycle which he completes by voiding his wastes into stream, ponds or irrigation ditches. This extremely debilitating disease is found throughout the whole of Africa, in the West Indies, Venezuela, Guayana, Surinam and French Guiana and wide areas of eastern Brazil, in irrigated areas in the Middle East, throughout the Indian sub-continent, Burma, most of South East Asia and in parts of Indonesia and the Philippines. As the still water of irrigated fields provides ideal conditions, bilharzia is a disease of tropical, irrigated lands and where economic development has extended irrigation, so too has the disease spread.

The third group of diseases are contagious diseases, commonly bacterial and viral, transmitted from person to person without necessrily the intermediary of insects, food or drink. They include leprosy, once not uncommon in Europe, yaws the spirochaete infection similar to syphillis though not venereal and associated with tropical regions experiencing average annual temperatures exceeding 25 °C, smallpox, influenza, measles, cerebro-spinal meningitis and tuberculosis. All are diseases which can kill, quickly or slowly, and most are not environmentally specific. Smallpox, until eliminated in the 1970s, reaped a heavy and continuous harvest and influenza has killed millions in its pandemics. Measles, rarely a killing disease today in the industrialized world, is still characterized by high mortality in the tropics and when introduced into communities which had previously not known it, death rates and demographic consequences similar to those of the Black Death have been experienced. The measles epidemic in Fiji of 1875, when by a most unfortunate mischance the disease was introduced from Australia, caused the deaths of some 30–40,000 persons out of a population of 135,000 and for some years subsequently deaths exceeded births because of the depletion of the reproductive capacity of the population (Derrick 1959; McDonald 1963). Tuberculosis most certainly is not a disease which has been confined to the Developing World but it is one very closely associated with poverty and with resulting poor nutrition, and crowded housing conditions. It is in consequence very much related to levels of economic development and has been widespread in many developing countries.

All the diseases cited are subject, in varying degrees, to amelioration by medical treatment. It is frequently stated that the medicine of the scientific industrialized world has been responsible for the dramatic upsurge in the population of developing countries because medical science has reduced mortality levels as it did in Europe a century or so ago. This will be examined in terms of the nature of the process and its timing and with regard to the three groups of diseases which have been described.

DISEASE AND POPULATION DYNAMICS IN BRITAIN

The analogy with the demographic situation in Europe merits discussion. It will be recalled that the population of England and Wales began to rise towards the end of the eighteenth century and continued the upward trend throughout the nineteenth. Though the data for the eighteenth century are unsatisfactory, some historical demographers have attributed the increase beginning then to an increase in birth rates and a fall in death rates with the latter as the most influential and attributable to improvements in medicine, social hygiene and hence health. Such developments were therefore not a direct consequence of the great structural change in the British economy which was taking place. Others claim that it was precisely these economic changes which encouraged larger families because of the greater employment opportunities they offered. It is difficult to see, however, how already high birth rates could be raised much further since there are physiological limits to reproduction. What can yield a big and rapid increase in population in circumstances of high birth rates is a fall in death rates. Holding the view that the latter is the more convincing explanation, McKeown and Brown have examined the role of medicine in the population dynamics of the eighteenth and early nineteenth century in England (McKeown and Brown 1965). They consider that the establishment of medical schools in the eighteenth century and the greater understanding of the body's structure and functions which resulted, desirable though it was, had little direct impact upon mortality rates nor did developments in surgery improve life expectancy. The nature and causes of diseases remained largely unknown, the virtue of asepsis was not appreciated until the work of Lister (1827–1912) and anaesthetics in surgery were rarely used until Simpson's applications of chloroform in 1847. The setting up of lying-in (maternity) hospitals in Britain and Europe increased rather than reduced mortality of both mother and the newborn by enhancing the risk of cross-infection of puerperal fever in circumstances where the role of hygiene and cleanliness was not appreciated. Likewise McKeown and Brown consider the role of General Hospitals to have been detrimental to health certainly up until the mid-nineteenth century. They became places where diseases could be contracted since the nature of disease transmission was not fully

21

understood and most medical drugs of the day were ineffective. With few exceptions, such as the pioneering work of Jenner in developing an effective vaccination against smallpox, the development of medical science up until the middle of the nineteenth century appears to have had little effect upon mortality rates yet these rates did fall with all evidence pointing to a steady decline between 1775 and 1850. Crude death rates stood at around 30 per 1000 in 1800, were 23 in 1850 and remained at that until 1870 and then fell steadily to 13 in the 1920s. If deaths from infectious diseases were not markedly reduced by medical treatment what was the cause? Mortality could be reduced by changes in the virulence of the disease or by the human population becoming more resistant. The virulence of scarlet fever and measles in Europe has diminished but in the twentieth rather than the nineteenth century. A better fed population could possess a higher resistance and so the economic development of the eighteenth and nineteenth centuries could, and probably did, have a role to play in disease diminution and in lowering mortality. Finally environmental improvements can serve to inhibit the transmission of diseases. These factors vary, however, in their significance from one disease to another.

Habakkuk considers that the falling death rates were due to improvements in environmental conditions (Habbakuk 1965 and 1971). Did living conditions improve? Did the increasing proportion of the population living in the new industrial towns run a lesser risk of infectious diseases than the largely rural population of earlier periods? The towns of the nineteenth century left much to be desired in health terms but it could have been that room space was greater, sewage disposal improved and separated from water supplies, and that as these utilities became more efficient the diseases of insanitation, the dysenteries, typhoid, hepatitis, cholera declined and the incidence of tuberculosis, the great killer of nineteenth-century cities, diminished as housing bye-laws were enforced and as in the latter part of the nineteenth century isolation hospitals removing infectious cases from the community came into being. The evidence is incomplete. What is certain is that in England and Wales the vulnerability to harvest failure disappeared by the nineteenth century as subsistence agriculture was replaced by more productive commercial forms and as the dependence of local demand on local production was reduced. Where it had not, as in Ireland, crop failure could produce death, disaster and emigration. Better nutrition, a rise in living standards, a greater appreciation of the need for cleanliness and hygiene translated into practice at family and public level and manifest in completed town sewerage and water-supply schemes and building regulations, all reduced the significance of the diseases of the environment and all were improvements characteristic of the whole of the nineteenth century. Medical science improved but the impact of prophylactic inoculations and therapeutic drugs was yet to come and in many diseases postdated 1945.

DISEASE CONQUEST AND FALLING DEATH RATES IN THE DEVELOPING COUNTRIES

Has this pattern of declining mortality initiated by improvements in living conditions and in public health facilities been replicated in the Developing World? In some countries it has been achieved but they are few. In most, public utilities of consequence for health, namely pure water supplies and adequate sanitation together with housing provision, are far from satisfactory. In 1897 the Annual Report for Lagos stated:

> Discussion is still going on as to a feasible scheme for the sanitary reform of Lagos town in connection with water supply and drainage that can be carried out reasonably within the means of the Colony. It will be easily comprehensible, that, on a malarial island a mile or two long by half a mile broad, with a population of 50,000 souls living on it and a much larger number of bodies dead and buried in it for many years past, disturbance of the soil is to be avoided by every possible means. No scheme has yet been approved
>
> (Thorp 1956).

Today, Lagos with several million inhabitants still has no comprehensive sewerage system, a feature common in both major and minor cities throughout the Developing World. Adequate water supply systems of pure water are likewise still rare and the diseases associated with these situations are still prevalent. The English pattern of a steady reduction in mortality from food, faeces and water-borne diseases as standards of living improved, does not characterize the rapid decline in mortality rates which has taken place in all developing countries since the Second World War. This decline, and it has been as dramatic as it has been swift, is the result of the application of modern scientific medicine with not only its understanding of the nature of diseases and their transmission but also armed with a weaponry of drugs and insecticides to combat them. It is a development which has been felt at one and the same time in both the affluent industrialized world and the poor developing countries.

The application of these remedies has varied in cost, ease and effectiveness across the disease spectrum. The most effective are those which immunize the individual. If the protection is secure, economically feasible and long-term, it obviates the need for other measures which may be more difficult and costly to implement. However, as Table 3 illustrates, the protection offered by modern vaccines varies considerably. Against the serious diseases associated with insanitary conditions, cholera and typhoid vaccination gives only short-term and, in cholera's case uncertain, protection. Effective protection is afforded against diphtheria, measles, whooping cough, poliomyelitis and against tuberculosis, the disease long-associated with overcrowded and poor living conditions. Smallpox defeated by the world's oldest vaccine has been totally eliminated. Notably absent from

23

Table 3 The degree of protection against major diseases affected by vaccinations

Disease	Degree of vaccination protection
Bubonic plague*	Six months approx.
Cholera	Six months approx.
Diphtheria	Long lasting
Influenza	Short time
Measles	Long lasting
Poliomyelitis	Long lasting
Rabies	Short time
Smallpox†	Long lasting
Tetanus	Long lasting
Tuberculosis	Long lasting
Typhoid	Short time
Whooping cough	Permanent
Yellow fever	Ten years approx.

* Uncertain protection
† Eliminated from world by 1977

Table 3 are trypanosomiasis, bilharzia, leprosy, filariasis, and most importantly malaria. All, except leprosy, involve an insect vector or an alternative
host and all have proved very difficult to eradicate. Yellow fever is the only
major insect-borne disease to be adequately counteracted by inoculation,
an immunization which was developed at the beginning of the twentieth
century. Bilharzia is in many respects a disease of rural insanitation. To
control it requires either the treatment by drugs of the infected population,
which as yet has not been successful, or the elimination of the snail, or the
provision of latrines and uninfected domestic water. These provisions are
complex, expensive and difficult to administer. Bilharzia remains a major
problem. Trypanosomiasis has presented problems. The tsetse fly can be
killed by insecticides or its habitat destroyed. In densely-settled, cultivated
areas it cannot live but such areas are few in Africa and the disease, particularly in the form affecting cattle is unsubdued. Malaria, the killer of many
throughout the Developing World presents the greatest challenge. During
the Second World War drugs were developed which by killing the pathogen
in the blood stream, if taken regularly, can protect the population at risk.
The anopheles mosquito can be killed by insecticides of which DDT was the
first effectively and extensively used. The breeding environment of the
many species of malarial mosquito can be destroyed though in practice this
is a near impossible task. All these approaches are commonly used with
insecticide spraying as the most widely applicable and cost-effective. The
World Health Organisation has mounted a series of malarial eradication
programmes which have done much to reduce the incidence of malaria but
the rate of success has been varied for several reasons. First, not all infected
areas, such as densely forested country, are amenable to spraying and

second, mosquito species are becoming resistant to insecticides. Third, resurgence has occurred, where the rigour of the eradication measures has slackened or lapsed. New drugs are required to be developed as the malarial plasmodia themselves develop resistance and finally and importantly, the movements of both man and mosquito greatly increase the problems presented in eradication. Infected persons, host to the plasmodium, move into cleared areas where the disease-free mosquito can take up the pathogen and re-infect the cleared population. Mosquitoes themselves know no political boundaries and an eradication programme in one country may be less than successful because its neighbour has no such programme. None the less the incidence of malaria has been dramatically reduced and this has been reflected in falling death rates (Prothero 1965; Learmonth 1957, 1978).

In Sri Lanka because it was an island where population movements could be controlled, because its dimensions allowed a comprehensive cover and because the vectors' habitats were easily identified and treatable, the eradication programme using DDT Sprays, a new insecticide against which no resistance had yet developed, was highly effective. Death rates showed a marked decline after 1945 but the precise role of malarial eradicated in the decline has been much investigated and deeply debated. In a sophisticated analysis, R. H. Gray has shown that malarial control in Ceylon was responsible for no less than 23 per cent of the post-war decline in mortality. As Gray indicates, the demographic consequences of malarial control in other countries such as Mauritius, Mexico, Venezuela and Guyana have been similar to those in Sri Lanka (Gray 1974).

Disease eradication by the application of modern scientific techniques of immunization, curative drugs and insect control has markedly reduced mortality levels in developing countries. The impact has been immediate and dramatic. It has not been the product of the economic and social developments which seemingly brought about the first and much more gradual falls in mortality characteristic of the demographic history of the industrialized nations. That stage is yet to come and with it, hopefully, the conquest of the diseases of insanitation and poverty. This reversal of the sequence has profound consequences for the Developing World's nations. The population of Ceylon in 1946 was 6.65 million. By 1953 it was 8.09 million and in 1963 had reached 10.58 million, an increase of 59 per cent in fourteen years. Sri Lanka's population in 1981 was 15 million. The increase is far from exceptional. It brings to the fore again the issues raised by the Malthusian model of population growth and population containment.

3 The Dimension of People: Birth Rates and Population Dynamics

'Impelled to the increase of his species by an equally powerful instinct, reason interrupts his career and asks him whether he may not bring beings into the world for whom he cannot provide the means of support'

Thomas Malthus
Essay on the Principle of Population 1798

In Britain birth rates remained high throughout the first eight decades of the nineteenth century and were over 35 per 1000 in 1880. Thereafter they began a steady decline, without interruption until 1940, a decline taking sixty years from 35 to reach 14. Overall national productivity was up and certainly from the 1880s living conditions were improving, yet the population did not respond in a Malthusian way and birth rates went down. This decline in fertility was characteristic of all the countries now characterized as developed and largely industrialized. What has made the decline difficult to interpret is that it does not correspond with the same stages of economic development in this group of European countries. In Britain industrialization and associated urbanization was characterized by high birth rates which did not begin to fall until 1880. In countries which industrialized after Britain, the same general fall in fertility took place from the late 1870s down to the 1940s. There were some variations, of course, but the trend was essentially the same as in Britain at the same time. This meant that in some cases it took place *during* their process of economic transformation which had taken place in Britain earlier. Falls in fertility took place in the Scandinavian countries, in Belgium and the Netherlands and also in France where birth rates had throughout the nineteenth century been lower than in England. All differed from England in natural endowments and in the chronology of their economic development.

Death is rarely a matter of choice. Whether or not to produce children can be. It is certainly incorrect to say of European populations that their physical ability to reproduce, their fecundity, diminished. Mitchison writes that changes in age distribution, resulting from higher life expectancy and from emigration, did not reduce the proportion of women in child-bearing age groups by more than 2–3 per cent between 1861 and 1901. Further she claims that although a rise in the age of marriage did take place it was not enough to affect fertility in a major way but contributed to that slow fall in fertility which did take place in England and Wales from the late 1870s on (Mitchison 1977). Clearly married couples were choosing to limit the size of their families and this was characteristic of all west European countries. The questions of how and why fertility rates fall, therefore, revolves around why potential parents choose to have fewer children. Habakkuk has attempted an explanation and considers a number of interacting factors which can be related to social and economic developments which may have influenced parents (Habakkuk 1971). Industrialization had meant more material wealth even for the manual workers but with even more available for the middle and upper classes. People, he suggests, were less tied by customs and traditions since they lived in towns and had broken with their rural past. In consequence, their decisions were more deliberate and they considered the issue of the relationship between the size of their families and their standard of living. As the economic structure evolved so the output of manufacturing industry broadened to include consumer goods and as they became available to a wider section of the population, they became first desirable and then, with the income elasticity of demand, necessities, and a call upon resources thus competing with cost of children. Also the acquisition of goods, the retention of money for investment, the increasing opportunity for house purchase meant that those who saw these opportunities realized that their attainment was easier with fewer children. This development would, of course, be more likely to manifest itself in the middle classes but as Habakkuk argues, the movement of people, the reduction of parochialism, both associated with urbanization, the spread of education and the growth of newspaper circulation all meant that new ideas, opportunities and knowledge of the norms of living of others become more rapidly and widely diffused.

Tranter in his work on the population of England and Wales since the Industrial Revolution is of the view that the enormous increase in opportunities for the employment of children positively encouraged both early marriages and the formation of larger families in the early phases of the Industrial Revolution. As the economy further matured changes in society led to circumstances which tended to reduce birth rates. Tranter refers to declining infant and child mortality rates, the way in which the state assumed greater responsibility for the elderly, and to the change in the status of women. He stresses that the most important influential factor was the growing desire for material possessions and social improvement (Tranter 1973). The temporal matching of economic events and demographic changes is, however, far from exact in Britain and when applied to other countries further mismatches occur. The relationship is exceedingly subtle and yet its analysis is important if the European experience is to further an understanding of the demographic changes taking place in the Developing World.

Causal factors, it may be hypothesized, fell into a number of inter-related groups. First those related to mortality. Throughout Europe significant falls in mortality preceded falls in fertility. The simple explanation refers to 'insurance births'. Since many would die, wives produced a large number of children to ensure sufficient survived to maintain the family and its labour force. When mortality rates fell, for the reasons discussed, the need for this 'insurance' margin was removed and fewer children were born because births were controlled. In reality the role of the mortality factor was more complex. Crude mortality rates conceal variations in age-specific rates. Mortality in Britain declined first, and sharply, in the 5–15 age group, then in the 15–24 in the late 1870s with the death rate for older persons not falling until the 1880s and 90s. Infant mortality rates which were very high in the mid-nineteenth century, 148 in 1860, fell hardly at all and were 146 in 1900 (Greenwood 1936). This meant that couples perceived mortality as remaining high and did not limit their families though a greater proportion of those who survived infancy lived. The drop in family size was thus retarded. It has been argued that amongst the better off, the middle classes, infant mortality did decline earlier so that their response in limiting their families likewise took place earlier. When overall infant mortality rates fell in the twentieth century then family sizes diminished and smaller families became the accepted norm. Age specific mortality rates are thus more significant than crude rates and their role is an interaction between economic and social factors.

The second group of factors are the economic which interlink with, because they are monetary evaluations of, other factors. In economic terms children, if they can be employed, are regarded as a resource by the family. Children can also be regarded as a form of consumption, a commodity which costs money, and so they are part of the demand pattern of the family and they compete with expenditure available for other goods. Families will therefore arrive at a mix of goods, including children, which they consider desirable. As income changes so the mix changes; as other conditions influencing society change, for example the mortality factor discussed, so again does the mix. If educational opportunities change this will feed back into the family decision. The value of more children which the family cannot afford to educate could be set against the improved and more valuable resource of children who after a non-productive period of education would, because of their training, have a greater capability of income-earning. Thus the loss of an immediate resource-gain would be set against a later but larger one. Similar economic ideas could be applied to the role of women. The woman giving birth to and bringing up a large number of children may be foregoing an income. She incurs an opportunity cost which must needs be taken into account in supporting the alternative of bearing fewer children. It can be argued that if incomes go up the need for investment in large families is lowered.

The third group of factors may be called social or cultural and likewise they involve both the mortality factors and economic valuations. For example the concept of status may in some societies find expression in the range and quality of material possessions. The middle class in nineteenth-century England might have wished to remain distinctive from the increasingly better off working classes and, to ensure this, substituted goods for children in their consumption pattern. The professional and middle class of Victorian England could also have been motivated by concern for their children, by the wish for them to benefit from the enlightenment of education or to have the opportunity for more fulfilling or remunerative occupations after, at considerable expense, they had been educated. Fewer children would make these goals more reachable. As a greater proportion of the population saw the possibility of such goals, the norm of the smaller family would characterize most strata of society. Changing attitudes to women and their role in society could have considerable repercussions upon birth rates and family size. The educated woman was more likely to wish to play roles in addition to those of wife and mother, to identify the opportunities for and needs of her children in terms of a fuller, healthier and educated life and to play an active part in society herself. All would be reasons for viewing the smaller family as desirable.

It may be wondered that there has been no mention of the development of contraceptive techniques. All the evidence shows that forms of family limitation had been practised over many centuries in many societies and techniques of contraception have improved markedly in their effectiveness particularly in the twentieth century. The central issue is, however, of the conditions which lead to the practice of family limitation, to the use of the available technology and it is these factors which have been discussed.

The multiple nature of these interlocking factors all influencing the trend towards fewer births meant that they could, and probably did, vary in their strength from country to country in Europe and that this accounts for the variations in the timing of the decline in fertility and its coincidence with economic and social developments. Clearly these groups of factors can apply to the situation in the Developing World and equally, the nature of their significance and their timing will vary throughout its many countries and cultures. In some cultures status may not be conferred by material possessions but by size of families. In others the impact of increasing numbers of children, as mortality rates fall, may bear not only on the nuclear family but upon the delicately balanced social systems of the extended family and wider society established to care for the welfare of dependants and unable to cope with a big increase in the younger dependent section of society. Long-established systems may begin to crumble under the pressure of the enlarging younger population. For all these reasons it is possible to argue that a similar fall in birth rates to that which took place in Europe may be characteristic of all the countries of the world. It can also be argued that the timing and character of the demographic change may well be as different as are conditions.

THE DEMOGRAPHIC TRANSITION

The population dynamics characteristic of Europe from the eighteenth to the twentieth century have been encapsulated in the well-known model, the demographic transition. It is shown in Fig. 5. A period of high birth rates and high death rates, essentially controlling the size of population, is followed by one in which a fall in mortality is experienced and, as birth rates remain high, the population increases, essentially the situation during most of the nineteenth century in Britain. There then follows a phase in which birth rates fall, death rates approach a very low level but the population continues to increase as the youth of its past become parents. Finally with both birth rates and death rates very low the population settles at a stationary level with death rates beginning to rise a little because the population is older. This transition has confounded Malthus; it is necessary to examine why.

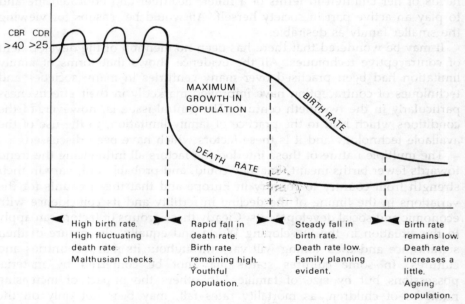

Figure 5 The demographic transition model

The Malthusian theorem did not work out in the country of its origin. Underlying his ideas on limits to the rate of production was the idea of diminishing returns. Applying a variable factor of production, it could be labour or manure or some other item, to a fixed factor of production namely land, would increase output by a certain amount for each unit of input. At first each unit of input would produce a big increase in yield but this amount of the increase would progressively decline as more units of input were applied, until a stage was reached when one additional unit of input

30

produced merely one unit of output. Beyond that point the curve tapers off and the amount of return on output becomes increasingly smaller than the unit input until eventually additional inputs actually produce a decline in output. The marginal product is the additional amount produced by each additional input and its curve shows precisely this diminishing effect until it passes below zero and becomes negative. Malthus saw this happening and postulated that the diminishing return would produce famine and malnutrition, death and a diminution in population to a point where production could sustain it. The population would then increase again and the whole process repeated so that the population was kept in check. This concept could, of course, be applied to other finite resources in addition to land. In the simplest terms two things happened which modified the Malthusian model. First the diminishing return effect did not manifest itself because that great assemblage of changes in technique, organization and economic restructuring called the agrarian and industrial revolutions, enormously increased the ability to produce per unit of population. The curve of production was raised above that of population increase so that the diminishing return curve did not bisect that of population and reduce its per capita benefits from production. Despite the fact that the population increased, not because of increased birth rates but because of reduced mortality, itself consequent upon economic changes and the reorganization of society, the scale and nature of economic development continued to stave off the critical conflict between size of population and resources to support it which Malthus had envisaged. Diminishing returns were continuously postponed by economic development, a feature of considerable significance for the Developing World. Secondly, the upsurge in population was contained not because it was cut back by famine and poverty but because, for the reasons discussed, couples chose to have smaller families. They made the choice under conditions of greater material prosperity and security; again a pointer for Developing Countries. Resources had been used more effectively and the nature of society had changed. Social and economic development had produced a demographic transition. The questions remain. Is the demographic transition of the kind experienced in Europe, North America and indeed Japan, the key to the understanding of the demographic situation in the Developing World? Is it an inevitable sequence of events? Will it, in the varied conditions of the many developing countries, take the same form as in Europe? Is a demographic transition of such a kind desirable? Has it a significance for the development process?

RESOURCES AND PEOPLE AND THE QUESTION OF OVERPOPULATION

In all countries of the Developing World populations are expanding and in many have been expanding rapidly since the Second World War. The

31

Average Annual Percentage Growth in Population 1970–81

> 3

2–3

1–19

< 1

n – No data

Source of data World Bank 1983

Equator

Figure 6 Population increase 1970–81

average annual growth rate in the decade 1960–70 in the low-income econo-mies was 2.3 per cent and in the lower middle-income 2.6 per cent, figures much higher than the maximum rate of 1.8 per cent ever reached by England and Wales. No less than eighteen of the seventy-three countries in these World Bank classifications demonstrated population increase of 3 per cent and over (Fig. 6). Their death rates have been quickly and markedly reduced by prophylactic medicine and the conquest of many major, infec-tious, zootic diseases, a conquest unrelated to the stage of their economic development and one mainly of diseases unrelated to living conditions. Their birth rates, in contrast, have remained high and, if the European experience is any guide, this is a feature very much related to the socio-economic development process. It could be said that many developing coun-tries are in the second phase of the demographic transition. The question is whether all, or some, will move into the stage where both deaths and birth rates are low and, if so, how quickly. This is a matter of some concern. The European transition is not inevitable. The conditions which pertained from the eighteenth to the twentieth century in Europe which saw popu-lation expansion associated with, and in large measure contemporaneous with, economic and social development as resources were assembled and utilized in a more productive way to sustain expansion, may not emerge in the countries of the Developing World. The population expansion there has largely preceded massive economic development because it was the product of non-associated external medical innovations. If, on the one hand, production can be raised to encompass the increased numbers and if, on the other, birth rates can be controlled to retard the rate of increase, a controlled transition can be brought about. If not, the spectre of Malthus will haunt the villages of the Developing World and stalk the streets of its growing cities and coldly calculate its ratios. It is the reason why population dynamics is so central to development planning.

Many of the subsequent chapters in this book will be concerned with the production side of the equation, with the lifting of the production curve of diminishing returns so that it encompasses the population dimension. Indeed underlying the ideas of Malthus, the demographic transition, concepts of over and under population, is the relationship between resources or supply and population or need.

Views on changing populations have varied in time and place. An increasing population, characteristic of most developing countries, could be regarded as an increasing asset, and source of power. Mussolini, the fascist dictator of Italy, is reported to have said in the 1920s that the population of Italy must grow if she was to be more powerful claiming 'with a falling population one does not create an empire but one becomes a colony'. A declining population can be regarded as a disaster. E. M. Hubback writing in 1947 states 'A Britain with a much smaller population would no longer be an important influence in world affairs either in peace or war. She would lose her status and power' (Hubback 1947). In the past at least, many governments in developing countries have held not dissimilar views. Some have said that the governments, economists and others in the industrialized countries who urge upon developing countries the pressing need to reduce birth rates and population growth are simply expressing the wish of the industrialized countries to remain dominant. They claim that larger populations are essential to stimulate economic development and state that industrialization in Europe was accompanied by the large growth in population which made it possible. Others in developing countries, expressing views like Mussolini and Hubback, state that young men are needed in greater numbers to sustain their status and power, and they are commonly referring to potential conflicts with each other. Similar concepts of the relationship between power and population size emerge in multi-racial countries or countries with several religious faiths, each race or faith fearful that if its numbers decline it will become under-privileged, disenfranchised or persecuted. Elements of truth exist in many of these views; fears of loss of ethnic, religious or indeed national identity are very real, if incomplete in some cases and unrealistic in others. They have certainly influenced the demographic policies of many countries. But to ignore the fast rising numbers, which have preceded the laying down of foundations for a sustained economic growth, is to become burdened with poverty rather than power. What has emerged, not only in the industrialized nations but also in the great majority of countries in the Developing World, is the need to reduce fertility rates and to do this quickly in order to make the size of the development task more manageable. This size has two demographic dimensions, the rate of population increase and the volume in absolute numbers. In some countries the numbers might be small but the speed of increase greater than the rate of possible resource development. In others the rate of increase might be less but the population base so large that the annual yield is vast. The population of tiny Fiji rises each year by an amount equal to the size of its second largest town. In the Fijian dimension it is significant. The population of India between 1981 and 1982 rose by some 17 million, more than the size of Australia's population. By any dimensions this is significant. The crucial relationship is the match between rates of population increase and rates of social and economic development.

4 The Dimension of People: A Travail of Transitions

THE DEMOGRAPHIC TRANSITION IN THE LATE TWENTIETH CENTURY

'Fertility is an area of human behaviour where individual tastes, religion, culture and social norms all play a major role. Yet evidence from large groups of people suggests that differences in fertility can be largely explained by differences in their social and economic environment.'

The World Bank
World Development Report 1980

It is possible to make a general statement as to the population dynamics of the developing countries in aggregate and to compare this with the situation in the industrialized economies, to compare the demographic transition. But the Developing World is vast, it embraces most of mankind and its nations. It is, therefore, important to examine its several components and to reveal any differences in both the form and speed in the demographic transitions which are taking place.

In its Development Report for 1980, the World Bank traced the progress of crude death and birth rates from the eighteenth century into the twenty-first for two aggregates of nations, the industrialized countries, including those of eastern Europe and the Soviet Union, and the developing countries. Projections beyond 1980 were based upon reasoned generalised assumptions of the performance of the population dynamic for each country. The graphical depiction of the situation is reproduced in Fig. 7. It indicates that a demographic transition, similar in its trends but displaced in time, will encompass the Developing World with net reproduction rates reaching unity between AD 2005 and AD 2045 and with stationary population being achieved between AD 2065 and AD 2175 (World Bank 1980a). The increase in population is at its maximum during the second half of the twentieth century when high, though falling, birth rates are associated with low, and still falling, death rates. Since China and India together accounted for 73.6 per cent of the developing countries' population in 1978, their demographic performance dominates the generalised transition shown in Fig. 7. The situation in other countries, areas or continents could differ appreciably and it is the situation within individual countries which bears upon their economic problems and possibilities. These variations will now be examined.

35

Per 1,000 population

Rate of population increase=birth rate−death rate

Crude birth and death rates. The projected increases in death rates after about 1980 reflect the rising proportion of older people in the population.
* Include industrialized countries, the USSR and Eastern Europe.

Source: World Bank 1980

Figure 7 The World Bank projection of the demographic transition

A TRAVAIL OF TRANSITIONS

The European model of the demographic transition contained the following sequence of cause and effect:

1. Socio-economic changes dominated mortality rates up until the First World War
2. Socio-economic changes influenced birth rates
3. Resulting declines first in mortality and subsequently fertility, produced the demographic transition with modern medical science playing its part in only the final stages.

The presumed demographic transition model for the Developing World contains the following elements:

1. Prior to the Second World War disease-ridden societies displayed the medieval European balance of high birth rates checked by high death rates
2. Medical science has dominated mortality rates since the Second World War and the rate of their decline has been much greater than in the European model because of this
3. Socio-economic changes will determine any further falls in death rates
4. Socio-economic development will influence birth rates and induce their decline

5. The demographic transition will be brought about by the interaction of (2) and (4) and, in its final stages, will be characterized by the operation of factor (3).

The European model of demographic transition is based upon events which have already taken place in the affluent industrialized nations of the world. The Developing World model presumes future developments. It is based on hypothesis. Its nature, or natures since many alternatives are possible, will depend upon the ways in which the variety of social and economic factors come together in the many countries of the Developing World and influence birth rates. The European model could be very much culture-related and the multitude of cultures in the model give birth to a multitude of transitions. In this cultural matrix there are many variables. Religion could play a part, the place of women in society could be influential, the adoption and rigour of family planning programmes could vary, the degree of urbanization might be influential. Culture in the widest sense, the civilizations of the world with their distinctive mores, could condition the way in which family size and birth rates are viewed. Even the nature of governments could play a part. The power-hungry totalitarian state might well take the Mussolini view of population. The state which put social provision and equity to the fore could strongly influence attitudes to family planning programmes and their provision. These are speculations but they are reasonable. Some are verifiable, others are not.

While in the immediate post-war period and into the 1950s there was much uncertainty about the demographic situation in the Developing World, since 1960 the wider availability of more reliable data is making the position clearer. A demographic transition in its broad outline similar to that of the European model *is* taking place but there are variations in both the speed of the transition and its dimensions. This situation will now be examined. The graphical device used to analyse the data is a development of that devised by Jakubowski (Jakubowski 1977). It allows both temporal and locational comparisons of individual countries and groups of countries. Countries in the pre-transitional, or early transitional stage, are characterized by high death rates and birth rates and will be located in the top left-hand corner of the graphs. Countries such as those of Europe which have passed through the transition to a period of very low death rates and birth rates appear towards the bottom right-hand corner. As their populations age, a function of their vital statistics, locations shift a little to the left into slightly higher death rates. The crescentic sweep of the transition curve can be detected in Fig. 8.

The first and coarsest analytical sieve is that of continental location. In 1960 the countries of Africa and most of those of Asia were bounded by dimensions of crude birth rates exceeding 40 per thousand and crude death rates in excess of 15. The birth rates were those of England a century earlier and the death rates of England in the nineteenth century, in most cases.

37

Figure 8 Crude birth and death rates by continents

Central and South America was displaced to the right, that is by lower death rates, but most countries still demonstrated birth rates in excess of 38. There were some notable exceptions and the Latin American countries of Argentina and Uruguay revealed population characteristics similar to those of the USA and the USSR. The European nations were characteristically bunched together in a zone of low death and birth rates and were joined by Japan. The countries of the Middle East all showed very high birth rates but ranged in death rates from the highest in the world, 31, to low European levels.

Twenty-one years later the situation had changed markedly (Fig. 8B). European birth rates had fallen still further and in all other continental areas death rates had declined. The compactness of the continental groupings had also been much reduced. Africa, and the Middle East each covered a much wider range of birth rates; Asia did so to a much greater extent; Central and Latin America as a whole had moved down in birth rate values but again a wide range is evident. What is discernible in all the continental areas is the characteristic crescent shape of the demographic transition with the crescent flattening as the range of death rates contract and lengthening as individual countries within the continents reduce their birth rates much more than others. The low birth-rate countries reach down to the European situation and the transition is much in evidence. It is necessary next to examine the reasons for the range in values within the continents.

On Fig. 9A, the weighted means for crude birth and death rates have

Figure 9 The demographic transition 1960–81

been plotted for each of the economic groups of the World Banks classification. India and China, both in the low-income group, are shown separately. The transitional crescent is evident with the economic groups ranged along it with the low income countries at its beginning, then the lower middle and upper middle-income groups with still some way to go to achieve the European situation which is evident in both the capitalist industrial economies and those of communist Eastern Europe. There is therefore a general demographic sorting according to GNP per capita income but there are exceptions. The high-income oil exporting countries, Libya, Saudi Arabia, Kuwait and the United Arab Emirates with incomes as high or higher than European countries, show a demographic path similar to that of the low-income countries. Secondly, India and China, though low-income, have distinctive paths. India is closer to the lower middle-income pattern but is moving rapidly towards the upper middle-income mean. China is truly exceptional. The world's most populous country has achieved the demographic transition in a brief span of some two decades. Figs. 10A and 10B show the situation more fully by demarcating the range of values of individual countries within each income group. In 1960 two countries lay exceptionally outside the main assembly of their appropriate group. Sri Lanka among low-income countries was distinguished by a very low death rate and birth rates low for a poor country. Cuba, a low middle-income

Figure 10 Crude birth and death rates by economy groups

country, lay in a similar fashion outside its group (Fig. 10A). China was not distinctive. In 1981 the separation of the income groups is more apparent and China joins Sri Lanka and Cuba in its distinctiveness. In terms of both continental and economic groups the early 1980s are witnessing the demographic transition in progress. The bunching together of the Developing World countries in the initial transition phase in 1960, has been replaced by a stretching of the field with the 'runners' as it were, spaced out along the track. As more countries approach the finishing post, if indeed the European situation is the terminal phase of demographic equilibrium, a new bunching is beginning to appear. Indeed the model would require the transition to be completed in such a way.

The analysis can be refined further by plotting the demographic shift for each country within each continental income-group (Figs. 11–13). The low-income economies of Africa which account for 21 of the 39 nations in the continent (of over 1 million population) are markedly similar in their demographic characteristics (Fig. 11A). All show continuing high birth rates with no marked decline and some increases. Death rates have fallen but, with one exception, exceed fifteen and many are still in excess of twenty. In Asia, the position is different. Only two countries have remained in the African situation; the others have moved markedly through the transitional phases, notably the world's most populous countries India, with still a long way to go to reduce birth rates, and China. In the next higher income groups

Figure 11 The demographic transition 1960–81

(Fig. 11C), the African countries show features similar to those of their low-income continental neighbours. Birth rates remain very high in all except Egypt and Tunisia and though death rates have fallen, most are above fifteen. Africa is clearly a continent where the demographic transition is in its early stages. The Asian income equivalents have all moved further along the transitional crescent with birth rates falling markedly (Figs. 11B and 11C). In the countries of Central and South America and the Caribbean the lower middle-income countries demonstrate features very similar to their Asian counterparts. All have cleared the initial phase of change and Cuba has essentially completed all but the terminal part of the transition (Fig 12A). The upper middle-income group for both Asia and Central and South America is shown in Fig. 12B. The two continental areas exhibit a wide range of birth rate values but a small spread in death rates. They cover essentially the same sector of the transitional crescent. Countries like Uruguay and Argentina in Latin America and Hong Kong and Singapore in Asia have all but completed the demographic transition.

The countries of the Middle East, undifferentiated by income group, are plotted on Fig. 9B. With four exceptions, Turkey, Lebanon, the United Arab Emirates and Israel, they all reveal characteristics similar to those in Africa with high birth rates persisting. The changing demographic situation in the

Figure 12 The demographic transition 1960–81

Figure 13 Crude birth and death rates by continental income-groups

countries of the Developing World between 1960 and 1981 is best summarised in Figs. 13A and 13B. In 1960 these countries were grouped together and all were characterized by high birth rates. The differentiation which is discernible is that lower death rates (and some of the lowest birth rates) were associated with the middle-income countries, the better off. The lower middle-income countries in Asia and Central and South America formed a short bridge to low and lower middle-incomes in Africa and low incomes in Asia. The exceptional countries of Sri Lanka, Cuba, Argentina and Uruguay were the isolated links in the continuum to the industrial market economies. By 1981 the same order of sequence was present but the countries of the Developing World stretched completely across the demographic spectrum as some countries pulled away from others in the extent to which they had reduced their birth rates and in their movement through the demographic transition.

The continental income-groups themselves encompass a wide range of values relating to birth rates quite apart from the exceptionally anomalous situations of countries like China, Cuba and Sri Lanka. Clearly, particular factors leading to a reduction in family size may well have been operative. A series of possible causative associations such as those to which reference has earlier been made will now be examined.

43

DIFFERENTIAL DECLINES IN FERTILITY: EXPLANATORY CORRELATIONS

GROSS NATIONAL PRODUCT PER CAPITA

A broad relationship between wealth measured in Gross National Product (GNP) per capita terms has been demonstrated at a continental level but there were exceptions. At country level this measure is graphed against total fertility rates (Fig. 14A). A general trend is discernible. The poorest countries with less than $1000 per capita are largely grouped in the above five fertility rates, whereas the rich countries, over $5000 per capita, are characterised by rates below three. But the correlation is a weak one. At all income levels there is a wide spread of values and this raises the issue of the many other putative factors to which reference has already been made. Clearly the distribution of wealth throughout the population rather than a simple average per capita is of likely significance. Countries with marked dual economies such as South Africa characterised by an affluent minority and a poor majority will have skewed-income effects upon family size. The origin and expenditure of national wealth will likewise determine the extent to which it influences standards of living amongst the majority. The rapid increase in national income of the oil exporting countries, consequent upon the great increase in oil prices in the 1970s, has not had time to be reflected in the overall betterment of family incomes. The distribution of income amongst the population and the purposes to which national income is allocated are likely to have greater significance for population dynamics rather than a simple average.

INCOME DISTRIBUTION

Data for income distribution are available for a minority of countries in the Developing World and the manner of their collection, significance and reliability inevitably varies. In Fig. 14B the percentage share of household incomes taken by the top 20 per cent of households is plotted against crude birth rates. The correlation is reasonably close giving some credence to the view that the spreading of developments throughout the population is a contributory factor to the lowering of birth rates.

GROWTH IN THE ECONOMY AND CHANGE IN BIRTH RATE

If the provision of health and social services and increases in disposable household incomes are related to economic growth, it would seem reasonable for it also to be associated with population change. Indeed, in a general way, the transition graphs reveal this. In Fig. 15 A the percentage change in crude birth rates, both increases and decreases, is plotted against the

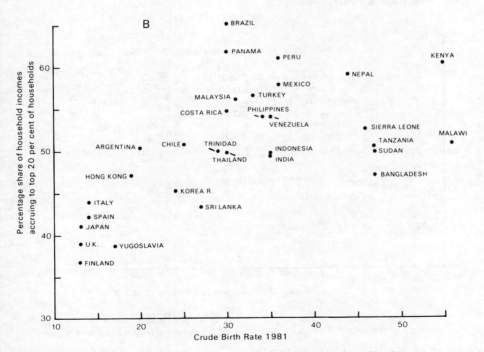

Figure 14 Fertility and birth rate correlations with incomes

Figure 15 (a) Birth rate change and GNP per capita change
(b) Birth rates and the agricultural labour force

percentage average annual growth, or decline, in per capita GNP between 1960 and 1981. There is a broad correlation from Niger and Ghana, with negative growths in GNP and near zero changes in birth rates, to Hong Kong and Singapore at the other extreme with very high increases in per capita GNP and dramatic reductions in the birth rate. However, in the tiers of lowest birth-rate decline, below 10 per cent, and birth-rate increase, the correlation falls away almost completely and this lack of correlation is almost entirely associated with African and Middle Eastern countries. Most are poor countries where percentage increases on very low absolute values will be of little significance. Others, like Libya and Saudi Arabia, demonstrate GNP increases in large measure due to oil wealth rather than the product of a more broadly based economy. Again it would appear that birth rate trends are wealth-related though the relationship is too complex and indirect to yield a strong, simple correlation.

AGRICULTURAL SOCIETIES AND URBANIZATION

The agricultural countries of the world are poorer and, for the most part, have diffused rather than concentrated populations which are, in consequence, more difficult to serve in terms of education, social and health provision. In discussing the British demographic transition reference was made, it will be recalled, to the view that agricultural communities adhered to old customs and values while the new town dwellers, in leaving their old societies, also abandoned their old ways including attitudes to family size. In Fig. 15B, the proportion of the labour force engaged in agriculture is compared with crude birth rates. There is a broad correlation with the curve steepening for countries with less than 30 per cent engaged in agriculture. Of the countries where over 50 per cent are agriculturalists the birth rate band is 30–55. Only two countries, Sri Lanka and China, are below this. It is significant also that the upper values in the band are overwhelmingly characterized by African and Middle Eastern countries whereas Asian and South American states occupy its lower margins. The largely agricultural countries are also the poorest. No country in the upper-middle income class has more than 50 per cent of its labour force in agriculture.

All the countries of the world are becoming more urbanized and so the developing countries are not exceptional. Their level of urbanization is, however, still low. Amongst the low-income countries the weighted average of urban dwellers rose from 17 to 21 per cent, and in the lower middle-income from 24 to 33 per cent, between 1960 and 1981. None the less, the range of the degree of urbanization remains very great from 2 per cent in the case of Burundi to 100 per cent in Singapore. As in other associations examined, a broad correlation rather than a narrow and exact one, characterizes the relationship with birth rates (Fig. 16A). The extremes of the curve are of low-income African countries at one end and the industrial economies

Figure 16 (a) Birth rates and urban population
(b) Birth rates and infant mortality rates

at the other. The correlation is broadened by the high birth rates of Middle Eastern and North African countries with urban population exceeding 40 per cent and by Asian countries with comparatively low birth rates which are largely rural for example Vietnam, Indonesia, Burma, India, Thailand, Malaysia and, of course, Sri Lanka and China. European countries reveal low birth rates regardless of the level of urbanization. Africa, the least urbanized of the continents exhibits the highest proportion of high birth rates. It is of interest that there is no correlation between urbanization and death rates. Low death rates, less than 9, are unrelated to urbanization and can be found in countries where 85 per cent of the population is rural as in Thailand, to where it is wholly urban, Singapore, and, indeed, higher death rates correspond more closely to income levels than to urbanization.

RELIGIOUS AND POLITICAL INFLUENCES

It is difficult to be precise in the categorization of whole nations in terms of religion or political affiliation. A country may have a Marxist government but may not be able to administer the economy in a rigorous Marxist fashion. All European countries are nominally Christian yet the vast majority of their populations do not attend church and many do not believe in the Divinity though most adhere to Christian moral values. In both examples it is the practice rather than the posture which is significant. Countries in which Buddhism is the main religion tend to have birth rates below the average of their income category and the Hindu countries likewise. Both are essentially Asian religions but there are marked exceptions to this tendency with birth rates of 44 per 1000 in Nepal; 43 in Lao, 40 in Bhutan contrasting with 30 in Thailand and 27 in Sri Lanka. Islamic countries where the majority of the population are devout believers are, as a group, characterized by above average birth rates for their income groups. There are exceptions. Egypt, Tunisia and Turkey are below the average for the lower-middle income groups.

In political terms it is not possible to cite easy correlations. It is true that China and Cuba with their Marxist-socialist systems both exhibit very low birth rates within their income groups but so too do Sri Lanka and Jamaica. In the Middle East the socialist Peoples Democratic Republic of the Yemen and the non-socialist Yemen Republic both exhibit, at 48, the characteristic high birth rates of Middle-Eastern Islamic countries. The communist state of the Korean Democratic Republic has a much higher birth rate, 31, than the capitalist Korean Republic with 24 while in Europe birth rates in Western non-communist countries are essentially similar to those in the Soviet bloc. What is important is the extent to which governments, whatever their political or religious label, incorporate into their views of, and plans for, their societies a deliberate social provision.

SOCIAL PROVISION

Social provision may be expressed in terms of education, of medical services for all and not simply for the urban rich, of maternity care and of family planning advice and facilities together with a policy related to a more even distribution of income. Among the countries of the Developing World, China, Sri Lanka, Cuba and Jamaica have been noticeably to the fore in this respect and this does much to explain their particular positions in the demographic transition. Three measures to assess this feature will be examined.

First, data is available on the number of persons in a country per physician as a measure of medical provision. It proves to be a very poor indicator of birth rates. In the low-income countries birth rates in excess of 40 are to be found in countries like Pakistan with one physician for every 3500 people and in countries like Niger, Upper Volta, Chad and Ethiopia where there is only one physician for between 38,500 and 53,000 persons. Lower middle-income countries again demonstrate a wide range of values. China with a birth rate of 21, has a large number of doctors, one for every 1920 persons, but Bolivia with a birth rate of 43 has even more per head of population, one for every 1850. Clearly much depends upon who has access to the physicians. Few developing countries have nationwide health services like the Chinese; in many, their physicians have urban practices and treatment is not free.

Second, the impact of medical care, of social provision, of improvement in living conditions and awareness of hygiene can be measured by levels of infant mortality as it was in Britain. Low levels consequent upon a complex of attitudes and facilities could well, as have been argued in the European context, lead to a lowering of birth rates as fewer 'insurance' births become necessary. Figure 16B illustrates a clear relationship existing between infant mortality and birth rates across the whole spectrum of low- and middle-income countries though, for obvious reasons, at very high mortality levels, high birth rates are characteristic regardless of the precise level.

Thirdly, it has been argued that the more educated the population, and in particular the women, the more likely they will be to evaluate the need to plan the size of families. Data adequately to measure comparative levels of education are lacking but utilizing data relating to females, the percentage of the primary school age group which attended school in 1960 has been compared with crude birth rates in 1981 and depicted in Fig. 17A. An association between a more educated female population and a reduction in birth rate is evident. There are anomalies such as Zimbabwe but it is of interest to see that in countries such as Sri Lanka, Jamaica, Cuba, Costa Rica and Lebanon, all with low birth rates for their respective groups, a large proportion of girls attend primary school. In contrast in most of the Islamic countries, Saudi Arabia, Libya, Sudan, Iran, Morocco, Syria, Algeria, less than

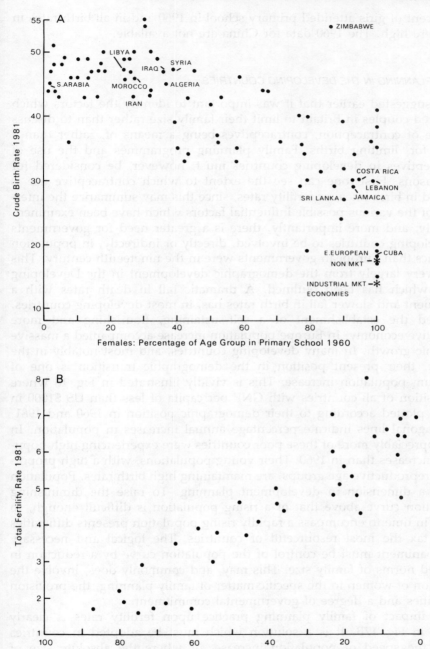

Figure 17 (a) Birth rates 1981 and females educated 1960
(b) Fertility rates and contraceptive use

40 per cent of girls attended primary school in 1960 and in all birth rates in 1981 were high. The 1960 data for China are not available.

FAMILY PLANNING IN THE DEVELOPING COUNTRIES

It was suggested earlier that it was important to identify the factors which motivated couples in Britain to limit their family size rather than to discuss the role of contraception, contraceptives being a means of, rather than a reason for, limiting births. Family planning programmes and the use of contraceptives in developing countries must, however, be considered for two reasons. First, one can see the extent to which contraceptive use is reflected in birth rates, or fertility rates, since this may summarize the inter-action of the various possible influential factors which have been examined. Secondly, and more importantly, there is a greater need for governments in developing countries to be involved, directly or indirectly, in population dynamics than European governments were in the nineteenth century. This stems very largely from the demographic development in the Developing World which has been outlined. A dramatic fall in death rates with a subsequent and slower fall in birth rates has, in most developing countries, preceded the establishment of a self-sustaining, flourishing and more productive economy. In Europe population increase accompanied a massive economic growth. In many developing countries, and most notably in the poorest, their present position in the demographic transition is one of maximum population increase. This is vividly illustrated in Fig. 18 where the position of all countries with GNP per capita of less than US $1000 in 1981 is plotted according to their demographic position in 1960 and 1981. The diagonal lines indicate percentage annual increases in population. In 1981 appreciably more of these poor countries were experiencing high popu-lation increases than in 1960. Their young populations, with a high propor-tion in reproductive age groups, are maintaining high birth rates. Population size is a dimension in development planning. To raise the diminishing production curve above that of a rising population is difficult enough, to raise it in time to encompass a rapidly rising population presents difficulties which tax the most resourceful of countries. The logical and necessary accompaniment must be control of the population curve by a reduction in accepted norms of family size. This may, and commonly does, involve the education of women in the specific matter of family planning, the provision of facilities and a degree of governmental commitment.

The impact of family planning practice upon fertility rates is clearly shown in Fig. 17B. It is a solution which must be adopted in countries where the speed of population increase, or where the absolute size of annual increases, are inhibiting social and economic development.

Two sets of forces are thus at work bringing about the reduction in birth rates in developing countries. One is the improvement in economic,

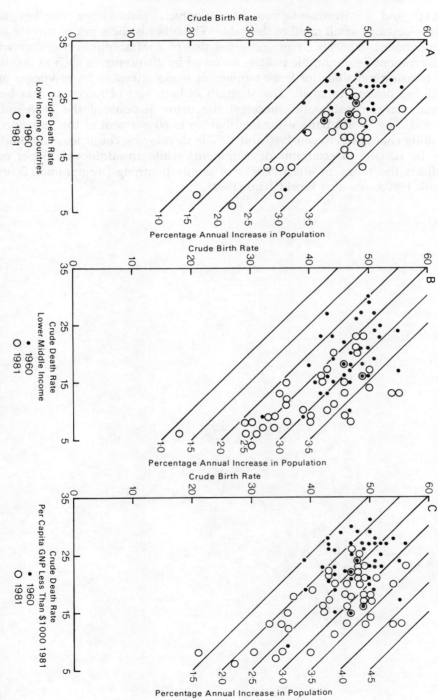

Figure 18 Crude birth and death rates and increases in population 1960–81

social and environmental conditions which make large families less necessary and small families desirable. The other is the work of private and government agencies to promote the use of contraceptives together with government demographic policies enforced by disincentives such as taxation or housing penalties for large families or made attractive by privileges and facilities offered to small. The strength of both sets of forces, as has been seen, varies considerably amongst the many nations of the Developing World. The World Bank estimates that up to 60 per cent of the variation in fertility changes between 1960 and 1977 in developing countries is accounted for by social and economic developments while an additional 15 per cent reflects the range of effectiveness of family planning programmes (World Bank 1980a; see also World Bank 1984).

5 Agriculture: the Environment and Indigenous Farming Systems

'And he gave it for his opinion, that whoever could make two ears of corn or two blades of grass to grow upon a spot of ground where only one grew before, would deserve better of mankind and do more essential service to his country than the whole race of politicians put together'

Jonathan Swift
Gulliver's Travels 1726

The countries of the Developing World are essentially agricultural in the sense that a large proportion of their populations work on the land to raise crops and stock. In 1980, in the low-income economies of the World Bank classification, 70 per cent of the labour force worked in agriculture. This group, since it includes India and China, represents almost half the world's population. In the slightly more affluent group of lower-middle income countries, the proportion in 1980 was 55 per cent though it had been as high as 71 per cent only twenty years earlier. These predominantly agricultural populations are in many cases inadequately fed. Per capita daily calorie supplies in over three-quarters of the low-income countries are below the necessary minimum for normal health and activity (see Figs. 2 and 3). Self-sufficiency in basic staple cereals has, furthermore, been declining in many developing countries in recent years. In an analysis of this situation, the United Nations Food and Agriculture Organization (FAO) has shown that over the period from 1961–65 to 1977–79, net cereal production failed to keep pace with both population growth and cereal demand in 73 out of 92 developing countries (FAO 1982).

Table 4 shows the continental variations in this situation which is at its worst in Africa where only three out of thirty-seven countries had raised cereal production sufficiently to meet rising populations and increased demand. In ten African countries cereal production actually declined. The most satisfactory situation pertains in Asia and the Far East but even there only half the countries maintained an adequate cereal output. As FAO point out, the fact that staple food production is below demand is not necessarily a problem if food imports can be paid for. The ability to pay will depend upon foreign exchange earnings and saving capacity. In examining seventy-two developing countries which were major cereal growers, FAO found that

Table 4 Growth in cereal production and growth in population and cereal demand 1961–65 to 1977–79

	Negative growth in cereal production	Growth did not keep pace with population growth	Growth kept pace with population but not with cereal demand	Growth kept pace with population and cereal demand	Totals
	Number of countries*				
Africa	10	20	4	3	37
Asia & Far East	—	8	—	8	16
Near East	7	3	1	3	14
Latin America	6	9	5	5	25
World	23	40	10	19	92

Source: FAO World Report 1981
* Refers to countries with market economies

in 58 per cent of them the self-sufficiency ratio in cereals declined between 1966–68 and 1978–80. (The self-sufficiency ratio is the production of cereals divided by the figure which represents production less exports plus imports by volume). In thirty-three of these countries this declining ratio was placing an increasing burden on their balance of payments. Small changes in the ratio can have a very marked effect upon the balance of payments particularly in countries with large populations. For example, in Bangladesh where over the period examined the self-sufficiency ratio fell from 94 to 89, the resulting cost of cereal imports to make up the deficiency absorbed no less than 58 per cent of Bangladesh's export earnings which could have been used in development investment (FAO 1982). Where large export earnings such as from oil are possible, food can be imported with little impact upon them. In the case of most developing countries this is not possible.

Two important issues stem from the situations which have been described. First, many developing countries, overwhelmingly agrarian though they may be, are unable to feed their populations securely and adequately. Second, the inadequacies of the agricultural production of food are retarding other economic developments. It is a situation which presents, head on, the question of raising the production curve, with its diminishing returns, above that of expanding populations. This, in turn, requires an assessment of the systems of farming which characterize the Developing World and the consideration of the extent to which they are adequate bases for a more productive development.

Agriculture and the rural economy is thus central to the problems of many developing countries. Food intake is lower in a calorific sense, is deficient in protein and lacks essential vitamins for optimum bodily health certainly amongst the Developing World's poor and they are many. Often food supply is seasonally varied and in some cases markedly so. Physical health does, as has been seen, reflect societal and environmental circumstances and this includes nutrition. Brain development can be retarded by malnutrition in infancy and its effect can be permanent. A famine can affect a whole generation. Poor nutrition does affect energy output, ability to work and susceptibility to disease. The securing of an adequate, balanced and nutritious diet is essential to the physical and mental well-being of the people of the Developing World and agriculture is clearly central to this situation. It is important in other respects in the processes of economic development but it is basic to the well-being of societies.

The majority of developing countries are not only less industrialized but are also less productive in agriculture than many so-called industrial countries. As their populations grow rapidly, so the pressure on inefficient and insecure food resources grows. The problem is not simply a matter of growing more food but also increasing the efficiency of harvesting, storing, transporting and marketing it and of using it more effectively. It is also a matter of the distribution of income and of the access to food of all sectors of the population both rural and urban.

The change in attitudes to new methods of production and to new organizational structures is a major one. Agriculture in the developing countries is very much a way of life of whole societies rather than simply a sector of an economy or an area of resource allocation. It embodies within it social structures, values and beliefs, prestige symbols and religious observances indeed all the strands of the fabric of life. To change within this situation is, perhaps, more difficult than moving out of it. To change within the extended family and the village may well present more of a problem than to migrate to a town to work in a factory or join the urban unemployed. Agriculture deals with the animate as well as the economic, with the life cycles of plants and animals, with the living soil and with climates the vagaries of which are difficult to predict and whose deficiencies are difficult to remedy. It is perhaps small wonder that governments so readily welcome, and invest in the factory, steel works and power station. It is not that these are not important, they clearly are, but that their apparent relative ease of construction and functioning, their openly declared manifestation of modernity and change may well lead governments to neglect the fundamental significance of agriculture with its multiplicity of production units and its association with a past rather than a future.

Agriculture in all economies and societies has, therefore, three components. One is physical, the role and influence of the physical environment. The second is social, reflecting systems and values at family and village level but also at national level as expressed in political ideologies. The third is economic. This is the dimension which not only calibrates the forces of the other two but also links agriculture to production and consumption activities at local, national and inter-national levels. The farming systems of the Developing World embody these dimensions.

FARMING AND THE PHYSICAL ENVIRONMENT

The Developing World is essentially a world of tropical climates though some of its countries extend into the sub-tropics. The issue has often been raised as to whether the climatic and edaphic environments of the tropics present particular difficulties which not only explain the relatively lower agricultural productivity of developing countries but also restrict further development.

The extreme situations of difficult environments are obvious whether in the polar regions of North America, Europe and Asia or the hot deserts of the tropics. In both cases populations are small and indigenous systems of food production from hunting, grazing or tillage are highly specialized. In countries where such areas are but a part of their territory, as in for example India, Pakistan and Chile, they tend to remain undeveloped. There are, however, developing countries which almost in their entirety are dominated by drought. Upper Volta, Mali, Chad and Niger are examples of independent countries desperately trying to manage their economies in the most difficult environmental conditions.

Apart from these obvious extremes the question as to whether environmental differences are important determinants of agricultural and other developments has been much debated by some and ignored by others. Andrew Kamarck, director of the Economic Development Institute of the World Bank has written:

> The effects of tropical climate are not absolute obstacles to economic development, but they do make many of the problems of economic development in the Tropics sufficiently different from those in the Temperate Zone countries so that an additional hurdle has to be overcome and, consequently, all other relevant factors being equal, the pace of development in tropical countries tends to be slower
>
> (Kamarck 1976).

Pierre Gourou has made equally positive statements as to the role of the physical environment stressing the poverty of many tropical soils: 'The poverty of tropical soils is often revealed quite unexpectedly by a yield often inferior to that in temperate soils' and 'For climatic reasons tropical soils and poor tend to become poorer quickly' (Gourou 1953).

Tosi and Voertmann have addressed themselves to this issue but with somewhat differing conclusions. They write:

> There is an informed judgement that the basic environmental traits which have historically restricted the productivity of tropical agriculture

also seriously impede the prospects of future development. But it is the opinion of the authors that this pessimism reflects a restricted conception of a high-productivity system tied to the crops, techniques, and organisation of the grain and pasture system. It is true that a high proportion of the plant species which form the basis of the high productivity system either will not grow at all in most of the tropical regions or else are very much less productive there. It is true that tropical soils are, for the most part, different in both physical and chemical make-up than the temperate region soils currently associated with high-productivity. It is also true that the dietary habits, food processing and raw material processing systems as well as agricultural machinery, land management techniques, and much else, are biased in favour of annual crops which, due to climate and costs differences have not prospered in the tropics generally. But all this is merely to admit that the land-use system, and indeed much else in the economic social and cultural life of the high income economies have been specialized by an environment structure quite unlike that of the tropics (Tosi and Voertmann 1964).

In other words, Tosi and Voertmann believe that a different situation may require a different approach from that in temperate areas and that which appears to be a deficiency or an inferiority may be simply a product of judging it by criteria which are not applicable. In their assessment, the humid tropics possess an enormous potential for production in terms of heat, radiant energy and water for plant growth.

A similar theme, but with different conclusions, is developed by Jen-hu Chang. His work is concerned with the humid tropics commonly associated with the rain forests and largely equatorial in location. Referring to the errors made by the disastrous ventures of the Ford Company's rubber plantation in the Amazon basin and the British groundnuts scheme in East Africa, Chang (1968) writes: 'Clearly, the principles of land use that have evolved from mid-latitude experience cannot be applied directly to the tropics; the efficiency of tropical agriculture must be judged by a different yardstick.' The equatorial forest areas he discusses are characterized by low population densities and low agricultural productivity in South America, Central Africa and in parts of the East Indies but by high population densities in other parts of the East Indies where rice, higher in calorie and protein content than other hot wet crops such as cassava though lower in protein than temperate grains, is successfully grown. He writes that 'in general, soils in the humid tropics have a distressingly low fertility'. There are, however, exceptions to this dictum notably on soils developed on mineral-rich recent lavas such as those of Java and the soils of flood plains and deltas of rivers which drain mineralogically varied areas. Unfortunately, in wide areas of tropical South America and Africa, the source materials for soils are the long-weathered pre-Cambrian rocks on ancient peneplanes. Of climate in the humid tropics Chang states:

'the much attenuated solar radiation, the persistently high night temperatures, the lack of seasonality, and the excessive rainfall, combine in one way or another to reduce the potential photosynthesis and to limit possibilities of diversified agriculture. The attainment of the potential yield prescribed by the thermal and radiation regime of a place is rendered more difficult by such factors as the intense oxidisation and leaching of soils, the lack of nitrogen-fixing legumes, the high cost of fertilizers, the troublesome weed problem, and the prevalence of pests and diseases. All in all, the humid tropics are regions of 'debilitation' in Fleure's sense where human effort has rarely been accorded favourable response

(Chang 1968; the reference is to Fleure 1919).

Chang recognizes that certain systems can succeed in the humid tropics but, unlike Tosi and Voertmann, does not see as yet a satisfactory solution. The systems which have developed successfully beyond shifting cultivation have commonly been tree and perennial crops for export which have little impact on food requirements, neither does Chang regard them as presenting a basis for a stable economy. The one big exception is paddy rice which can give higher yields, which conserves soil fertility and which has for centuries sustained large populations.

We have, therefore, on the one hand the view that it is not the tropical environment which presents great difficulties, it is simply a matter of doing the wrong things, and on the other the widely held view that the environment is difficult and restrictive. Of the humid tropics Chang writes 'the natural choices are fewer and less appealing in the humid tropics than in most other climatic regions on the earth' (Chang 1968). This latter view would appear to be the more realistic. It is the view taken by Lee in his book *Climate and Economic Development in the Tropics* (Lee 1957). More recently the work of Eden on the Amazonian rain forest indicates the fragility of its agro-eco-systems and the extent to which they are vulnerable to the various forms of development (Eden 1978). It would seem that the 'informed judgement' to which Tosi and Voertmann questioningly refer is not only informed but accurate and realistic.

Much of this discussion has been concerned with the humid tropics. Great parts of the Developing World lie in the less humid, seasonally arid tropics. Here the environment also presents difficulties. The availability of water, not temperature, determines the start and finish of the growing seasons. Lower rainfalls are commonly characterized by greater variations in annual amounts by, in other words, lower reliability. In the tropics not only is this the case but the soil water regime, in contrast to that in temperate regions, tends to accentuate rather than compensate for, rainfall deficiencies. In Western Europe, the lower temperatures of winter mean that precipitation exceeds evapotranspiration and tops up the soil moisture levels which thus provide a reservoir of moisture to be drawn upon during the warmer growing season with its higher evapotranspiration losses. In the seasonally arid tropics soil moisture is adequate during the growing season but the rains cease before harvest. A season with no rainfall follows, soil moisture is lost and the sowings for the next season take place in soils with no water reserves. In such circumstances, the time and nature of the first onset of the rains is crucial. If, as in the savanna zones of West Africa, the first downpours can be followed in some years by rainless days or weeks before a second fall, the precious seed corn having been sown can be lost. The rain itself, essential though it is, can cause problems. It effectively leaches the soil of nutrients as it exceeds evapotranspiration and causes soil erosion by its characteristically torrential nature. The extensive savanna areas of other parts of the tropics all face these problems to a greater or lesser degree (Kenworthy and Glover 1958; Kowal and Kassam 1978; Agnew 1982).

Levels of agricultural productivity, success and failure, do, however, vary within the same edapho-climatic environments since social, tenurial, economic and political systems themselves vary and strongly influence the response to the environment. The problems presented by tropical environments become questions of how to improve existing systems, of how to introduce new, of how to create new agrarian and rural economies within environments which are far from supportive.

INDIGENOUS AGRICULTURAL SYSTEMS AND THEIR DEVELOPMENT

At the least developed level of subsistence, man has practised collecting and hunting and developed a culture designed to abstract from the natural environment a harvest of plant and animal food without the intermediary function of agriculture. Such systems exist today in a few localities but most have gone (Forde 1934). Both activities are still widely practised to augment agricultural harvests in dry seasons and in droughts. The bulk of the people of the Developing World, however, feed themselves on farming produce. What is grown and when, and whether livestock form part of the economy, depends in large measure upon climate and culture and historical experience.

According to climate a range of environments is presented:

1. Areas which are too dry or too mountainous for cultivation in which some grazing is practised and which may be punctuated by oases in which groundwater can sustain crops and around which distinctive cultures and agrarian systems develop. Example areas occur in the Sahara, Arabia, parts of India and Pakistan, Afghanistan and in Mexico.
2. Areas which are seasonally arid but where temperatures are sufficiently high to allow all-year crop growth. Wet season rain-fed cropping is practised and, where irrigation is possible, dry season irrigation farming in

more restricted localities. This is characteristic of much of the African savanna. The grazing of livestock, though often in systems and societies divorced from cultivation, is widespread.

3. Areas with sufficient heat for all year cropping and with a rainfall regime which allows two cropping seasons. Examples include much of Brazil, large areas in inter-tropical Africa, India and South East Asia. Cattle farming tends to be limited except in South America.

4. Areas which lie towards the tropical extremities such as northern India, southern Brazil, Uruguay and Paraguay experience a hot and a cool season which, while allowing all year cropping where rainfall is adequate or irrigation possible, means that the two seasons are characterized by quite different crops.

5. Areas experiencing the equatorial rainfall regime which are constantly humid with little seasonality in temperatures or day length. Such areas as in southern Nigeria and Cameroon, the Congo basin, Amazonia and the East Indies are essentially characterized by cultivation and few if any livestock though the nature of the crops grown and the manner of their cultivation may vary.

This broad and elementary classification gives some indication of range of environments, further modified by altitudinal variations, present in the wide expanse of the Developing World. These environmental variations demand and have produced different responses. A range of agricultural systems has resulted with some adjusting to the environment and altering it little while others involve major environmental modifications. Within this variety, common themes, goals and methods are discernible and it is more relevant to development issues to consider the major farming systems functioning in the Developing World rather than attempt a comprehensive description of their many regional manifestations.

The main aim of the indigenous farming systems of the developing countries is to produce food, chiefly carbohydrates, in sufficient quantity and as securely as possible, to feed the population. The central, crucial purpose is to produce enough food to survive. Additional to the staple diet will be plants grown, or collected, to make the diet more palatable, more interesting and, indeed, often more nutritious. Goats, sheep, pigs, poultry and dogs are often kept to provide a limited amount of animal protein to which can be added the meat of rats, lizards, snakes, monkeys, birds and, importantly where possible, fish. The keeping of large livestock such as cattle and camels is commonly a separate activity associated with distinctive cultures. Where they are kept by cultivators it is generally for use as draught animals. While pure subsistence economies are becoming relatively rare, part-subsistence economies are common and within them the first aim is still that of securing the basic food supply. Beyond that, other crops will be grown for family consumption and partly for sale and these will include non-food crops such as coffee, cotton or sisal. The growth of a cash sector is the first stage in economic and social development leading to an interdependence of societies and areas, to the development of marketing, to the emergence of compara- tive advantage playing its role in regional specialisation and trade, and to the development of a space economy incorporating both town and country. The dramatic impact of largely European contacts, first in trade and then in the form of colonial development, in many areas accelerated this trans- formation to part-subsistence or indeed wholly cash economies as well as, in some cases, introducing totally new and alien systems of farming linked to external markets.

SHIFTING CULTIVATION AND BUSH FALLOWING

Shifting cultivation and bush fallowing is a farming system and agricultural practice which attempts to meet food needs by a husbandry which recog- nizes and is adjusted to the fragility of tropical eco-systems. Land is rotated rather than crops, acknowledging the limited resource of the soil without the application of inputs to replenish the drain upon it though some crop rotation may be practised. Throughout the humid tropics with heavy rainfall and high temperature the weathering of rocks is rapid and the leaching of exposed soils is pronounced. Soils quickly lose their productive capacity and yields equally rapidly diminish. In seasonally arid areas yields also fall off quickly under continuous cropping. William Allan in his authoritative work, *The African Husbandman*, on the basis of field evidence from Zambia, has produced a set of hypothetical fertility gradients on a range of Zambian soils (Allan 1965). His graph of the yield performance under maize in normal years is the basis of Fig. 19. The minimum yield on which the subsistence

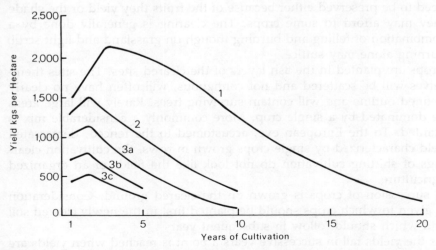

Figure 19 Falling crop yields under shifting cultivation in Zambia (adapted from Allan 1965)

cultivators of these soils can exist is of the order of 560–670 kg per hectare. The poorest soil, 3c, therefore cannot be cultivated, 3b is abandoned after two or three years, 3a after four while class 2 soils can be cultivated for up to six or seven years. The class 1 soils are commonly tilled for only five years, though their yields would not fall to subsistence limits for some fifteen years, and are put into a natural grass fallow before being reculti-vated. The speed of fertility decline thus varies according to the original nutritional status of the soil and to its textural and structural characteristics since these control the degree of leaching. When yields approach the critical minimum level the land is abandoned to be recolonised by natural vegetation.

Throughout the tropical world, shifting cultivation is widespread and is practised by both subsistence and semi-subsistence farmer in all its main essentials though elaborations of the system occur and the name, of course, varies. In Brazil it is known as *roca*, in Mexico *milpa*, as *masole* in Zaire, *chena* in Sri-Lanka, *kumri* in India, *ladang* in Malaysia and the term *swidden* has been applied to its practice in Sarawak and the Philippines. It should be remembered that bush fallowing is not peculiar to the tropics. It was prac-tised in Britain up until medieval times and survived in other parts of Europe much longer. It is a simple and land extravagant method of land rotation which can be very successful. The basic procedure and sequence of events is as follows:

1. The existing vegetation is cleared. If this is woodland it commonly means that some trees are left standing since on the one hand there is the consideration of costs and benefits in terms of the time and labour available for more complete clearance and on the other some trees may need to be preserved either because of the fruits they yield or the shade they may afford to some crops. The clearing is generally done by a combination of felling and burning though on grassland and light scrub burning alone may suffice.
2. Crops are planted in the ash layers of the cleared sites. The sites them-selves will be scattered and not contiguous, will often have no clearly defined outline and will contain surviving trees. Rarely will large areas be dominated by a single crop. More commonly a considerable mix is planted. To the European eye, accustomed to the fenced, demarcated field characterized by single crops grown in rows, the cultivation clear-ings of shifting cultivation do not look like the fields of an organized agriculture.
3. A succession of crops is grown on the cleared ground. Consideration is given to which crops should be planted first in the newly cleared soil and which should follow in subsequent years.
4. As the yields fall in successive years a point is reached when yields are so low, and the problem of weed infestation so great, that the plot must

be abandoned to recolonisation by natural vegetation under which the soil can recuperate.
5. A new site is selected and cleared.

It will be appreciated that the family and the village involved will have, at any one time, a considerable number of plots at various stages in this cycle of cropping and exhaustion. It is not a case of total food supply increasing and declining in cyclic succession. (For a further consideration of the processes involved see: de Schlippe 1956; Nye and Greenland 1960; Miracle 1957; Spencer 1966; Allan 1965; 1969; Ruthenberg 1971; Webster and Wilson 1980.)

The length of time the land is left uncultivated will depend on two things, the nature of the soils and vegetation and the amount of land available to the particular community. In consequence fallow periods vary considerably tending to be longer in woodland areas and shorter on grasslands. In the Philippines, Conklin reports a cycle of some 12–14 years on good volcanic soils with the fallow or recuperative period occupying 8–12 years of the cycle (Conklin 1957). Peters found the Lala of Zambia to practice a 17 year fallow and that yields fell by 25 per cent to below the subsistence level if the fallow was reduced to 9–12 years (Peters 1950). Freeman, working among the Iban of Sarawak, observed a fallow of 20 years on poor soils and 10 on rich with cropping periods being either two years when natural forest was cleared or only one in the case of secondary forest (Freeman 1955). A large area in Mexico is reported to be under a 10-year shifting cultivation cycle with only 2–3 years in crops (Clark and Haswell 1970). Eden states that on the *terra firme*, the non-alluvial soils of the Amazon basin, 'indigenous recultivation is usually delayed for at least 15 years' (Eden 1978). It is clear from all these examples that under shifting cultivation only a small proportion of the land used for cultivation is in production at any one time. It is a system which requires a very large input of land, indeed land is used as *the* input rather than fertilizer and intensity of cultivation. Laborious though the initial clearing may be and time-demanding the subsequent weeding, total labour input in systems of shifting cultivation is less than in sedentary forms of all-year agricultural production.

The vegetation cleared may be virgin woodland or grassland or some intermediate vegetational association. It may be, and commonly is, a regrowth of vegetation after fallowing; tall secondary forest will develop if time is allowed, shorter fallows will yield an immature forest or indeed allow regrowth only to an early succession phase of scrub with grass and bushes rather than trees. On grassland, short fallows will revegetate with grassland of a different flora than in the complete vegetational succession. It is commonly reported that in woodland areas the farmers prefer to clear secondary rather than virgin forest because it is easier. The shorter the fallow, the more intensive the use of land and the closer the system approximates sedentary cultivation. Short fallows without the support of additional inputs such as fertilizer represent a heavy drain on soil resources. In the area which a village or tribe has at its disposal for cultivation, that is an area recognized by its nearest neighbours as its territory with rights of usufruct, the villagers will clear plots first in close proximity to the village. As these are abandoned to revert to fallow, sites more distant will be cleared and cultivated until the distance-decay of effective input is such that it is more reasonable to move the whole village to a central position within a new area. An intermediary stage with the setting up of a daughter settlement to initiate cultivation may precede the final move of the village.

In true shifting cultivation there is thus a combination of the rotation of land around the settlement, bush fallowing, and the rotation of the movement of the settlement through the land at its disposal. This is shown in a highly diagrammatic form in Fig. 20. The result is a longer period of rest for any one area of land with the corollary that very large amounts of land are required for the production of crops.

In reality the practice is complex and sophisticated with many variations throughout the tropical world. Crops such as yams are planted in mounds or ridges incorporating compost or green manure. Sometimes pits are dug and the crops are planted in a mix of soil and vegetable remains. In other cases organic trash is piled into heaps, covered by soil, and then fired within the mound. Crops are planted in the resulting ash. All are attempts at fertilization to augment the soil and retard the drain on nutrients. The combination of bush fallowing with intensively cultivated gardens in and near the village is widespread. Because of their proximity they can receive not only food remains, domestic rubbish, animal dung and night soil, greatly to increase their nutrient status, they can also receive much greater attention resulting in better weeding and the scaring away of birds and other predators. Old village sites when abandoned commonly remain in cultivation for a period of years precisely because of the higher organic content of the soil. Shifting cultivators are able to identify by the natural flora the most suitable sites for clearing and within them the best areas for particular crops just as they can tell the stage of soil recovery by the vegetational succession on the abandoned sites. Cropping will reflect the need to secure a basic quantity of food but with some variety. The great intermixture of crops so often found reflects a knowledge of the micro-climate and edaphic needs of particular crops; it also minimizes the risk of diseases and pests, specific to particular crops, decimating a whole harvest. This mixture also ensures a near-continuous soil cover which inhibits soil erosion and leaching and results from the varying growth rates and manner of growth of individual plants. The variety of crops helps to spread out labour demands for planting and harvest while a more continuous yield reduces the need for storage capacity and the risk of destruction by insect and animal pests during storage. As the soil deteriorates the less demanding crops will be planted. Cassava, though native to South America, is now

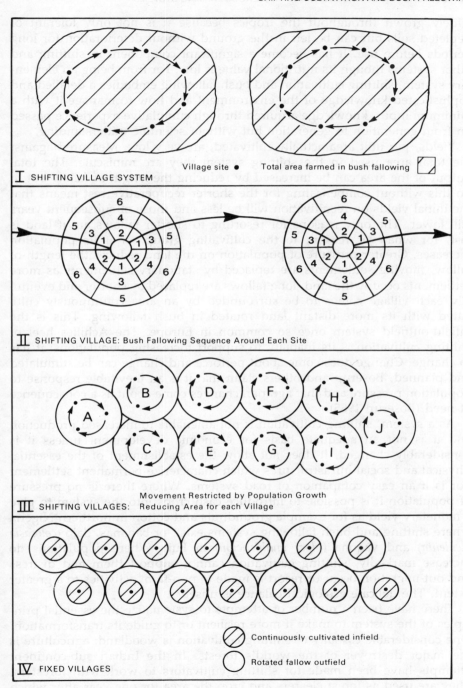

I SHIFTING VILLAGE SYSTEM

Village site ●   Total area farmed in bush fallowing ▨

II SHIFTING VILLAGE: Bush Fallowing Sequence Around Each Site

III SHIFTING VILLAGES: Movement Restricted by Population Growth Reducing Area for each Village

IV FIXED VILLAGES

▨ Continuously cultivated infield

○ Rotated fallow outfield

Figure 20 The transition from shifting to fixed villages

widely grown throughout the tropics because it is not only tolerant of depleted soils but can be left in the ground without deterioration for long periods before use. It has become a significant component in shifting and other systems though its nutritional value is low. Far from being an elementary system, shifting cultivation and bush fallowing embodies a detailed and sophisticated knowledge of the environment and how to manage it with a minimum input, knowledge acquired through cumulative experience passed on from generation to generation but without scientific understanding.

Yields, per unit area actually cultivated, are very low. Measured against the total area used in the shifting system they are miniscule. The total output of the area can be increased by reducing the length of fallow but to do this without compensating for the shorter recuperative rest means that the initial yields on recultivation will be less and those of subsequent years still lower. The only reasons for resorting to shorter fallows are if land is lost, for whatever reason, to the cultivating group, or if its population increases. Greater pressure of population on the land reduces the length of fallow, moving settlements are replaced by stationary settlements as more settlements occupy the land, long fallows are replaced by shorter and eventually each village comes to be surrounded by an area continuously cultivated with its more distant land rotated in bush fallowing. This is the infield-outfield system once so common in Europe. The Achilles heel of shifting cultivation is its inability to support increasing populations; it has to change. Change does come about perforce and change can be stimulated and planned. Boserup and others claim that it is an inevitable response to population pressure and that agrarian changes come about as a consequence of need (Boserup 1965).

As a system, shifting cultivation is not amenable to increased production and it is not an adequate basis for economic development unless it is considerably changed. It does not allow the establishment of the essential physical and social infrastructures which characterize permanent settlement nor is it an easy companion of road systems. Where there is no pressure of population it is possible to introduce cash crops into the system to give a monetary yield as for example groundnuts and cotton in northern Nigeria where shifting and bush fallowing systems exist, or bananas, dalo (*colocasia esculenta*) and yaqona (*piper mythisticum*) in Fuji. Where populations do increase markedly, shifting cultivation cannot support them and distress and out-migration occur or resort is made to non-farm activities to a greater extent. The delicate ecological balance is upset.

There have been a number of attempts to systematize the essential principles of the system to make it more resilient or to guide its transformation. One considerable casualty of shifting cultivation is woodland; agriculture is the major destroyer of the world's forests. In the Indian sub-continent attempts have been made for shifting cultivators to work with foresters. They are used as forest clearers and crop the area for one year after which the foresters take over and plant commercial timber and the area is restored to forest for seventy years or so (Ruthenberg 1971). In Fiji the Lomaivuna scheme in the 1960s attempted to resettle individual farmers from communal village communities in a forest area by allocating them 4 hectare blocks with 2.5 hectares to be devoted to the cash crop bananas, 0.8–1.2 hectares to subsistence crops with the rest in woodland. The bananas were intended for export, the project was supervised and the aim was to produce sedentary individual farms. Soil depletion and banana diseases caused the scheme to fail but the individual farms persisted with the farmers identifying cash crops for which there was a local demand. Supervision of the project became unnecessary. It highlights the need to appreciate that the indigenous farmer is often capable of responding to opportunities if circumstances allow. In the former Belgian Congo, now Zaire, attempts were made to systematize forest clearing in the so-called *couloir* system whereby corridors of cultivation were driven through woodland in surveyed plots at right angles to the direction of advance. Unfelled areas separated each strip which was subject to a planned sequence of crop growth so that an individual cultivator had in any one year a sequence of strips with the allocated crop for the particular year of rotation. Each strip reverted to forest for some nineteen years (Dumont 1957). The benefits of the organization were rotations that could be practised using better varieties, with a more effective control over cultivation techniques, while the compact nature of the corridor of advance meant that roads could be used and marketing made more effective. Yields were increased but the system had all the land-extravagant characteristics of shifting cultivation and eventually administration declined and the system is no longer practised in Zaire.

The inability of shifting cultivation to sustain larger populations is obviously a Developing World problem. In many places it has changed and in others the process in under way. The first obvious transition is to the situation in which the village becomes permanent and with it the notion of a village area in which its inhabitants have rights of use, though land ownership in the European sense may not develop. Permanently cultivated land surrounds the village with fallow periods in a crop rotation while further out longer fallows characterize bush fallowing on land which will commonly abut against that of neighbouring villages. Areas become demarcated and village territories characterized by a zonation of use (Prothero 1957; Blaikie 1971). Features of the transitional stage are the greater use of inputs to compensate for shorter rest periods by adding green and animal manure, greater care in planting, the sowing of row crops, more weeding and a greater tendency to grow blocks of the same crop. It can result in a more stable system supporting a higher population density particularly if the soils are intrinsically of above-average and fertility and if the climate is less debilitating.

Before considering the nature of the transition to permanent agricultural types reference must be made to the livestock analogue of shifting culti-vation, namely nomadism, which in some parts of the Developing World is the major form of livestock husbandry.

NOMADIC CATTLE-KEEPING

Nomadic herdsmen are essentially confined to Africa, the Middle East and central Asia. In Africa where cattle-keeping is restricted by the tsetse fly, the system is confined to areas too high or too dry for the tsetse fly to persist though in their journeys the nomads will cross infested country. The Fulani of West Africa exemplify the system. In the Sahel and Guinea Savanna zones the Fulani practise the animal equivalent of shifting cultivation. They use wide areas of poor territory, put nothing into the land and graze their cattle on natural and man-modified vegetation. The movement is a continual search for fresh vegetative growth and hence they follow the rains in their seasonal movement north and south across West Africa from the forest edge to the desert fringe. They occupy largely tsetse-free areas but are obliged to cross the Guinea Savanna areas which are notoriously tsetse infested, to market their cattle in the more densely populated south. In Nigeria nomadic Fulani account for over 90 per cent of the country's cattle stock. Cattle provide food for the families, milk and butter for cash sales to agricultural-ists or for food by barter; the sales of cattle for slaughter is a further source of income.

Cattle are owned by individual families and their number is an indication of a person's prestige. They are transacted in social obligations such as dowry gifts and are the centre, indeed the raison d'etre, of the whole way of life. As a consequence in many nomadic societies cattle are rarely sold, but amongst the Fulani selling has become a fundamental part of their economy. They may sell directly to the butcher in the towns of the South and receive a high price. In doing so they run the risk of their cattle dying, or becoming diseased and certainly of losing weight, as they move through the tsetse areas. The alternative, increasingly taken, is to sell to local merchants in the North for a lower price but without the losses of the long journey, and the cattle are transported by road or rail.

Grazing is carried out communally with whole clans moving together and sharing tasks. The system depends upon a delicate ecological balance between grazing available, intensity of grazing, and the need to move. The input into this system is what the land and climate offers. Commonly the group will be focused in one area, trekking through it in a form of grazing. rotation but it will also travel long distances in search of water and grazing. The parallel with the move–rotate–move sequence of shifting cultivation is strong. The Fulani family's wealth is stock not land. The animals must possess the ability to survive rather than the capability to yield heavily. Stocking densities necessitated by the poor quality of the vegetation grazed are, or should be, low. Generally they are of the order of one cow per eight or nine hectares and in poor dry areas much lower. In northern Nigeria a symbiotic relationship has developed between the Fulani herdsmen and the Hausa cultivators. Their cattle are allowed to graze on the fallows, commonly the stubble of the Guinea corn (*Sorghum* spp) which they improve with their manure and help soil consolidation by treading.

The Fulani practise a system which is vulnerable to economic and political change and to any developments which restrict mobility or the land available to the herdsman or which disrupt the symbiotic relationship. As more land is brought under cultivation, as forestry areas are demarcated, this resource base is eroded. Land developments can prevent Fulani movements and hence restrict access to grazing areas. Political boundaries lie across and hinder the free movement of a culture based on movement. As cattle keeping and mixed farming develops, the need to allow Fulani cattle to graze stubble diminishes. They become a nuisance rather than a benefit and a disease risk to sedentary livestock. As grazing is restricted so pressure on the remaining land increases, vegetational yield is less and soil erosion more (Stenning 1959; Davies 1966). The system is not compatible with the changes taking place. It can be converted to a form of ranching but in the conversion a way of life and a culture would disappear. The Fulani and their like run the real risk of being left out of development and they have little political cohesion or strength to state their case. The ranch may well emerge. It is a transformation with parallels in the American West where the cattle trail was essentially nomadic grazing over a vast unrestricted area. It was brought to an end by the spread of the cultivator and the invention of barbed wire. It was replaced by the fenced ranch and produces store cattle to be fattened on arable farms in the Corn Belt. The future of the Fulani and other nomadic grazers may be similar.

TRANSITION TO SEDENTARY AGRICULTURE

As shifting cultivation is unable to sustain large increases in population the changes forced upon it may lead to a deterioration of the environment, to a situation of permanently low yields, to poverty and distress. Change for the better requires a re-appraisal of cultivation techniques, of fertilizer practice, of plant and animal selective breeding. It demands innovations in labour use, the consideration of non-human sources of energy and a change both in the organisation of production and the marketing of produce. In short it requires one good form of husbandry to be replaced by another and not by an inferior form.

There is evidence which suggests that the pressures of population can lead to innovative changes by which farmers effectively transform their systems into sedentary forms capable of sustaining large populations. The dense rural populations of India and China bear witness to this. Esther Boserup in her book *The Conditions of Agricultural Growth* states simply 'One of the main contentions of this book is that the growth of population is a major determinant of technological change in agriculture' (Boserup 1965). If one puts aside, for a moment, the long-established rice cultivations of Asia, the question can be asked as to whether the process is discernible in the much more lightly populated Africa.

In what has become a classic study, Mortimore and Wilson examined the area around the ancient city of Kano in Northern Nigeria which they describe as the Kano close-settled zone (Mortimore and Wilson 1965). Here the population is very dense by African standards. In the innermost zone, rural densities are greater than 190 per square kilometre while densities still exceed 55 per square kilometre at distances of 50–65 kilometres from the city. Mortimore stresses that these are rural and not suburban densities; by contrast in the Guinea Savanna 'middle belt' of Nigeria the average density is 10 per square kilometre or less.

In the close-settled zone shifting cultivation and bush fallowing have been replaced by permanent occupation of the land using methods developed over generations. The soils are essentially light and are physically capable of intensive working but, being sandy, are not intrinsically fertile. The rainy season is short, May to September at the maximum; the rainfall low, 33 inches in conditions of high evapo-transpiration, and highly variable. In winter the desiccating, dust-laden Harmattan blows across the area from the Sahara. Walled villages are characteristic though isolated compounds do occur and land is, obviously, in short supply. There are two distinctive categories. *Fadama* is the land along the streams with access to their water and during the dry season this means the sub-alluvial water below their dried beds. It is the most valuable and productive land because of this. The much more extensive category is made up of the low interfluves between the streams beyond access to their water. On this land the staple grains, Guinea corn (*sorghum* spp.) and millet (*pennisetum* spp.) are grown together with cow peas (*vigna sinensis*) and ground nuts (*arachis hypogea*). The latter two are important sources of vegetable protein and ground nuts are not only the main cash crop of the area but also of Nigeria. On these interfluves seasonal aridity prevents the year-round growth of crops though temperatures would allow it. The *Fadama* is intensively cultivated in tiny plots throughout the year producing a range of vegetables for the Kano market. Population pressure has resulted in the emergence of the idea of individual land owning. In northern Nigeria tenure has become a blend of traditional African forms of communal ownership, with individual use, and Islamic views on the laws of tenure and inheritance which stress order and organisation. So totally is the land farmed that use and occupation have become coincident. Until the Nigerian Government nationalized all land, the land in the Kano Emirate belonged to the Emir. However, long before the government edict all plots were registered and the use of them could be inherited and indeed rights of use could be transferred. Associated with these developments was the demarcation of plots by low hedges generally of useful shrubs or grasses. Land came to be used for such things as security for loans and since 1945 the sale of land has become common indicating the strength of the idea of ownership. Progressive farmers can enlarge their holdings by buying and renting but as Islamic law requires a subdivision amongst all inheritors upon death, holdings go through a cycle of enlargement, fragmentation and consolidation. There is no spare land. As the population grows enlargements can only take place at the expense of others. Holdings are approximately half the size of the average for Northern Nigeria.

The dense populations are supported by an intensive and careful cultivation of fixed plots in which the users can invest which they come to know intimately. The land is manured particularly the *Fadama* which in addition receives the benefits of water and silt. Crops are row planted and intercropping is characteristic on both *Fadama* and interfluves. The ground nuts are, however mono-cropped since they are grown essentially for sale. Manure is the key to success. The holdings are too small, 1.5 to 2.5 hectares, and less in solely *Fadama* plots, to make the keeping of draught cattle possible. Sheep and goats are kept and Fulani herds graze the interfluves in winter. But Kano is *the* important source of manure. The city (population 250,000 in 1962) has a very large animal population of donkeys, goats and sheep and is a source of town refuse. This assemblage of organic manures helps to replenish the drain on the light soils while the incorporation of legumes in the rotation further assists them. The town manure is the result of a reciprocal trade in firewood and manure carried on donkey back. From distances of five to ten miles and more, strings of donkeys move in each day throughout the year carrying fuelwood. During the season when manure is applied to the fields, from January to March, they return with manure sacks on their backs. Mortimore has calculated that some 27,800 tonnes of manure are carried in this way each season and spread onto the surrounding land. Areas outside Kano also supply manure. Agriculture thus supports a large population but it is poor rather than affluent. Some farms are large enough to occupy fully the family labour resources. Others are too small and their cultivators commonly have non-agricultural additional employment particularly hand-loom weaving. The *Fadama* areas more remote from Kano grow fewer vegetables and more sugar cane, rice and winter wheat on their irrigated plots. A fixed form of farming has thus evolved but further changes are difficult to introduce. Holdings are too small to develop mixed farming and it is difficult to create larger holdings unless a satisfactory alternative to farming is available for displaced farmers. Yields can be increased if new high yielding varieties can be developed, if artificial fertilizer can be applied, and insecticides used. Further technical development can allow a greater intensity of land use; without it regression may take place.

It is possible to hypothesize that some situations are more conducive to change and development than others. The Kano close-settled zone was favoured by the proximity of a market, a source of manure and by soils which could respond to intensive cultivation. The impact of these attributes decayed with distance from Kano. The Rural Economy Research Unit of Ahmadu Bello University, of which the author was a co-director when first it was established, has further explored this question around Zaria and near Sokoto and demonstrated the importance of location and access in agricultural change. The greatest modification was evident in areas of urban proximity and next where road access was good. Areas remote in terms of accessibility, and not simply distance, exhibited the least change in agricultural systems from bush fallowing to sedentary types and in the extent to which non-farm activities were present in villages (Norman 1967; Goddard, Fine and Norman 1971; Norman 1972; Goddard 1974; Norman *et al.* 1976). Gleave has reviewed the literature relating to population pressure and agriculture change in West Africa and concludes:

> The intensification of agriculture is not the panacea for agricultural development by itself since 'progressive' areas in West Africa have affected it. The difference between the most successful and least successful areas . . . is their position relative to markets both urban, national and international, in the level of their infrastructural provision in terms of factors such as roads and sources of inputs and in the willingness of their population to adopt new and improved methods.
>
> (Gleave 1980)

SYSTEMS OF PERMANENT CULTIVATION

Permanent cultivation does not, of course, mean necessarily development in the sense of improved economic and social conditions or in well-being. It can simply be the end product of the pressure on land resources when no land is available to be brought into cultivation for shifting systems and less land becomes available per person. It can be characterized by rock-bottom yields and returns on labour input as, for example, in parts of India and Pakistan where population pressure has removed shifting cultivation and sedentary systems are insufficiently productive. Development should mean a permanent occupation of the land coincident with increasing yields to raise the food intake, to produce a surplus for sale and to enable additional labour inputs to become economically productive. It is not a process insulated from other sectors of the economy.

There are two major categories of farming systems which permanently occupy the same land, those which rely on rainfall and those which are based on irrigation. The two practices are not mutually exclusive and indeed farmers will practice irrigation, whenever possible, if only on a small part of their land. Within the two categories there are many regional variations throughout the Developing World. Asian examples will be used to illustrate the types since Asia is overwhelmingly characterized by fixed rather than shifting systems, since population densities are high and because Asia provides examples of long-established and sophisticated irrigation systems.

On the Deccan Plateau of India where the black *regur* soils have developed on the Deccan lavas, and in adjacent parts of peninsular India where red sandier soils are associated with metamorphic rocks, small sedentary farms are characteristic. The soils present difficulties. The *regurs* though intrinsically the more fertile, are clay soils difficult to cultivate and indeed almost impossible to till without the plough and draught animals. In the characteristic monsoonal oscillation between a very wet season and a very dry and hot season, the clays either bake hard or deflocculate into a plastic sticky mass. The red soils are easier to cultivate but lack plant nutrients. The population is numerous and holdings are very small. The average for India is 3 hectares but is much lower in the peninsula, 0.6 hectares being the average in Mysore. Most farmers in India, some 80 per cent, are owner occupiers. In the absence of land for bush fallowing the problem is of inputs to sustain output. Animal and vegetable manure can be added. Draught animals, zebu cattle (*Bos indicus*) and the water buffalo (*Bos bubalis*) are much more commonly used than in Africa. They can provide manure but they also require to eat. They can graze on any scrub or waste land, they can be fed on the by-products of crops grown for human comsumption, like grain-straw, or they can be fed or fodder grown for them. Fodder crops take land out of use for human consumption and there is therefore a reduction in human food supply even if the cattle are eaten or their milk consumed because of the energy used in the conversion. The calorific yield per hectare is less. In India, however, cattle are not eaten since it is prohibited by the Hindu faith and the slaughter of cattle is forbidden in the Indian constitution. Cattle supply milk and this is nutritionally important though yields are low due to inadequate feeding, the poor quality of peasant cattle, and energy lost in working fields. Overall they make a negative contribution to India's food output. On the Deccan laval soils where cattle are needed to plough, they consume up to 30 per cent of the farm output. Breeding cows serve only to supply new draught animals and cattle surplus to this need, and cattle too old to work, are a further drain on very limited resources. In areas long deafforested, cattle dung is a major source of fuel and so does not find its way back to the soil to replenish it. The poor farmers on smaller plots cannot afford to keep cattle and if they cannot hire them are compelled to use hoes for cultivation. The dry central parts of the Deccan are characterized chiefly by, millet, bulrush millet (*Pennisetum typhoideum*) and finger millet (*Eleusine coracana*) while wheat is the main crop further north. Maize is widely grown both as a fodder crop and a food crop. Despite manuring practices, crop rotation, the use of draught animals and steps taken to control soil erosion, yields are low. Nutritional levels are at a correspondingly low level and poverty is widespread. Cassava had been introduced to replace grains in many areas because of its high yields in difficult conditions. If a patch of land can be irrigated from 'tanks', small reservoirs to retain the monsoonal rain, or from wells, the situation can be improved. Not only can a range of vegetable crops be grown but also, where possible rice. Tanks are widespread in the Indian sub-continent not only allowing irrigation downstream of the *bunds* (dams) but also the growth of crops on their beds after the surface water has been used. In addition to the staple grains the leguminous crops, chick peas (*Cicer arietinum*) and pidgeon peas (*Cajanus cajan*) are grown on most holdings and are invaluable sources of protein.

India supports a very large population at a low level of nutrition. Wheat millet, maize and rice supply between 70 and 90 per cent of her population's food. The need is to improve the output of these many small farms in the rain fed areas. This requires a range of innovations easier to cite than to implement and India has made strenuous efforts to do so since her independence. First crop varieties can be improved by selective breeding. It can and has been done in research stations but the transfer to the farming community raises further problems. Likewise, selective breeding can be applied to livestock though, in India's case this clearly, in relation to cattle, applies to milk production only but dairy farming has much to recommend it as a form of Developing World farming. It provides a nutritious product with an important role to play in the improvement of health, and it yields a cash product with, in India's case, a ready market in towns. Importantly, also, it is a means of introducing an organized and demanding form of production which can do much to stimulate agrarian development in appropriate situations (Whyte 1967).

Improvements on the one hand require improvements on the other. Higher yields of new crop varieties can only be sustained by improvements in other aspects of farm practice. They require a greater input of fertilizer, a greater care in weeding, an ability to control pests and diseases and in some cases the use of improved agricultural implements. Livestock developments require improvements not only in livestock husbandry but also in fodder production, feeding skills and the availability of veterinary expertise. This all requires time, training and importantly capital, an assemblage of inputs to improve an unsatisfactory agrarian structure within a difficult environment.

The great concentrations of Asia's populations are not in the rain-fed areas but on the irrigated lands of the valley bottoms, the coastal plains and the deltas, indeed the population distribution of south and east Asia has been described as topographic. It is a valid description whether one applies it to the Indian sub-continent, to China or to south-east Asia. Even these areas are characterized by low material living standards though they have given given rise to and supported, some of the world's greatest cultures in the so-called 'hydraulic civilisations'. The obvious advantage of irrigation in tropical Asia is the coincidence of water availability throughout the year with all-year growing temperatures. More than one crop can be grown in the year and in some areas several. The area cropped is thus considerably greater than the area cultivated. It is precisely the reverse of the situation found in shifting cultivation. The production from a given area of land is thus much increased. In addition it is possible to obtain much higher yields of crops grown under irrigation since, other things being equal, water availability is the common restriction on plant growth. Fallowing is less necessary and sometimes unnecessary. It is possible to have a continuous, sometimes multi-sequential, schedule of cropping with the possibility of higher yields for each crop compared with the dry-land equivalent. Irrigation agriculture is much more responsive to increasing inputs be they of fertilizer or labour; in economic terms it is characterized by high marginal returns. There are additional and obvious advantages. Apart from exceptional situations of widespread and prolonged drought, dependency upon rainfall is much reduced. Variations in yields from year to year are on a small scale and this reliability lessens the need to divert resources into contingency strategies and so allows a fuller more productive use of them. Food is available throughout the year and so also are incomes from cash crops while labour inputs are more evenly spread.

Central to Asian irrigation is, of course, rice. It has sustained large populations over centuries allowing a permanent occupation of the land characterized by high yields and without soil fertility dropping to disastrously low levels. Whole holdings may be irrigated or only part as topography and tenure patterns dictate. The explanation of irrigated, or paddy rice, productivity lies in its maintenance of soil fertility. The land is levelled and sudivided by low-banks, features which inhibit soil erosion, while the application of water provides nutrients in solution. On river flood-plains and in deltas, annual flooding may provide nutritious silt as well as water. These nutrient supplies do much to replenish the loss consequent upon harvest. In addition, stubble is not burned but ploughed into the puddled bed of the growing basin adding organic material. While fertility is thus maintained it can be increased by the addition of animal manure, household refuse, night soil, composted vegetable matter and, in some areas, by green-manure crops grown to be ploughed in. Where continuous cropping is practised with other crops alternating with rice, as in the most intensive systems, the detailed control of water, the great attention paid to crops and the large input of care and attention, all serve to suppress weeds and reduce pests. When water is impounded in paddy fields, nitrogen-fixing algae further enrich both water and soil (De and Mandal 1956; Grist 1975; Webster and Wilson 1980).

This level of care is reflected in crop rotations. Two crops of rice followed by a green crop may characterize the sequence found in a single year on ill-drained areas. On better land two crops of irrigated rice may be followed by a non-irrigated crop, wheat or maize or a root crop in the cooler season, again within one year. A greater flow of cropping can be achieved by sequential planting in which a following crop is planted before its predecessor has been harvested. A sequence of harvests is thus possible and on land irrigated throughout the year as many as four crops, occasionally more, or as few as three, can be raised. On seasonally irrigated land two or three crops are more usual. With some crops, notably sugar cane and rice, and occasionally the sorghums, ratooning is possible, that is vegetative re-growth rather than replanting. This speeds up the sequence but yields successively fall and so it is not the most intensive form of cultivation. The use of nursery beds to grow the seedlings allows very intensive production and is widely practised with rice. In all these systems interplanting is used as it is on dry-land permanent farms. Row planting is characteristic with each row given the particular attention it requires in a carefully organized system. In some areas inundated land yields fish, and ponds are rotated through the cycle of cultivation. The input of labour is high and the intensive nature of the system gives a large output which supports dense rural populations which because of their size, however, can only experience low material standards of living. Holdings are small and are sub-divided as populations grow. The requirements of water management and civil engineering have been associated with the development of social, economic and political institutions but these have been essentially of a non-industrial nature. The pressure of population means that Asian irrigation agriculture continually needs to become more productive despite its intensity, as do all other farming systems in the Developing World. Within South and East Asia, the range of productivity and the degree of agricultural intensity is considerable. Even within such involved and sophisticated systems as irrigated multi-cropping there is room for increased efficiency and productivity. The challenge for future development is there.

INITIATING THE DEVELOPMENT OF AGRICULTURE

The development process in agriculture can be conceived of as incorporating the means to increase the production of crops and livestock, the ways by which the farmer may be drawn into the cash economy so that his products may be sold in exchange for non-agricultural commodities and services, the establishment of systems of marketing whereby he obtains a fair price for his product and the creation of rural credit facilities which enable him to finance his developments without the evils of usury. Some techniques aim at an increased output from the land, others at increased production per worker; some involve completely new systems of farming, others modifications to the indigenous systems which have been described. The common goal is an increase in total production.

These various processes and techniques can touch upon every aspect of farming and agrarian society. So far-reaching and so intertwined are they, that it could be said that the only way forward is to change radically the whole rural scene. The tangle of tenurial constraints, fragmentation of holdings, absence of capital inputs, of plant and animal breeding, of fertilizer and insecticide use, the inadequate cultivation practices, the rudimentary economic schedules could suggest that existing systems must be swept aside. In their place would be established large consolidated units, carefully planned, efficiently managed, soundly financed, embodying technical skills and using an appropriate mix of mechanization and paid-labour force. These large units, with a market identity, would be owned and operated by companies be they private, co-operative or state. It has been tried in one form in the Soviet Union with its state collective farms and in another and completely different way in China with her communes (Chapter 16). In both cases the entire agrarian economy has been changed. In Ghana where state farms and Workers' Brigades were established by President Nkrumah they met with an almost complete lack of success (Killick 1978). In some developing countries the plantation, either nationalized or left in private hands, is a model of the system. Government-implemented schemes of agricultural development may take the form of capital-intensive and large-scale environmental modifications the object of which, and irrigation schemes are the obvious example, is to extend the cultivatable area. Indeed, it is only governments which can raise the capital required. There are notable examples in India and Pakistan. The Gezira scheme is the Sudan is another where over three-quarters of a million hectares have been reclaimed from desert land by canal construction and irrigation. The land is divided into surveyed tenant plots, all operations are determined by a central management including water supply and cropping rotations. Inputs of seed and fertilizer are provided and soil preparation is carried out by the central tractors organisation. The major crops are cotton, sorghum and a fodder legume (*Dolichos lablab*). The tenants can keep cattle on the fallow stubbles. Marketing of cotton is carried out by the managerial body upon which tenants are represented. The sorghum harvest and that of other crops belongs to the tenant and he receives a share of cotton sales (see Gaitskell 1959). In many ways it is a successful scheme greatly increasing the secure output of cotton and grain in Sudan. Guy Hunter, however feels that this scheme with its high degree of central control has inhibited local commercial and economic enterprise (Hunter 1969). It raises the wider issue of the role of the state in fostering or stifling human endeavour.

The alternative approach to agricultural development is to address the problems of the multitude of individual small farmers and to attempt to improve their conditions by increasing output and enhancing marketing opportunities and to do this with a smaller injection of capital and a less involved technology than in the large modernization projects. This approach is made more difficult because it deals with a very large number of individuals and families embedded within the social and economic fabric of their traditional societies. It has to cope with ignorance, it has to be seen to be meaningful by the people for whom it is intended, it has to produce results in order to convince. This second approach puts to the fore the goal of increasing the income of the many peasant families which make up the majority of the Developing World's population and so of bringing benefits, albeit modest, directly and quickly to them. It is not the panacea for all the ills of the Developing World's rural communities but it is an approach which acknowledges that their condition cannot simply await the completion of some massive scheme or some long-term plan for structural changes in the national economy. It is an approach which everywhere has proved difficult partly because it deals with the disaggregated multitude and partly because many, perhaps most, governments have given it a low priority and viewed it with little enthusiasm. In many countries it requires radical changes in land ownership and tenurial systems notably, but not exclusively, those of Latin America, and is therefore a development which impinges upon long-established relationships between hierarchical social structures and wealth.

As has been seen, almost all indigenous forms of agriculture are, without change and additional inputs, subject to limitations on their productivity. Increased production can take two forms, increased output from the land and increased output per worker. These increases can be the product of using improved methods, adopting new but appropriate technology, incorporating where possible livestock into cropping systems to provide animal protein, manure and draught power, of using improved breeds of livestock and varieties of crops and of applying fertilizers and insecticides. Throughout this century agricultural research stations have been working to this end. In too many cases the innovations have not been adopted and in most it has been because the society for which they were intended has not been involved and its priorities and its economic and social structures not understood. Potential blockages in the adoption process have not been identified. All the evidence points to the need to involve the small farmer in the changes which are purported to be his benefit. G. Benneh, reporting upon a scheme to introduce mixed farming in northern Ghana, states 'illiterate small-scale farmers are responsive to agricultural innovations provided that the benefits of the recommended practices are demonstrated to them, the introduced technology is not too much above the level of that which is being replaced and an attempt is made to study the problems which the recommended practices aim at solving before they are introduced' (Benneh 1972).

In practice one innovation requires others to become fully effective; an improved variety or crop may demand a greater application of fertilizer and water, an improved breed of cow a more nutritious diet in order that its yield potential might be realized. The well-known high-yielding variety seed programme (HVP) introduced into the Indian sub-continent in 1966–67 exemplifies this situation. It was an attempt to increase production from the land in countries where land is limited and mostly fully used, and where the pressure of population upon resources is very great. This 'Green Revolution' Chakravarti describes as a 'a significant breakthrough in feed grain production' and says that 'it appears to be a turning point in stagnating Indian agriculture' (Chakravarti 1973; Brown 1970; Frankel 1971; Johnson 1972; Nulty 1972). The traditional varieties of seeds used for the main crops, wheat, rice, maize, jowar (sorghum) and bajra (bullrush millet, *Pennisetum typhoideum*), were incapable of high yields as they had evolved over a long period of time as crops able to continue to yield under conditions of poor husbandry, drought and on infertile soils. The HVP introduced new hybrid varieties of these five cereals which were drought resistant with the exception of rice, were very responsive to the application of fertilizers and had a shorter growing cycle which made multi-cropping more feasible. Importantly they were capable of yields twice to four times greater than that of the traditional varieties. The success of these varieties depended, however, on the availability of other inputs notably of water, fertilizer and insecticides. These required access to capital the consequence of which was that the programme was most successful on the larger and more commercialized farms and least in the areas of poor small holdings where most help was needed. It was not a matter of progressive farmers and conservative peasants but one of money. The implementation of the programme was hindered in its nationwide impact by the incomplete distribution of fertilizer centres and by the inadequacy of provision for credit and loans to adopting farmers. The sub-continent is, of course, cursed by the unreliability of rainfall over much of the area and the HVP came to have its greatest impact upon intensively cultivated irrigation areas and indeed led to an accentuation of regional disparities in agricultural production. The wheat growing areas most successfully adopted the new seed (a Mexican hybrid dwarf wheat). In the rice areas the new varieties were less successful being very susceptible to pests and diseases and less acceptable in taste. Their shorter straw meant less fodder for cattle. As Chakravarti points out, disparities were enlarged not only at regional level but also within village communities in which poor low-caste farmers unable to buy the inputs became increasingly disadvantaged compared with their wealthy neighbours who grew the new varieties. Indeed much has been written criticising this differential effect of the Green Revolution not only in India and Pakistan but also in the Philippines. The HVP requires further work on the breeding side to produce more disease resistant and palatable varieties. It has demonstrated the crucial need for ancillary facilities of fertilizer, water and financial help and these, particularly the need for water, inhibit its application. It has, however, been a development which *has* increased the production of the staple food grains. To be critical of the high-yielding variety seed programmes, to condemn them because of their flaws is too easy. A.H. Bunting has put the case in a different way.

Whatever the weaknesses, errors and difficulties which, with hindsight can now be identified, and which in future must be corrected or avoided, the initial decisions were taken by Ministers and governments. One may fairly ask the Western critic one single question: had he been Minister of Agriculture in India or Pakistan, or Turkey, in the mid- sixties, would he have refused to accept the new technology, and if so what reasons would he have given to the public and to the world? And what would the consequences have been?

(Hunter, Bunting and Bottrall 1976)

It is, of course, possible for developments on the macro-scale to be paralleled by efforts at the individual farmer level. Indeed it is important that this should be so. The work carried out by Bradley, Raynaut and Torrealba in Mauritania illustrates this situation and shows what can be done with minimum capital input (Bradley, Raynaut, Torrealba 1977; Bradley 1980). Mauritania is largely desert, has limited resources to expand food production and is obliged to import food. Areas of potential expansion are the alluvium of the Senegal Valley and its levees and a narrow band along the Malian border in the south and east. The valley alluvium is the more fertile and has access to more water for a larger period of the year. The dry land of the south and east can support only rain-fed agriculture of the dry-land type with poor yields on infertile soils. The Government with financial aid from the World Bank and other agencies, has focused its development activities on the valley of the Senegal river in irrigation projects in which Mali, Senegal and Mauritania are involved. Bradley argues that the dry-land farming of cereals is totally neglected and yet could provide the greater part of the country's grain requirements. He and his colleagues chose to live amongst the Soninke people of the area and assess how the prevailing system functioned rather than to take in pre-conceived new methods to promote change. They discovered a system delicately balanced with the environment but disturbed by the emigration of males to work in French factories. Having been accepted into the community they identified constraints and bottle-necks in the system, tested out their ideas with the local community, modified them in the light of the feedback and were able to see them taken up by the local farmers and rapidly diffused throughout the area. Ensuing problems were again handled in the same way and by the end of four years an effective assemblage of new techniques had emerged. The result was an appreciable improvement in crop yields and the even wider adoption of the new techniques by surrounding villages which had not previously been interested. This work, involving the community in feeling its way to developments, is an example of success at the peasant community level. It has stimulated amongst the Soninke a dynamic attitude to agriculture which is evident in the continuing flow of new ideas and practices which have ensued. Alongside this work and in contrast to it, the Societé Nationale de Developpement Rural in Mauritania has set up pump-irrigated schemes in the river valley. Bradley found the targets set for production and financial return had not been met. He attributes this to the absence of infrastructural developments, physical, such as roads, and commercial, such as marketing arrangements, and to the lack of technical and mechanical support in a scheme where they were essential. All are deficiencies which could be remedied; as it is this more capital-intensive scheme has proved less effective. Bradley argues that the irrigation scheme promotes too much dependence upon outside help and influences instead of promoting self-reliance. It is a consideration which underlies all development issues and not solely those of the agriculture sector.

The individual farmer approach which has been discussed, has however, its limitations. It can improve the conditions of the many, it can promote self-reliance and, perhaps, stimulate initiatives but it cannot put within reach the greater opportunities for further economic and social progress which exist. These require a much more profound change in society and economy. It can be regarded, however, as a stage, indeed an essential stage, which so many countries have attempted to pass by, that is preliminary to and lays the foundations for a more broadly based development. Much the same could be said of agricultural and rural development as a whole. The People's Republic of China identified the role of this stage and has used it as a means of egalitarian progress and a platform for further development. In many countries of the Developing World, the over-reach for industrialization and the failure to conceive of the development of a rural economy, has placed an albatross around the neck of their development plans.

6 Agriculture: The European Imprint

'The main influence upon the organisation of agriculture and the distribution of its products is the system of land tenure. Geography and climate are obviously of great importance, but different types of organisation can produce different consequences in the same natural conditions'

J Robinson
Aspects of Development and Underdevelopment 1979

The influence of Europeans, or peoples of European stock upon the agricultural systems and economies of developing countries has been great. It has taken three main forms. First, it created a market for the Developing World's agricultural produce external to the producing countries. Second, in some areas, it took the form of European settlement where Europeans acquired ownership of the land which has remained in the hands of their descendants. Thirdly, in some countries, the European impact resulted from the establishment of the plantation system. European land acquisition and settlement will be discussed in the context of Latin America and of the Kenyan White Highlands. Plantation agriculture will be considered in terms of its role in economic development.

LAND TENURE IN LATIN AMERICA

European settlement took place earliest, and had its most profound and lasting impact, in central and southern America where the Spanish and Portuguese conquered and destroyed pre-existing political systems, claimed title to the land and established colonies characterized by economies and systems of land-holding transplanted from Iberia. The independent countries of Latin America are heirs to these colonies and have shared an experience which has given the region its distinctive agricultural problems which bring to the fore the issues of land tenure in agrarian development. (Barraclough and Domike 1966). Latin America is vast, its environments varied and its forms of agriculture many. As a continental area it is lightly populated. In pre-conquest times the small population was essentially peripheral with the greatest concentrations in the Andean valleys and plateaux and along the Pacific coast. The Spanish conquest, primarily interested in precious metals, focused upon this Andean area and made use of local labour. Interest in agriculture was secondary and rarely was it developed to produce crops or livestock products for export. Large land grants were made to Spanish settlers and were valued as much for the status they conferred on the recipients as for their productive capacity. The local Indian population was used as labour but the use of land on the *hacienda* or *estancia* was extensive rather than intensive except in proximity to the mining centres and administrative cities. The colonial economy continued to be based on mining rather than on agriculture. Plantations, in the modern sense, did not develop in Spanish America until the mid-nineteenth century when its countries were independent of Spain. The Portuguese in their Brazilian territory were far more concerned with land settlement and agricultural production and cultivated crops, such as sugar, for export. As in Spanish territory large land grants were made by the Crown.

The conquests in Latin America markedly reduced the indigenous populations and led to the bringing in of negro slaves from West and Central Africa to work on plantations (Odell and Preston 1973). The large estates worked by labourers yielded their owners a satisfactory living because of their size even when worked inefficiently and at a low tempo. There was little incentive to develop an efficient and productive agriculture. In some cases the estate owners rented their land to workers in share-cropping or cash-rent arrangements and, as time went on, a proportion of land-owners became absentee land-owners. The surviving Indian population was relegated to the more difficult and less rewarding territory where they continued to practise their largely subsistence farming by traditional methods. Indians, Indian-Hispanic people, the *mestizo*, the mixed negro groups, the *mulatto*, came to be the poor agriculturalists farming small rented or share-cropped plots, or tiny holdings on infertile soils or steep slopes, or became the forest clearers nibbling away at the woodland edge. The division of the agricultural land of so many Latin American countries between a few, wealthy landowners, owning most of the best land, and a large number of small impoverished farmers came about. To the poor farmers must be added the landless agricultural labourers who worked on estates large and small and on plantations. Many of these hired labourers lost all knowledge of how to operate a farm on their own account. The history of colonization in Latin America has left, though there are variations and exceptions, a continental area whose agrarian structure is characterized by an inequitable distribution of land, wealth and opportunity for development. Land tenure has become a major obstacle to the progress of agrarian society and the development of more productive farming systems in a region where land is in abundance. It is small wonder that many of the countries of Latin America are characterized by a most skewed distribution of income, and by a rural population in a state of unrest (Paige 1975).

The first report of the Independent Commission on International Development Issues popularly known as the Brandt Report stated:

In many countries, there are sharp disparities in land ownership: a minority of landowners and large farmers, often 5 to 10 per cent of the rural households, may own 40 to 60 per cent of arable land. The rest of the rural populations is crowded on small, often fragmented pieces of land; many own no land at all. In many cases, a high proportion of rural land is held on a tenant or share-cropping basis with the landlord appropriating large shares of the total crop. Such agrarian structures are unjust and inefficient. In some countries, the large holdings are under utilized and output per acre is lower than on small holdings. To reduce poverty and increase food production, agrarian reform and the promotion of farmers' and workers' organisations are priority issues

(Brandt 1980)

It is a comment which appropriately describes the situation in many Latin American countries where much land exists in very large estates, the *latifundia*, worked in the manner described with the remaining farmed land sub-divided into the tiny holdings, the *minifundia*. In Brazil in 1950 almost 60 per cent of the agricultural land was accounted for by only 4.7 per cent of the land holdings. In Chile in 1955 some 7 per cent of farm units farmed over 80 per cent of the land while in Peru in 1961 just over 1 per cent of farm holdings accounted for three-quarters of the farmed land. This inequitable distribution of land ownership and production was similarly evident in other Central and South American countries though to a less pronounced degree. The converse is the very large number of small farms which account for a very small proportion of the total agricultural land.

Clearly such situations represent obstacles in the way of economic and social development since on the one hand neither the large estates nor the small farms represent an efficient use of resources and advanced farming techniques while on the other the egalitarian objectives of social development are frustrated. In the several countries of Latin America attempts have been made to modify the agrarian structures. It is a difficult process since the major landowners are both wealthy and politically powerful with every reason to favour the status quo. As S. L. Barraclough states –'most Latin American countries have favoured large landowners and relatively well-off urban groups instead of the small farmers and workers . . . Traditionally-oriented Latin American governments will not normally permit any type of *campensino* (small farmers and farm worker) movement that would seriously threaten established power relationships' (Barraclough 1976).

In Mexico after the revolution of 1910, large *estancias* were confiscated and re-allocated to peasant farmers in communities known as *ejidos*. Most of the *ejidos* are cultivated by individuals in separate plots though the land is owned by the community. In a minority of cases, chiefly on irrigated lands, the *ejidos* are operated as very large farms with the *ejido* members working as labourers on them in what are essentially worker-owned collectives. In the Yaqui Valley, by 1940, about one-third of the irrigated land was worked by collectives which co-operatively owned cotton gins, machinery and service centres. Changes in the Government lessened the support of the *ejidos* and led to their breakdown. In the late 1970s a Government more anxious to promote agrarian reform, resuscitated and modernised the *ejidos* (Barraclough 1976). Preston describes similar developments taking place in the Fuerte Valley in the 1950s (Odell and Preston 1973).

Other examples of the promotion of co-operatives to achieve a more equitable sharing both of land and the opportunity for economic advancement are to be found in Peru where, by the early 1970s, some 1700 co-operatives had been created but Barraclough reports that decision-making by members remained minimal. In Chile the Christian Democrat government during the 1960s had expropriated a large number of big estates, which covered 14 per cent of the nation's agricultural land, and reorganized them into a form of co-operative called *asentamientos*. These units were jointly administered by government officials and a committee representing the farmers. The *asentamientos* came to be advantaged groups when compared with the bulk of poor peasants and their members came to operate more for individual rather than corporate interest. The Allende regime carried out much more extensive land appropriation taking in 40 per cent of the agricultural area and in addition set up 100 state farms. When the Allende regime was overthrown many confiscated estates were returned to their former owners and on the surviving co-operatives, farmers were encouraged to work individual plots (Barraclough 1976). Similar sequences of events have taken place in other Latin American countries where reforming legislation has been passed but rarely have subsequent substantial modifications of land holding followed. The great exception is, of course, Cuba where the Marxist revolution of 1959 took over all means of production. By 1968, 70 per cent of Cuba's agricultural land was farmed in state-owned and managed units by wage-labourers. One form of estate had been replaced by another.

EUROPEAN SETTLEMENT IN THE HIGHLANDS OF KENYA

A second example of European agricultural settlement in the tropics may be taken from Africa. Over much of Africa, European colonialists did not settle because of climate and disease-risk. Where altitude and location ameliorate the extremes of climate, colonialism in the twentieth century was associated not only with administration, mineral extraction and trade, but also with permanent agricultural settlements, notably in what were then the Rhodesias, and Kenya. In the latter, the high altitudes along the equator produced a climate attractive to Europeans and offering a range of agricultural possibilities from the production of tropical cash crops such as tea and coffee to temperate crops such as wheat and potatoes as well as the rearing of livestock using both temperate and tropical breeds. The Crown Land

Ordinance of 1902 gave the colonial government total ownership of all land. This allowed the alienation of specific areas of land for British settlers. By 1914 there were over 1000 settlers in the Kenya Highlands which came to be known as the White Highlands. In 1960 there were 3600 agricultural land holders in the Highlands owning 548,400 hectares of arable land and 2,193,200 hectares of pasture. In terms of area, the main crop was wheat but other important crops included coffee, sisal, tea, wattle, maize and pyrethrum. Odingo, in a very full account of the agriculture of the Kenya Highlands, describes how the crop cultivation in the area evolved as two distinct systems. One was a large-scale plantation system producing coffee and sisal, the other of smaller-scale arable farming growing wheat, maize and pyrethrum together with some coffee (Odingo 1971). In addition there was livestock farming, since almost all the area was tsetse free, and by 1960 over 1 million head of cattle and half a million sheep grazed on permanent grasslands and cultivated ley grasses. Dairy and beef cattle were kept both on specialist stock farms and on mixed arable-livestock holdings. The ownership and management was in the hands of European settlers. The labourers were hired Africans. There thus emerged an enclave of a productive, efficient, commercial and essentially European agriculture in a country otherwise characterized by traditional forms of African tillage and livestock economies.

In an Order in Council of 1938–39 non-Europeans had been excluded from land-ownership and farming in the Highlands. Subsequent to the Mau-Mau disturbances, this Order was rescinded in 1960 and from 1961 the area was opened to all races and the British Government agreed to sub-divide the mixed farming areas in the Highlands and to redistribute the land among peasant farmers. In 1962 over 500,000 hectares were allocated for resettlement. Subsequently very large areas were purchased by Kenyan Africans and Asians from those European owners who left Kenya after independence. These changes in land-ownership were almost entirely focused upon the mixed farming areas; the plantations and ranching areas remaining unaffected by either the resettlement schemes or land purchase. The Government of independent Kenya maintained this emphasis by sub-dividing the mixed farming areas. Population pressure on the land could be released as these areas were taken up by part-subsistence African farmers. At the same time the large coffee and tea plantations so vital to the export sector of Kenya's economy, were left, largely British managed and owned, as efficient producers (Paige 1975). As the transitional phase since independence has passed, the Government has encouraged the growing of both tea and coffee on small holdings, particularly the latter, so that gradually the dominance of British planters in the agrarian sector of the Kenyan economy has been diminished. It is a transformation which has taken place smoothly; its initiation was very largely the product of political independence.

PLANTATIONS AND THE PLANTATION ECONOMY

Reference has been made to plantations established in the Spanish and Portuguese conquests of Latin America and the British settlement of Kenya. They are a form of land holding, agricultural organization, production and marketing which has a long history and distinctive features. Plantations have, amongst some, become an emotive topic since they have associated them with a foreign exploitation of land and resources. They still exist in developing countries and in some are of great importance not only within the agricultural sector but also to the national economy.

Prior to the nineteenth century plantations were essentially associated with the Americas. In consolidating their position on the coast of Brazil, and thereby protecting their trade routes, the Portuguese colonial nobility began to organize sugar plantations in north-east Brazil as early as the sixteenth century coming to use negro slave labour from their African territories. The plantations were all small with several supplying a central cane mill. In the seventeenth century the Dutch acquired for a time the Portuguese territory around Pernambuco and, together with Britain and France, began to take possession of the islands of the West Indies. Subsistence activities by the settlers were replaced first by tobacco and then sugar as cash crops for the European market. Small holdings were amalgamated by successful planters and large plantations worked by negro slaves became characteristic by the eighteenth century (Angier 1960; Courtenay 1965). When slavery was abolished, in most cases by the 1860s, many of the smaller islands of the Caribbean became small-holder and largely subsistence communities. In the case of Trinidad and British Guiana, Chinese and, notably, Indians were brought in as indentured labourers to work on what became increasingly large sugar plantations. In Jamaica, sugar production declined and was overtaken by small-holder production of bananas for large marketing companies, notably those which merged eventually to form the United Fruit Company, which shipped the fruit to the United States. Cuba remained a colony of Spain where sugar was produced by negro slaves on large plantations, slavery not being abolished by the Spanish until 1885, and with large areas of suitable land experienced the greatest growth in plantation sugar production. The system remained after the emancipation of the slaves. Independent Cuba was the recipient of much American investment and its sugar output became tied to the American market by preferential tariff arrangements.

While the nineteenth century saw changes in the old plantation areas and in the scale of the plantation economy, it also witnessed the European initiation of plantation production in Africa, Asia, the Indian Ocean and the Pacific involving a wider range of crops produced for the growing European domestic and industrial market. Coffee, and later tea plantations were established in Ceylon (Ch. 14) and India by the British. The Dutch were involved in a variety of products in Java particularly coffee, sugar and indigo but including tea, cinnamon, cloves and nutmegs. At a later date they began to produce rubber and cinchona. The British established rubber plantations in Ceylon and Malaya, sugar plantations in Mauritius, Fiji and South Africa and coffee and tea in Nyasaland (Robequin 1954; Courtenay 1965; Chs. 11 and 14). Plantations were established in other colonial areas. The Belgians in the Congo set up large-scale oil palm plantations, the Americans in Hawaii grew sugar cane, the Germans and French in the Cameroons and Togo established plantations to produce rubber, palm oil and cocoa. In Brazil, where plantations began and where slavery was not abolished until 1888, sugar began to give way to coffee production which became the country's major export crop. Increasingly the coffee plantations were established in the more temperate southern parts of the country on plateaux in the State of Sao Paulo. The labour force was provided by European immigrants largely from Italy.

By the Second World War, plantations and plantation economies, were to be found in all the continental areas of the Developing World and though their histories had been varied, their impact in colonial territories had been considerable and they came to share a number of common attributes. With some exceptions they overwhelmingly bore the stamp of the industrial nations which operated them and have, indeed, been described as industrial forms of agriculture. In countries otherwise characterized by small-scale farming, they were large units manned by wage-labourers. They tended to be set up in sparsely populated and little cultivated areas and represented, therefore, additions to the farmed land. In the majority of cases it is incorrect to claim that they took land out of peasant food production. Shortage of local labour was a characteristic problem which plantation estates faced. Local farmers were either too few or saw no advantage in working on the plantations or were considered, in some cases, unsuitable. Whatever the reasons the large plantations of the world were worked by immigrant labour. At first, as has been seen, they were slaves from Africa. From the mid-nineteenth century they were usually hired labourers often indentured for a period of years after which they could return home passage-paid. They came overwhelmingly from the densely populated countries of the Indian sub-continent and China. In Ceylon, Indian Tamils from south India were used on the tea-plantations. Indians were shipped to Mauritius, to Fiji, to Trinidad, to British Guiana and to East and South Africa. Indians and Chinese were used in Malaya, Africans in South America, the Caribbean and Mauritius. Chinese, Japanese and Filipinos were taken to Hawaii. In India itself the tea plantations of Assam were worked not by local inhabitants but by the peoples of the Ganges plain and peninsular India. The movement of workers in this way, most of whom remained in the plantation countries, was on a large scale and has had not inconsiderable consequences for both race-relations and economic development in subsequent years. The plantations were not only large-scale implants of new forms of economy they also constituted enclaves of alien people.

All the plantations produced crops in demand in the industrialized countries and while the market was not entirely external it was overwhelmingly so. Mono-cropping was characteristic and to it scientific methods of cultivation were applied utilizing fertilizer and insecticides together with the selective breeding of plants to maximize production, disease resistance and ease of processing. None of the crops were basic and essential staple foods and though they included food crops such as bananas and sugar cane, the non-essential commodities such as tea, coffee and cocoa became important plantation products increasingly consumed in Europe and North America. With the introduction of the motor vehicle and the invention of the pneumatic tyre, rubber became a dominant plantation crop in south-east Asia in the twentieth century. Palm oil, copra and coconut oil both foods and industrial materials, sisal, cinchona, cinnamon, pyrethrum have all been cultivated on plantations as well as small-holdings. Many of these products require one or more industrial processes before they are exported and the necessary industrial plant operates most efficiently if it can achieve economies of scale and a year-round rather than a seasonal harvest function. Tree products which yield throughout the year lend themselves to this requirement notably tea, rubber, coconuts and oil palm. In short, plantations were, and many still are, large, foreign-owned and managed, funded by external capital and worked by paid labourers who were immigrants or descendants of immigrants. Their cropping is scientifically based and managed, is specialized and is commonly concerned with only one commodity; there are exceptions such as the estates in Malaya which grow both rubber and oil palm. The majority of plantation products are exported and often their profits repatriated. It is an economy which can be insulated from its host country. In newly independent countries this poses problems.

It is possible to argue a case for the positive contributions of plantations to the development process in developing countries. They introduce new ideas of how to manage soils and crops, of insecticides, fertilizer and cultivation techniques. They link the host country to an external market and hence can earn exchange revenue. The wage-labour they employ itself creates a local market for food and consumer products and exemplifies the ideas of the sub-division of labour and its organisation. In its activities the plantation invests in infrastructural developments such as roads, railways, docks, warehouses and factories. It builds settlements to house its workers, schools for their children and medical facilities for all. It becomes a source of scientific advice on crop husbandry and of economic advice on business administration. These positive benefits are manifest in most regions of plantation agriculture. There is, however, another side to their operation and this has become more evident during the twentieth century as the companies operating plantations have become much larger and more complex.

G. L. Beckford has drawn attention to the 'plantation economy' practised by multi-national companies, an economy which doubly divorces them from the national economies of the countries in which they operate (Beckford

1969, 1972). Plantations can be operated as part of the function of large, and often multi-national, companies. Reference has been made to the associated manufacturing element such as drying, blending, packing in the case of tea, of milling, refining, re-refining, packing, in the case of sugar, plus the processing of the by-product molasses into rum or other alcohols, while with the growing of coconuts there are the necessary processes of copra production and drying, of oil milling and of copra-cake production. This has led to these many activities becoming vertically integrated both technically and economically within a single company. In addition the products require transport and marketing and again these services have tended to be handled within the company, indeed in the case of some companies of which the United Fruit Company is an example, their initial involvement in the plantation economy was as a carrier rather than a producer. The integration has thus been backward as well as forward. These vertically organized companies link not only the plantation products of the tropics to the markets of the industrialized world but also integrate the economies of the producer countries into a wider multi-national company economy. Beckford argues that even after political colonial control was relinquished and with it, in many cases, land-ownership, the economic relationships have persisted. He claims that the independent countries of Central America can be regarded as extensions of the economic system of the United States and the sugar plantations of the Caribbean as part of an economy which absorbs them within that of the United States and the United Kingdom. In some countries the role of plantations constitutes such a major part of their national economy that this becomes very much influenced by the activities and fortunes of the plantation company. Where this company is large and multi-national in its operations, the individual country's economy becomes but part of that larger operation (Beckford 1969, 1972; Heady 1952; Jones 1968). Large companies, such as the British-based Tate and Lyle, Lever Brothers and Booker Brothers, McConnell and Company and the United Fruit Company, are not only characterized by vertically organized functions but also by a geographical spread of operations with their farming activities taking place in several countries. Beckford quotes, for example, the activities of the firm Booker Bros, McConnell and Company as involving the growing of sugar cane, the manufacture of raw sugar, the distillation of rum and other spirits and alcohol and the manufacture of machinery for sugar making. In addition the company provides bulk storage for sugar, owns wharfs, handles the ocean transport of sugar, acts as shipping agent and insurer, and as merchant for agricultural equipment. This company produced over 80 per cent of Guyana's sugar in the 1960s and accounted for the greater part of that country's exports. It was the biggest employer of labour and owned all the sugar storage and shipping facilities. Essentially this company dominated Guyana's economy; it operated also in Barbados, Canada, India, Jamaica, Malawi, Nigeria, St. Lucia, Trinidad and also Zambia though largely in a non-agricultural sense. The Tate and Lyle company is much bigger and more complex and is involved in sugar plantations in Jamaica, Honduras and Trinidad, with sugar refining in the United Kingdom, Canada, Zambia and what is now Zimbabwe and with sugar storage and distribution, molasses products and other activities in Africa, Asia, the Caribbean, North America and Europe. In the 1960s, it possessed eleven sugar ships and handled 65 per cent of sugar refining in Britain and 30 per cent in Canada (Beckford 1969, 1972). The United Fruit Company is much concerned with the banana production of Central America and their import into the United States. In 1966 it handled 55 per cent of all bananas imported into the USA and controlled all the area devoted to growing bananas for export in Guatemala as well as 70 per cent of that in Costa Rica and Panama and 56 per cent of that in Honduras. Of the fruit it handled, 47 per cent was grown on its own plantations, the rest coming from other growers.

Each of these firms is thus involved, to a major degree, in the economies of the developing countries in which they operate. Their range of activities extends beyond these individual countries and in their total activities the agricultural section, the plantation, does not represent the major part of their investment. The overall economy of the company relates to all its activities and not simply to agriculture and since the firms' decisions relate to the promotion of an economy which spans several countries, the company's view of its economic development may not necessarily be coincident with that of a particular country in which they operate. A plantation may be well-run and efficient and yet its contribution to the social and economic development of its host country may be limited. The company will look, naturally, at its allocation of resources of land, labour and capital in terms of the functioning of the company and, since it functions in several countries, it will view the separate components in its integrated operation in an international rather than individual country sense. It will not be concerned with the question, in terms of comparative advantage, of whether a particular country might better use the resources in growing rice rather than sugar or bananas or directing investment to the manufacture of shoes or transistors rather than raw sugar or rum. Profit maximization within the company will be related to all its operations and not solely its agricultural sector. It can draw the raw materials from a range of sources and not only from its own several holdings but from other supplies. A low price for raw sugar may reduce the returns to the farming function but means a low cost for the raw materials of its refining and distilling activities. Thus in this hypothetical situation while the company's profit may be up the beneficial spin-offs of its plantation activities in its host countries may be reduced. The risk of harvest failure in an individual country is cushioned for the company by its involvement in several though the stricken country suffers, while in less dramatic but equally significant terms, the large multi-national company expands or contracts its activities as it sees its own best interests served which are not necessarily those of the host country.

These features are not peculiar to multi-national plantation companies but can be the product of any transnational activity. What is particular to them is that their contribution to economic development, though it can be considerable, is constrained by the nature of their operations. Not only are they concerned with products with are not staple foods and hence do not directly contribute to alleviating food shortages but with methods and processes which are very specific to the crops grown. The technical spin-off is limited whether it relates to agricultural machinery, plant breeding or industrial processes. The vertical integration reduces the opportunity for ancillary supporting industries to develop so again the multiplier-effect is constrained. Even the exchange revenue earned by exports may be offset by the need to import food and equipment to sustain the work force and the plantation. While they provide employment opportunities for the local population it is largely as unskilled labourers, the managerial, scientific and technical functions remaining mainly in the hands of expatriate employees.

The greater part of these disadvantages are the product of the multi-national nature of the large foreign plantation companies such as these described by Beckford. As a farming system it can have much to recommend it in its role in agrarian development. It encompasses techniques and concepts which can do much to promote agricultural productivity. If it is considered in terms of the development of plant breeding, of fertilizer and insecticide practices, cultivation techniques, land conservation, labour organisation, the quality control of output and processing, and the development of management and entrepreneurial skills then the plantation by its scale and its semi-industrial nature has a place in the economy of developing countries. If it can attract supporting industries and services it can further galvanize developments. In some developing countries former foreign-owned plantations have been acquired and sub-divided amongst small holders or operated by state or private local companies. In other countries, agricultural development projects have been implemented which are, in everything but name, plantations. The plantation can play a part in the transformation of the agrarian economies of the Developing World.

7 Industrialization

'Your worship is your furnaces
which, like old idols, lost obscenes,
have molten bowels; your vision is
Machines for making more machines'

G Bottomley (1874–1948)
To Iron Founders and Others.

'successful development in virtually all countries has been characterized
by an increase in the share of manufacturing in total output. This
structural change, is both a cause and effect of rising incomes.'

H Chenery
Structural Change and Development Policy 1979.

The countries of the Developing World, many of them former colonial
territories recently independent, saw themselves in the years after the
Second World War as markedly different from the nations of Europe and
North America in two central ways. They were poorer and less industrialized. The way forward, in planning their own destinies, seemed to many
to be the machine, the factory and the power station. Industrialization was
the way to a secure and less dependent future, to the creation of wealth and
the removal of poverty. Both politicians within, and economists without, the
developing countries regarded industrialization as having the key role to
play in development planning. Kwame Nkrumah, President of Ghana,
wrote of a 'rapidly increasing industrialization that will break the neo-colo-
nial pattern which at present operates' (Nkrumah 1965). In 1967 the economist D. W. Jorgenson was stating 'The process of economic development
may be studied as an increase in income per head or as an increase in the
role of industrial activity to that is agriculture' (Jorgenson 1967). Others have
argued that industrialization is essential to absorb the 'surplus' population
of the underemployed and unemployed of the agrarian economies of the
tropics. These views have raised considerable debate and in the light of
experience and with the wisdom of hindsight they can be evaluated but first
it is useful to examine the bases for industrial development present in the
mid-twentieth century.

They are strong parallels in indigenous industry with the agricultural
sector. Indigenous manufacturing fits into the same pattern of social and
economic relationships of those of farming. Capital input is mininal, technological sophistication is absent inanimate power is rarely used and the

scale of production is small. The major inputs are labour and skill, the skills once possessed by the craftsmen of Europe and now largely lost. Some developing countries, and China and India are notable examples, represent the last great reservoirs of craft skills. The level of production is, in the main, geared to local demand and local raw material resources too small to sustain a large modern manufacturing plant, take on a special significance. The sporadic occurrence of rarer minerals or crops related to specific environments gives rise to regional specialization and trade but essentially, industrial production is concerned with disaggregated local economies. Demand is the other dimension and it is an expression of the way of life in terms of habitation, of domestic utensils, of clothing, foodstuffs, and of agricultural implements and craft tools. The demands made upon industry are limited by this way of life and industry has grown up and responded to it. Manufacture has been attuned to agriculture and integrated into society throughout the cultures of the Developing World. In such societies the demand for non-agricultural goods refers not only to family and house-hold requirements in the home and the field but also to the non-essentials such as jewellery and ornaments which can identify status and give expression to individuality. Many of the raw materials are the products of agriculture such as oils, fibres and leather or of the forest, while the rest are common minerals such as clay or lean iron-stones.

In Africa, the least industrialized and urbanized of continents, these characteristics of indigenous local industry are still widely evident. The towns and villages of West Africa exhibit such a range of domestic indus-tries. Hand spinning and weaving using cotton, camel hair or wool fibres produce cloths for clothing and bedding. Clothes are embroidered in tradi-tional designs some indicating class and status (Heathcote 1972). Fabrics are coloured with vegetable dyes by specialist dyers. The products based on agricultural materials serve a general demand with some degree of market sophistication. The cattle, goats and sheep, which are slaughtered for their meat, yield hides and skins which by elementary forms of tanning are converted to leather for saddles, harnesses, cushions, belts and shoes in a sequence from primary processing through to skilled making-up and the application or artistic talents. Lean, lateritic iron ores worked from shallow surface pits are smelted at low temperatures and beaten to a purity which enables iron worked by village smiths to produce tools for the home and agriculture including hoes of sophisticated designs. Brass and copper working produces prestige goods such as the brass pots given in marriage dowries, potters either resident in large settlements or itinerant workers serving many small villages produce more mundane vessels from local clays. Carpenters make furniture and vehicles from local, not imported, timbers. Food processing, producing commodities such as groundnut and palm oil, and yam flour, compose another group. The essential salt is manufactured wherever possible and is traded over long distance, where not; soap manufacture also uses an amalgam of local materials. Beads, bracelets and musical instruments further diversify production. Some of these activities are recognised artisan skills practised by families through which the skills are passed from parent to child. Some are protected by trade guilds. Many are part-time activities practised by farmers during slack periods in the agricultural year. These activities are as characteristic of towns as of villages. Mabogunje reports a similar spectrum in the 1960s in Ibadan the largest indigenous city in sub-Saharan Africa with a population of over half a million in 1963 (Mabogunje 1968).

THE COLONIAL IMPACT AND NASCENT INDUSTRIALIZATION

What has been described, though there will be differences according to environment, culture and historical experience, can be found throughout many countries of the Developing World. It still survives but it has been and is being profoundly altered by external influences. As in the case of agriculture, the colonial experience and the impact of the industrialized world have made their mark as the localised equilibrium of agriculture and industry, supply and demand has been shattered by competing supplies and demands. Industrialization outside the Developing World rather than within it has profoundly altered its economies and this took place before independence opened the door to planned developments. The increase in the capacity to manufacture which Europe experienced in the nineteenth century created a demand for raw materials from the tropics, as has been seen in the case of agricultural products but it, of course, also included minerals in short supply in Europe. An enlarged market for European manufacturers also became necessary. These manufactures were often superior to goods made by the domestic industries of the Developing World and increasingly replaced them so that what survives is but a relic of a former economy. In West Africa the smith turns from the manufacture of hoes and adzes to the repair of bicycles of other imported machines. The tinker uses as his materials the scrap of imported tin boxes and cans. The wood-carver becomes a furniture maker and repairer. The weaver buys European or Far Eastern fabrics, invests in a sewing machine and becomes a tailor. The non-agricultural spectrum is enlarged, not so much by manufacturing as by service industries as imported watches, vehicles, printing machines, electrical appliances and a host of other machines are serviced and repaired. In Ibadan as recently as 1963 there were only forty-seven industrial establishments employing over ten persons and of these in only nine did employment exceed one hundred. The larger firms included soft drink manufacturers, tyre treading and furniture makers (Mabogunje 1968).

Some suggest that the mass of small industrial enterprises, present not only in Africa but throughout the Developing World, represent the fertile, bubbling concoction out of which industrial society grows arguing that the scene of domestic, artisan industry described was characteristic of pre-industrial Europe. Is this the breeding ground of industrialization in the Developing World? It may be in terms of individual entrepreneurial aptitudes but it cannot be as a system. The parallel with the birth of the mechanical factory industry in Europe, so dear to economic historians, omits one crucial component, namely the contemporaneous existence of the Industrialized World vastly more possessive of a present productive capacity let alone a future one. It is the need to encompass this situation which presents the industrialization of the Developing World with a major, perhaps *the* major problem.

The amount and character of industrialization varies throughout the range of developing countries. Some are characterized by industrial developments initiated by the industrial nations during the colonial period. These are most commonly associated with the extraction of minerals and represent the industrial equivalent of the plantation. Examples in Africa are the copper mines and smelters of Zaire and Zambia and the tin mines of Nigeria dating from the early years of this century. In Asia the placer deposits of tin in the Malay peninsula and Sumatra and in South America the tin, lead and silver of Bolivia and Peru and the copper ores of Chile are further examples. It will be noted that these examples are characteristically of relatively high-value metals the value of which could help offset the remoteness of their locations from the processing industries which would use them. They were also minerals becoming in increasingly short supply in Europe. Like the plantation, the mining industries, their associated smelters and the settlements of their workers, became enclaves of modern industrial technology in otherwise non-industrialized countries. Their subsequent development has had, however, in many cases, profound repercussions upon the development paths of the countries in which they were located (Ch. 10).

Manufacturing industry in colonial territories was inhibited rather than encouraged since it could serve to reduce the market opportunities open to the industries of the colonial powers. None the less in some countries European techniques of manufacturing and factory methods of production were adopted and took root. In Brazil, where there had been a considerable influx of Europeans to establish and work coffee plantations in the late nineteenth century, the development of coffee production and marketing not only raised capital but provided commercial and managerial experience upon which other industries could be based. Characteristically they first produced consumer goods, notably textiles. The manufacturing activity was then extended into iron-making, using local raw materials but in a modern high-technology manner, and into engineering. In the Indian sub-continent domestic cottage industry dominated the industrial sector throughout the nineteenth and early twentieth century. In an attempt to encourage small industrial developments protective measures were enacted in 1922 to allow Indian textile factories to develop, modernize and grow and the iron and steel industry, using the coal and iron deposits of the Damodar-Jamshedpur area of the peninsula, to begin to supply the local demand for iron and steel manufacture. On independence in 1947 both India and Pakistan were still however, essentially agricultural countries.

The colonial episode did stimulate economic development, including that of manufacturing, in many countries though the effect varied considerably. Capital and expertise were injected and methods for the large scale utilization of the physical resources of agriculture, timber and minerals introduced. Factory organized wage-labour systems were set up in some countries and enlarged the size of the domestic market while, importantly, concepts of economic administration and business management were implanted. Some of these introductions withered; others such as the infrastructural developments of road and rail systems and dock installations remained. But overall the economic developments of the colonial era bear the mark of their external origin and focus. The transport development was essentially designed to extracts resources and products and transport them to the new ports for shipment to the markets of the industrialized nations. The railway map of Africa demonstrates this most clearly with its series of isolated railway systems connecting interior to the coast but rarely country with country. It is a physical expression of economic developments skewed by a particular intent (Taaffe, Morrill and Gould 1963). Capital formation took place outside the developing countries and ancillary developments, as with plantations, were restricted if they had advanced technological requirements. Indeed, most industrial developments were manifestations of the plantation type of economy; they were designed to further and sustain the industrial economies of Europe, North America and, latterly, Japan.

INDEPENDENCE AND THE LURE OF INDUSTRIALIZATION

Manufacturing industry, the missing element which seems to distinguish the rich from the poor nations of the world presents a development problem different from that faced by agriculture. In its scale, its technological reguirements, in its organization and concept of management, it is something so very different from what has gone before that it can be regarded as something totally new. It is an addition to, rather than a modification of, pre-existing economies. For all these reasons it has been put to the fore in developing strategies by most governments either in state enterprises or in their encouragement of private endeavour. In the context of political economies, industrialization is the banner of modernization and to the new politicians of the recently independent countries it appeared to have four outstanding attributes which could be proclaimed in speech and writ large on banners. First, that it is the missing element which, when introduced, will disrupt the equilibrium between subsistence agriculture and cottage industry. It is a thing of the new future rather than the stagnant past. Second it can provide goods either directly or indirectly for the enlargement of material possessions. It is the way to wealth. Third it can provide employment for the unemployed and underemployed. Fourth, it is the way to free developing countries from the yoke of the Industrial World, from the 'neo-colonialism' of which Nkrumah wrote. These are powerful notions which catch the imagination and offer hope; their translation into practice has proved a difficult matter.

The countries of the Developing World possess in varying degrees the factors of industrial production, raw materials, labour, energy resources and capital. These relative factor endowments will condition the form which their development path, including industrialization, takes. These endowments will have been influenced by their particular historical experience,, including colonialism. The many countries in the Developing World differ from each other not only in their natural resource endowments but also in their size, their access to capital from outside the country and in their political ideologies, social goals and attitudes to economic and social planning. The consequent opportunities, and problems, will thus vary considerably for industrialization as for agricultural development and the past three to four decades have illustrated this. Despite its inauspicious beginnings amidst inadequate social and physical infrastructures, capital deficiencies and untrained work forces, industrialization has been taking place to some degree in all developing countries. Some have become fully industrialized nations, for example Hong Kong, Singapore and Taiwan for which the acronym NIC, Newly Industrialized Country, has been coined. Other have a large industrial component in their economy and can be described as semi-industrialized. South Korea, Argentina, Brazil, Chile, Mexico and Uruguay together with Jordan and Lebanon would seem to fit this description. Both India and China despite their huge agrarian populations which define them as agricultural, have developed large industrial sectors incorporating all stages of manufacturing. The majority of developing countries in the 1980s still, however, employ less than a quarter of their work forces in manufacturing, and in many cases much less, and derive the greater part of their export revenue from the export of primary products (Table 7, Ch. 9).

The economist, Hollis Chenery, has for over thirty years been involved in the investigation of structural changes in the economies of developing countries and has attempted to establish what could be regarded as 'normal growth functions'. By examining a range of data from a large number of countries using multiple regression analyses, he suggested that at per capita annual income levels of US $100 (1950s values) the contribution of manufacturing was 12 per cent but that rises in per capita incomes were associated with an increase in manufacturing so that at levels of US $1000 per capita the characteristic proportion of manufacturing in the GDP was 33 per cent. The contribution of primary production fell over the same income change from 45 to 15 per cent of GDP. Furthermore Chenery was able to correlate changes in the nature of the manufacturing industry with increases in average per capita incomes. In a country of some 10 million people with per capita incomes at the US $100 level most manufacturing (65 per cent of output) would be concerned with consumer goods and only 20 per cent with intermediate goods, that is goods used to make other goods such as rubber or chemicals. Manufacturing devoted to the production of investment goods such as the making of machines to manufacture products or generate energy or the production of metals such as iron and steel, would account for the remainder. As per capita income rose this would be associated with a much smaller proportion of manufacturing concentrating on consumer goods, 43 per cent, while the basic investment goods would account for 35 per cent and intermediate goods for 23 per cent (Chenery 1960). Chenery and Taylor then took the analysis further and categorized countries into three types, large countries whose populations exceeded 15 million, small countries whose export trade was largely concerned with manufactured goods and small countries where exports were of the primary products of farm, forest and mine (Chenery and Taylor 1968). In both the large countries and the small industrialized countries the patterns of industrializations were similiar with industrial share of GNP rising rapidly from 16 per cent of GNP at incomes of US $100 to 32 per cent at US $400. Thereafter, the rise in the share of industry was much slower reaching 37 per cent at US $1200. Primary production's contribution fell from 45 per cent at the US $100 level to 12 per cent at US $1200. In the third category of country, the small primary export nation, the changes were different. Primary production remained more important than that of manufacturing up to the US $800 income level falling from 50 per cent at US $100 to 30 per cent at US $500 while industry rose from some 17 to 19 per cent. Chenery and Taylor's analysis covered fifty-seven countries of which thirty-nine were developing nations. Fourteen were of the small primary export type in which industrialization is likely to present the greatest problems and twenty-five were developing countries in whom, it would seem, industrialization has a very positive contribution to make to development.

Chenery has extended his work still further and in 1975 published a wide-ranging statistical analysis of development patterns and processes over the period 1950 to 1970 (Chenery and Syrquin 1975). He and Syrquin were attempting, by examining the experience of over one hundred countries, to identify universal patterns of economic structural change which are associated with rises in per capita income in what has been described as 'modern economic growth'. The development of the industrial sector is an important part of that structural change. Its precise character reflects not only the abundance or scarcity of the factor endowments of raw materials, energy resources, and labour supplies in particular countries but also the development path which they have identified. Chenery has sub-divided the three categories of country he defined in 1960, the large, the small industrialized and the small primary producer, according to the development strategy the particular country has adopted. These are primary specialization, import substitution, balanced production and trade and lastly industrial specialization. The categories are based on coincidences with or deviations from normal average patterns of production and exports with the data relating to 1965 (Chenery 1979). It will be apparent that involvement in trade is an essential characteristic of these strategies though the amount and the nature varies considerably. It reflects the alternative decisions of nations either to choose an absolutely, or relatively, self-contained existence, a choice normally open to large countries with a rich and varied resource base, or to opt for participation in the world economy and with all that that implies in terms of imports, export opportunities, loans and foreign investments. In the political context of newly acquired independence, the majority of developing countries sought to achieve some degree of economic independence in terms of industrial goods from the industrialized countries. Some with the essential resource base attempted to lay the foundation of a vertically-integrated manufacturing structure and established capital-intensive basic industries such as iron and steel, heavy engineering and heavy chemicals. This was similar to the pattern used by the Soviet Union and India followed it (Chapter 15). Others, the majority, sought to establish import-substituting industries producing consumer goods essentially for the home market but also generating capital which could be used, where possible, in a backward extension of linkages through intermediate to basic industries; the reverse of the Soviet model. Import-substitution appeared both from political and economic viewpoints to be the way to spear-head industrialization.

IMPORT-SUBSTITUTION INDUSTRIALIZATION AND PROTECTIONISM

A degree of economic independence from the industrial nations was regarded as a means of both demonstrating the new political independence and of reducing the drain on scarce resources. Most developing countries were primary producers and the export of primary products was their major, often only, source of exchange needed to energize economic development. The import of manufactured goods from abroad not only limited this opportunity but also could, and often did, lead to crises in the balance of payments. Two concerted actions were open to countries in such situations. First, industries could be set up to produce goods at home replace some of those imported and, second, tarriffs quotas and other measures taken, could be implemented to keep out a wide range of 'non-essential' manufactured goods and at the same time protect the infant home industries. This need for protection has often been increased in developing countries because they have over-valued their currencies. This meant the imports appeared as particularly low-cost competitors to home products. It continued to be the case of all imported commodities not covered by the protective measures. These could include raw materials and components used in the manufacture of 'inessential industries' and so their use would be encouraged. Griffin and Enos, who take a jaundiced view of the efficacy of import-substitution, point out that in such situations home industries develop production techniques based upon imported materials with the result that a greater use is made of imported inputs. Protecting the balance of payments may result in both the development of 'inessential industries' (that is industries which are considered of low priority either in laying the foundations of economic development or characterized by a low industrial linkage propensity) and a greater use of imports. So while the output of home-produced goods increases, being based upon imports it uses exchange revenue and does much to defeat the purpose of import-substitution. They argue that most new industrial ventures in developing countries are markedly less efficient than their counterparts in the Industrial World. In consequence the ratio of inputs to outputs is greater and their use of the imported raw materials much more extravagant. The net result is that, in money terms, the import-substitution effect is very low (Griffin and Enos 1970; Bernstein 1973). There is another possible consequence. Devoting a great amount of investment capital to the import-substituting consumer goods industries means less is available to establish capital goods industries. If these basic industries do not exist, or cannot expand, they are able neither to serve the import-substitute industries nor initiate the establishment of any others. Capital goods have, therefore, to be imported and increase still further import costs. It is true, of course, that this investment in imported capital goods will, in the long run, help sustain output. Indeed it can be argued that is preferable to invest *ab initio* in capital goods industries and in manufacturing designed to produce competitive exports rather than to encourage a large domestic demand for consumer goods which, since it cannot be met adequately from home industries, will maintain a taste for imported items.

In the 1950s a large proportion of developing countries chose the path of import-substituting industrialization and protectionism. Behind tariff barriers they further assisted the new home industries by granting them tax exemption and providing capital loans at low interest rates. In some countries the state was directly involved, in others private enterprises and in most a mix of the two. Protectionism it was felt would allow the new industries, with their inexperienced management and workforce, to establish themselves securely, iron out difficulties and become increasingly efficient so that they could eventually withstand the competition. This approach was adopted both by countries following the consumer-goods approach and by those taking the basic-industries road. Its effectiveness in allowing the development of efficiency proved to be a far from unqualified success. Griffin and Enos quote examples from Ghana where in 1964 twenty-two out of thirty-one state industries not only failed to make a profit but achieved massive losses, from Chile where the privately owned motor vehicle industry in the 1960s was grossly inefficient in its use of resources and from Pakistan where inefficiency was present in a large proportion of industries (Griffin and Enos 1970; Islam 1967; Johnson, H. G. 1964; Johnson,

L. L. 1967; Sologo and Stern 1965). The evidence appears to indicate a greater tendency to inefficiency in the consumer-goods sectors. It should be pointed out, however, that initial inefficiencies are to be expected; the question is the extent to which they are unduly prolonged by excessive protection. Continuing inefficiency and hence high unit costs together with an over-valued currency acts as a positive disincentive to the export of manufactures.

DEVELOPMENT PATHS OF INDUSTRIALIZATION

Chenery's classification of development paths, to which reference has been made, provides a convenient summary of the progress of industrialization and structural transformation in developing countries (Chenery 1979). He points out that most countries begin by specializing in the export of primary products which result from their natural resources. Of the countries he analysed, those who remained in this category from 1960 until 1975 were either small countries or those with a particularly valuable mineral to export. The exceptions were the three oil exporters Nigeria, Iran and Indonesia. In other countries the phase of primary export specialization had been succeeded by other developments; indeed Chenery describes primary specialization as a 'strategy of deferred industrialization' that is it is used to accumulate investments and to raise income levels so as subsequently to allow industrial developments. Clearly the rate at which this takes place will depend upon the size and value of the primary resource, the world demand for it and the ability to re-invest the derived income effectively. Malaysia and the Cote d'Ivoire are examples of countries who have been particularly successful in stimulating industrial growth by investing income from agricultural exports.

The second of Chenery's categories was that of balanced development. This essentially represents a combination of primary export and a manufacturing development which has not resulted in industrial specialization. Within this group Chenery distinguishes a sub-category of nations which have opted for a deliberate policy of import-substitution. He writes:

> Over time these policies lead to relatively low levels of exports, diversion of resources from agriculture, and ultimately a slowdown in the growth of industry and of GNP as the possibilities for import substitution are progressively exhausted. Because of this market limit, the strategy of inward-looking development usually succeeds in eliminating the specialization in primary production but not in achieving manufactured exports
>
> (Chenery 1979).

Large countries, that is those with populations exceeding 15 million in 1965, have tended to be those which have persisted with import-substitution and to have been more successful with it because of their larger home markets which offer scale-economies to scale-sensitive industries. For other countries it does not appear to have been a self-recommending policy. The other balanced-development countries though engaging, at least initially, in some import-substitution activities, have retained a more open economy and with it a much greater incentive to export manufactured goods.

In the third category of industrial specialization are found countries which, having initially in some instances been concerned with some primary exports and indeed with the home market, have sought to manufacture goods for the international market and to seek their salvation in trade. A limited resource base has, of course, stimulated this course of action in a number of instances. This path requires the assemblage of entrepreneurial abilities, industrial skills and adaptive labour force which characterizes the industrial nation. It is not a package which is easily put together. Hong Kong and Singapore, notably deficient in natural resources, together with Taiwan have been equally notably successful.

Fifty countries in Chenery's analysis are depicted in Table 5. It is important to note that this classification is of policies and not of attainment. It, therefore, does not mean that Kenya, for example, is to be regarded as an industrial country. It is suggestive of a ladder of structural change and development though it does not purport to cover all dimensions of devel-

Table 5 The Chenery classification of development strategies

Primary specialisation	Balanced development Import substitution	Other balanced	Industrial specialisation
Algeria	Argentina*	Costa Rica	Egypt*
Bolivia	Brazil*	El Salvador	Hong Kong
Dominican Rep.	Chile	Greece	Israel†
Indonesia*	Colombia*	Guatemala	Kenya
Iran*	Ecuador	Ireland	Lebanon
Iraq	Ghana	Jamaica	Pakistan*†
Ivory Coast	India*	Morocco	Portugal†
Malaysia	Mexico*	Peru	Singapore
Nicaragua	Turkey*	Phillipines*	South Korea*†
Nigeria*	Uruguay	South Africa*	Taiwan
Sri Lanka		Spain*	Tunisia†
Saudi Arabia		Syria	Yugoslavia*
Tanzania		Thailand*	
Venezuela			
Zambia			

Source: Chenery 1979
* Population exceeding 15 million in 1965
† Countries in which the net resource inflow as a share of gross domestic product was high, ie a high capital inflow.

Figure 21 Employment in manufacturing 1980

Percentage of Labour Force Employed in Manufacturing 1980

< 15

15 – 24

25 – 34

> 34

n – No data

Equator

Source of data World Bank 1983

opment. The proportion of the labour force in industry is some measure of the degree of industrialization. In 1980 in the low-income economies of the World Bank's classification, excluding India and China, 11 per cent of the labour force was engaged in industry. This description includes mining and construction work as well as manufacturing. In India the figure was 13 per cent and in China 19 per cent. The average percentage for the low-middle income countries was 17 and the upper-middle income 28 whereas in the industrial market economies the average was 38 per cent. This measure of the degree of industrialization is shown in Fig. 21. In the twenty years from 1960 to 1980 throughout most of the Developing World industrial work increased its contribution to employment by 6 per cent though in the upper-middle income group the increase was 8 per cent. During the same period, in the industrial market economies as a whole there was no increase though employment in agriculture continued to fall. The major employment opportunities in the so-called industrial economies were in the service sector which is by far the largest employer. This is suggestive of a further stage of development in structural transformation which in large measure is a product of the efficiency of capital-intensive means of manufacture and raises questions of the role of appropriate technology in the development process.

For the majority of the countries of the Developing World manufacturing remains an undeveloped sector which must be further stimulated to energize the development process and fulfil as yet unfulfilled hopes. As Hughes has written 'the most rapidly growing developing countries have been those that, without neglecting other sectors, have achieved the most efficient and rapid growth in manufacturing industries' (Cody, Hughes and Wall 1980).

Clearly to be considered adequately, the role of industrialization, the addition of large-scale manufacturing to essentially agrarian economies, must be viewed in the context of overall development policies. These policies embrace all sectors of the economy and all aspects of society since a development in one will have consequences for the others. Issues of population have been discussed and their relevance to social and economic development stressed. The nature of agricultural systems, and their potential for change, has been reviewed. Traditional indigenous industries have been described and the question of industrialization raised. These separate considerations are parts of one entity and it is with the development of this, the political economy, that the peoples and the governments of developing countries are concerned. It is the question of stimulating, guiding or controlling this development process which will now be considered.

8 The Development Process and Development Planning

'I have a Vision of the Future, chum,
The workers' flats in fields of soya beans
Tower up like silver pencils, score on score:
And Surging Millions hear the Challenge come
From microphones in communal canteens
"No Right! No Wrong! All's perfect, evermore

J Betjeman
The Planster's Vision 1945

'What is the essential of planning economic development? I would say
that the essential consists in assuring an amount of productive
investment which is sufficient to provide for a rise of national income
substantially in excess of the rise in population so that per capita
income increases.'

O Lange
Essays on Economic Planning 1960

'One must avoid the persistent confusion of growth with development'
Brandt Report 1980

DEVELOPMENT PLANNING

Development planning has itself grown out of other developments. These
include the study and increasing understanding of economic processes; the
increasing internal integration of national economies which have replaced
relatively discrete, disaggregated local economies; the increasing acceptance
of the role of the state in the welfare of society; the development of administrative abilities and professional and technical skills to manage large and
complex structures. These developments have all been encapsulated in the
concept of the nation state. They became essentially characteristic of the
industrialized countries of North America, Europe and Japan. In the Soviet
Union, incorporated in the Marxist ideology, these trends were brought
together into a totally planned economy, the command economy which was

implemented after 1918. They appeared, for different reasons and purposes, in the fascist states of Germany and Italy in the interwar period, while at the same time increasing state intervention in the economy, in an attempt to mitigate the effects of the economic slump and to restore economic growth, became characteristic of the democratic countries of western Europe. The prosecution of the Second World War itself forged instruments of national, concerted economic effort in all the belligerent nations from the United States in the West to Japan in the East. The countries of the Developing World were not part of these developments quite simply because most were not independent. In those that were, notably in Latin America, neither their organs of government, nor their political systems nor yet their economic structures were conducive to the emergence of development planning. In the greater part of the Developing World, up until the end of the Second World War, independent countries and distinctive national economies did not exist. National plans, where formulated, consisted of accounting exercises by the colonial governments.

The twenty five years between 1945 and 1970 saw the vast majority of colonial territories achieve independence. Abruptly new sovereign states came into existence, new governments were faced with the task, for the first time, of administering their countries. They came into existence at a time when the acceptance of some form of economic planning was commonplace and when belief in the efficacy of planning was widespread. The populations of the developing countries looked to their new rulers, now their own kind and not foreign, for a promise of better things and of the means to obtain them. In retrospect it is possible to see how daunting, how formidable, this prospect was for the newly established and often inexperienced politicians, inexperienced, that is, in governing rather than political activism. Some were supported by their ignorance of the problems faced, others by the strength of their ideological beliefs, others conscious of their inadequacies, not of leadership but in technical competence, sought help from international agencies such as the World Bank, from the former colonial power which had ruled them and from economic advisers both imported and home-grown. Their aim was to diminish rapidly the difference in the levels of economic attainment, standard of living, technical sophistication and economic independence between their country and that of the 'western' industrialized world. This was regarded as a goal which was not only attainable but as one which could be reached quickly. Development planning was to be the answer.

While these events were taking place in country after country in the Caribbean, Latin America, Africa, Asia and Oceania, scholars in the affluent world were increasingly turning their attention to this issue of development. Was there a discernible and inevitable process which transformed a technically backward, impoverished society into a more productive affluent organism? Was not the sequence of events which had taken place in Western Europe the apposite analogy? Could components of the European economic transition be isolated, examined, understood and re-assembled into a model which would not only describe the process but give indications of how it should be initiated in the new nation states of the 'underdeveloped world'?

The intellectual interest of economists had long been in the mechanism of growth which had brought about the transformation of the economies of the industrial countries. It now embraced the question as to why so many nations had not experienced this transformation. The theories of growth and non-growth were the obvious source-material for economic development planning.

It can be argued that poor countries are poor because they are poor, that poverty is a self-perpetuating condition. At its simplest, the argument would take the form that low productivity means an insufficient food supply, that this leads to malnutrition and ill-health which in turn reduces the ability to work effectively resulting in a maintenance of low productivity. On the one hand this low productivity leaves no surplus of production which can be diverted to other and additional forms of production and on the other means that the producer has no means of purchase and so the total market is small and locked into a situation of a low-level equilibrium between supply and demand. The conditions of subsistence agriculture and domestic industry which have been described bear some of the marks of this condition. Nurkse developed this idea in his book *Problems of Capital Formation in Underdeveloped Countries* (Nurkse 1953; Mountjoy 1971). He writes:

> Perhaps the most important circular relationships of this kind are those that afflict the accumulation of capital in economically backward countries. The supply of capital is governed by the ability and willingness to save; the demand for capital is governed by the incentives to invest. A circular relationship exists on both sides of the problem of capital formation in the poverty-ridden areas of the world
>
> (Nurkse 1953)

He makes the point that some countries are poor because they lack mineral resources and because their environments are hostile to agriculture but that the lack of capital applies to their condition also. Leibenstein and Nelson have been associated with a further development of this circular relationship in the formulation of the theory of the low-level equilibrium trap (Leibenstein 1954, 1957; Nelson 1956). This theory bears upon the issues raised in considering the economic implications of population dynamics referred to in Chapters 2 and 3.

It states that as incomes rise populations will grow; the Malthusian proposition that populations grow and press up against the subsistence level. Malthus, it will be recalled, argued that this will then result in a reduction in per capita income, distress and a fall in population. Leibenstein's view is that since there is a physiological limit to the rate of population expansion (in the absence of immigration) to certainly not above 4 per cent per annum, this identifies the level of increase of per capita income below which the low-level equilibrium trap will operate. Increases up to this level will mean that population will expand in response to the income increase and, by absorbing the national income, again produce a situation in which savings approach zero and once more hold development down. The low level equilibrium trap is shown graphically in Fig. 22 and is explained in the caption. Leibenstein was, however, not only concerned with the role of capital in a financial and physical sense but also as applied to the concept of the human resource, its skills, aptitudes and innovative energy.

Figure 22 The low-level equilibrium trap (after Todaro 1977)

In this diagram the rate of increase of production, (O_1), is shown as demonstrating characteristic diminishing returns. The rate of increase of population (P) is plotted against per capita income. The curve assumes that as per capita income increases so the population will grow until it reaches the physiological limit around 3.5 per cent. The two curves interact with each other. As per capita incomes grow from a very low level at A to a slightly higher level at B, greater affluence allows more to survive and the rate of population increase rises sharply in Malthusian fashion. At X the rate of population increase exceeds that of production and prevents a further rise in per capita incomes. As population continues to expand increasing poverty operates its Malthusian checks cutting back population so that it and production fall to a low level. Output and population increases oscillate, therefore, around X in a low-level equilibrium trap. If, for some reason, it is possible to continue to increase production until population increase reaches its physiological limit at Y then per capita income can reach C and continue to increase until D. Thereafter because of the operation of diminishing returns the production curve declines and crosses the curve of stable maximum increase in population at Z. At this point per capita incomes begin to decline and the rate of population increase likewise falls until a further equilibrium is reached oscillating around Z a second equilibrium trap. To break this containment of population-output equilibrium it is necessary to be able to harness the means of production so as to raise the production curve (O_2) so that it always exceeds that of population with the result that as population declines output continues to exceed it and per capita income increases. Continuing aggregated developments, when the development process is fully launched, will ensure that the diminution in returns on inputs are continually postponed as one form and means of production shifts into another. The model assumes, wrongly, that average per capita income, derived from the division of national output by national population, is the influence upon the size of family and hence the population curve. It is the actual family income which produces conditions favourable or contrary to, the formation of small families (see Chapter 3). The distribution of family income therefore modifies considerably the relationships depicted in this figure.

THE ROSTOWIAN MODEL

These views all centred around the difficulty of accumulating capital for investment for further development in countries which were initially characterized by poverty. The issue became one of how to break through this containment. Nurkse and Lewis could not see how a subsistence community could ever generate capital and therefore it must be an activity associated with some other sector, cash agriculture, mineral export, either privately or state operated. This in turn implied that one sector would become more affluent. Arthur Lewis regarded rates of saving as central to the issue of economic development. In his paper *Economic development with unlimited supplies of labour* (Lewis 1954) he states that economic development is characterized by rapid capital accumulation. He associates this with increases in the rate of domestic savings. It therefore follows that if it can be explained why countries with previous low levels of saving and investment are transformed into nations with much higher levels, the levels he refers to are from 4 or 5 per cent or less of the national income to 12 to 15 per cent or more, then a greater understanding of the process of economic development can be achieved.

There are two points to note in Lewis's views. First, there is stress not only on saving as a source of investment but also the need for a *rapid* accumulation of capital. Second, Lewis was referring to the experience of the capitalist industrial countries and their structural transformation as possible guides to the explanation of 'development'. As applied to the less developed countries it implies that the opportunities for worthwhile investment exist; it is the capital which is lacking. When these views are tied to Leibenstein's exposition of the low-level equilibrium trap possible explanations begin to emerge. What is needed is a massive investment over a short period to raise income levels above the containment rate. Thereafter, since it was believed that savings levels and hence opportunities for capital accumulation were determined by per capita income, this would allow a continuing growth of the economy so that it always exceeded any population expansion. Indeed as we saw in Chapter 3, the rate of population increase would tend to decrease as its members became more affluent.

The ideas incorporated in theories of growth therefore suggested a succession of stages in what was conceived of as 'development' analogous to what had happened in Europe and it is with this concept that the name of Walt Whitman Rostow is most closely identified. Rostow progressively formulated his thesis in a number of works. (Rostow 1952, 1956, 1960, 1963). Approaching the problem as an economic historian and examining the development process in Europe, North America and Japan, Rostow put forward the hypothesis that:

> The process of economic growth can usefully be regarded as centring on a relatively brief time interval of two or three decades when the economy and the society of which it is a part transform themselves in such ways that economic growth is, subsequently, more or less automatic. This decisive transformation is here called the take-off
>
> (Rostow 1956).

Rostow is concerned with rates of investment rising and being employed effectively so that per capita output in real terms rises and that this crucial level of investment is such that it leads to fundamental changes in production and in the disposition of the resulting income which in turn will lead to further investment, further increases of income and so on in a self-perpetuating manner. He says:

> Initial changes in method require that some new group in the society have the will and the authority to install and diffuse new production techniques; and a perpetuation of the growth process requires that such a leading group expand in authority and that the society as a whole respond to the impulses set up by the initial changes. . . .
>
> (Rostow 1956).

In the course of a sophisticated thesis, Rostow examines historical analogies and identifies a series of stages of development of which the first two, the 'pre-conditions' and the 'take-off' he considered particularly relevant to the Developing World. The first referred to slow economic and social developments of a century or more when conditions for 'take-off' were established; the second to the twenty or thirty years referred to above. The third stage was the subsequent period of self-sustaining growth. According to Rostow 'take-off' requires three conditions:

(a) a rise in the rate of productive investment from (say) 5 per cent or less to over 10 per cent of national income (or net national product).

(b) the development of one or more substantial manufacturing sectors with a high rate of growth.

(c) the existence or quick emergence of a political, social and institutional framework which exploits the impulses to expansion in the modern sector and the potential external economy effects of the 'take-off' and gives to growth an on-going character. The third condition implies a considerable capability to mobilise capital from domestic sources

(Rostow 1956).

Rostow makes the last point because he believes that while foreign capital can help to establish the pre-conditions for 'take-off' it cannot institute 'take-off' itself. This is the product of an internal transformation which subsequently allows a high marginal rate of savings. Rostow concludes:

> This hypothesis is, then, a return to a rather old-fashioned way of looking at economic development. The take-off is defined as an industrial revolution, tied directly to radical changes in methods of production, having their decisive consequences over relatively short periods of time.
>
> This view would not deny the role of larger, slower change in the whole process of economic growth. On the contrary, take-off requires a massive set of pre-conditions going to the heart of a society's economic organisation and its effective scale of values. Moreover for the take-off to be successful, it must lead on progressively to sustained growth; and this implies further deep and often slow-moving changes in the economy and the society as a whole

(Rostow 1956).

It is important to recognize two issues in this quotation. One is the recognition that economic development can be regarded as a discontinuous process of structural transformation. It is not the same as economic growth which may be simply enlargement without change or development. It is a view expressed as early as 1911 by J. A. Schumpeter whose work was translated into English by R. Opie in 1934 (Schumpeter 1911, 1934). Secondly, and related, Rostow refers to a 'massive set of pre-conditions'. It is this requirement which was so often to be forgotten. Too frequently attention has been focused only on part of Rostow's carefully considered arguments which were very persuasive and influential. Too many saw only the 10 per cent savings rate as the key to success and remembered the conclusion to his article of 1956 which reads:

> What this argument does assert is that the rapid growth of one or more new manufacturing sectors is a powerful and essential engine of economic transformation. Its power derives from the multiplicity of its forms of impact, when a society is prepared to respond positively from this impact. Growth in such sectors, with new production functions of

high productivity, in itself tends to raise output per head; it places income in the hands of men who will not merely save a high proportion of an expanding income but who will plough it into highly productive investment; it sets up a chain of effective demand for other manufactured products; it sets up a requirement for enlarged urban areas, whose capital costs may be high but whose population and market organisation helps to make industrialization an ongoing process; and finally it opens up a range of external economy effects which, in the end, help to produce leading sectors when the initial impulse of the take-off's leading sectors begins to wane

(Rostow 1956).

The argument is very plausible, the sequence sounds inevitable, the historical analogy is strong. It is a logical presentation of events amongst which the 10 per cent saving rate and industrial sector development stand out strongly. The ideas were taken up and followed by many. The word 'take-off' evokes the parallel with aircraft. A critical power level or thrust has to be reached before an aircraft can take off. All manner of lower level inputs will not achieve this; the aircraft will merely taxi around but not become airborne and self-sustaining. But Rostow's hypothesis has vital provisos, first the true nature of development and second the crucial pre-conditions. It is not how much can be saved. Countries with large raw material export resources can and do experience savings of over 10 per cent of GNP and yet not move into the take-off stage. They can experience growth without development. It is possible to mistake the appearance for the reality of development. Some countries are rapidly developing with savings rates of less than 10 per cent. What is important is how the savings are productivity invested. This, in part, depends upon 'the massive set of pre-conditions' in the pre-take-off stage. These have to be created. They involve favourable political, administrative and social organizations. They involve infra-structural developments but more importantly they involve changes in attitudes and values which create a new awareness of how to do things differently and result in an ability to do so. The creation of take-off conditions and the controlling of the aircraft of development in its ascent requires a complex and delicate balance of considerations. These are the essentials of development theory and practice. As Paul Streeten says:

All thought presupposes implicit or explicit model building or model using. Rigorous abstraction, simplification and quantification are necessary conditions of analysis and policy. But models must be realistic, relevant and useful. The trouble with many current models is that they are shapely and elegant but lack the vital organs

(Streeten 1972).

The economists of the 1950s and 60s came forward with their models of development designed to rupture that ceiling of containment, to create the

115

conditions of development and achieve the state of take-off. The approaches varied as their authors laid stress on differing factors and emphasized different goals. They were intended to form the basis of national development plans.

PLANNING INVESTMENTS

Essentially development strategies are concerned with making a country more productive by making a fuller use of its resources with the aid of more efficient economic processes. The strategy implements a certain pattern of investment designed to initiate certain forms of economic activity, to stimulate particular sectors which, it is hoped, will create a favourable economic, social and psychological environment to bring about the 'quick emergence of a political, social and institutional framework which exploits the impulses to expansion' (Rostow 1956). The mechanics of the strategy are capital investments in land for agriculture, in forestry, mineral and energy resources to make a fuller use of these resources and also to make a fuller and more productive use of the resource of labour. The productivity of labour is thus increased by a considerable margin, be it in agriculture, mining or in manufacturing, to a level over and above the previously pertaining. These developments make infrastructural demands. Capital is required to be invested in the transport infrastructure in road, rail networks, rolling stock and vehicle resources, in ports and port facilities. Energy supplies of a scale vastly greater than those made available by wood fuel, become necessary as factory production is introduced and as transport modernizes. Power stations, transmission and distribution networks, appear in sectoral development plans. Beyond these directly productive investments come the demands of the social infrastructure for education, training and health facilities, and for administrative functions.

All these investments, these economic injections and activities, are interrelated. All are calls upon scarce resources. The issue becomes one of how to balance them and arrive at the right mix to promote true development. Such true development would not only encompass the definitions of Schumpeter but also the dimensions of equity and social considerations which would influence who receives the benefits of development. The considerations in the 1950s and early 60s came to centre around three main ideas. First that the break-out of the low-level equilibrium trap of Nurkse and Leibenstein required a concentrated major economic effort, the so-called 'big push'. Second that the need to raise the level of savings relative to national income described by Lewis would be the means of financing the 'big push'. Third that industrialization would be the major part of that thrust and that the output of industry would be essentially for the home market to further stimulate structural transformation. As has been noted Chenery's work has done much to identify the role of manufacturing in structural changes (Chenery 1960, 1979, Chenery and Taylor 1968, Chenery and Syrquin 1975). It was felt that planning would more quickly and effectively initiate these developments than the operation of free market forces, indeed that it was necessary to initiate the process of developments.

It is important to return to the role of savings and capital investment since this was central to all theories of growth and development. The work of R. F. Harrod and E. Domar on the theory of growth, though carried out independently, covered such common ground that it became known as the Harrod–Domar growth model (Harrod 1948; Domar 1957). This model states that the national rate of growth, that is the rate of growth of the Gross National Product (GNP), is the product of the ratio of savings to national income and the national capital-output ratio. It appeared, therefore, to provide the rationale behind the savings-capital-investment argument. As Myint so pertinently comments, it was a model based upon the analysis of mature economies with stable capital-output ratios and therefore not necessarily applicable to the stage of rapid structural change during take-off which Rostow's model required (Myint 1964). None the less the concept of the capital output ratio is of significance in the understanding of development strategies and can be applied to the take-off stage if a non-stable ratio is involved. Simply, the ratio refers to the amount of capital investment required to produce a unit of output. If one unit of investment produced one unit of output the ratio would be one. If it required five units of investment to produce one unit of output the ratio would be five. In other words activities which required a large amount of investment to produce a small output would be characterized by high capital-output ratios. From the concept it follows that, in theory, it would be possible to estimate the amount of national investment necessary to give a desired increase in the GNP and therefore an increase in per capita income. It could set the dimensions of investment. Investment added to investment would further increase output so as savings were re-invested the self-sustaining growth characteristic of Rostow's final stage could be achieved, indeed the capital-output ratio came to be described as the incremental capital-output ratio (ICOR).

It has been shown that the populations of almost all developing countries are growing rapidly; to achieve increases in per capita income this must be included in the calculation. In a situation where the population is growing by 2.5 per cent per year, as in Nigeria between 1970 and 1980, to keep average per capita incomes at their present level the national income must grow by 2.5 per cent otherwise population increase outstrips income and there is less to share out. This leads to a deterioration in conditions, the reverse of development. Even maintaining an output commensurate with the increase in population means only an attainment of equilibrium – or stagnation. How much investment is required to maintain this state of equilibrium turns, therefore, on the national ICOR. If it is, eg, four, this would require 4 per cent of the national income to be invested to raise output by 1 per cent and to raise it by 2.5 per cent, that is to maintain the status quo with a 2.5 per cent population increase, would require an investment of 10 per cent of the national income. To move into a growth situation with a 3.5 per cent increase, would require a 14 per cent investment ratio. Rostow's and Lewis's figures of 10 to 15 per cent of national income being required to be invested reflect this concept of ICOR.

The ICOR does, of course, vary from activity to activity. What has been referred to so far is capital-output ratio in a gross or national sense, a figure arrived at from a wide range of values. The national ICOR will be the result of the particular mix of activities prevailing in the particular country. The ICOR is characteristically high for infrastructural developments in transport, for public utilities such as water supply, for the energy industries and some of the heavy industries. It is high for social investments in education and health facilities. In the case of the agricultural sector it can be very low. Other instances occur between these extremes. Investments in the less directly productive enterprises tend to be characterized by slow returns in output resulting from their implementation. Clearly these differences in ICOR and in return times raise the crucial question of the balance or mix of investments incorporated in a nation's development plan. There is another matter. Between the developing countries and those of the technically and financially advanced countries of the industrialized world there are differences, many of which have been discussed. These differences include differences in capital-output ratios. Not only do capital-output ratios differ from sector to sector but they are also subject to change. As technologies change so does the ratio. The most profound changes take place precisely during the take-off stage of major structural transformation and the emergence of new values, attitudes and institutions. As a country changes from elementary subsistence-cash agriculture to commercial farming, from handicraft cottage industries to factories supplied by power stations, as transport changes from head loads to railroads, so the ICOR for each of its activities will change and they will not all change at the same time and in the same way. The nature of change will depend upon the nature of the activity. In the case of a manufacturing and assembly industry, such as motor-vehicle manufacturing, economies of scale with increasing size consequent upon additional investment, will result in a continuing benefit from capital injections. It will result in the ICOR becoming lower. If the activity is one of primary production, such as agriculture using the resource of land, or forestry or mining developing mineral resources, the law of diminishing returns applies much more forcibly. Increasing investments produce diminishing returns so that the ICOR increases as the process goes on. As many developing countries emerged as independent nations with the colonial legacy of a focus upon primary production, this factor is important. In the advanced industrialized economies capital investments can be reallocated into continuously arising new opportunities so that specific capital-output ratios do not go up and, in consequence, neither does the national ICOR. In such situations the self-sustaining and continuous development is characteristic and is a manifestation of this flexibility. Indeed it is of interest that inflexibility is not only characteristic of primary industry economies of the Developing World but also of the least successful countries and areas among the the industrial nations of Europe in the continuing industrial revolution. The situation is made particularly difficult in developing countries where populations are not only increasing but where the resource base is diminishing as soils are over-utilized, forests cleared and mineral resources exhausted by primary export activities. There would seem, therefore, to be a case for instituting developments which would broaden the range of economic activities away from those characterized by diminishing returns to those where inputs of capital and labour were more significant than natural resources and where scarce capital could be used more effectively.

The study of the ICOR, the Harrod–Domar model of growth, the ideas of Lewis, Rostow, Leibenstein and others, all involve the effective use of capital and indeed in being able to generate capital for investment. The theory says this is derived from earnings. The problem occurs where national earnings are too low to allow enough to be put aside for investment to start the process going. The process needs to be started since the concensus opinion is that development is a discontinuous process of transformation. One side of the problem is therefore the generation of capital or access to it. The wealthy industrialized world is one possible source and this raises the issue of borrowing on economic terms, of receiving interest free loans, of being given aid in money or capital equipment or in the form of tecnhical assistance to save on capital which would otherwise be committed to this need. Trade is another possible source of capital accumulation. Activities can be promoted specifically to achieve earnings which can be re-invested. Obvious examples are the encouragement of foreign enterprises to develop mineral resources, of which oil is currently the best example, so that the exchange revenue derived from their sale can be allocated development investments. Other instances are the development of commodity exports, generally of primary produce, for sale under international agreements or on the competitive open market; sugar, tea and coffee are examples. In these cases the use is often being made of earlier capital investment of the colonial period which, as has been seen, was essentially concerned with primary rather than manufacturing industries. As a consequence initial export earning has rarely involved manufacturing unless the capital for its installation has come from foreign and multinational investment. A further source of earnings has come from the development of tourism, where the physical and social environment has been conducive to its development, since it is an activity with a relatively low ICOR. These issues will be returned to later and more fully discussed.

If capital acquisition is one side of the problem the other is its effective disposition and investment. Importantly, as has been exemplified in the discussion of agriculture, it is not simply a question of investment allocation to separate sectors since none is truly independent. It is a question of the interaction of investments as commonly the full utility of investment in one sector requires development in others. It is an obvious point but one which has often gone unheeded by the governments of developing countries. It is also an issue which underlies much of thinking which has been devoted to the question of appropriate development strategies. There was a general agreement that an initial, large-scale investment was necessary, the 'big push'. There was agreement also that industrializing action should be the major component in the investment programme. Where the views of the strategists of the 1950s differed most was in how sectoral developments should be designed to interact.

THE BROAD-FRONT BALANCED-GROWTH APPROACH

Nurkse in his concern for the difficulties in generating capital in low-income countries was of the view that incentives to invest were limited because of the small domestic market which developing countries offered. In most of them the national population was small and being composed of poor people in economic terms was a very small market but Nurkse argues that his view applies to large countries, like China and India, also. The small market is a product of low productivity. He is referring to the 'vicious circle of poverty' (Nurkse 1953). By enlarging the market the incentive to invest would increase and this could be achieved by stimulating development along a broad front of activities. To make his point Nurkse hypothesizes the case of the establishment of a single factory to produce one product, say shoes. The factory workers earn wages which give them the ability to buy shoes but their demand for shoes is far smaller than the factory's output and they need to spend their wages on items in addition to shoes. Unless other developments are simultaneously taking place increasing the ability of other workers to buy shoes these other workers will not divert their income to footwear purchase from other needs such as food or housing. As Nurske comments at low income levels demands are inelastic. The solution he claims is to establish a wide range of industries since this will enlarge the market. 'People working with more and better tools in a number of complementary projects become each other's customers. Most industries catering for mass consumption are complementary in the sense that they provide a market for, and thus support, each other'. He quotes John Stuart Mill's formulation of the classical Say's Law of Markets 'Every increase in production, if distributed without miscalculation among all kinds of produce in the proportion which private interest would dictate, creates, or rather constitutes, its own demand.' Nurkse continues 'Here, in a nutshell, is the case for balanced growth. An increase in the production of shoes alone does not create its own demand. An increase in the production over a wider range of consumables, so proportional as to correspond with the pattern of consumer preferences, does create its own demand'.

(Nurkse 1953). A further supporting argument in the case Nurkse presents is that of 'external economies'. He is using the term in a special sense namely that each industry, in the wide range he envisages, by enlarging the market is creating economies external to itself. The more conventional meaning of external economies such as derive from the joint use of transport facilities, banking, communication and pools of skilled labour also, of course, can be advanced as benefits of the broad front approach.

At first sight Nurkse's views may seem somewhat divorced from the reality of development planning and indeed their implications have been questioned. Myint questions the ways in which the establishment of a wide range of essentially consumer industries work (Myint 1964). He points out that if the new consumer goods industries are more efficient in the use of their resources than the domestic or handicraft industries they replace, then the extent that their products replace ones made in the traditional way rather than augment them, will create some unemployment. If they use labour more efficiently then a smaller labour force can produce the same amount and since the factory labour force it envisages is itself part of the market, then the contribution of the new industry in enlarging the market will depend upon it being able to produce more and find a market for the increase. Nurkse's case is that the increased market is provided by the workers of other industries. However, if one product can be produced at unit costs well below pre-existing costs or if it has a particular attraction, it may siphon off the demand for other consumer goods the effect depending upon price-demand elasticity and cross-elasticity relationships. The favoured industry could, of course, invest its income in other industries and so enlarge the consumer market and employment opportunities but only if it did so. New industries which are not markedly more cost-effective than their competitors will not put them out of business and in Nurkse's concept will enlarge the total market by the total numbers of their employees. This is the total market for all goods including food and in reality it is composed of a whole set of individual markets for individual groups of products. Even if the total market is enlarged it may still mean that the individual markets are too small for the efficient use of industrial plant though industries do vary in their sensitivity to scale economies. For some industries, therefore, it will be possible for them to operate successfully in the conditions of the Developing World. Others, because of their scale, technical needs and skill requirements, may be difficult to incorporate in this balanced growth.

In a broad front approach aiming at setting up a range of consumer goods industries, essentially substituting for imports, producing for and creating a market by enlarging the industrial wage-labour force, it is not possible to keep them advancing at the same rate. Adjustments and re-adjustments will have to take place continuously due to differing levels of efficiency and productivity resulting in differential movements of prices which in turn will result in changes in expenditure and demand patterns. It is a form of industrially-based development which is subject to a number of constraints (Myint

1964). Although in Nurkse's argument it is a means of generating capital and investment, the initial availability of capital for a wide range of enterprises is an obvious difficulty. Secondly, it is not realistic to assume that there exists an instant, ready-made labour force. The work in the factory may well be of a completely different order from that in handicrafts and agriculture. Labour may not be readily forthcoming from the land. Suitable labour may require training and particular skills and aptitudes may be in short supply so that competition for them may raise labour costs and send up manufacturing costs. The precise effect will vary from industry to industry. As with capital this is a constraint which is most forcibly felt at the beginning of the process. Over the longer term a pool of industrial labour would have been created which by its very existence would facilitate industrial changes. The broad front approach envisaging a whole series of endeavours is particularly demanding of managerial resources and these tend to be scarce in developing countries because of their economic histories. Experienced expatriate managers have often been employed to overcome this constraint.

Much of the thinking behind this broad front approach has been focused upon manufacturing. The balanced growth was thought of as essentially one between manufacturing industries. Their successful development obviously is conditioned by the extent of the supporting infrastructure. It is something which requires not only the creation of a new kind of labour force but also the physical infrastructure of transport facilities, appropriate supply of energy and water, the economic infrastructure of financial and information facilities and the administrative infrastructure of government. As industry's requirements become more sophisticated, the infrastructural need incorporates the dimension of education and training. The compass of balanced growth spreads. But this is not all. One crucial dimension has often been neglected, that of the agricultural economy. The new, non-agricultural labour force requires to buy food. If in condition of an expanding market agricultural production cannot increase without unit costs going up as diminishing returns apply, then food costs go up. The increased food prices may feed back to the farmer and be regarded as a beneficial spread effect of industrialization. If agricultural production cannot meet the needs of the enlarging industrial and urban population as well as those of the vast rural community, then food imports become necessary and the economic development, so earnestly desired, may fall behind. What is vitally necessary is a planned development which incorporates agriculture and the rural sector. It must be part of any balanced growth programme. It so rarely is.

Development planning, therefore, requires, first, a balance between components in the productive sectors of industry, second, a balance between industry and agriculture, between urban and rural communities, and third, a balance between investments in the directly productive sector and infrastructural investments. The latter present particular problems. It will be recalled that the ICOR is high and the return indirect and long-term for such projects. They demand large amounts of initial capital and this is made particularly difficult because, like some manufacturing plant, they are subject to scale requirements. A road to connect A to B is not a meaningful investment if it only goes half-way. A dam for a hydro-electric project cannot partially cross a valley or be below a certain height. Infrastructural investments tend to come in big blocks. All manner of sub-optimum compromises can, of course, be used such as the building of a single-tracked railway which can be upgraded to two tracks at a later date when more capital is available, or the construction of low-cost roads with a low axle-load capability with the intent of strengthening them at some later date. It is true also that in many developing countries colonial infrastructural investments will have taken place so the task is of augmenting them rather than starting from scratch. None the less infrastructural investment presents problems. Unavoidably it makes too great a demand on scarce capital at first without immediate returns but if it is neglected it creates bottlenecks which impede subsequent developments.

Balanced development planning presents a broad spectrum of developments and involves the concept of inter-related and consequential developments over time. The question becomes one of which existing facilities to develop and by how much, which productive enterprises to encourage, how to smooth out the calls upon investment capital over time and how to react to inevitably changing situations as the economy progresses. It is a matter of integrated planning based upon a design but with flexibility. The structure being erected will include the basic foundations, the infrastructure which enables other activities to develop more readily, such capital and intermediate product industries supplying basic goods or semi-manufactured as are deemed feasible, and finally the consumer goods industries whose role, at least initially, will be to produce goods previously imported. It is a very demanding programme and in developing countries one very difficult to implement. Data sources and data collecting services such as exist in most industrialized countries are sparse or non-existent. It therefore becomes difficult to monitor progress and yet the balanced growth programme requires this if it is to respond in a meaningful way to changing situations for change there will be. Inefficiencies in some activities will upset balances; technical problems will disturb nicely balanced predictions. The management of national economies has proved equally difficult in the free-enterprise countries of Western Europe and the command economies of the communist states of Eastern Europe and the Soviet Union. Many developing countries do not have the personnel to mount a development programme across the whole range of activities particularly if the state is attempting to implement it. It places too great a burden on the civil service. In practice broad-front balanced planning commonly involves both governmental and private enterprise as for example in India and Nigeria. In some the state is largely concerned in infrastructural projects, not only the obvious social investments in education but also in the major energy and irrigation schemes, land reclamation, large agricultural estates and in the transport provision. Some governments also set up State-run heavy industrial projects. The state is involved in these activities largely because they are characterized by a high ICOR and involve large sums though in some instances the government may assume such functions for ideological reasons. While the state is thus involved, private enterprise will concentrate upon intermediate and consumer-good industries. In such situations there arises not only the phasing of these several initiatives into development plans but also the relationship between government operated enterprises and private businesses since technical and economical vertical linkages may be involved.

Broad front strategies have become the most widely adopted though they vary greatly in their degree of sophistication, the effectiveness of the control of development and the range of activities involved. There are also variations which reflect how governments identify their goals and the means of achieving them. There are those who see their investment priorities in basic industries and infrastructures giving a low priority for consumer goods and present material well-being. Their vision is of laying secure foundations for future developments rather than of providing for current tastes. This has an element of what might be called the Soviet model. There are those who, on the other hand, see a need for the population involved in the development process to experience some return for their efforts which benefits them, that all planning cannot be solely for one's descendants. Between the extremes of all for the future and all for now lies the way which most countries have taken and, indeed, in democratic societies it must be so.

UNBALANCED GROWTH

The difficulties of maintaining the balances which, when applied, the balanced growth theory encountered gave rise to some scepticism as to its practicality. It was argued by some that it is precisely the wrong way to stimulate the economic energies and initiatives necessary to propel development forward. Hirschman makes the point that in any economy its component sectors, and indeed activities within each, will develop at different rates. They do not advance together in a continuing balance. He writes:

> Just as on the demand side the market can absorb 'unbalanced' advances in output because of cost-reducing innovations, new products and import substitution, so we can have isolated forward thrusts on the supply side as inputs are redistributed among users through price changes, and or the cost of some temporary shortages and disequilibria in the balance of payments or elsewhere. In fact, development has of course proceeded this way, with growth being communicated from the leading sectors of the economy to the followers, from one industry to

another, from one firm to another. . . . The advantage of this kind of seesaw advance, over 'balanced growth' where every activity expands perfectly in step with every other, is that it leaves considerable scope to *induced* investment decisions and therefore economises our principal scarce resource, namely, genuine decision-making

(Hirschman 1958; Myint 1964; Mathur 1966).

By 'induced investment' Hirschman was referring to a chain reaction whereby investment and growth in one activity would stimulate development in others.

This view is not the complete rejection of development planning which it may seem to be at first sight. Essentially it says that since developing countries have neither the state nor private capital to invest over a wide range of activities, nor yet the technical and managerial capacity to handle them, a selection of priorities becomes inevitable. In the absence of adequate capital and expertise, a balanced growth path will be impossible to follow, the programme will begin to break up and an unbalanced growth will result so why not plan an unbalanced growth rather than let it emerge out of chaos? Why not select a group of industries which have significant horizontal and vertical linkages, where economies can be achieved because of them, both internal and external, where comparative advantage exists, and concentrate on that group, focus the investment there and apply to it the scarce entrepreneurial and managerial skills? This group of industries, or activities, are more likely to succeed and pull ahead of the rest of the economic structure, break away from the old balanced relationships, produce a state of disequilibrium and by doing so stimulate other activities and sectors to catch up and readjust. It is the concept of the lead sector and it is an attractive thesis. In reality it presumes too much. It relies upon the ability to select the most significant growth sectors and to an even greater extent it relies on the emergence of new 'stimulated' activities of development significance. It demonstrates too little concern with the time-lags involved in 'backward' sectors catching up with the leaders. It presumes that a 'surplus' labour force exists in agriculture which can be drawn upon and then fed by those remaining. This cannot be done unless agricultural developments also take place and keep pace. Attention therefore *must* be paid to agriculture even though it may not be regarded as a lead sector. Infrastructural investments will be necessary to facilitate the forward thrust of the manufacturing sector and will make a call upon investment. Elements of a balanced programme begin to appear, a balance which must incorporate agriculture which, as has been discussed, is the keeper of old values, traditional societies and cultural identity and is often the most difficult and slowest to change. This essential agricultural component will set some limits on the rate of change. Many programmes have neglected it and it has remained out of balance. The difficulty with the unbalanced approach is not that it embraces the reality of continual change but that some sectors *are* left

125

behind and do not catch up. It is a feature which underlies the problems of many developing countries today.

Whatever particular strategy is adopted, any development programme must address a complex of considerations. First there is that of the generation of capital internally and access to external capital. Second, the choice of investments in the situation of limited capital and managerial and technical ability. Third, there is the need to balance investments between infrastructural needs, production activities and social investments in education and health. Fourth, it is necessary to pay particular attention to agricultural productivity and the role of the rural community in overall economic development. Fifth, there is the need to consider the balance between basic, intermediate and consumer goods industries. Sixth, in all activities the issue of capital-intensive or labour-intensive strategies will need to be evaluated and with it the question of appropriate technologies. Lastly, all these considerations must be viewed in the context of the relationship between the nation's economy and that of the rest of the world. In this must be weighed issues of comparative advantage, of export earnings and import substitution. All development plans also require a time dimension in which stages of attainment can be phased. It appears complex because it is.

The discussion presented has been essentially of development of national economies en blocs as it were. This was the approach adopted by many economists in the 1950s and early 60s and it has not completely disappeared. But what of other dimensions of development? What of the spatial or regional applications of development planning? What of backward areas characterized by lagging sectors of the economy? What of the people for the benefit of whom the plans are ostensibly designed? What of the issue of the distribution of these benefits among people? The peoples of the Developing World are not a homogenous mass in social and economic terms nor in many other respects. What of tribal or religious divisions expressed in political power groups and which may have a spatial identity? What of racial duality particularly if it is associated with differences in economic opportunity? These features are the stuff of development situations which armchair panaceas tend to neglect but with which governments in the implementation of their development plans have to contend. These issues will be considered in subsequent chapters and exemplified in the case studies discussed in the latter part of this book.

9 The External Dimension

'Neither a borrower nor a lender be,
For loan oft loses both itself and friend,
And borrowing dulleth edge of husbandry'

Shakespeare
Hamlet

'Above all, we believe that a large-scale transfer of resources to the
South can make a major impact on growth in both the South and the
North and help to revive a flagging economy'

Brandt Report 1980

Much has been made of the central role of investment in the promotion of
economic development. It is important to draw the distinction between
capital in the sense of finance and capital as a means of production. Finance
can be obtained to cover debts or deficits but it does not remove them; only
the creation of real wealth by production can do so. Finance can be invested
in productive capital developments which can create real wealth. The ability
to invest can be acquired by earning it. The ability to earn it can be achieved
by the appropriate investment of available finance. The finance can be
derived from domestic savings, from trade and by borrowing. To contribute
to the development process it must be productively invested. Developing
Countries can earn exchange revenue from their export activities be they of
primary commodities or manufactured goods. With this they can purchase
goods from other countries both to satisfy consumer demand for goods not
produced at home and, in the case of imported capital investment goods,
to further strengthen their productive capacity. Trade can, therefore,
generate finance for capital investment and promote growth. However, as
has been seen, the creation of this situation is not without its difficulties.
Time lags in returns on infrastructural investments may, for example, hold
up other developments intended to generate productive capital. Trade may
not be able to develop sufficiently, for external reasons, to generate the
necessary income for investment. These and other bottlenecks which
balanced-growth policies need to avoid are of common occurrence so much
so that the majority of developing countries have had to seek external
finances to maintain their development programmes. The problems of the
Developing World's countries and their development paths thus acquire an
external or international dimension. They are part of the world economic

community. This dimension has two facets. One is the use of foreign resources. These include gifts, loans and aid in the form of technical assistance. The other is participation in world trade and it is this feature which will be discussed first.

WORLD TRADE AND THE DEVELOPING COUNTRIES

Long-range world trade of large dimensions is of comparatively recent origin. It essentially began and was associated with the industrial revolution in Europe. As it spread throughout Europe and crossed the Atlantic into North America, trade itself grew in volume and reach. The new industries created new resources, new demands for new materials and new markets for their products. New technologies enhanced the capacity of international transport and new areas were drawn into an ever-growing system of trading links. As has already been discussed, the great upsurge of colonial activity was very much associated with acquiring access to new raw material and controlling new markets. Much of the development, through its beginnings were earlier, dates from the mid-nineteenth century. Compared with today, trade was very small but it continued to grow rapidly until the First World War and it was essentially a European affair. In 1914 European nations accounted for around one half of the world's export trade and some 58 per cent, by value, of all imports. Much of this trade was *between* European countries. The countries now called the developing countries played only a very small part in this world trade but it was a growing part. In 1900 they accounted for around 16 per cent and in 1913 for 19 per cent of world trade. Between the wars world trade declined because of the economic recession in the industrial nations and did not begin to revive until the late 1930s. The trade of the developing countries had risen to 25 per cent of world exports by 1938 (Bairoch 1975).

After the Second World War, considerable changes took place in world trade. The need for recovery stimulated both manufacturing and trade but it was within a new situation. There began the, at first gradual, and then rapid, dismantling of colonial empires. By the 1950s a large number of countries had achieved their political independence and by 1970 almost all. These new developing countries could view trade in a different manner. Industrial developments in Europe, North America and Japan created a new demand for raw materials. Some of this was due to technological developments such as those which created new uses for aluminium and thus a greater demand for bauxite and some due to the increasing exhaustion of European mineral resources. Importantly there developed a growing and voracious appetite for oil in the industrial nations of the world. These events involved those developing countries endowed with the resources in demand. The impact was obviously first, and greatest, in the oil-rich countries of the Middle East. The post-war recovery led to an enormous increase in production in the industrialized countries, the like of which the world had never seen before, and to a big upsurge in trade. Much of this trade was, however, concerned with manufactured products. The nature of manufacturing industry was changing. Processing was becoming a much larger part of input as products became more sophisticated. The relative contribution of raw materials fell away so that as total trade increased that in raw materials, though it rose, did so by a smaller amount. In this trade in manufactured goods the developing countries were little involved. so as the world trade grew, and with it that of developing countries, their share of the total fell. From being 25 per cent of world exports in 1938 and 31 per cent in 1950 it had fallen to 21.3 per cent by 1960 and 17.8 per cent in 1970. (These figures exclude China though her trade was very small despite her size). From a situation which had existed in the 1930s of a positive balance of trade the developing countries, as a group, moved into the situation of negative balances which has persisted since the early 1950s. In the developing countries as a whole, the rate of growth of their trade was less than that of their Gross Domestic Product. It is important to stress that this general description conceals important differences. Those countries which possessed valuable primary products in great demand did not experience this decline and adverse balances of trade. In the rest of the developing countries trade was thus even less buoyant. By 1970 Latin American countries demonstrated trade deficits and so did those of Asia; Africa was in slight credit and the Middle East showed a major credit balance.

The big growth in world trade has been, therefore, mostly in manufactured products and has been between the industrialized nations. At the end of the Second World War most developing countries were largely primary producers and many still are; their participation has therefore been of a different kind and on a smaller scale but has been changing. Four main trade groups have emerged, the industrialized nations dominating world exports and imports, the Communist Soviet bloc countries characterized by very low levels of trade, the oil-producers of the Developing World, most notably the high-income oil producers whose exports of a highly marketable primary product have been massive and sustained until the recession of the 1980s, and lastly the developing countries. How, therefore, has trade evolved in the developing countries since 1945 and how has it been incorporated in their developing strategies?

The economies of the vast majority of developing countries are open economies, part and parcel of the world's economy and linked to it by trade. This offers possibilities for the pursuit of balanced growth with an unbalanced internal economy. One obvious path is to identify any comparative advantage which may exist and afford export opportunities; it could be the export of primary produce from farm, forest or mine or, indeed, it could be a manufactured product. These commodities could be produced by focused internal developments, exported and earn revenue which could then be used to buy in items not produced at home because of the unbalanced concentration on exports. These imports could be of consumer goods or of capital goods designed to broaden the basis of the home economy. If the exports were primary products the strategy would be that of the Chenery's primary specialization category.

To follow the path of export-led development meant for most developing countries, the export of primary products such as sugar from Guyana, cocoa from Ghana, tea from Ceylon, bauxite from Jamaica, copper from Zambia or rubber from Malaysia. This policy has faced a number of difficulties. First, over a long period of time the value of raw materials relative to manufactured products has declined (United Nations 1949). The effect has been for primary exports to buy increasingly less of manufactured imports in exchange. It is a process tending to retard the rate of development. Second, the world market for primary products is notoriously volatile. In agricultural products it may be a reflection of weather-induced good years and bad years. Periods of shortage may influence new developments in other developing countries as they see emerging market opportunities and, as result, similar environments in tropical South America, Africa and Asia will be competing with each other in commodities with inelastic demands. Supply shortages stimulate the search for substitutes, the development of synthetic rubber being an example. Technical developments in manufacturing may increase the demand for a particular raw material, say tin, to the disadvantage of another, say copper. The very nature of agricultural production, particularly when it involves tree or bush crops such as rubber, cocoa or coffee means that it is difficult to react readily to changing market conditions. The alternative markets for cocoa, tea and coffee, for example, are singularly limited yet it is not possible in the short-term to grub up the tea plantations and plant cocoa trees even if it were environmentally feasible. In mineral production capital investment is commonly on a large scale and is very specific to the enterprise. A copper mine and its equipment is designed solely to produce copper ore. It is this lack of flexibility in alternative output which makes the primary producer especially vulnerable to the viscissitudes of the world market but it is particularly significant in the context of the characteristically undiversified economies of low-income developing countries. The primary products exported often account for a very high proportion of the exchange revenue which is earned. In 1960, for example, cocoa exports in Ghana accounted for 60 per cent of the country's foreign exchange revenue. In Zambia copper represented 97 per cent in 1979 and in Nigeria in 1960, before the growth of oil exports, cotton, groundnuts, cocoa and other crops accounted for 89 per cent of such earnings. This means that if prices for these commodities fall the impact upon the national economy is dramatic. Home markets are usually too small to absorb the surplus production and to act as a buffer; fluctuations in world trade are thus felt immediately.

In these circumstances, the need is to plan for a more diversified economy, and to establish manufacturing which can itself absorb some of the primary production, by import-substitution save on exchange currency and, subsequently, enter the market of industrial exports. Clearly the export of primary products must not, however, be lightly abandoned since the ability to enter the market for manufactured goods will depend upon their competitiveness. To maintain an effort on all three fronts of primary exports, import-substitution and manufacturing for export, is demanding of capital investment and requires unceasing vigilance over standards of production and market opportunities. It is possible to lose, with some commodities, as for example has happened with sugar, even the possibilities of primary production to the industrialized nations but it is also possible to succeed in the face of such competition. When the development of synthetic rubber threatened the Malaysian rubber growers, Malaysia devoted much research to the growing of natural rubber, introduced technical improvements, and successfully maintained her competitive position as a rubber producer.

Enlarging the manufacturing sector is therefore a process of diversification which helps to reduce the extreme vulnerability to market oscillations which primary producers face. To become even more industrialized, and fuel development by manufacturing for export, is a further stage in the structural transformation of developing economies. It is difficult because it has to take place in the face of the competition of the large, technically and commercially sophisticated industrial nations. It has been done and new industrial nations have emerged from the Developing World.

Table 6 World trade in merchandise 1981

Country group	Exports		Imports	
	Value: (millions US$)	Percentage share	Value: (millions US$)	Percentage share
Low income	42,444	2.21	60,117	3.04
(India and China)*	(29,624)	(1.54)	(36,567)	(1.85)
Low-middle	98,497	5.14	122,588	6.21
Upper-middle income	238,675	12.46	283,141	14.30
High-income oil exporters†	174,131	9.09	58,249	3.46
Industrial market economies	1,210,104	63.21	1,290,415	65.45
E. European non-market economies‡	150,270	7.85	146,968	7.45
World	1,914,121	100	1,971,478	100

Source: World Bank Development Report 1983
* Figures for India and China are included in the low-income economy totals
† Libya, Saudi Arabia, Kuwait, United Arab Emirates
‡ Includes the Soviet Union

The development strategies and trading endeavours have produced significant changes in the past three decades. Table 6 depicts the situation in 1981 in which the continuing dominance of the industrial world is shown. If all countries in the World Bank's classification of low and middle income countries are equated with the Developing World, its share of exports in 1981 was 19.81 per cent of the world total. If, however, oil exporters are omitted from this group the share falls to only 12.17 per cent. What, however, has changed is the relative importance of primary commodity and manufactured exports from developing countries. Though there is much variation in the importance of manufactured exports among these countries, in almost all they were very much more important in 1980 than in 1960 as Table 7 shows. This reflects both the relative fall in the demand for raw materials, with the exception of oil, compared with manufacturing growth, and the extent to which developing countries have succeeded in exporting manufactured products. There has been a further change. While most of the exports of the developing countries still go to the industrial market economies of the so-called 'western' nations, this proportion fell appreciably

Table 7 The structure of merchandise exports 1960 and 1980

| | Percentage of commodity exports | | | |
| | Primary commodities | | Manufactured goods | |
	1960	1980	1960	1980
Low-income economies excluding China and India	91	71	9	29
China and India		50		50
Low middle-income*	96	82	4	18
Upper middle-income*	84	55	16	45

Source: World Bank Development Report 1983
* Primary exports include the oil exports from major producers except Libya, Kuwait, Saudi Arabia and United Arab Emirates which are classified as high income.

Table 8 The destination of merchandise exports 1960 and 1980

| Source | Destination (percentage of total) | | | | | | | |
| | Industrial market economies | | E. European non-market | | High income oil exporters | | Developing economies | |
	1960	1981	1960	1981	1960	1981	1960	1981
Low-income economies	51	50	21	5	1	4	27	41
Low middle-income	73	70	7	3	1	2	19	25
Upper middle-income	67	63	6	4	—	3	28	30

Source: World Bank Development Report 1983

between 1960 and 1980. To an increasing extent, Developing World exports are being absorbed by developing countries (Table 8).

Despite these developments primary commodities have remained the dominant exports most obviously in the least industrialized low-income and low-middle income countries. The attendant disadvantages with the persistence of adverse trading balances has led many developing countries to feel that the international trading situation is working to their continuing disadvantage. The first meeting of the United Nations Conference on Trade and Development, UNCTAD, called in 1964, became very critical of the trading policies of the industrialized nations. The import-substitution policies protected by tariffs in so many developing countries were resulting in goods being manufactured at home at a much higher cost than if imported. Tariff barriers were being raised against their manufactured exports by the industrialized nations and as a result their ability to sustain development with the help of export earnings was much diminished. The argument presented by developing nations at the conference was for a re-structuring of the international trading situation which would allow them a greater chance of growing through trade. The so-called North–South situation was developing. In 1976 the Conference on International Economic Co-operation also addressed this problem as it was increasingly realised that some transformation of the world structure of trade was desirable. Such a transformation will be inevitably slow and indeed it has been further retarded by the economic recession in the industrial countries which have been tempted to protect themselves by tariffs and quota allocations from the exports of the newly industrializing countries.

There are those, however, who view the international dimension and the role of trade as sinister and indeed some who attribute to it a counter-developing function which produces underdevelopment or, at very least, holds developing countries in a permanently tributary position. Three attitudes to trade have thus emerged; that of those who see it as a proven way of economic advancement as demonstrated by the industrial countries; second of those who concede that it can be of help but who claim that this is limited because the developing countries were in a colonial status, are in an economic colonial position and will remain so; third that of those who take the extreme view and see current trading structures as one of the worst manifestations of economic imperialism and claim that developing countries can only develop by realising their own potentials in a self-reliant, independent way. The latter group recommend a withdrawal from world trade and the world economy, unless the world's economic structure, and with it trade, can be radically altered (Frank 1967, 1969; Dos Santos 1970, 1978; Amin 1972, 1974).

Are the developing nations locked into a world economic structure and trade pattern which either limits of reverses their chance of development? Morton and Tulloch address this question in their study of trade and the developing countries and, indeed, query whether their terms of trade are deteriorating in the manner alleged by the more radical commentators (Morton and Tulloch 1977). Prebisch and Singer initiated the thesis of deteriorating terms of trade referred to earlier and related it to the differing labour conditions pertaining between the industrialized and the developing nations (Singer 1950; Prebisch 1959). It was argued that since unionised labour was powerful in the industrialized countries, revenues which resulted from improvements in productive efficiency accrued to the wage earners. As unit costs of production went down prices did not while wages went up. The consumer, therefore, did not benefit from continuing improvements in productivity and, if he happened to be a customer in a developing country, faced either sustained or increasing price levels without the benefit of higher income. In the developing countries, increases in efficiency in manufacturing had the reverse effect. Because labour was in plentiful supply, the thesis said that it could not raise its wages and any improvement in efficiency could thus be reflected in lower prices. Goods exported from developing countries thus became characterized by falling prices while goods imported by them featured rising prices. Prebisch was therefore of the view that the continued progress of the industrialized world seemed to make its own workers more prosperous but, at the same time, produced the reverse effect among the labour force of developing countries. This argument has been countered by the application of the classical model of supply and demand. In such a situation this predicts that the world demand would be satisfied by obtaining its goods from the cheapest sources so that where certain commodities were available cheaply in the Developing World demand for them would rise and prevent a deterioration in terms of trade. The developing countries would be able to take advantage where their low labour costs led to low priced but technically acceptable products. As comparative advantages came into play the industrialized countries would specialize in goods which were competitive despite their high labour costs because they would be produced by capital-intensive means of production. However, this state of equilibrium has not been reached. In developing countries primary products are still the major exports and manufactures the major imports with all the consequent difficulties which have been discussed. Morton and Tulloch claim, however, that the thesis of Prebisch and Singer remains unsubstantiated. Deteriorations in trade terms have occurred but so too have marked improvements. The case remains unproven.

Emmanuel's argument, to which Morton and Tulloch also refer, again questions the beneficial effects of trade (Emmanuel 1972). Like Prebisch and Singer he argues that it is the level of wages in a country which determines the prices of the goods it produces. These wage rates he claims, are not related to productivity but to factors, such as the role of trade unions, which are peculiar to an individual country. The price of exported goods is, therefore, little to do with their supply and demand but instead reflects the supply and demand for labour within individual separate countries. The stress is on individual countries because labour is regarded as internationally immobile; if it were mobile its movement would eliminate differences in labour costs from country to country. Since labour is not freely mobile while capital is, it is labour-cost differentials which produce international price differences. Emmanuel argues that since developing countries are characterized by abundant cheap labour their goods will always be characterized by low prices and that this results in an unequal exchange in trade if they trade with the rich, industrialized nations. He sees only two remedies to this situation, either the withdrawal from world trade with development based entirely on internal self-sufficiency, or the development of trade with other developing countries in which similar labour and other conditions pertain. The two approaches can be modified so that they combine. There are a number of questionable issues in Emmanuel's argument. It is predicated upon the belief that differential wage rates are the product of institutional differences, such as union influence, and not of differences in worker productivity. All the evidence suggests that the latter is the explanation (Morton and Tulloch 1977). Low wage rates cannot be equated with low labour costs; it turns on productivity. Neither is labour, in the sense of suitable labour, as readily available in all developing countries as Emmanuel believes. The alternative of a self-sufficient economy which is compatible with prospects of economic development does not exist for any but the largest and best-endowed nations; for most countries their resource base and domestic markets are too small and restricted.

Still other anti-trade arguments have attributed to imported manufactures from the industrialized world another undesirable role. Not only are they regarded as usurping home market opportunities but also are accused of creating a taste for manufactured goods which, coming from the industrial countries, have been made by sophisticated technologies. There can thus be two results. First, this addiction will create a market within developing countries which they cannot themselves, at first, supply. As was described in Chapter seven they become repairers of imported machines rather than manufacturers themselves. Second, so it is argued, in order to manufacture these goods themselves rather than remain dependent upon imports, the developing countries have to adopt the production methods, often capital-intensive and of high technology, used in the industrialized countries. These methods developed under very different conditions may be most inappropriate for the developing nations and may not coincide with their own natural endowments of cheap labour. But it is, of course, possible in the case of many products to adopt labour-intensive means of manufacturing the same goods. These can be used to supply the home-market (import-substitution) of if their quality and specifications are acceptable, to compete in the export market. This has indeed taken place as the newly industrialized nations have demonstrated and as China has done to some extent and will certainly do to a greater extent as she enters into world trade.

The situation is not, therefore, as bleak and restrictive as the critics of growth and development through trade would have. It would be equally unrealistic to claim that the process is without its difficulties and that the present structure of world trade is satisfactory. Since self-reliance is not a feasible proposition for most countries some form of participation in trade would seem essential. Trade between developing countries is certainly a way forward and, as has been seen, this is growing. The development of appropriate technologies, which will be discussed in a later chapter, may be of help in reducing technological dependence. But also, to quote Morton and Tulloch, 'Some trade, at least, with developed countries would seem necessary unless the baby of economic development (including economic growth as one element) is to be thrown out with the bathwater of socio-economic inequality' (Morton and Tulloch 1977).

The restructuring of world trade relationships in a way which deliberately takes into account the problems of developing countries is widely considered as something which is desirable. The Report of the Independent Commission on International Development Issues, the Brandt report, considers this issue and states:

Action for the stabilization of commodity prices at remunerative levels should be undertaken as a matter of urgency. Measures to facilitate the participation of developing countries in processing and marketing should include the removal of tariff and other trade barriers against developing countries' processed products, the establishment of fair and equitable international transport rates, the abolition of restrictive business practices, and improved financial arrangements for facilitating processing and marketing
(Brandt 1980).

In the case of manufactured products the Report states:

The industrialization of developing countries, as a means of their overall development efforts, will provide increasing opportunities for world trade and need not conflict with the long-term interests of developed countries. It should be facilitated as a matter of international policy.
   Protectionism threatens the future of the world economy and is inimical to the long-term interests of developing and developed countries alike. Protectionism by industrialized countries against the exports of developing countries should be rolled back; this should be facilitated by improved institutional machinery and new trading rates and principles.
(Brandt 1980).

Alas it is all too easy to make recommendations; to achieve international agreement in world of apparently conflicting interests is a different matter.

THE USE OF FOREIGN RESOURCES

Financial aid from foreign countries which assists in the promotion of development has been a characteristic of the developing countries' economies in the post-war period. It may be said to have had its origins in the Marshall Plan under which American aid was given to assist the recovery of the war-ravaged economies of western Europe. Such assistance has been seen, and sought, by its recipients variously as a pump-priming resource to establish initial developments, or as a means of augmenting revenue from trade or indeed, as a necessary and continuing transfer of assets to help counter-balance the imbalance between development opportunities seen to exist between the Industrial and the Developing Worlds. Aid becomes more necessary when earnings from trade decline; when insufficient aid is forthcoming the developing nations argue the more strongly the case for a reorganization of world trade to allow them a more equal share of opportunities.

The oil-exporting countries have had little need to call upon external capital resources in the form of aid and have, indeed, become donors. The higher middle-income countries, which have most successfully industrialized and enjoyed a trade-led development based upon the export of manufactures, have been able to sustain growth with less help from aid programmes. None the less, almost all developing countries have since 1945 made use of foreign resources whether it be aid in the form of scientific, commercial and technical manpower, grants, low interest loans, or whether loans obtained on the commercial market or direct foreign investment in economic activities within their borders. The use of such resources has become an integral part of the economic and development plans of developing countries with few exceptions. The need is felt to utilize this externally derived capital in order to sustain the impetus of development until a self-sustaining situation can be reached where, perhaps, savings will allow internally derived capital to suffice. This need clearly becomes greater in periods of world economic recession when earnings from trade fall but at such times it is less forthcoming as all nations retrench and take refuge in protectionism.

The supply of foreign capital takes several forms. Funds which are multilateral can be channelled through international agencies of which the International Bank for Reconstruction and Development, commonly referred to as the World Bank, is the most important. Official funds can be made available in bilateral agreements with individual developing countries. Outside this official aid, individual countries can borrow on the international money markets at commercial rates. Lastly, capital investments can be made by private firms which set up manufacturing, mining or other economic activities within developing countries.

Aid, as opposed to commercial loans and private investment, has been given for a number of reasons. Some is undoubtedly given for humanitarian reasons to assist poor countries to break out of the low-level equilibrium trap and to offer hope to their peoples. Some aid, notably by charitable organisations such as Oxfam and Christian Aid in Britain and similar bodies in other countries, is given specifically to help the diseased and most poverty-stricken and is often given to relieve emergency situations. It deals, of course, with the symptoms and not the cause. Other aid is given because it helps the donor. The cynical point to the loans given with one hand and the tariff barriers erected against exports from the Developing World with the other. Aid can be given for specific purposes such as the construction of irrigation schemes, the building of hydro-electric installations or a factory but given on the condition that the necessary equipment is purchased from the donor country. Again the cynic would describe this as a form of market creation and a means of ensuring employment in industrial countries. Help is also given for political and strategic reasons, to buy friends, secure allies or placate the neutral. The democratic nations of the capitalist world have given aid for these purposes, so too have the totalitarian states of the Soviet bloc though in the case of the latter it has commonly taken the form of military aid. Politically aligned aid is a very uncertain source since political shifts in ideology within recipient countries can easily result in its withdrawal. While such motivations still exist much aid is genuinely given to assist the recipient countries. A greater source of concern is not that of motives behind the assistance but of its effective use. In the early years of donor schemes too little attention was paid to assessing the proposed use of aid and grandiose status-seeking projects resulted and littered the capitals and airports of the Developing World. In more recent years financial aid has been associated with assessment and advice in project design and implementation, the World Bank making notable contributions in this respect. As developing countries have gained experience, often bitter, of the difficulties in effectively using investment, so also have they become more efficient.

Who should receive aid has been a subject of much debate. To suggest that all developing countries, regardless of size, resources, or political alignment, should receive an equal, presumably per capita, share may appear equitable but it raises the problem of the definition of development status and would result in such a thinly spread capital augmentation as to be useless. Should the very poorest nations receive all the aid since their need is the greatest? The effectiveness of such a policy would turn upon how efficiently they could absorb aid and use it for development. Not to be able to do so would convert aid into poor relief and while this is a good cause it is not to be confused with capital transfers to fuel the engine of growth. Andrew Shonfield suggested that aid be focused upon two or three countries which were within reach of continuing development, which could effectively use capital loans and which, being focused upon them, could be given in such quantity as to provide an externally derived 'big push'. (Shonfield 1960). None of these suggestions have materialized but official aid giving has persisted.

Official Development Assistance (ODA), funded by members of the Organization for Economic Co-operation and Development (OECD) which is composed of the world's affluent nations, is distinguished from strictly commercial loans by its low interest rates and favourable terms of repayment. It can take the form of bilateral assistance between donor and recipient or be a multilateral activity. In the early 1980s some two thirds of ODA bilateral aid went to the middle-income countries. These same countries in addition borrowed on the commercial market to an extent which accounted for 80 per cent of their use of foreign resources. In contrast the low-income countries relied much more heavily on ODA and received over three-quarters of their foreign loans in the form of multilateral ODA assistance even though this totalled only one third of ODA capital lending (World Bank 1983). Among these low-income countries the significance of this capital inflow varied considerably. In the large, heavily populated countries of South Asia it represented only 5 per cent of gross domestic investment whilst in Africa it was as much as 40 per cent (World Bank 1983).

The United States has been one of the major sources of aid to developing countries since it is the world's wealthiest nation. Much of its aid has been tied to purchase of American goods and equipment. Most countries in western Europe have likewise given aid while the members of OPEC, the Oil Producing and Exporting Countries, began to give aid generously after the escalation of oil prices in the early 1970s, most of it going to other Arab or Islamic nations. The aid from the Soviet bloc to developing countries has been very limited. The amount of ODA in selected years since 1960 and the proportion it forms of the GNP of donor countries is shown in Table 9. Few OECD countries have allocated more than 1 per cent of their GNP to aid programmes.

Access to foreign resources of capital in the form of aid can clearly be important and helpful to developing countries but there are obvious provisos. Aid freely given without restrictive conditions can be the most effective in promoting development provided that the recipient government and its economic planners can identify the most significant investment and implement it. Sound economic advice, accompanied by technical support, can play an important role in this regard. There is, however, always the risk, in the view of some, that the continued receipt of aid tends to make internally derived capital less forthcoming and that it is an experience which dulls the incentive to progress independently. As Jean de la Fontaine has it, 'Aide-toi, le ciel t'aidera'.

Capital borrowed in the world's money markets is a different matter; it is borrowed on strictly commercial terms. It is, of course, common practice in all lands and, in theory it can allow investment in productive enterprises which will, by increasing production and earning revenue, pay the interest, that is, the debt service cost. As production aggregates it will allow the repayment of the capital over the agreed period. Crucially such borrowing is dependent upon the success of the investment in earning revenue. This

Table 9 Official development assistance from OECD and OPEC countries

	1960	1965	1970	1975	1980	1982
Millions US $						
OECD						
Australia	59 (0.37)	119 (0.53)	212 (0.59)	552 (0.65)	667 (0.48)	882 (0.5)
Austria		10 (0.11)	11 (0.07)	89 (0.31)	178 (0.23)	361 (0.5)
Belgium	101 (0.88)	102 (0.60)	120 (0.46)	378 (0.59)	595 (0.50)	497 (0.5)
Canada	75 (0.19)	96 (0.19)	337 (0.41)	880 (0.54)	1075 (0.43)	1185 (0.4)
Denmark	5 (0.09)	13 (0.13)	59 (0.38)	205 (0.58)	481 (0.74)	415 (0.7)
Finland		2 (0.02)	7 (0.06)	48 (0.18)	110 (0.22)	144 (0.3)
France	823 (1.35)	732 (0.76)	971 (0.66)	2093 (0.62)	4162 (0.64)	3991 (0.7)
Germany FR	223 (0.31)	456 (0.40)	599 (0.32)	1689 (0.40)	3567 (0.44)	3163 (0.4)
Italy	77 (0.22)	60 (0.10)	147 (0.16)	182 (0.11)	683 (0.17)	820 (0.2)
Japan	105 (0.24)	244 (0.27)	458 (0.23)	1148 (0.23)	3353 (0.32)	3023 (0.2)
Netherlands	35 (0.31)	70 (0.36)	196 (0.61)	608 (0.75)	1630 (1.03)	1473 (1.0)
New Zealand			14 (0.23)	66 (0.52)	72 (0.33)	65 (0.2)
Norway	5 (0.11)	11 (0.16)	37 (0.32)	184 (0.66)	486 (0.85)	566 (1.0)
Sweden	7 (0.05)	38 (0.19)	117 (0.38)	566 (0.82)	962 (0.79)	987 (1.0)
Switzerland	4 (0.04)	12 (0.09)	30 (0.15)	104 (0.19)	253 (0.24)	251 (0.2)
United Kingdom	407 (0.56)	472 (0.47)	500 (0.41)	904 (0.39)	1852 (0.35)	1794 (0.3)
United States	2702 (0.53)	4023 (0.58)	3153 (0.32)	4161 (0.27)	7138 (0.27)	8302 (0.2)
OPEC						
Algeria				41 (0.27)	65 (0.17)	65*
Iran				593 (1.13)	7 (0.01)	−150†*
Iraq				215 (1.63)	829 (2.13)	143*
Kuwait				946 (7.40)	645 (2.04)	685*
Libya				259 (2.29)	282 (0.92)	105*
Nigeria				14 (0.04)	42 (0.05)	149
Qatar				338 (15.58)	284 (4.25)	175*
Saudi Arabia				2756 (7.76)	5944 (5.09)	5798*
U. Arab Emirates				1046 (11.69)	906 (3.38)	799*
Venezuela				31 (0.11)	125 (0.21)	67

Source: World Bank Development Report 1983
(Figures in brackets express assistance as percentage of donor GNP)
* 1981
† net recipient

in turn depends not only on the cost effectiveness of production but also in securing markets for the products. A situation can arise, and indeed, has arisen, when the prospective income does not materialize in sufficient amount even to service the debt. This may be the product of world recession which restricts market opportunities, or of production inefficiencies, or both. In such circumstances the debtor country may borrow more in order to service the debt and negotiate for extended repayment terms. This means more money is leaving the country in order to pay for imported capital and a stage may be reached when more is flowing out than coming in and an adverse balance of payments results. It is vital that export earnings are at a sufficient level, and that investment of borrowed capital is sufficiently productive as to reduce the need for imports financed by capital inflows; then borrowing can continue since it will not get out of control (Scammell 1980; Mikesell 1968).

The recession in industrial countries in the early 1980s by reducing the export opportunities of developing countries produced such a crisis of debt servicing and payment balance in a number of developing nations. As the World bank has indicated, whereas medium and long term debt incurred by developing countries increased by 20 per cent per year in the 1970s, the increase in their resources and ability to repay capital and service debt was adequate. Interest rates on loans increased by a smaller amount than prices and were less than the rate of inflation in the industrialized countries. The Bank goes on to say:

> After 1980 the position changed. Although the rate of growth of debt halved to an estimated 11 per cent in 1982, the slowdown in export earnings was sharper. As a result the ratio of debt to exports rose from 76 per cent to 104 per cent between 1980 and 1982; . . . For oil-importing countries, the ratio was far higher than at any time since 1970; for oil exporters it was no lower than it had been before the 1973–74 oil price rise . . . Boosted by higher interest rates, the ratio of debt-service obligations rose sharply from 13.6 per cent in 1980 to 20.7 per cent in 1982 . . . had export earnings risen at 10 per cent a year in 1980–82 (about half the average increase in the 1970s), the debt-service ratio would have risen by less than three percentage points instead of the seven points it actually did.
>
> (World Bank 1983).

The situation is shown in Table 10. As a result more than twenty developing countries have, since 1980, attempted to reschedule their debts. The international dimension of the developing countries' development dilemmas

Table 10 Debt-service ratios 1970–82

	1970	1980	1981	1982*
All developing countries	13.5	13.6	16.3	20.7
Low-income Asia	13.3	7.9	8.4	10.1
Low-income Africa	6.5	8.8	11.6	28.3
Middle-income oil importers	14.0	14.9	18.0	25.0
East Asia	6.7	7.0	7.6	8.6
Latin America	13.0	33.3	39.6	53.2
Oil exporters	13.9	13.0	15.7	19.1

Source: World Bank Development Report 1983
* Estimated

could hardly be more clearly indicated. It reinforces the case for a greater degree of international co-operation and understanding.

FOREIGN FIRMS WITHIN DEVELOPING ECONOMIES

Foreign companies which set up manufacturing or other plant in developing countries represent the third method of capital inflow. The outsider identifies a business opportunity either related to natural resources or a suitable labour force and with market potential either domestic or export. He goes to the developing country to make money but his presence has a manifold effect. He brings in all or most of the necessary capital and so helps to offset this characteristic deficiency. Second, he establishes linkages with the Industrial World. Third, he brings in experience of both manufacturing and commerce. He can thus help in the transfer of technology and the process of modernization by being part of it. The potential benefits from this use of foreign resources are considerable, particularly in the early stage of the development process. There are disadvantages which have already been discussed in the context of industrialization. To contribute to economic development, the foreign enterprise must either demonstrate a multiplier effect which stimulates other developments or its operation must allow capital which would otherwise have been invested in its function to be re-deployed, or it must earn revenue which can be re-invested in local development. Preferably it must do all three. If the foreign company repatriates the greater part of its profit there is a loss of income to the home country. If it re-invests most of its earnings in the host country it serves to increase the ratio of foreign to indigenous capital and if sufficient foreign firms set up this could lead to a large part of productive capital investment becoming foreign owned. If for nationalist or political reasons or on grounds of prudence, this is considered undesirable and is limited, then remittances must be allowed on a sufficient scale to persuade companies to set up and stay. So while benefits can result from the use of external capital in this way, export earnings on a large scale is not one of them. The potential for dispute between host governments fearful of foreign domination or neo-colonialism on the one hand and foreign companies wary of nationalization or a moratorium on remittances on the other, is considerable. Nkrumah claimed that foreign capital was used for 'the exploitation rather than for the development of the less developed parts of the world' (Nkrumah 1965). In reality there is often a concidence of interest between the political power groups in developing countries and the foreign investor. Exploitation undoubtedly takes place in some instances but on balance, adequately controlled by mutually agreeable terms, the foreign investor setting up and operating plant in a developing country has a beneficial effect.

The companies which have attracted most attention and aroused most suspicion in the Developing World are the so-called multinational or transnational corporations (Tugendhat 1973; UN 1973, 1978; Windstrand 1975; Lall and Streeten 1977; Vernon 1977; Siddayao 1978). Having grown considerably since 1945 their activities are such that it has been estimated that around one half of the world's trade, by value, was taking place within transnational companies in 1975 and the proportion is growing. They display all the characteristics of the 'plantation' type of economy which has been discussed and because of their economic autonomy and insulate their activities to a large extent from the economies of the countries in which they operate. They extend into the Developing World to develop tropical crops, scarce minerals and to acquire new markets but it must be stressed that the greater part by far of their interests is *not* in the Developing World indeed only 25 per cent of multinational corporate investments take place there. Where they do exist, the very nature of their operations means that their goals need not be coincident, in anything but the most indirect way, with the investment priorities of a struggling developing nation. The incorporation of the functions of multinationals in national development strategies is far from easy, big fish are liable to eat small ones, but it can be done as countries as dissimilar as China and Singapore or Taiwan and Sri Lanka have shown. There are risks and benefits. As Lall and Streeten say 'The skill in framing a policy and in negotiating a contract with multinational com-

Figure 23 A schema of economic development

panies is to maximize the surplus of beneficial over detrimental effects that is still acceptable to the TNC. The key to policy then, is selectively, not ideology' (Lall and Streeten 1977).

Trade, aid, loans and foreign capitalized enterprises are, therefore, all sources of the necessary capital so strongly identified in the early post-war theories of development. Each presents its own challenges and opportunities, each involves risk and uncertainty but all are manifestations of the international dimension of the Developing World's development. Their role in the development model is shown diagrammatically in Fig. 23.

These features have been discussed in the firm belief that they can contribute to economic progress and enhanced productivity but with an equal awareness that these goals in themselves do not constitute development. It is the latter issue which brings into question the adequacy of the economic development models formulated in the 1950s and 1960s. There are indeed dimensions other than that of growth and these must be examined.

Plates 1 and ***2*** **The future of the Developing World.**
Children in China (above) and Fiji.

Plates 3 and ***4*** **The problem of poverty.**
Villagers on the Jos Plateau, Nigeria. (above)
A village in Malawi.

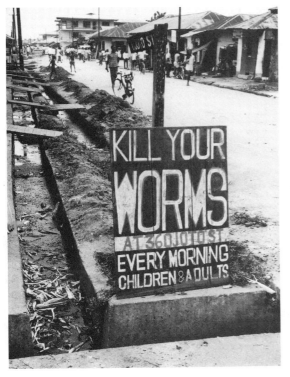

Plates 5 and **6 The problem of disease.**
An anti-filariasis poster in Fiji (above). Combating parasitic worms. Note the open sewer behind the notice. Port Harcourt, Nigeria. (opposite)

Plates *7* and ***8*** **The problem of population.**
Family-planning posters in the world's largest country, China (above) and one of the smallest, Tonga.

Plates *9* and ***10* Shifting cultivation.**
Clearance by burning in Guinea savanna forest (above) and cultivation mounds in a
forest clearing. Central Nigeria.

Plates 11 and ***12*** **Nomadic livestock economies.**
Fulani cattle on the move (above) and grazing Guinea corn stubble on Hausa fields.
Northern Nigeria.

Plates 13 and ***14*** **Cash crops in indigenous agriculture.**
Cotton (above) and groundnuts in Northern Nigeria. The pyramids are of groundnut
sacks awaiting transport.

Plates 15 and ***16*** **Intensive sedentary agriculture.**
Irrigated vegetable crops, Kano close-settled zone Nigeria (above). Terraced
vegetable small holdings, Sri Lanka.

10 The Dimension of Space

SPATIAL ASPECTS OF DEVELOPMENT AND DEVELOPMENT PLANNING

'The spatial pattern will change with shifts in the structure of demand and production, in the level of technology, and in the social and political organisation of the nations'

J Friedmann and W Alonso
Regional Development and Planning 1964

Much of the thinking of development economists and much of what has been discussed so far, has been concerned with national economies. Particular attention has been given to the manipulation of sectoral investments in 'big-push', 'minimum critical effort' investment schemes utilising balanced or unbalanced approaches but with no mention of their spatial characteristics. Yet economic developments have a spatial dimension. Resource bases have one, the population for whom one is planning has one, economic activities possess one, existing levels of development display a spatial dimension. To analyse or to plan en bloc a nation's economy involves spatial dimensions and consequences whether they are anticipated or not. This raises the issue as to whether the resulting spatial patterns are seen as desirable and, if so, whether they can be promoted, or if they appear undesirable, whether development plans can incorporate measures to modify them.

The most casual inspection shows that in all countries levels of economic activity are unevenly distributed. It can be argued that this represents the optimum activity-pattern which corresponds with the pattern of production based on the disposition of resources of soil, climate and minerals, influenced by comparative advantage, infrastructural facilities, transport structures and distribution of population. It is, however, a pattern observed at one point of time; all the components in the matrix, including the economic significance of the seemingly immutable deposits of minerals or fertile soils, can change. The significance of locations change, the dimensions of space change. Since the essence of development is change it must necessarily be concerned with changing spatial patterns of economic activity, with the space economy.

Societies and their economies change and develop at varying rates in the course of their history. There are periods of relatively little change when all

145

economic activities are spatially attuned to each other and a state of near spatial equilibrium exists. One can hypothesise a pre-colonial, pre-industrial, situation in the Developing World characterized by a series of localized and almost discrete economies, though with some marketing activities over-spanning them and some centres possessing particular focus because they were centres of political and administrative power. The same could be said of medieval Europe. If this somnolescent period is disrupted by some significant new development which has spatial attributes, the equilibrium is broken and a new pattern of activity takes shape. In eighteenth-century Britain this took place with the invention of the steam-engine, the use of coal for iron-making and the emergence of a machine age which gave greatly enhanced significance to the coalfields so much so that their location became coincident with the main and growing areas of economic activity. The industrial revolution possessed a spatial dimension and an activity-pattern quite different from that which it had displaced. In many of the developing countries, a similar disruption of a period of little change in the spatial equilibrium took place with the advent of colonial penetration. Particular areas, because of the crops they could grow or the minerals they possessed, took on a new economic significance and new spatial patterns were formed. Those who subscribe to the idea of spatial equilibrium would argue that such disruptions are inevitable if there is to be change but that the competitive market processes will, in time, balance resources, needs, markets and employment opportunities, so that a new spatial pattern of economic activity emerges which represents the optimum activity-pattern coincident with optimum economic efficiency. In reality in most economies, and certainly in countries actively stimulating economic development, the process is one of continual change. At any one time there will always be areas of a country which are less active than others because there is not the national need to utilize their resources since they are not competitive in terms of returns on investment compared with others. The rate of change is crucially important and its significance varies between political, social and economic components. For example, an economic shift to achieve the optimum mix in terms of the use of factors of production may take place rapidly while the social or political response to the movement takes place slowly. The resulting mismatch can produce social distress and create a potential for political conflict. It is this situation which poses a dilemma for all concerned with the spatial consequences of development strategies. Its neglect has produced major problems in many developing countries and led to tragedies in some. If the readjustments to a new spatial equilibrium are natural ones which maximize the economic attributes of locations, the ques-tion is whether they should be tampered with. To do so would impede a process designed to achieve economic efficiency and with it the maximisa-tion of growth. Where maximum, unimpeded growth is the sole objective of development strategies there is no problem. If development embraces goals additional to growth, such as an equitable participation in growth, interference may become necessary. In short, regional development cannot be divorced from the objectives incorporated in a national development policy.

The emergence of distinctive economic regions requires explanation and it is one which involves movement. There is a need to explain why labour moves from one area to another, why capital is redeployed in a new location, why business enterprise shifts from one place to another. The so-called regional export or export-base model does this (Tiebout 1956, 1968; Hirschman 1958; Moses 1955; North 1964; Baldwin 1964; Perloff and Wingo 1964.) Put at its simplest, it presumes factors of production to be mobile and states than an area will grow by developing the production of a commodity or range of goods in which it specializes and in which it has a comparative advantage either because of the natural resources it possesses or because of its access to markets. These advantages, by allowing it to produce these goods efficiently and cheaply, increase its competitiveness and sustain further expansion. As it grows it begins to experience scale economies, to attract skilled personnel and becomes able to introduce a continuing series of innovations which further reduce its unit costs and enhance its ability to penetrate additional markets in surrounding regions. This increased market opportunity feeds back to stimulate further production and a chain of cumulative causation is established. The group of growing industries attract ancillary and supporting industries and services and the spin-off still further increases economic growth and employment opportunity. This process involves other regions because in order to maintain growth it not only requires access to markets in other regions but also access to their resources. The burgeoning growth may begin to draw in labour and attract capital from other parts of the country; it has an impact beyond its own bounds. Returns on investment in the growth region may become so attractive compared with others that it draws in capital which would otherwise have been invested elsewhere and its wage rates and employment opportunities tempt people to leave their home regions and seek a better future in its boom towns. According to their relative accessibility, resource endowment and the strength and growth of their own economies, the other regions of the country will be affected by the growth region's emergence. Few, if any, will be able to compete with its specialist products and will cease to make them and instead buy them in from it. These regions may possess advantages themselves over other more remote or less endowed areas and may be able to export products to them. Most regions will, however, furnish the dominant region with the resources and labour which it requires and will themselves decline, or at least remain static, requiring less capital and using a small workforce as these assets move away until, in theory, a balance is reached when production and employment is spatially arranged in the optimum economic manner and capital is invested accordingly. There can be, of course, more than one growth region and each can exhibit a wide range of sizes and shapes. For example, a growth region can be ultra-linear aligned along a transport axis, or semi-circular centred upon a port. The model, therefore, involves the concept of a regional hierarchy of major growing or core regions, secondary and tertiary tributary regions, and peripheral regions which are the most remote and backward in the sense that they are participating less actively in economic growth. The international parallel of world trade and development is clear (Hirschman 1958). There exists, therefore, a space economy which interlinks activities within a country by strands of varying strengths. This economic space has also an expression in physical space. In the advanced economies of the highly urbanized, industrial nations, the disposition of towns and cities holds and emcompasses this network of linkages and the bulk of the population.

It was Walter Isard who did much to develop a general theory of spatial equilibrium and the concept of the space economy (Isard 1956). In writing of him Friedmann has said 'His graphic representations of the topography of the space economy were particularly suggestive ... For the first time, planners could actually "see" a regional landscpae that had "structure" but no boundaries' (Friedmann and Weaver 1979). But over half a century earlier the perceptive Mackinder had described the evolving space economy of Britain though in terms of the physical manifestations which connect the abstract space economy to reality:

At first a number of small market towns . . . were scattered all over the more fertile parts of the country. They were local distribution centres at nodal points. Then a few of them, placed upon coalfields, grew as though to rival the metropolis, yet possessing no equivalent nodality. And now a certain number of the remainder are being selected for city growth, while the rest dwindle with the general loss of rural population and the improvement of communications, which tend everywhere to eliminate the middlemen. But it is characteristic of the rising places that, like the industrial towns of the coalfields, they obtain their renewed importance no longer as general distributors of the second or third grade but by specialisation of some different type . . . It follows that they are not self-sufficing after the manner of the old market towns but must supplement one another, or depend on some vast neighbouring city. Thus a continuous organisation, with clearly articulated parts, is beginning to spread over groups of counties, binding them together into great loosely-knit urban federations

(Mackinder 1902).

It is a lucid description of the evolution of a space economy.

These ideas have been developed in the context of mature integrated societies. What of their relevance to the emerging economic structures of developing societies? Three stages can be identified:- first, the pre-colonial space economy with near equilibrium established; second, that of the colonial impact which disrupted this; third, the post-colonial situation with the

persistence of the colonial spatial pattern of development and the consequences of that pattern for the new nation's progress.

Beginning with the second stage, it can be seen that new regions of
development were identified by colonial merchants. These were the source
areas of minerals or where particular crops could be grown. In addition
there were contact areas, the interface between the economies of the colonial
territories and those of Europe. Most commonly these were coastal contact
areas. The space economies associated with these external initiatives were
associated with production for export. Infrastructural developments took
two main forms – first, and most importantly, the construction of transport
facilities to move the products out and second, in the case of mineral exploitation, the building of mining settlements. Both were specific to the new
economic activities though transport facilities could be, and were, used for
additional purposes. To large extent, distinct, separate enclave activities
were established. This new space economy was not linked into the pre-
existing one except where, in the case of agriculture, peasant farmers were
involved rather than plantations. Two space economies emerged, one
developing and externally linked, the other changing but slowly and inward-
looking; and two groups in the population became distinct, those participating in these new colonial activities and those who were not. Unequal
development began to take place and this had spatial dimensions. In so
much as the new economic activities gave better economic returns and often
greater influence, regions of growth stood out like mountains on a plain of
traditional harmonised economies. They were the nodal growth points on
the development surface. Regional equilibrium theory would have it that by
the movement of people, capital and technology, regional disparities in
affluence, or poverty, would be diminished as the economy readjusted. But
the colonial economy was geared to an external linkage rather than an
internalized one so that the distinctions tended to persist.

This general statement on the emergence of the colonial space economy
requires to be linked to geographical space, the situation described so
eloquently by Mackinder, to alignments on the ground and the tangible
manifestation of settlements. In this the role of transport is crucial. It was
particularly important in this phase because the new transport network
implanted by the colonial powers was so totally different from that otherwise prevailing. Railways, vastly greater in carrying capacity, replaced
bullock carts and head loads. These traffic arteries possessed a great significance in the focusing of the new space economy. They created growth
regions, growth alignments and growth nodes. Areas distant from them
were given a new inaccessibility and became peripheral areas. The friction
of space was recalibrated in a way which markedly distinguished those areas
on or near the railway route from those which were not. In consequence,
the existence, alignment and density of transport networks, came to be
related not only to the new alien space economy but also to the way in
which the indigenous space economy could readjust. Being the product of

colonial initiative concerned with exporting goods out of the country, the transport systems were not designed primarily to promote regional development in an articulated sense. Inevitably, however, an evolving space economy grew around them. In a classic paper, Taaffe, Morrill and Gould have postulated a model which describes these developments and exemplifies them with reference to Ghana and Nigeria (Taaffe, Morrill and Gould 1963). Figure 24 depicts the essential components of their model of the evolution of transport networks.

As transport networks developed they created new aligned accessibility and low-cost axes; in economic terms, *economic rent* increased along their routes. The ports of their coastal termini took on a new significance and grew rapidly while other indigenous coastal settlements stagnated. Towns along the railways likewise prospered, especially at intersections. Mabogunje writing of Nigeria says:

> irrespective of their size, traditional urban centres which were not on the rail-line or on any other major routeway found themselves shunted into the backwater or economic decadence, losing many of their virile young men to centres now being favoured locationally. To make the situation more serious, the new type of trade based on export and import, exposed traditional manufacturers to competition from better finished articles. The result was the undermining of traditional craft and a worsening position in the decadent urban centres
>
> (Mabogunje 1965).

Economic growth is, therefore, characterized by spatial development which is essentially one of regional differentiation marked by the emergence of urban centres which, as concentrations of economic activity, become the foci of the emerging growth-regions. Developing countries exhibit such a pattern and it is commonly one set by the colonial phase of development as is illustrated in the case studies presented in the second part of this book. It becomes the spatial pattern upon which the post-colonial developments must be subsequently based when goals of development are often different from those pertaining in colonial times. The very nature of the space economy in the industrialized and urbanized nations of the 'North' and the history of its growth has suggested that the urban concentrations of economic activity are the natural centres of innovation and change. In them new ideas develop, new technologies emerge and spread from one to the other involving the whole space economy in a continuing development (Berry 1972). So much so has this idea been promoted that 'urbanization' has been equated by some with 'modernization' where modernization is regarded as a comprehensive description of true development in which all attitudes and aptitudes are geared to a well-organized, technologically-based and highly productive society (Soja and Tobin 1975). Urban centres thus become the vehicles of change and it is but a short step to the concept of using them

Figure 24 Transport and the regionalisation of development

as spatial tools in the development process and in the creation of an integrated space economy.

Central to these ideas is that of movement; the movement of physical things such as people and goods; the movement of financial energy, of capital; the movement of methods; the movement of the vital intangibles of ideas, attitudes and values. Mobility is of the essence. This transfer of things, people and ideas gives dynamism to space economies and their physical manifestations. As Friedmann and Alonso express it:

> Spatial patterns will change with shifts in the structure of demand and or production, in the level of technology; and in the social and political organisation of the nation. The economic and social development of the nation is reflected in its patterns of settlement; its systems of flow and exchange of commodities, money and information; its patterns of commuting and migration; and its reticulation of areas of urban influence. And if there is a pattern corresponding to each 'stage' of development, it may further be suggested that there is an optimal strategy for spatial transformation from one stage to the next . . . At an advanced stage of development, the national economy will appear as a fully integrated hierarchy of functional areas, with most of the population and activities polarized in metropolitan areas
>
> (Friedmann and Alonso 1964).

Emerging out of such statements is the spatial analogy of unbalanced growth strategies. Centres grow because they are the natural foci of development, their growth should be encouraged rather than restrained since this will maximize growth opportunities. If this means that some areas are left behind and regional inequalities appear, there is little cause for concern since the benefits of growth will spread out from the growth centres and eventually diminish the regional disparities. This argument, therefore, presumes flow and mobility which restore a balance. But do they? Are the factors of production freely mobile? Capital seeks out opportunities. It will move freely into growth centres. Will it as readily disperse into the surrounding areas where perhaps the certainty of return on investment is less? The labour force will see better incomes. The farmer will leave his subsistence holding for another operation if he sees a worthwhile differential of income in prospect. The evidence shows that much labour movement is short-distance and localized and this is largely because in developing countries, even with radio for the illiterate and newspapers for the schooled, knowledge and awareness of opportunities is limited. But the big cities are known by repute. They can pull in labour from great distances, not by the reality of job-opportunity, but because they are perceived as places of betterment. Labour demand is an aggregate of differing aptitudes and skills and so opportunities are not coincident with gross numbers. Labour migration does not efficiently redistribute supply and demand and allow a balanced equilibrium to be reached. Material resources do move but overwhelmingly it is an inward movement. Indeed, it is the inward movement of capital, labour and materials which predominates for technical and commercial innovations are adopted more readily and are more meaningful in the complexity of interactions characteristic of the large centre rather than the surrounding areas.

In all these cases the issue centres upon the transfer of information, information about investment opportunities, job opportunities, information about markets for materials, information on the latest technological and commercial developments. Mobility is related to the diffusion process. The equilibrium theory and the views of those who mistook Perroux's abstract mathematical space economy with its growth poles for what he called *geonomic* space, or the space of reality, postulates that ideas and benefits will diffuse outwards from growth centres (Perroux 1950; Boudeville 1966; Darwent 1969). This 'spread effect', as experience has shown, is greater in the immediate proximity of the growth region or city, the *core*, and diminishes rapidly with distance into the *periphery*. The 'backwash', the drawing into the *core* of people and resources from the *periphery*, has a longer reach but it too is subject to a distance-decay effect (Soja 1968; Riddell 1970; Gould 1970; Weinand 1973 writing on Kenya, Sierra Leone, Tanzania and Nigeria respectively; Robinson and Salih 1971; Parr 1973; Gilbert 1975).

Increasingly the evidence in the Developing World is that nicely balanced and integrated space economies have not emerged. It would appear that the backwash effect often does mean the sucking out of resources and that the movement to the centre is not compensated by the spread effect. Indeed it was Myrdal who as early as 1957 had coined the terms 'spread' and 'backwash' choosing the latter to stress the draining of resources. The surrounding areas lose, in Mabogunje's words 'their virile young men', their business entrepreneurs, their physical resources which move to the town for processing. Since essentially the comparison is between big cities on the one hand and the rural areas and small country towns on the other, the process is one in which the differences between rural and urban levels of earning widen appreciably. This stimulates a movement to the big cities where the rural migrant tries to find work and leads to a mushrooming urban growth, increasing urban unemployment and a failure of urban facilities to cope with the influx. On the one hand inward migration and rapid urban growth presents problems, while on the other the benefits of the spread effect into the countryside is impeded by the need for radical changes in the rural economy and society effectively to accommodate the spread benefits. These changes, as has been discussed, cannot take place readily; the many blockages in the path of agricultural and rural development such as the need for land-tenure and land-consolidation reforms restrict the take-up of opportunities. As Friedmann puts it: 'for "spread" to occur, the structure of the rural economy must be thoroughly isomorphic with that of the city; it must be organized (or capable of being organized) along commercial, capitalistic lines. In addition, the periphery must be econo-

153

mically accessible to the core area' (Friedmann and Wulff 1976).

There are additional obstacles to the diffusion of ideas and economic transformation. Since spread effects are spatially limited, the process is most effective when it can take place around a series of towns which form part of a hierarchical network. This network of towns constitutes the paths which the diffusion process can take and it can, in the Mackinder fashion, bind them together 'into loosely-knit urban federations' (Mackinder 1902). Such networks in most developing countries are conspicuous by their absence. Their economic history has produced in most cases few urban centres. Often one single centre has grown so that it dominates all others. Urban primacy is common and forms a singularly inadequate mechanism for the diffusion of benefit and innovation in all but the territorially smallest countries.

Not only is the urban network unsatisfactory, but the slopes of the diffusion surface down which ideas, innovations and benefits can, as it were, slide, are neither regular nor continuous. In the abstract world they might be so; in the reality of the Developing World they are not. Distinctive divisions within the population are common. Tribal differences, religious divisions, ethnic plurality are frequent and significant. The importance of information flow has been stressed. This tends to occur within communities, within tribes, religious and ethnic groups, in other words, diffusion is often culture related. In so much as there may also be strata of society related to status and wealth this may further break up the diffusion surface. The spread effect is selective and travels at different speeds in the distinctive groups. Its impact will, therefore, tend to disaggregate the periphery rather than weld it into the fabric of the space economy since cross-cultural flows are impeded. Because these distinctive groupings of the population are often spatially specific this means that some parts of the peripheral zones will be quicker, and others slower, in adopting innovations. Even when they are not, it is possible to see in many parts of the Developing World evidence, albeit superficial, of the extent to which 'modernization' has varied between distinctive communities in the same area.

Throughout the Developing World the population is becoming increasingly urbanized. Between 1970 and 1981 the rate of growth of the urban population in the low-income economies averaged 4.4 per cent per year compared with 1.9 per cent for the total population. In the lower middle-income countries the rates were 4.3 per cent for the urban and 2.6 for the total population. Much of this urban population is accumulating in a few cities, often a port established in colonial times or the capital. In 1980 in 40 of the 68 low-income and low middle-income countries for which data are available, the largest city itself accounted for one third or more of the urban population, and in 17 the proportion was at least 50 per cent (Table 11). This marked concentration has not produced an adequate involvement of the peripheral areas. Existing urban hierarchies have not proved to be the efficient machine of diffusion the model describes.

McGee indeed challenged the assumption that the large cities of the

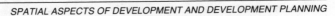

Table 11 Large cities and urban populations

Country	Urban as % of total pop.	1970–81 Average annual growth		Largest city	Percentage of urban pop. in largest city
		Total pop.	Urban pop.		
Mozambique	9	4.2	8.2	Maputo	83
Guinea	20	2.9	6.0	Conakry	80
Thailand	15	2.5	3.4	Bangkok	69
Jamaica	42	1.5	2.5	Kingston	66
Senegal	34	2.7	3.7	Dakar	65
Angola	22	2.5	5.8	Luanda	64
Costa Rica	44	2.8	3.6	San Jose	64
Benin	15	2.7	4.1	Cotonou	63
Togo	21	2.5	6.6	Lome	60
Kenya	15	4.0	7.3	Nairobi	57
Haiti	28	1.7	4.7	Port au Prince	56
Congo P.R.	46	2.9	4.4	Brazzaville	56
Dominican R.	52	3.0	5.3	Santo Domingo	54
Uganda	9	2.6	3.4	Kampala	52
Mongolia	51	2.9	4.0	Ulan Batar	52
Tanzania	12	3.4	8.6	Dar es Salaam	50
Zimbabwe	24	3.2	6.3	Harare	50
Yemen P.D.R.	37	2.5	3.8	Aden	49
Laos P.D.R.	14	1.9	5.2	Vientiane	48
Sierra Leone	22	2.6	4.4	Freetown	47
Nicaragua	54	3.9	5.0	Managua	47
Bolivia	45	2.6	6.9	La Paz	44
Paraguay	40	2.6	3.3	Asuncion	44
Upper Volta	11	2.0	6.0	Ouagadougou	41
Chad	19	2.0	6.5	N'Djamena	39
Mauritania	24	2.3	8.1	Nouckchott	39
Egypt	44	2.5	2.9	Cairo	39
Peru	66	2.6	3.5	Lima	39
Cuba	66	1.1	1.9	Havana	38
Ethiopia	14	3.5	5.5	Addis Ababa	37
Jordan	57	3.5	4.7	Amman	37
Madagascar	19	2.6	5.2	Tananarive	36
Guatemala	39	3.1	3.9	Guatemala	36
Ghana	37	3.0	5.0	Accra	35
Zambia	44	3.1	6.5	Lusaka	35
Somalia	31	2.8	5.4	Mogadishu	34
Ivory Coast	41	5.0	8.3	Abidjan	34
Honduras	36	3.4	5.5	Tegucigalpa	33
Syria	49	3.7	4.6	Damascus	33

Developing World would generate development writing 'in the context of the majority of the Third World Countries, it seems that a theoretical framework which regards the city as the prime catalyst of change must be disregarded' (McGee 1971). He regarded these cities as parasitic upon surrounding areas rather than the diffusion centres of development. Gottman, on the other hand, holds fast to the view that large cities are an essential component in development.

In the last 500 years no country in the world has achieved an advanced status without relatively large cities. In the twentieth century, urbanization has been the major characteristic of the acquisition of national wealth. No backward country pulled itself out of such status without large cities . . . . Large cities do not solve the problems. But cities are the instruments of development, lasting wealth and, with their turbulence, of social dynamics. There has been no known alternative for the masses

(Gottmann 1983).

Two problems have emerged. On the one hand a few cities in each developing country have grown so quickly and become so large that the expansion has outstripped the ability of the city to provide adequate housing, facilities and formal employment. The movement to the city has not been one of universal benefit and opportunity. On the other hand, the existence in the periphery of vast tracts of territory and people in a state of stagnation, or indeed decline as their resources drain away, presents a problem of human, economic and political dimensions. For many the promised new world of independent development and affluence is still but a dream; for even more it appears a cruel delusion.

To tackle these problems embedded in the spatial dimension of development, the issues have been reconsidered by scholars and by governments which have made attempts to remedy them. Three particular areas of concern have drawn attention. One is that of the spatial imbalance produced by primacy coupled to which has been the strategy of urban implantations in undeveloped areas to act as major growth poles. A second is the inadequacy of the urban hierarchy to diffuse developments. The third is the problem internal to the big cities themselves and this will be discussed first.

THIRD WORLD MILLIONAIRES?

Most of the Developing World's population does not, of course, live in towns. The percentage of urban dwellers is only 21 in low-income countries and 33 in the lower middle-income economies. The towns which do exist include some very large settlements. China and India, the world's most populous nations, have respectively, seventy-eight and thirty-six towns exceeding half a million. A further thirty-one half-million cities exist in the other low-income nations and sixty in the lower middle-income group. Between 1960 and 1980 the number of these cities in these two groups of the world's poorer nations rose from seventy-seven to 205. This number includes even larger cities, most in India, China and south-east Asia but Latin America and the Caribbean boast fifteen cities exceeding one million and even Africa outside South Africa, has no less than seven.

Cities in the developing countries are growing for two reasons. One is natural increase but the other is migration. This inward movement is part of Myrdal's 'backwash', the sucking in of resources from surrounding areas. The migrant moves because he perceives better opportunities than in his home village or rural town. Income differentials do exist but the job opportunities available do not match the scale of influx so urban unemployment and poverty are a major characteristic of developing countries. Some, the neo-Marxists, see this as a further manifestation of capitalist exploitation of the Developing World. In their eyes most of the large cities of the developing countries owe their economic character to the investment and activities of foreign firms of the kind discussed in the previous chapter. These firms, they argue, adopt capital-intensive forms of manufacturing brought in, unchanged, from their industrial homelands with the result that not enough jobs are provided. It can, of course, equally be argued that the excess of people over jobs is the product of false expectations on the one hand and the lack of opportunities and the poor quality of life in rural areas on the other. People may move because they feel it cannot be worse and may conceivably be better.

This in-migration takes several forms. Much of it is short distance and may be a direct rural to urban movement. This is true of the immediate surroundings of towns whether large or small. In other cases where a more comprehensive urban hierarchy exists, the movement may be from small town to larger and eventually to the giant city. The urban experience gives the taste for the urban life. Wilkinson, for example, has shown that in Lesotho migrant workers who have experienced wage-labour and urban life in South Africa, where, of course, they cannot stay permanently, upon return do not rejoin their old village communities but settle in Maseru the capital and largest city (Wilkinson 1983). Neither is all urban settlement permanent. In Africa particularly, but also in the Indian sub-continent, the migrant may return to his rural origins after a period of years whereas in Latin America, the move is commonly permanent. The explanation may lie in differences in agricultural practice. In Latin America the male is often a paid farm labourer whereas in Africa and the Indian sub-continent family small holdings are more common and the women work the land while the men are away. The majority of migrants are young and in the child-bearing age groups so that they further increase the potential for growth of the cities.

Whatever the reason, and investigators of them have been many (Simmons, Diaz-Briquets and Laguian 1977), the city pulls in migrants in their thousands as individuals, in families and in kinship groups, all of whom identify better prospects there. They often join relatives or former neighbours and the feed-back of experience further stimulates migration. What then is the problem? It has two parts. First, immigration has not been produced by a demand to fill available vacancies in the industrial sector or indeed in other activities. The influx has far exceeded the capacity of manufacturing industry, located in the cities, to absorb it. Even the servicing sector, which in most cities in developing countries is large and is more labour intensive than manufacturing, cannot absorb all immigrants. Many immigrants have neither the training nor aptitude for the jobs which do become available. Formal unemployment is thus a problem and can be a source of poverty. The second part of the problem relates to both the speed and the magnitude of the growth of city populations and to urban poverty. There is a mismatch between housing demand and housing supply. This raises property prices and rents. The low-paid and unemployed can neither rent nor buy. The city authorities cannot build sufficient public housing. The result is a spread of squatter settlements, that is settlements without legal title to the land used, around the cities, within it on sites too difficult for conventional housing and, indeed, on any vacant lots.

There has emerged, and this is characteristic of nearly all cities in the Developing World, a local, immigrant-produced and unconventional solution to these two problems. They create their own jobs and build their own housing. They are solutions often viewed with suspicion, apprehension or outright opposition by the municipal authorities. The immigrants create 'informal', as opposed to conventional settlements and engage in an 'informal' economy to solve the employment problem. Two cultures and two economies operating within the same social and economic complex have thus emerged. One is made up of the salaried and wage-earners who derive regular incomes from conventional occupations be they bank managers or bus drivers, factory workers or company directors, civil servants or house servants. They live in private houses or apartments as owners or tenants or in municipal housing; they utilize and pay for public utilities and they pay local taxes. The other is composed of those with no conventional income and no accommodation other than that which they have built. Their huts are made of scrapwood and metal; any electricity used is pirated from illegal mains connections; sewage disposal is non-existent and water supplies at best will be the occasional stand-pipe; rather than on paved streets, their shacks stand on tracks dusty in drought and bemired in the rains. It is an assemblage characteristic of the shanty towns of Latin America, Africa and Asia. The inhabitants of these places engage in petty trading, in menial irregular services, in manufacturing at home in a putting-out system practised by small manufacturers, in salvage sorting and collection from refuse dumps and, in some instances, in prostitution and crime. They use their ingenuity, tenacity and capacity for hard work to survive in a situation which would otherwise crush them.

The scene depicted is, inevitably, full of generalisations. Between the formal and informal sectors the divide is not so sharp. The inhabitants of the shanty towns can, and do, get formal employment in shops, office and factory though they may still be unable to buy into the conventional housing market. Others with entrepreneurial talents may be so successful in their informal activities as to be able so to improve their houses as to make them indistinguishable from those in the conventionally-built streets and some may increase their incomes by sub-letting. The shanty towns are not static sites of festering poverty. There is much evidence of their self-improvement, their consolidation, which encompasses better housing, laid-out and paved streets, electricity and water supplies and sometimes sewerage. They are converted into self-built and unplanned suburbs. Since this metamorphosis turns upon the acquisition of wealth it is by no means inevitable nor does it involve all and in the sifting process, the unsuccessful, the poor, drop out into a grim poverty. For those who stress this aspect it is, of course, useful to remember that the quality of life in, say, a poor Indian village on the Deccan is hardly one of comfort, affluence and rustic charm. None the less the vast areas of slum property and urban degradation which characterize such great cities as Calcutta and Bombay, or the large cities of Africa such as Kinshasa and Addis Ababa, can only be described as a problem, 'informal' solutions or not. As E. H. J Johnson puts it.

> More than one Asian or African country is discovering that a planless drift of workers in the prime years of their potential productiveness to sprawling, slum-cursed cities, where huge manpower reserves already exist, may mean not only a tragic misuse of human resources but an equally prodigal wastage of scarce capital by reason of unwarranted pressure in all varieties of municipal facilities. Maintenance, repair, and depreciation costs accelerate; the costs of public surveillance, sanitation, and welfare escalate at rates wholly out of proportion to the growth in the public revenue-yielding capacity of the urban economy. The presumed beneficence of urbanization is not very evident in Manila, Jakarta, or Calcutta!
> (Johnson 1970).

The problem described is the problem of underdevelopment and the difficulty of developing. The fact that it exists in the proximity of modern factories, high-rise buildings, international banks and streets jammed with motor cars should not obscure this truth. The rapid rate of population increase in developing countries had been identified as an impediment to progress. In their great cities this rate of increase is much faster. Concentrating so many into so few places sharply focuses and exacerbates the problem and it becomes a microcosm of the national and international scene of underdevelopment and the development process. What are the solutions? Several lines of action have been taken and none have been wholly, or even largely, successful.

A possible approach is to focus all attention and resources on the city problem. But to build more accommodation, even at low cost, does not build jobs and it is the lack of adequately remunerated employment which is at the root of the problem. Attempts to create more jobs in productive industry, particularly if using labour-intensive methods, encounter all the problems of industrialization which have been discussed so it is not a quick and easy solution. The provision of non-productive jobs in the administrative and servicing sector which *is* labour-intensive, can provide additional employment and has done so in many of the large cities of the Developing World where overmanning is so visually evident. But this increasing sub-division of employment does little to raise levels of income and it still leaves the question as to who is to pay the piper. Investment directed into the city still further deprives the non-urban areas and smaller towns of the oppor-tunity for advancement and exacerbates the problems of urban primacy. Yet the problem of these big cities cannot remain untouched. The few major successes include the city states of Hong Kong and Singapore where essen-tially there is no periphery, it is all core, and where the ability continually to increase productive capacity has been established and investment is all urban-focused (Chapter 20). In the face of massive inflows of refugees Hong Kong has accommodated most of its dwellers in public and private accommodation though it has not totally eliminated squatter settlement. Singapore, without such immigration problems, has successfully housed its population and whereas Frazer in 1952 was able to report of thousands living in squalid conditions the same is not true of the much larger city of today (Frazer 1952). Other cities in less favourable circumstances and less buoyant economies have met with little success. The building of low-cost housing has been widely practiced though it does not always solve the prob-lems of the most poor, of those who need to live near to where their formal or informal activities are practiced, nor is it a solution which can be imple-mented on a wide scale (Gilbert and Gugler 1981). Some countries have sought to assist the squatters to help themselves by giving support at varying levels. It may be that title is given to existing squatter plots or that this, plus the provision of electricity, water supply and refuse collection, is arranged. In other words that squatting is accepted, legalized and incor-porated in the city service and administrative structure. In some countries land is demarcated for squatting; in others to this is added the laying out of streets and plots with basic services provided; the incomer has only to build his house. Zambia has, for example, incorporated all these approaches in its attempt to accomodate the squatting influx into Lusaka. It has even built schools on the fringes of existing squatter settlements in anticipation of the inevitable further inflows. Most attempts by city authorities to ameli-orate the 'squatter problem' are characterized, understandably, by a wish to create order and regulation where there appears to be chaos.

It is important to note two characteristics of the shanty towns and the squatting population. First, the population, because it is poor, is not neces-sarily, incompetent, feckless and lacking in purpose or ingenuity. It is, after all, composed in part of Mabogunje's 'virile young men'. Second, both this population and the shanty settlements they inhabit are not static but in continual change. The initiatives demonstrated in devising employment and accommodation are evidence of this. The community will evolve its own evaluation of the relative importance of housing, its size, quality and cost, of proximity to a job, of educational opportunity, of entrepreneurial initiative, of job in the town rather than life in the country. These evaluations may be totally different from those imagined by city officials, urban planners — or 'western' scholars. Furthermore, they will change as individuals' life patterns and prospects change. There are stages of evolution in the world of the city dwellers of the developing countries as of other worlds. The squatter shack, the shanty town, the informal sector could well be regarded as forms of appropriate technology. While other solutions but partially succeed or become pale palliatives, these autochthonous developments must be allowed to continue though they will never solve the problem completely.

An alternative course of action is to try to stop the big cities growing further by preventing in-migration. This can be done by prohibiting movement, an action only possible where a strongly authoritarian government can effectively enforce its laws either by force or by a political indoctrination which produces compliance or by a combination of both. This degree of control and administrative efficiency is rare in developing countries even those ruled by military regimes. Its requirements are most closely met in socialist totalitarian states of which the Peoples Republic of China is the most noteworthy. China has controlled, in large measure, internal migration but as part of a wider management of people and the space economy (Chapter 16). The Kampuchean policy of rustication of the mid-1970s, which emptied the cities, can only be regarded as a disaster produced by a political and malign bigotry, misguided and ruthlessly applied. For most countries an imposed control of internal-migration is not a feasible solution. But there are further and obvious alternatives. These relate to the creation of more growth centres, either by stimulating the economies of existing but small towns or by building new; in other words, a policy distributing urban populations more widely and more thinly. This resurrects the wider spatial issues of the urban hierarchy and of counterbalancing poles of development.

CAPITAL IDEAS

As has been seen, in most developing countries, urban primacy is associated not only with urban squalor but also with marked differences in regional development. The primate city, often a port or the capital, frequently both, is the dominant in the space economy. To overcome the problems of the ever-enlarging city and regional disparities a number of countries have selected sites in less-developed regions and built new towns to which in some cases the capital has been moved. Friedmann was involved in such a project in Venezuela. There, a new city, Ciudad Guayana, was to be built utilizing local undeveloped mineral resources of iron ore and bauxite in the industries which were to give it life. Energy was to be derived from hydroelectric installations. This new growth pole would help counterbalance the foci of urban and industrial development along Venezuela's north coast around Caracas and Maracaibo (Friedmann 1966). A new industrial city of over a third of a million people has emerged contributing notably to the Venezuelan economy but it has not disminished the strength of the Caracas–Maracaibo axis nor disseminated development into the surrounding countryside. The most famous, or notorious, example of a new city, Brasilia, was built to a grand architectural design by Lucio Costa on essentially virgin land in Brazil's interior and away from the great port of Rio de Janeiro and the industrial agglomeration of Sao Paulo. Its spectacular buildings contain the offices of government, and the houses and apartments of civil servants and others line its boulevards. This new capital, while it functions effectively as the seat of government, has done little to counterbalance the continuing growth of Brazil's great urban agglomerates or to open up Brazil's vast interior. The architectural showpiece made little provision for the work-force of its developing economy with the result that all the manifestations of the Latin American shanty towns are discernible around the periphery.

In Africa both the largest country, Nigeria, and one of the smallest, Malawi, have relocated their capitals in planned new towns. In Malawi the new capital of Lilongwe has been constructed alongside an old-established provincial town in the central part of the country in an attempt to initiate an urban growth-pole away from the major urban and industrial centre of Blantyre in the south. Spacious and well laid out, new Lilongwe is a beautiful city. Its houses, hotels and public buildings compare favourably with most countries and it is served by a new modern international airport. But it gives the impression of a city of residence rather than work, a place for car-owner rather than of workers using public transport, a place with even less industry and commerce than the old town alongside which it has grown. It is early to judge, but unless Lilongwe generates more industrial and commercial growth and houses the associated workers, its impact on the regional spread of development will be limited. Nigeria is vastly more well-endowed and populous than Malawi but despite its greater spread of large towns it too experiences a pronounced regional imbalance and exhibits in Lagos a huge port-capital development with all the ills of the Third World city. The new capital at Abuja in the underdeveloped central belt is an ambitious project designed precisely to counterbalance the political and economic concentration of power in Lagos. More thought, however, has gone into its own town plan than into the economic rationale and its completion is currently in doubt (Chapter 12). Elsewhere new city prospects have likewise been less successful. Those in the populous countries of India and China have essentially been over-spill, satellite towns rather than cities designed to give additional and alternative poles of development.

THE IMPERFECT HIERARCHY

Friedmann's experience in Venezuela led him to believe that the free operation of economic forces would continue to reinforce the strength of the cores at the expense of the periphery. He concluded that 'Economic growth tends to occur in the matrix of urban regions. It is through this matrix that the evolving space economy is organized' (Friedmann 1966). He was thinking in terms of a hierarchical central-place system in the Christaller mode. This represents the third of the three areas of interest and concern, that of the inadequacy of urban hierarchies in developing countries to serve as diffusers of development.

The idea of establishing new urban centres, or stimulating the growth of old smaller centres, the decadent towns, to make a more complete framework for the spread effect has much to commend it but its effectiveness depends entirely on how it is done. It is not simply a matter of establishing middle-sized settlements, which are missing in the rank-size distribution between the giant cities and the small quasi-village towns, and placing them at intervals at central points throughout the less-developed regions of a country. That is drawing-board geometry. It is a matter of creating centres of economic growth which, certainly after the initial phase, will be self-sustaining and *will relate* to the surrounding area, their hinterlands. They can create markets for hinterland-produce and offer services of health, education and commerce and while they will draw in resources and labour, they will none the less, integrate their tributary areas into the development process because these new minor centres will more adequately divide up the modernization surface into smaller area units in which meaningful linkages can be established.

Since private capital tends to move to the cores and neglect the periphery, the role of the state, whether it is central or local government, is often seen to be crucial in this attempt to decentralize development. Public investment can be seen as less overtly economic, at least in the short term. It can be regarded as having a part to play in the laying of foundations and in the creation of a favourable economic environment which will make the new regional growth centres more attractive and persuade private capital to follow it. Public funds can, for example, be invested in infrastructural developments characterized, it will be recalled, by high ICOR and slow returns and often requiring large blocks of capital which are more difficult to generate privately. Transport facilities, energy supplies, public utilities, telecommunications, all sometimes encapsulated into industrial estates, represent such 'pump-priming' infrastructural investments. More directly productive state capital investments can also be made in precisely those areas where private capital is less likely to go. The private industrialist can be induced to set up plant in these new centres by grants, low-interest loans, tax concessions, low rents on sites and a whole range of temptations. It is a scene all too familiar to those acquainted with regional policies in the United Kingdom and western Europe, policies far from distinguished by unqualified success. As yet in the Developing World there is also little evidence of this policy's successful implementation with the exception of the special case of China discussed in the second part of this book.

What then have been the limitations placed upon this strategy of decentralized development? Economic science is the science of scarcities and hence of choosing between alternatives. The developing countries do not possess unlimited capital whether self-generated or borrowed; capital is scarce. Decentralized development may spread this limited resource so thinly as to make it ineffective in all places rather than effective in some. Secondly it could be argued that the periphery is by definition a sub-optimal area in the space economy and is indeed seen as such by private entrepreneurs. It is the area of slower, smaller and less secure returns. Therefore, the allocation of a proportion of the national investment and developing these areas, it would seem, can only be done at the expense of retarding the rate of national development. In other words a distortion or manipulation of the optimum activity-pattern exacts a price. Any government must therefore balance the benefits of regional development policies against that of the overall national good. But what is this national good? Is it the GNP or does it embrace wider issues? This at once moves regional development into the political arena and the question of the goals of development policy. What then are the conceivable reasons for embarking upon a policy of regional decentralized development? First, it could be argued on grounds of equity, to improve the lot of the many and not the few. It should be noted, however, that spatial equity is not necessarily coincident with social and demographic equity though in the largely rural conditions of most developing countries that is more likely the case than not. Second, it could be said that regional development allows the use of otherwise unutilized resources which might be of land, people or minerals. This would certainly be a valid reason in these countries with large areas undeveloped but potentially developable territory. Outside South America and in some areas of tropical Africa, such as Zaire, few countries fall into this category. A third reason for promoting regional development would be to obtain political support. Reasons for not following such policies, in addition to their retardation of national growth, might be advanced by economic power groups within the country who regarded deviations from the apparent economic optimum as an unnecessary and too costly a philanthropy. Governments too might be influenced by the wish, or indeed the need, to see benefits go to their supportive tribal, religious or ethnic groups rather than be distributed solely in terms of impartial equity.

These factors both for and against may account for the lack of enthusiasm and lack of success of regional development policies in so many countries but there are more fundamental basic requirements if these policies are adopted and are to be successful. First, it is essential to identify accurately areas with a growth potential. Second, this growth must be a regional feeder rather than an enclave activity with metropolitan roots and connections. Branch-plant outliers of core companies are notoriously vulnerable to closure whenever the tide of prosperity recedes. Branch-plant management and government officials putting in their time in provincial outposts before returning to the core, are too centre-orientated effectively to stimulate the essential interactions between the regional centre and its region. Different attitudes are necessary. It would seem that the plugging of the gaps in the urban hierarchy has been an unsuccessful measure because alternative evaluations of development have maimed it, because most governments have neither the means nor the will to implement it, but most importantly because it is an insufficiently radical re-organization of the space economy in a manner appropriate for most developing countries. It produces the frame of the umbrella without the fabric.

Part 2 The practice

Let observation with extensive view
Survey mankind from China to Peru
Remark each anxious toil, each eager strife,
And watch the busy scenes of crowded life.

Samuel Johnson
The Vanity of Human Wishes 1749

11 Fiji and Tonga

'. . . it may be that for many of you the passage of time has dimmed the memory of the initial thrill of independence: our experience is that the feeling of independence is rather like that of leaving the cramped compartment of a jet liner. First the exhilarating and heady gulps of fresh air: then the cautious steps down to earth: and suddenly and immediately the need for direction, the offered hands to help with the burden – and then, I presume, a place in the rat race'

Ratu Sir Kamisese Mara,
Prime Minister of Fiji
Address to the General Assembly of the United Nations on the
occasion of Fiji's admission
21 October 1970

By the end of the eighteenth century, mercantile adventure, imperialism and the driving curiosity of exploration had all but tidied up the world into the 'known' and the 'unknown'. It was essentially a Eurocentric view and the 'unknown' was, in the main, the continental interiors of South America, Africa, Australia and Asia where climate, terrain and difficulties of over-land transport made access less easy to the European. But there was another area little known, that of the Pacific whose very vastness meant that its scattered island communities could be as easily missed as found. Gradually the empty charts were filled and throughout the late eighteenth and the nineteenth century the flags of European empires together with that of the United States were raised on volcanic islands and coral atolls and beneath them was preached the Christian faith by missionaries each according to his sect. An alien culture, a sophisticated technology, new dimensions of a wider world were introduced into the small isolated communities and foreign names, New Caledonia, New Hebrides, Cook Islands, Gilbert and Ellice Islands were intermixed with or replaced the old.

These islands of the South Seas, of all the islands of the world, possess the most romantic image. To the urbanized populations of Europe and North America they have an attraction made up of more than a physical beauty compounded of palm trees, coral sand, white surf and blue seas for many islands can boast as much. Few can, however, conjure up such images of the unspoilt life, of peaceful undisturbed remoteness, of mankind at ease with itself and nature, of life as it once was and, perhaps, still ought to be. Yet these islands are not the fictitious lands of some romantic tale but the homes of peoples with their distinctive cultures and traditions, people who are kindly, courteous and hospitable but people who are of today with today's problems, hopes and aspirations. They are not the inhabitants of some open-air museum simply to be looked at.

In the second half of the twentieth century these communities have become separate sovereign nations aware of other things and other places, of standards of living different from their own. They cannot revert to whatever former ways they had, though their cultures can and must remain alive and vibrant, nor can they remain static. The islands of the South Pacific present, literally, a microcosm of the problems and challenges of the Developing World. Their governments and people are planning and striving within the development process. Amongst the palm fronds and hibiscus flowers are prices and income policies, trade agreements and employment problems. They illustrate the ubiquitous Third World issues discussed in the first part of this book but they also highlight the special problems of small nations for all of them are small in area and population. All have very limited natural resources and in all cases these problems of size have been exacerbated by remoteness in the world's largest ocean where distance impresses itself even in the days of jet aircraft. The Pacific south of the equator is as large as Asia, Africa and Europe combined while its island communities total less than two million people. Two countries have been selected which encapsulate the issues of development and illustrate the problems of scale. One, Fiji, is large enough, sufficiently endowed and compact, to offer opportunities for substantially development. The second, Tonga, treated here briefly, is an example of an ancient and proud nation which in the twentieth century is very much restricted by its geography and the paucity of its resources. It raises the issue of nations which might be too small and remote to allow their inhabitants hopes for a better future unless help is given from the world at large.

FIJI

Until the latter part of the nineteenth century when Fiji became a British colony, there was not a nation in the modern political sense but an archipelago of several hundred islands inhabited by peoples of Melanesian stock with a Polynesian component whom today are called Fijians. They had no written history but a rich oral tradition which attributed to them a common and divine ancestry and they had acquired a reputation as a fierce, warlike people hostile to outsiders. Their first contact with Europeans dates from the early years of the nineteenth century when traders came to the islands seeking sandalwood, and later bêche-de-mer, for the lucrative trade with China. The interest of the British Government was drawn to Fiji by the activities of its Australian colonists in the mid-nineteenth century but an expedition sent to survey to group's potential for colonial development reported unfavourably. It was not until 1874 that Fiji was ceded to Britain, at the request of the dominant Fijian leaders of the day, after a period of unsavoury, unofficial European speculation in Fiji. With Victorian precision an area of Pacific ocean almost the size of Texas was defined as the Colony of Fiji. Less than three per cent of it was land.

After ninety-six years of colonial rule Fiji became an independent nation in October 1970. In this period there had been significant changes. Fiji had acquired new peoples and a broader resource base as commercial agriculture, mining and tourism were added to the subsistence economies of former days. The future was now in the hands of the peoples of Fiji themselves and a programme for economic development was mapped out. Development Plan Six (DP6), some eighteen months in the making, appeared within a month of independence and marked the watershed between the period of colonial rule and the independent future.

DEVELOPMENT ISSUES

Fiji has development problems much in common with other countries of the developing world. There is a need to raise the material standard of living though in Fiji per capita incomes are on average much higher than in most of Asia and higher than in any country in Africa save South Africa and Libya. The average is, of course, weighted by an affluent commercial, professional and industrial sector whose higher earnings offset the low monetary income of the farming community which still contains a large subsistence element. The income disparity between the various sectors of the economy had considerable implications for any planned development policy. Secondly, Fiji's earnings of foreign exchange had been, and still are, closely associated with the export of a few basic commodities, sugar, coconut products and gold. Sugar alone accounted for two-thirds of the value of commodity exports in 1970. In none of these exports was Fiji's position secure. There was an obvious need for the diversification of the country's economic activities. Thirdly Fiji's population was expanding rapidly. The need to provide increasing opportunities for employment clearly required a major effort.

In addition Fiji faced problems less ubiquitous. First, as a South Pacific community she was isolated in a vast ocean. Second, she was small. With an area of 18,332 square kilometres and a population of some 527,000 in 1970, Fiji was a small nation in which economies of scale would be difficult to achieve over a wide range of activities. The problem was aggravated by the country's archipelagic nature which breaks the country up into several still smaller units. Unlike other South Pacific countries Fiji is a country of racial duality. Over half the population consists of Indians, descendants, in the main, of the indentured labourers brought in to work sugar plantations between 1870 and 1921. In so much as the original Fijian population and the introduced Indian group are distinguished from each other in terms of land

tenure, participation in the cash economy and the extent of their urbanization, racial duality is a factor in development planning. Lastly, Fiji, in
becoming a tourist centre since the Second World War, has not only developed a previously untapped resource which now contributes significantly
to the country's invisible exports, but has also accentuated the problems of
what might be called her 'threshold' situation. This has two facets. The first
is that though small, Fiji is not too small to rule out any considerable prospect of development. She has hopes for the future which appear attainable
and the earnings from tourism have helped to place her on this threshold.
The second facet is sharply cut by tourism; it is that of subjective or
comparative poverty. Into an island community of subsistence farmers, fish-
ermen and peasant cane growers has come the epitome and caricature of
twentieth-century affluence, the tourist. Coming from the more prosperous
sections of the more prosperous countries, the tourist in his mood of
holiday-spending highlights the contrast between the affluent society and
that of the Third World. His presence demonstrates the comparative poverty
of the peoples of Fiji and raises their level of expectations. In so much as
these expectations may not be realisable in the short-term, development
planning, if it is concerned solely with laying a secure foundation for
sustained growth, may appear too restrictive and too slow. It must needs
incorporate provision for the present as well as the future.

RESOURCES FOR DEVELOPMENT

Fiji is an agricultural country; 70 per cent of its population live in rural areas
and these are almost entirely agriculturalists. Agricultural commodities have
long dominated the export trade so clearly land is a basic and fundamental
resource for Fiji's development yet much of Fiji is steep and mountainous
country and a tenth of the Dominion's area is in scattered groups of small
islands. The small area of the country is an even smaller resource. Twyford
and Wright classified 70 per cent of Fiji as difficult land including 40 per cent
considered to be quite unsuitable for agriculture (Twyford and Wright 1965).
The best quality land covers 20 per cent of the total area and the second class
10 per cent, including some areas in the mountainous interiors of the two
large islands, Viti Levu and Vanua Levu, the use of which is restricted by
their inaccessibility, and other areas in small islands too fragmented and
remote to be significant (Fig. 25B). The first agriculture census, taken in
1968, revealed that the total area under cultivation was some 146,000
hectares of which 42 per cent was on Viti Levu and 40 per cent on Vanua
Levu. This represents only 8 per cent of the total area and only 26 per cent
of the two better quality land categories. Of this area around 125,000
hectares were under sugar cane, coconuts or rice, the remaining 21,300

Figure 25 Fiji (a) location (b) land quality (after Twyford and Wright 1965)

0° EQUATOR

KIRIBATI

NAURU Ocean

SOLOMON

ISLANDS

PHOENIX IS.

TUVALU

TOKELAU IS.

ROTUMA

WESTERN
SAMOA

AMERICAN
SAMOA

FIJI

VANUATU

COOK IS.

Niue

TONGA

NEW
CALEDONIA

AUSTRALIA

Norfolk

Kermadec Is.

Lord Howe

Sydney

NEW ZEALAND

0   800 Km

Auckland

A

0°

B

Labasa

VANUA LEVU

YASAWA

GROUP

TAVEUNI

VITI LEVU

Koro

Lautoka

OVALAU

Nadi

Gau

Suva

Land Quality

Class I

Classes II & III

Class IV

0   80 Km

being devoted to a wide variety of crops including village crops grown in systems of bush fallowing. Since the ratio of cultivated area to fallow is one to seven, the maximum area required for the growing of these crops could be as high as 151,500 hectares giving a total area devoted to cultivation of perhaps 276,200 hectares. This is still only half the area of the better land. Pasture land, other than common grazing, accounted for a further 37,000 hectares. In Fiji there was, and is, clearly considerable scope both for the extension and the intensification of agricultural production.

Much of the land unsuitable for agriculture on the steep slopes of the wetter areas is clothed in rain forest of a varied flora while secondary forest covers cut-over areas. Indigenous species include both valuable hard and soft woods the commercial properties of which were imperfectly known until the 1960s. Approximately 248,500 hectares contain commercial species. Extraction without replanting had been common even after the Second World War but the Forestry Department began to establish a number of plantations, chiefly of the exotics Caribbean Pine and Mahogany, so that forest resources would not be prematurely and unnecessarily exhausted. The wet Fijian climate promotes rapid tree growth. It is estimated that pines can be grown on rotations as short as 25 years for timber and 10 to 15 years for pulp-wood. Some 810,000 hectares are considered as suitable for forestry without any encroachment being made on land of good agricultural quality. The land potential of Fiji is thus considerably increased by its ability to produce commercial timber.

Fiji's outstanding natural beauty is a further attribute of its land resources and one for which the word 'recreational' seems hardly adequate. From its coral coasts and sandy beaches to the rugged interiors of the larger islands the Fijian archipelago delights the eye with its natural beauty; the warm climate and long hours of sunshine, particularly in the northern and western parts of the larger islands is a further attraction. These are not the only qualities which bring in tourists in considerable numbers but they are fundamental and represent a land resource which requires to be husbanded as carefully as those of farm or forest.

The development of these resources of the land is, however, conditioned by the character of land tenure. As a result of British policy designed to ensure that land ownership remained in the hands of the indigenous Fijian people, and because individual land ownership was unknown in Fijian society, some 84 per cent of the land area was at the time of independence communally owned by Fijian village communities and could not be sold. This Fijian owned land was administered by the Native Lands Trust Board which placed a large proportion into the category of Native Reserve. This land could not even be leased to anyone other than a member of the Fijian race; at least three-quarters of the total area of Fiji could only be developed by Fijians who represented 42 per cent of the population. The government of independent Fiji did not change this situation. The remaining quarter of the country included Crown Land (now Fiji Government land), freehold and leasehold land, much of the latter two categories being of high quality. It is upon this land that most of the sugar cane and rice is grown and beef and dairy cattle kept. Clearly in realising the full potential of Fiji's land resources particularly attention must needs be paid to the communally held Fijian land.

Mineralization in Fiji has been on a small scale and scattered. Gold, because of its value, has been least affected by this situation and is still the only mineral of significance mined. First worked in Vanua Levu, the only gold mining remaining is at Vatukoula in northern Viti Levu. By 1970 the economic ore reserves were already approaching exhaustion. The static world price of gold and rising costs, made inevitable as increasingly leaner ores are worked, produced a financial crisis in the industry and the new government of independent Fiji in its first year of office gave the mining company a considerable subsidy to maintain operations. Other minerals, manganese and copper, have been mined on a small scale but neither has been significant.

THE PEOPLE IN THE DEVELOPMENT PROCESS

Central to the development goals and strategies of any country is its population. As has been discussed in chapters three and eight its size, distribution and demographic characteristics establish parameters for economic growth. Its health and education are both development goals and development resources. In Fiji's case racial duality has also its socio-economic and political implications.

At the time of the first census in 1881, 127,500 people were enumerated of whom 115,000 were Fijian and 500 were Indians brought in under the indentured labour scheme. The growth of the Indian population to 1921 when the scheme ended was largely the result of immigration. At the time of independence Indians totalled 263,500 (50 per cent of the population) and Fijians 220,000 (42 per cent) out of a total population of 527,000. The rapid population increase had produced a youthful population with 57.4 per cent under the age of 19 in 1966 and an estimated annual growth rate of 3.3 per cent. In consequence the population was estimated to reach between 717,000 and 742,000 by 1985 depending upon the effect of the birth control programme and other influences on fertility rates. Birth rates have been brought down and the population at the end of 1984 was estimated at around 695,000. None the less the potential labour force has been growing faster than the population and the rate of population increase sets, of course, the lower limits to the rate at which national productivity must grow.

Differences in the socio-economic characteristics of the racial groups have a considerable significance for planning. Both major groups are overwhelmingly employed in agriculture. The Indians are concerned mainly with cane growing and to a lesser extent rice and vegetable production and they are commercial rather than subsistence farmers. The Fijians are predominantly subsistence or part-subsistence farmers within the traditional village economy but they produce about half of coconuts exported from Fiji, almost all the bananas and cocoa and a range of other crops for the internal market. The Indian population is largely confined to the two main islands, particularly the cane areas, whereas the Fijians are more widely distributed and are the dominant group in all the smaller islands (Fig. 26B). Since there was little additional land available to Indian cultivators, extra employment on the land could not be readily provided. This situation channelled many Indians into non-agricultural occupations for which they were suited by aptitude and inclination. Indians became active in commerce, industry and the professions and became highly successful as small entrepreneurs. At the managerial level, Indians outnumbered Fijians by 3 to 1 in primary industry, 11 to 1 in construction, 8 to 1 in commerce and 7 to 1 in transport. At supervisory and clerical levels and among skilled workers there were twice as many Indians as Fijians. Most of these activities are urban-based and consequently Indians became the more urbanized group.

Education is easier and cheaper to provide in towns than in rural areas. As the 1969 Commission on Education pointed out, the scattered and rural character of the Fijian population presents severe logistic and scale problems for education (Fiji Education Commission 1970). There are 55 separate islands with Fijian schools and 130 Fijian schools can only be reached by sea. Fijian schools averaged only half the size of Indian and their isolated or rural character has often meant that both teacher and pupils are deprived of outside stimulus. Conditions for study in villages are most unsatisfactory and rural poverty makes difficult the maintenance of adequate standards. Secondary education for rural areas can be provided, in the main, only by boarding schools and increased expenditure. The Indian rural population is less scattered and though rural poverty presents problems, it is not to the same extent aggravated by the geography of the population of Fiji. The Commission stated that a disparity did exist in 'education, opportunity and achievement between Fijians and other races of the country' (Fiji Education Commission 1970). This situation is one which bears directly upon the quality of manpower available as a resource for economic development and it began to receive urgent attention.

In contrast to the situation in many parts of the Developing World, the population of Fiji is healthy. There is no malaria, leprosy and filariasis are declining diseases while tuberculosis which had long been a major disease, had been brought under control and was residual in a decreasing number of adults.

Figure 26 (opposite) Fiji (a) sugar areas (b) ethnic distribution

Plates 17 and **18 Rice the great food staple of Asia.**
Rice nursery beds in southern China (above). Paddy fields amidst coconut groves Sri
Lanka.

Plates 19 and 20 Small holder cash cropping.
Coconut husking on a small holding Vanua Levu, Fiji (above). Sugar cane harvesting on an Indian 4 hectare holding Viti Levu, Fiji.

Plates 21 and **22 Plantation Agriculture.**
A tea estate in Malawi (above). Within a rubber tree plantation Malaysia (below).

Plates 23 and
24 Traditional indigenous manufacturing.
Hand-spinning and hand-loom weaving by Hausa people in northern Nigeria.

Plates 25 and **26 Contrasting technologies.**
Labour intensive and capital intensive tin mining on the Jos Plateau, Nigeria.

Plates 27 and **28 Appropriate technologies.**
A mini hydro-electricity station in China serving a village of 300 people (above).
A gas-turbine electricity generator in the Nigerian oilfields (below).

Plates 29 and ***30*** **Decentralized development: industry in the countryside.**
Rural brickworks (previous page) and a fan-making factory in the Chinese
countryside.

A

Labasa

Penang

Rarawai

Lautoka

● Sugar Mills

Cane Land

Land over 1000 feet

Cane Railway

100 inch Isohyet

0   80 Km

B

VANUA LEVU

TAVEUNI

YASAWAS

KORO

Percentage of Total Population

FIJIAN >50

INDIAN >50

NEITHER >50

OVALAU

VITI LEVU

GAU

KADAVU

0   80 Km

DEVELOPMENT STRATEGIES AND DEVELOPMENT PLANS

The United Kingdom's Commonwealth Development and Welfare aid programme which functioned after the Second World War required potential recipients to submit plans of expenditure. Such was the case in Fiji and led to its series of five-year plans, the first of which was submitted in 1949. The first four plans were essentially proposals for government expenditure and capital investments in social services and infrastructure. In 1966 the new C.D. and W. Act required that a comprehensive development plan be prepared in support of all requests for aid. Fiji's first integrated plan Development Plan Five (DP5) covered the period 1966–70. The Sixth Development Plan (DP6) was published in November 1970 by the newly independent government and was both far-reaching and sophisticated. It assessed the achievements under DP5, considered the economic position at the time of independence and presented proposals which attended to both short-term problems and long-term developments.

In making its proposals Fiji was very much conditioned by her particular circumstances, her resources, remoteness, scale, racial duality and the need to achieve fair and equitable opportunities for employment as her population expanded. The classical free-trade approach to Fiji's situation would be to stress her international comparative advantage in her export commodities and use the earnings from these to correct any domestic imbalances. Tourism could be viewed in a similar light. Over the years this, in fact, had been the situation. Earnings from sugar exports and to a lesser extent from coconut products and gold exports had fuelled the Fijian economy and paid for increasing quantities of imports. Good progress had been made in recent years which had witnessed both a considerable expansion of sugar exports and an increasing efficiency in its production but the situation had obvious weaknesses. Too much of the national revenue and foreign earnings was derived from one commodity and that a primary agricultural crop, subject to diminishing returns, and with a future market less certain than in the past. Secondly, as raw materials, consumer goods and indeed capital goods for investment programmes, were to a large extent imported, their costs, including transport charges, were out of the control of the Fijian economy. The country was vulnerable on two fronts. It was essential, therefore, to diversify the economy; first to extend the range of exports and so reduce the risk (tourism can be viewed as a beneficial development in this context); second to reduce dependence upon imports by the creation of import-substitute activities in both industrial and agricultural sectors; thirdly, by enlarging the field of activity to provide greater employment opportunity in the cash sector.

This was broad-front planning involving a balance between internal and export activities and industrial and agricultural sectors. It is the balance between those developments which calls for the most careful assessment and the most delicate of decisions. It was not possible to advance at all points. Capital availability and resources were restricted and priorities had to be allocated. Fiji was hoping for capital to be made available in two ways; first from overseas aid, essentially for government-controlled spending in developing the infrastructure of communications and public utilities but also for major agricultural projects; secondly from private investment, particularly in tourism and industry, for which the essential prerequisites were the creation of an infrastructure to make the capital productive and the maintenance of political stability. It can be argued that the execution of such a broad development plan makes calls upon administrative and organizational resources beyond the capability of a small and newly independent country. Indeed, for this reason the activity of private enterprise was to be encouraged since it would release the government from some of the burden. However, this also has its drawbacks. Local entrepreneurs and administrators are as likely to be as much in short supply in industry as in government. Secondly, the private capital available was mainly foreign. In consequence both investors and management over wide areas of private enterprise could well be foreign and so raise fears of foreign domination of the economy. It will be recalled that in theory at least, broad-front development creates economic cross-stimuli between agriculture and industry and within industry allows the development of horizontal and vertical integration.

The alternative strategy to this broad front approach, that of a focus upon one sector in which interrelations of activities are likely to be fruitful with the resulting rapid growth upsetting the economic equilibrium and stimulating further change, was an alternative not available to Fiji. The sector would have had to be manufacturing since its level of activity responds more quickly to growth stimulus and holds prospects of an import-substitution role and even of exports. As manufacturing is more flexible in adapting to market changes than primary production it would enable the country to cushion itself more effectively against changing world market conditions. Such a focus would have implied, however, a capital emphasis upon this one sector to the extent that others would be starved of it. In Fiji, manufacturing, excluding the processing of sugar and coconut products, contributed only 5 per cent to the GDP. Wage earners made up only 7.2 per cent of the employed population, the remainder being self-employed and essentially agriculturalist. Of the 48,100 farming mainly for cash, 15,600 were cane-growers. A further 29,000 were subsistence farmers. To concentrate upon a narrow-front development of industry would be to accentuate the income disparity between town and country, between main islands and minor and, to some extent, between Fijian and Indian. The Sixth Development Plan recommended a broader approach. It attempted to embrace the problems of racial and economic duality, of geographical dispersion and urban-rural contrast and of over-dependence upon the export of a primary product, sugar, whose growth potential was considered to be severely limited.

DEVELOPMENT PLAN SIX

In discussing its objectives, the authors of the plan point out that economic development must needs encompass social development and is therefore concerned with the optimum use of resources both human and physical. They stated that the moderation of increasing income disparities was perhaps the most important single objective of DP6 (Fiji Parl 1970). From this single objective stemmed many of the Plan's proposals. As the disparity was a rural-urban one and as agriculture was the predominant activity of the country and land one of its major resources, it followed that agriculture must be given special attention. A more prosperous rural population would mean a greater market for home-produced manufactures and a more secure food supply for the urban worker. It also implied the bringing into the cash economy of the subsistence farmer. As these farmers were located in the more inaccessible areas and in the outer islands, the effort for agricultural development embraced the need to improve transport and marketing conditions in these areas and so to tackle the spatial problems inherent in Fiji's geography. The agricultural effort was not considered to require putting more land in Fiji's most lucrative crop, sugar-cane. Indeed, as production per hectare was increasing as a result of the technological advances made in cane growing, the area under sugar was thought likely to decline. The need was for agricultural alternatives to sugar. As is so often the case, agriculture presented the greatest problems for resource development. The plan balanced this agricultural effort by envisaging industrial and service developments which would help to provide additional employment opportunities in urban areas.

Central to the whole agricultural scene was the position of the giant sugar industry. The plan assumed a 1975 sugar production of 368,000 tonnes based upon the maximum export quota allowed under the International Sugar Agreement and including 25,400 tonnes for home consumption. The sugar-milling company, which initiated the industry in Fiji and operated it for 90 years, decided to withdraw from Fiji because it considered the new contract apportioning sugar proceeds between itself and the growers formulated under the Denning Award of 1970, to be unacceptable. After DP6 was published the milling company sold its interests to the Fiji Government. The state thus became involved in a financial commitment of some F$10 million not allowed for in the plan and the owner of the country's major industry the uncertain future of which made all the more imperative agricultural expansion on other fronts.

Agricultural proposals fell into two categories. One was of small-scale investments characterized by low ICORs and the other of large infrastructural developments with higher ICORs. On the one hand the detailed proposals for agriculture make reference to training programmes to improve the small farmers' techniques, extension work to change 'value and behaviour patterns' and to facilitate the introduction of new ideas, to the provision of rural credit to finance small-scale investment in agriculture and to the need to continue and extend subsidy and price support schemes to provide financial incentives for cash farming and farm improvement. Such proposals would relate to the bulk of the farming population. On the other hand the plan incorporated a major commitment to the development of irrigation schemes for paddy rice in three of the nation's major river valleys. These schemes, far beyond the capacity of individual farmers, were designed to boost the production of rice and so reduce the need for imports.

The aim of the effort in agriculture was, therefore, to improve the income of the farming community and so reduce the drift to the towns and to prepare for a future in which the expansion of sugar production was thought unlikely and a contraction possible. The improvement in agricultural efficiency and the diversification of agriculture was not something to be achieved quickly as progress in the preceding plan's period had shown. The small scale of activities and the fragmentation of the land resource meant that more efficient marketing arrangements were imperative if improvement were to be encouraged. The plan described them as poor and uncoordinated and stated 'the creation of an efficient marketing system is the single most pressing requirement to stimulate agricultural production' (Fiji Parl. 1970). Proposals for a national marketing authority and for the development of co-operatives were made. On land tenure there were no specific proposals but the plan said 'It is in the national interest that arrangements for the use of the limited agricultural lands of Fiji be designed to preserve and develop their productivity' (Fiji Parl. 1970).

The plan's proposals for the development of Fiji's forest potential were muted because an F.A.O. team was assessing it at the time of the plan. It was, of course, another primary resource but forestry development could offer a much needed diversification of land use, provide opportunities for employment and contribute to exports. Steps had already been taken in DP5 to further these ends including the extension of a plantation programme and the restriction of lumber exports so the value added by sawing and processing could accrue to Fiji.

Manufacturing industry was described as 'not a key component'. It had, and has, however several important roles to play. For example, the gold industry was in difficulties and receiving government help. While the mine is producing gold the industry earns foreign currency so that governmental assistance may be regarded as a conversion exercise transforming Fiji's natural resources into exchangeable earnings. There is clearly, an opportunity cost limit to such an operation. The Government had, however, another objective. It regarded its assistance as a short-term bridging operation to prolong the life of the mine so that alternative employment could be created for the mine workers by the time the ore was exhausted. It was important to maintain the Vatukoula community, which totalled some 5,000 persons, with its infrastructure of housing, roads, power and public utilities and to prevent the dispersal of that rare commodity in so many developing countries, a trained and organized work force. The mining company made land available for an industrial estate which could use the power, services and training facilities at Vatukoula.

Manufacturing clearly had a role in providing additional opportunities for employment at Vatukoula and in urban areas yet it was little developed. Like agriculture, it was dominated by the sugar industry which accounted for nearly sixty per cent of the net output and forty per cent of employment in manufacturing industry. As has been seen, industrialization is so often thought of as synonymous with economic development that it may seem surprising that more was not made of it in DP6. The appraisal was, however, realistic and the problems of industrial development, certainly over the period of the plan, were recognized as considerable. It is in this field of activity where Fiji's small size hits hardest because it directly affects her international competitiveness. Fiji had neither the manpower, energy resources nor capital for large-scale production nor a large domestic market to support it. The possibility of import-substitute industries is often canvassed as a means of providing employment and as a saving in import costs. However, Fiji did not have a balance of payments problem and to produce goods at home more expensively than they could be imported would have been an extravagant way of providing employment in the circumstances. There were, however, other possibilities; if import-substitute industries could also command a local export market in the South Pacific this would recommend their development, particularly if they were of a nature in which scale-economies were not important. Secondly, industries processing the country's agricultural and forestry products would be viable projects if the requisite quality control were established. Such industries would add value to exports and provide employment. They would include fruit and meat canning, coconut desiccation, and, using timber, wood pulp manufacture, ply-wood and fibre-board making. The authors of DP6 in outlining these possibilities stressed the need for a careful scrutiny of proposals and for government help by way of tax concessions to new establishments. Already government-developed trading estates, to assist industrial development had been established in Suva and other towns. Labour-intensive techniques were recommended where possible though this was not considered to be the major criterion for development.

The activity which was the most buoyant and required guidance rather than stimulus was tourism. The 1960s had seen a spectacular rise in tourist numbers, averaging 23 per cent per annum. Total spending by tourists rose from F$7.5 million in 1965 to F$26 million in 1970. However, tourist spending was on duty-free goods which were imported so that the net benefit to the Fiji economy was much less. None the less net tourist receipts served to offset the large adverse balance in commodity trading which had developed in Fiji and which was expected to increase further as imports necessary to support the proposals in DP6 were brought in. Clearly tourism is a most welcome diversification of the economy. Its contribution was small

(3.5 per cent of the GDP in 1970 compared with 20 per cent for sugar) but its growth potential was considerable. Furthermore, if carefully directed it could help in the development of the rural areas, including those of the smaller islands, both directly and by providing a local market for vegetables and craft goods. Like every silver lining tourism has its clouds. In the first place unless guided and controlled it could destroy the beauty and exoticism which gave it birth and detract from land development for other purposes. Land use planning is essential; this was proposed in the plan and technical assistance for an overall survey of tourism in Fiji was sought from the United Nations Organisation. Secondly, tourism must not be allowed to distort the use of scarce resources so that other essential developments suffer. The social repercussions of tourism are commonly great and some may create difficulties; the development of subjective poverty has been mentioned. Others may be undesirable and require control but given forethought and planning, tourism can be a valuable part of an economy. It is essential, however, that participation in this industry, and not merely as wage-earners but as partners, is open to the people of Fiji. Tourism, like commodity exports, is subject to external influences. The size of its clientele depends upon taste, fashion, and the changing prosperity of the countries from which the visitors come. It is also dependent upon transport technology. Most of Fiji's visitors come by air and stay for a few days en route for another destination because Fiji is a staging point on the trans-Pacific routes. Developments in aircraft technology could result in the overflying of Fiji to the detriment of its short-stay tourist traffic.

DEVELOPMENT PLAN SEVEN

The first plan of independent Fiji thus addressed the crucial components in its development process. A well-conceived and balanced plan which proved to have laid secure foundations for Fiji's further development, it was not successful upon all fronts. Its implementation was facilitated by the maintenance of racial harmony though the disparities between the races were not removed. It initiated the diversification of the economy though in its short span it could hardly produce significant changes and it acknowledged the problems of the increasing movement from outer islands to the main island of Viti Levu and from the countryside to the towns but it did little to stop it. The distribution of land ownership was mentioned only in passing. External influence affected the plan considerably. While tourism did well, financed largely by foreign capital, the major sugar industry performed less well and the increase in oil-prices contributed to a further enlargement of the import bill. The subsequent plan, DP7, attempted to correct some of these trends. It recommended that foreign investment should not exceed 50 per cent of capital finance, that a hydro-electric station be developed to reduce dependency on oil imports, and that a greater proportion of the earnings from tourism be retained in the country. But as the international economy went into recession so the tourist trade suffered. Output from the newly acquired sugar industry declined and inflation pressures, part imported and part created by demands, increased rapidly. The trough in annual growth was reached in 1975 with GDP experiencing a decline in that year. Thereafter the economy became much more buoyant largely due to improvements in the fortunes of the sugar industry.

DP7 setting out the plans for development until 1980 contained many of the objectives of its predecessor. It aimed to increase employment opportunities, to encourage a more equal participation of the races in the cash economy and to improve conditions in the rural areas. It differed importantly in laying greater stress on regional development seeing it not simply in terms of rural-urban differences but in the income differentials which existed on a wider regional basis within and between the large islands and the many smaller ones. Importantly the idea of developing manufacturing industries within the rural areas began to emerge.

In addition to this concern with regional disparities, DP7 couched its proposals in such a way as to maintain or increase Fiji's ability to meet its own requirements. The reasons were obvious; the more that could be produced at home the more employment could be created, imports could be reduced and the balance of payments situation improved. However, the very nature of the capital goods required to support development objectives meant that they could not be manufactured in Fiji. The same was true of a range of consumer goods. As oil prices further increased in the late 1970s the import bill continued to grow and helped further reduce national economic self-sufficiency. By the terminal year of DP7 there had occurred some slight structural changes in the Fijian economy which included a fall in the contribution of primary industries to the GDP and a slight increase in the role of non-resource based manufacturing.

Despite these changes Fiji remained in 1980 a country dependent upon the export of primary products with sugar remaining strongly dominant. Manufacturing was not on a scale which could significantly engender pronounced economic development and structural change. Though the annual increase in population had fallen, the high birth rates of earlier years meant that the labour force has continued to expand at a greater and indeed rapid rate and unemployment emerged as a major economic and social problem.

DEVELOPMENT PLAN EIGHT

For the planning period 1980–85 Fiji's planners, having analysed the first ten years of progress since independence, set out objectives similar to those expressed in earlier plans but with a greater stress on issues of the political economy and social justice. Notably the plan incorporates a shrewd evaluation of the psychology of development. It is a plan more ambitious, far reaching and more detailed in its proposals than its predecessors. It recognises six major components in its development strategy. It recognizes the need to grow economically, to generate more true wealth so that there is wealth to be distributed. It recommends a reduction of the dependency on Fiji's two major sources of wealth, sugar and tourism, and this means a diversification of the economy in all sectors. For example, within the sugar industry itself, it argues the case for the greater processing of sugar products within Fiji instead of a reliance on raw sugar exports and hence the production of sugar-based spirits such as rum, of ethanol for motor fuel, of particle board from the cane stalk, and of animal feed from molasses. Such developments will increase self-reliance, create employment, substitute for imports and also widen the range of exports.

Secondly, the plan stresses the need for greater economic and social equity achieved by a wider participation in the development process. It draws attention to welfare provision for the poorest to cater for their basic needs. It stresses the significance of location policies in industrial development, agricultural investments and service provision which will stimulate new developments in the disadvantaged regions and islands. So significant is this issue regarded that the plan's authors devote a second volume of their plan entirely to a comprehensive system of regional economic planning which involves the deliberate planting of manufacturing and service units in identified growth centres throughout the main islands and the archipelago. These rural growth centres are the most recent and significant developments in economic planning in Fiji.

Sectoral change, regional developments and the goal of greater equity all have a bearing upon the increasingly grave unemployment problem which is emerging since this manifestation is the outcome of the present inadequacies in Fiji's development path. The plan points out that increasing incomes among the employed have created consumption tastes for goods which can only be imported, that too rapid an adoption of mechanized techniques in some industries has also reduced employment opportunity, that the attraction of the towns has pulled in young people from rural communities where they could be employed, to the towns where they could not, and that the education system plays a vital role in differential employment opportunity. These are features common to many developing countries and DP8 seeks to modify their effects and 'provide access to productive activities for individuals' (Fiji Parl 1980–81).

Thirdly, the plan reaffirms the need for greater self-reliance particularly by changing policies and attitudes. It states:

efforts will be concentrated upon increased community participation in development activities and decision-making; discouragement of reliance on non-essential imported goods and services; careful monitoring of Government assistance to ensure against reliance on hand-outs; increasing local people's ownership of assets and total investment using appropriate fiscal policies and institutional arrangements; careful screening of foreign investment proposals as to their social and economic benefits; assessment of the appropriateness of technologies imported and used and also greater local capacity to design and manufacture simple tools and implements; careful monitoring and evaluation of external assistance programmes especially their necessity and adaptability to local needs and conditions

(Fiji Parl 1980–81)

It is a wide-ranging package of recommendations with equity and social considerations at its heart and more closely approaches concepts of full development as opposed to growth than a simple development plan for economic growth would do. The plan also stresses the need for cultivating the feeling of national unity in a nation so divided into two distinctive major racial groups. The two races have existed in harmony over the years and a conflict would be disastrous; the plan advocates the greater understanding of each other's cultures and views and encourages positive steps to this end to be taken in the field of education, the press and the radio.

The many detailed recommendations contained in the plan are designed to achieve these major goals. Primary products will continue to play a major role in fuelling the engine of development with the sugar industry, which became much more productive in the late 1970s, being the lead component though agriculture is being diversified by developments in cocoa, coffee and tea plantations which will come into production during the period of DP9.

By far the most sophisticated of Fiji's development plans, DP8 has identified significant goals in the development process which, if achieved, will do much to ensure a steady transformation of Fiji's economy and society in a way which is acceptable to its peoples because they both participate in it and benefit from it. It is of interest that in a small country with a population of less than 700,000 so many of the dimensions of Third World development are present. It is to the country's credit that the significant problems have been identified and solutions to them approached in such a thoughtful and effective way.

TONGA

If Fiji illustrates the problems of small and remote countries, Tonga demonstrates them in a much more extreme form. Though not the smallest nation in the South Pacific, by any standards Tonga is a small country. Its islands number 150 and yet their total area is only 696 square kilometres. In 1981 the country's population was estimated at 98,000 living on 36 of the islands. Lying some 720 kilometres to the south east of Fiji, the Tongan islands form three main groups, Vava'u in the north, Ha'apai in the middle and Tongatapu in the south, stretching over 640 kilometres of the Pacific. Tongatapu is the largest island some 29 kilometres by 14 and a mere 256 square kilometres in extent. It carries the capital Nuku'alofa and 63 per cent of the total population.

Some islands are high and steep-sided volcanic islands, with a few being active volcanoes, but most Tongan islands are uplifted coral reefs on still submerged volcanic foundations and form low-lying flat, limestone islands. On the more numerous coralian islands the soils are of two types. The most significant is the soil, known in Polynesian as *kelefatu*, derived from volcanic ash overlying the limestone. It is the dominant soil on Tongatapu, Vava'u, 'Eua and many of the Ha'apai group, islands which in total support 90 per cent of the population. A deep, mature soil of moderate to high fertility it is texturally capable of intensive cultivation. The other soil, *tou'one* developed on coral sands behind the beaches is most widespread in the Ha'apai group and is far less productive. Together with the harvest of the sea, these soils constitute Tonga's only resources apart from her people.

The natural vegetation of Tonga has been completely cleared except on some of the steep-sided volcanic islands notably Tofua and Late and on 'Eua which is a high island (300 metres) where the volcanic rock is covered by limestone. On them tropical rain forest, of the kind found in Fiji, survives. The total area of this unmanaged forest is 9700 hectares. For the rest the land of the inhabited islands is cultivated with occasional patches of secondary scrubland. Coconut plantations cover wide areas under-cropped with a variety of other crops. Agriculture is central to Tonga's economy and culture. The coconut is both a traditional subsistence crop and the major export commodity. Bananas and tomatoes likewise contribute substantially to exports with vanilla as a minor item but the remainder of the agriculture effort is to produce subsistence crops. To the fore are the basic carbohydrate root crops taro (*colocasia* spp), yams (*dioscoria* spp), kumala, the sweet potato (*ipomaea batatas*) and cassava (*manoic* spp). Pawpaw (*carica papaya*), pineapples and water-melons are fruits commonly grown and small areas are devoted to maize and tobacco. A few cattle are kept for beef but the country is not self-sufficient in meat. The surrounding seas are rich in fish but the Tongans practise only inshore subsistence fishing. The Government operates a long-line fishing vessel bought in 1966 but this has not led to any great development in the harvesting of pelagic fish from the deep Pacific. An Australian concern runs the only commercial fishery venture and exports crayfish. Manufacturing is essentially at a cottage-industry level making bread, biscuits, soft drinks, soap, furniture and banana boxes. Tobacco is processed, fruit juices canned and vanilla cured. Most production is for the domestic market. A larger unit is the desiccated coconut factory opened in 1962 and operated for export by the Tonga Copra Board which handles the export of copra. The economy is thus simple, agriculturally-based and small in scale.

Despite the small size of its population, because of its limited and fragmented land area Tonga is faced with problems of population pressure which bears most upon the provision of opportunities for employment. In the period from 1956–66 the annual rate of population increase averaged 3.14 per cent. A vigorous family-planning campaign has contributed to a significant reduction in the rate of increase which is now down to 1.4 per cent. This fall has yet to relieve the pressures on land and employment. In a system of land-tenure which is peculiar to Tonga, all males over the age of sixteen are classified as tax-payers and as such are entitled to some 3.25 hectares of *api tukuhau*, or tax-land, which they can farm and so make their contribution to society (Maude 1973). Such has been the growth of population that the number of tax-payers now far exceeds that of tax-land allotments. In 1966, 59 per cent of entitled males were landless (Fiefia 1968). This situation has contributed to the movement of population, particularly of young people, to the largest island Tongatapu. There the capital Nuku'alofa, is seen to offer prospects of education, better services, a greater opportunity for wage-labour employment and is perceived as the national centre of economic and recreational activities. It is an interesting reflection on comparative values that a quiet and beautiful little town (15,685 in 1966) of leafy lanes, wooden houses set in gardens, a few shops, two hotels and a cinema, should be seen as a metropolitan attraction. This movement has relieved land pressure in some islands though it has affected it little in the Ha'apai group and, of course, increased it on Tongatapu. The landless can, and do, borrow land from relatives or rent it from others but this increases pressure rather than relieves it if small-holdings are sub-divided further. Opportunities for employment in industry, tourism, transport and public utilities and in government service are limited even in the capital and are insufficient to take up the surplus. In such a situation the provision of employment opportunities must be central to any development plan.

The ancient kingdom of Tonga which was a British Protectorate from 1900 to 1970 produced its first formal development plan in 1965 (Tonga Kingdom 1966). A modest venture in a small country it set out to address the problems of four main areas of concern. First it funded developments designed to enlarge and improve the country's agricultural output since the subsistence of a growing population and exports depended upon it. Rehabilitation plans were implemented for ageing coconut groves and the agricultural advisory services were enhanced. Second, it planned to improve both the physical and the social infrastructure in such a way both to facilitate economic development in an archipelagic community and to provide for a fuller life for the people of Tonga. Capital investments were made in airport facilities, the road network and wharves and jetties in the islands. Hospitals were built and child welfare schemes established. Education provision was enlarged particularly in the field of technical training. As the first and subsequent plans have indicated, the manpower of Tonga is insufficiently educated and trained to make substantial contributions in the professions or the technically skilled and semi-skilled activities. The Tonga Technical College has now catered for the latter while high level tertiary education is available in the University of the South Pacific in Fiji which is a federal university serving many of the Pacific's small island communities. The third problem faced was that of the balance of payments. The visible trade balance was in deficit and was offset by foreign aid largely from the United Kingdom which began in 1965, from tourism and to this end a modern 100-bed hotel was built in Nuku'alofa, and from the sale of stamps and coins to overseas collectors.

The expenditure upon social services in the first plan proved to be an effective use of capital and later plans have attempted to increase local production both in scale and variety so as to reduce the element of dependence on foreign aid. The emphasis was, naturally, upon agriculture and fisheries together with the stimulation of industries to process their products and, in a modest way, to allow a substitution for imports. For example, a saw-mill began to use Tongan timber to make banana boxes where previously imported wood had been used. Infrastructural investments continued to be focused upon transport improvements in part to stem the influx into Tongatapu by making the other islands less remote and therefore more able to participate in tourism. Airstrips were built and inter-island sea services increased.

An economy based on a small agricultural production is subject to the limitations of diminishing returns and a country so small, so little endowed with resources and so remote from other centres of economic activity, can have but limited opportunities for material advancement. Tonga's culture is rich, harmonious and sophisticated; it has a wholesomeness. But it is a culture whose equilibrium can be disturbed if its young people are unable to see a future of fulfilment before them. Tonga is no longer in a state of isolation from cultures other than those of its own Polynesia. The pace of life is leisurely and the environment idyllic but unemployment is a problem and idleness is neither leisurely nor idyllic. There is no easy solution. Emigration can provide some easing of population pressure if there are recipient countries available. A redistribution of population to the islands losing population is a formidable regional development task for it is counter to perception and preferences but it could make a limited contribution and investments have been directed to this end. Tonga has received substantial external aid and this must needs continue, not to relegate her to the position of a recipient of poor-relief but to enable her to fund developments which will make her more self-reliant. In the Developing World there are countries too small in resources to reach out for and attain the level of material affluence experienced by the large and rich nations. Tonga is such a country. There must be a middle-road which allows those poor in the material resources necessary for the technological society but who are rich in culture, to live in dignity and with self-respect.

12 Nigeria

'. . . wonder is packed every morning into the birth of an African day.
Heat and sweat and weariness come later . . .'

Elspeth Huxley
The Mottled Lizard 1962

Nigeria is the largest of African nations and with a population estimated at
87.6 millions in 1981, is the ninth most populous country in the world. This
African giant covers 923,768 square kilometres of territory and though some
of it presents environmental difficulties they are not of the severity experienced by her Saharan neighbours of Niger and Chad. Her resource base is
varied and, importantly, Nigeria possesses large reserves of oil. Yet
Nigeria's development path has been far from easy. Her problems and
experience exemplify many of the central issues in Third World development and demonstrate vividly the difficulties of translating development
models into practice. In particular Nigeria illustrates two facets of development, first that of the spatial dimension and the question of regional
development and second of effective sectoral investments.

Upon independence in 1960, Nigeria was an assemblage of lands and
peoples on the coast of West Africa demarcated by the boundaries of colonial parcellation. Her economy and political structure reflected both her pre-
colonial and colonial history, histories which have produced patterns significant today. It is important to stress two elementary geographical characteristics of Nigeria. First Nigeria has a coast and was thus accessible by sea
to Europeans from as early as the fifteenth century. Second, gradual but
pronounced changes in the environment take place from Nigeria's Guinea
coast on the Bight of Benin to her northern limits on the edge of the Sahara.
The climate becomes increasingly drier with a more seasonal and uncertain
rainfall ranging from over 2500 mm per year in the south to less than
500 mm in the north. Natural vegetation correspondingly changes from high
rain forest through the more open woodland of the Guinea Savanna forest
to grassland with trees and eventually passes into thorn scrub in the
Sahelian zone (Fig. 27).

Agricultural potential and practice likewise varies. A series of east-west
zones thus present contrasted environments and opportunities. The first
Europeans along Nigeria's coast sought slaves and ivory but later traders
came to know of, and barter for, the products of the interior. In West Africa
there developed two contact zones. One, the older, was along the Saharan

Figure 27 Nigeria: natural vegetation

edge where the contrasted environments of the desert and the more humid south come together and where a whole string of trading cities grew up. In Nigeria they included Zegzeg, now Zaria, Katsina, and, most important, Kano. This same contact zone traded products across the Sahara to the Mediterranean cultural area as well as east-west along the Sahelian edge. In the south the second contact zone was manifest in coastal towns and villages where the products of Europe were traded for the exotic commodities of tropical Africa. Between these two zones internal trade existed to some extent since within Nigeria's climatic range crops were of contrasting types.

The Portuguese made their first contact with the Nigerian coast in 1471 and were followed in turn by the English, French and Dutch. The early and notorious interest was in slaves but this traffic was totally abolished by all European nations, except the Spanish and Portuguese, in 1815. It was trade in ivory and palm-oil which claimed British interest in the Bight of Benin where towns like Calabar, Bonny and Brass grew up and prospered from the trade on this inhospitable coast much of it backed by the mangrove wastes of the Niger delta. Further west on its lagoonal site, the fishing village of Lagos also participated in trade, first as a slave port but later for the export of palm-oil and other products from the Yoruba country to its north. Since its contact with the interior was not restricted by deltaic mangrove swamps, Lagos came to be the increasing focus of trade.

THE COLONIAL EXPERIENCE

The British interest was essentially mercantile with trade penetration conducted through companies set up for the purpose. The first territorial annexation took place in 1862 when Britain acquired Lagos so as to secure it as a trading base. In 1884 Britain declared the Oil Rivers, that is the southern palm-oil producing country, a protectorate and by the end of the century exerted political control over southern Nigeria. After a series of military forays into the north to forestall the French moving south across the Sahara, the British government created three protectorates to govern the whole of what is essentially the Nigeria of today. Parts of Cameroon were transferred to Nigeria after the First World War. British colonial rule of a territory called Nigeria, the name was invented by Flora Shaw in an article in The Times newspaper in 1897, dates, therefore, from 1900. Lagos was made the capital in 1914. Nigeria's development throughout the twentieth century has been very much influenced by this colonial presence. A colonial power had implanted itself on the coast of West Africa primarily because of trading interests, had demarcated a territory over which it secured political and economic control and was able to promote a colonial form of development by infrastructural investment and the organization of production designed to this end. The structure and shape of Nigeria's economy for the next sixty years was being forged.

The British were concerned with the extraction of raw materials, mainly crops, with an initial concern with palm-oil from the wild trees of the oil-palm bush. The potential of Nigeria for the growth of cotton, groundnuts and cocoa was later developed together with the mining of tin from the deposits on the Jos Plateau. Areas which could produce these commodities received the economic stimulus of the British demand. They were linked to the coast by transport developments specifically designed to facilitate export. The construction of a railway from Lagos northwards was begun in 1898, reached the Niger at Jebba in 1909, Zaria in 1912 and the ancient northern city of Kano a short time later. Coal was discovered in 1913 near Enugu which was then joined to the new port, Port Harcourt, by rail in 1916. Tin from Jos left the plateau by a circuitous rail link to Zaria, now abandoned, but in 1927 Jos was connected directly to the Port Harcourt line (Fig. 28A). This rail network has proved to be important in establishing spatial patterns of development.

The companies handling the growing export trade and which enjoyed tax exemption until 1939, invested little in Nigeria, their activities being essentially extractive. Nigerian cotton went to Lancashire mills, groundnuts, palm-oil and cocoa to British and European factories and tin to British industry.

Figure 28 Nigeria (a) minerals (b) cash crops

193

By 1939 the United Africa Company, the largest involved, was itself handling over 40 per cent of Nigeria's export trade.

The British involvement in Nigeria has, however, a distinctive and significant feature. While tin mining was essentially in British hands, though there were a few small Nigerian operators, and while trade for export was overwhelmingly dominated by British companies, there was no British settlement, no taking over of agricultural land to produce export crops and no plantations. Agricultural production including that of export crops was left entirely in the hands of the village farmers. This meant that the demand stimulus of the export market was felt at the small farmer level. Agricultural systems did not change in any profound way and cash crops were incorporated in bush fallowing, but it did bring numbers of peasants into the cash economy who, though their purchasing power was low, themselves became a market for low-cost manufactured goods. In the Kano close-settled zone these developments stimulated intensification but, for the most part, since population pressure over much of Nigeria was low, the increase in demand created by the export market was met by extending the area under cultivation rather than by the intensification of inputs. Wider areas and more farmers thus became involved. The rail-lines were subsequently augmented by roads motorable in the dry season. These feeder-road networks further diffused production since they could reach and serve the extensive agricultural zones whereas railways were essentially the main arteries of transport linking them to the modern ports of Lagos and Port Harcourt. The former was the more important because it was established earlier, was the capital and terminated the most significant rail link to the cocoa, cotton and groundnut areas. Not only did these transport connections give the two ports growth-potential they also gave locational significance to towns upon them such as Kaduna, Zaria and Kano. Towns not linked like Sokoto, Katsina and Maiduguri stagnated and became Mobogunje's 'decadent cities' though Maiduguri was later stimulated by a rail connection after independence.

Axes of economic development began to be discernible along the transport arteries and was thus skewed or aligned by this particular situation. In it the peasant farmers were the major productive agents. A separate development such as that of Kenya, Rhodesia and Zambia with their white farmers did not take place. The cocooned economy of the foreign plantation was avoided and the road network and peasant production spread the developmental impact of the colonial cash economy widely. Some farmers, notably the cocoa growers with their lucrative crop, became commercial farmers, most grew cash crops along with their subsistence cultivations, some remained untouched. Prior to the discovery of mineral oil, the small independent farmers of independent Nigeria accounted for 70 per cent of her exports. In the early 1960s it was estimated that some 6 million persons depended upon the sale of groundnuts for their cash income. Cotton production grew rapidly after the Second World War. The collection of raw cotton was organized by a Cotton Marketing Board and the British Cotton Growers' Association which ran the ginneries. This central organization co-ordinated the production of the many farmers, supplied them with high-yielding cotton varieties and gave advice on cultivation techniques. A major industry of minor producers was thus created. Cocoa and rubber production was again associated with small holdings though there were a few larger plantations of rubber.

The colonial period saw the emergence of spatially specific export crop regions and, of course, of tin mining. The transport system stimulated the growth of towns along its routes. Overall, however, there was little marked differentiation in regional affluence though the South was demonstrating a greater awareness of European methods. Little had been invested which could create development in its full sense, the economy being extractive rather than constructive. Importantly that distinctive feature of the affluent societies of Western Europe, manufacturing industry, was but little developed until the 1950s. Mabogunje makes the point that it was the Mac-Pherson Constitution of 1951 which began the process of self-government which culminated in independence in 1960 (Mabogunje 1978). During this nine-year period the newly-established federal and regional legislative assemblies were able effectively to govern Nigeria and marked its economic transmutation from a colonial to a national economy. It is significant that by almost all economic measures, the economic progress of Nigeria mark-edly accelerated after 1951. In this period regional differences in economic opportunity began to appear. Manufacturing started to grow and was essen-tially an urban phenomenon. The transport network by giving a new centrality to towns on its routes influenced the spatial pattern of these developments.

There was, however, another spatial manifestation which was a product of Nigeria's history and has proved to be of a very special significance. It has raised dramatically the issue of regional development. The British deli-neation of that part of West Africa now called Nigeria encompassed a large number of distinctive tribes each having its own language, its own customs and its own territory (Fig. 29). Upon this tribal variety had been imposed the Islamic conquest of the early-nineteenth century when the Fulani horsemen in a *jihad*, or holy war, conquered and converted to Islam the greater part of the population of the northern two-thirds of Nigeria. The British contacts throughout the nineteenth century had been with the non-Islamic south which became more fully acquainted with European commer-cial organisation, production methods and transport. With the merchants had come the missionaries who converted the southern tribes to Christi-anity. Importantly, mission schools were established in many villages and rural towns. English was taught and with it came the European mind and European ideas of society and means of production. It was an education which equipped the young Nigerian more readily to participate in the process of modernization, to become a clerk or an artisan in the European

Figure 29 Nigeria: distribution of the main tribes

mode. The British did not occupy the North until the twentieth century and there was, by agreement with the emirates, no setting-up of missions and mission schools in Islamic areas. Islamic schools did not, understandably, teach English nor equip children for participation in the process of Europeanisation. These two factors, the longer duration of the British presence in the South and the exclusion of European forms of education from wide areas of the North contributed to significant differences in the ability of people to participate in modern economic and technological developments.

On the eve of independence, the South was coming to have the attributes of the 'core' and the North of the 'periphery'. Within this broad division there were exceptions. The major northern towns of Kaduna, Zaria and Kano, all on the railway, and Jos, the tin town, were centres of growth and industrial development. In the South, sizeable areas in the Niger delta and the remaining high forest were areas of relative backwardness. The country was still overwhelmingly agricultural and though farming was far from sophisticated, Nigeria could feed itself and crops were the major source of export revenue. Energy resources though largely undeveloped had considerable potential. Bituminous coal deposits around Enugu possessed reserves of 364 million tonnes, the largest in Africa north of the Equator though small by European standards (the Netherlands' reserves total 3764 million tonnes).

This coal fuelled Nigeria's railways until they were dieselized and fired the main thermal electricity stations in Lagos, Ibadan, Port Harcourt, Kano and Enugu itself (Simpson 1969, 1988). Large lignite deposits lay untouched to the north of the delta and hydro power was developed along the Jos Plateau's edge for use by the tin industry. Other resources were limited. Oolitic ironstones of the Kabba province were low quality ores. The high forest timber, though valuable, was not abundant while that of the Savannah woodland was of little value other than as woodfuel. The harnessing of these resources began before independence. Investigations into the development of the large hydroelectric potential of the Niger and Kaduna rivers began as early as 1953 though it was the independent Federal Government which passed the approving act in 1962 and work on the Kainji Dam began in 1964. Factories had been established in Kano and Kaduna in the North and in the capital, Lagos. A long and expensive search for oil was rewarded in the middle 1950s by the first commercial production by the Shell-BP company from a field in the delta. A grid network for electricity distribution was beginning in the urbanized south-west while the Kainji Dam Project on the Niger in the empty Middle Belt was of such magnitude that the establishment of a national electricity grid was essential.

The sum total of these developments meant that in the newly independent Nigeria a strong pattern of regional differentiation in terms of manufacturing industry, power supply and utilization and oil-based developments had emerged and was to influence all subsequent developments. In the period 1958–62 three-quarters of all manufacturing employment occurred in a belt across the most southern part of the country (Fig. 30B). Almost all the remainder was associated with the northern towns of Kaduna, Zaria and Kano, all on the main northern railway route. The proposals for electricity transmission developments by the mid-1960s reinforced both the east-west axis and the northern Lagos to Kano axis as foci of industrial and urban development (Fig. 28A). Since these spatial differences were identified with tribal distributions when tribal feelings of identity were strong, the coincidence of tribal distributions with levels of development took on a political significance. The new independent Nigeria of 1960 was faced not only with the development of its natural resources, the husbanding of its work force and the enlargement of its productive capacity in a manner which would initiate true development, but was confronted with the need to produce a distinctively Nigerian political economy. The hopes and aspirations of diverse peoples whose loyalties were first to tribe and region and only second to Nigeria, had to be encompassed within the new nation. It has proved a difficult task.

INDEPENDENT NIGERIA AND THE PROBLEMS OF POLITICAL ECONOMY

Nigeria inherited and retained the three regional governments of the pre-

A

SOKOTO

KANO

MAIDUGURI

KADUNA

JOS

IBADAN

LAGOS

CALABAR

PORT HARCOURT

0   200 Km

Factor scores in standard
deviation units

1.0 or more

0.99–0.30

0.29––0.30

– 0.31––0.70

increasing
spread

– 0.71 or less

B

KANO

ZARIA

KADUNA

JOS

ABEOKUTA   IBADAN

LAGOS

BENIN

ENUGU

PORT HARCOURT   CALABAR

0   200 Km

Area containing 76% of all
Manufacturing Employment
1958-62

independence period within a federal constitution. Each region had considerable economic autonomy and sought to promote its own development. Representation in the Federal parliament was proportional to population and attempts were made to falsify the population census of 1962 for political advantage and the census was abandoned. In 1963 a second census was carried out. Its results were disputed and subsequent analysis has revealed that it too was manipulated. None the less it remains the only accepted Nigerian census, and the size of Nigeria's population is extrapolated from it since that of 1973 was similarly rejected on grounds of falsification. Also in 1963 after a plebiscite, a fourth region, the Mid-West, was created to give identity to a group of peoples who felt distinct from the Yorubas, the majority tribe of the Western Region. These events give some indication of the political ferment in the new nation.

An uneasy alliance between the Northern People's Congress (NPC), the political party dominant in the Northern Region, and the National Council of Nigeria and the Cameroons (NCNC), that of the Eastern Region, formed the first federal government. This coalition broke up in 1964 and put the country in a state of political turmoil. It was out of the unstable political alliance of NPC and NCNC that Nigeria's first development plan was born in 1962. As its objective the plan put 'the achievement and maintenance of the highest possible rate of increase in the standard of living' (Nigeria Fed 1962). The goal was laudable but imprecise. The plan was to run until 1968 funded by a series of sectoral investments over half of which were to be in the public sector. Half the necessary finance was to be obtained abroad but oil production rose appreciably and its revenue gave promise for the future funding of Nigerian development. The plan set out and achieved major infrastructural investments in increasing the carrying capacity of the road network, in the establishment of more schools and four new universities and in the harnessing of hydro-power. Its targets in primary production and manufacturing were not reached.

In the event this first plan, unrelated to regional issues and with all the uncertainties of any initial plan, never ran its full course. The first of a long series of violent political events cut it short. In a coup organized by Ibo army officers, the Federal Prime Minister and those of the Northern and Western Regions were killed as were many senior Northern army commanders. When the coup was suppressed, General Ironsi, himself an Ibo, was asked to head a military government. It was January 1966 and parliamentary democracy had lasted less than six years. The new regime stressed the need for national unity. The people of northern Nigeria saw the change as a take-over by the Ibos not only of the nation but of their own Northern Region. They had already found themselves as second-class citizens in their own

Figure 30 Nigeria (a) diffusion of development (after Weinand 1973)
(b) manufacturing employment 1958–62

state where jobs requiring the skills and education they did not possess went to those from the South. Southerners were the office-workers, the artisans, the engineers and train-drivers; the Northerners were peasant farmers and labourers. Now they saw the Ibos coming to rule over them. In June 1966 the Northerners began to massacre the Ibos in their midst. In July Ironsi was killed and a young northerner, General Gowon, from a Christian minority tribe and hence regarded as impartial in the North-South clash, became the supreme military governor of Nigeria. In September a second massacre of Ibos occurred in every town throughout northern Nigeria and the Ibos in their thousands fled to their home areas in the south-east. The regional differentiation in development and the political divisions along regional and tribal lines had found expression in a national tragedy. No greater case could be put for the development of a political economy which embraced place and people.

Gowan, acutely aware of the need both for national unity and the regional and tribal expression of identity and participation, proclaimed in May 1967 that Nigeria's four regional states would be replaced by twelve (Fig. 31). The Ibos saw themselves identified with one small state, the East Central, essentially outside the oil-field areas. Ojukwu, the army officer who had become leader of the Ibos, proclaimed South East Nigeria as the separate nation of Biafra and in the same month the Nigerian civil war began. The war has been explained in terms of the dispute over Nigeria's new oil wealth but to explain Biafra's secession and the war to re-incorporate it in terms of a conflict over oil is too facile. It was more deeply rooted in the complexities of Nigeria's history, her polyglot composition, the political manoeuvrings within a new country and the manifest uneveness of opportunity amongst her people.

THE AFTERMATH OF WAR

The civil war, bitter and destructive, halted Nigerian progress and set back her achievements. In the aftermath of war the Second National Development Plan for 1970–74 was a plan of reconstruction as well as development. The twelve states proclaimed by Gowan in 1967 held, in theory at least, the prospect of more disaggregated regional development. The stress was, however, upon the restoration of national growth. The plan stated 'replacement of assets cannot be undertaken indiscriminately because they have been destroyed by war action. Damages need not be replaced at all or replaced in the form or place of the original asset. The crucial test for replacement is contribution to the growth of the national economy' (Nigerian Federal Republic 1970). The projects which were to be emphasized were those estimated to give 'the highest linkage with growth effects' (Nigerian Federal Republic 1970).

The emphasis in the plan was upon urban-located developments despite

Figure 31 Nigeria: the subdivision into States

the acknowledged problems of rural areas and the increasing drift to the towns. While the twelve states offered the prospect of a diffusion of development with their regional capitals acting as growth poles, this was at variance with the developed economic axes and as such was pitting the role of regional against national growth. According to the plan, regional disparities were to be reduced but it stated that this would not be pursued 'at the cost of stagnation in areas which are presumed to be relatively more developed. To do so would be to slow down the rate of development for the national economy as a whole' (Nigerian Federal Republic 1970). This understandable stress none the less served to reinforce the status quo. Investments implemented tend to persist and become permanent parts of the economic pattern and to emphasize regional differences as the colonial infrastructural legacy had done. The regional problem again emerged. People in the lessdeveloped areas could move to restore the spatial equilibrium but what if there are strong tribal identities and local allegiances which the civil war revealed only too cruelly? These issues and those of urban-rural polarisation were not tackled by the plan.

Weinand's work referring to conditions in the late 1960s demonstrates the spatial dimension of development in Nigeria and the extent of 'spread' and 'backwash' (Weinand 1973). Using a multivariate analysis he assembles characteristics which measure spread such as primary education, health services and road densities, since these were infrastructural developments, and characteristics such as numbers of banks, shops, telephones, vehicles, market activities which he regarded as indicating levels of economic activity. By the absence of the latter he measured 'backwash'. His 'spread' surface is shown in Fig. 30A and emphasises the core area of the South of Nigeria and the rapid diminution of its influence to the North with an enclave around the Jos tin centre. The sucking out or 'backwash' he found to be strongest in the immediate vicinity of the growth centres leaving the more distant areas untouched.

Nigeria's second development plan was born out of trauma. Time allowed some of the wounds of war to heal and the fountain of oil wealth was more than a salve, it gave Nigeria that element missing in so many developing countries, the wealth to finance her economy. It was a wealth further increased by the upsurge in oil prices brought about by OPEC of which Nigeria was a member. Here was a chance to transform Nigeria's status from that of a Third World nation into one of sophisticated advancement and self-sustaining growth. It was time rather than capital which was in short supply and the wise spending of oil money proved more difficult than its acquisition.

THE OIL BOOM AND THE THIRD NATIONAL PLAN

The second of Nigeria's plans had aimed to reduce regional disparities but did not provide the means. The third plan had the means and was designed within a framework of regional intent. Like its predecessors its passage was jolted by political events. The tiger of military coup let out of its cage in 1966 proved a difficult animal to recapture. Gowon was deposed in a bloodless coup in July 1975 and the third development plan was implemented by his successor Brigadier Murtala Muhammad. He created twenty states more closely to reflect local interests (Fig. 31B). It was proposed that Lagos should cease to be the capital and that a new capital be built at Abuja at the geographical centre of Nigeria and in the midst of the under-developed Middle Belt. These measures would help reduce the dominance of Lagos and the south and create a regional vehicle for the dissemination of development though Kaduna, Port Harcourt and Lagos were also to receive special federal aid. A new constitution was designed to accommodate the new government arrangements.

Nigeria's population increase was put at 2.5 per cent per annum and the new plan's objective was to increase GDP by 9 per cent per annum. Between 1960 and 1970 the growth rate in GDP had been 3.1 per cent per annum. The main thrust of the plan was industrialization in a 'big push' approach but with some balance. Oil revenues were no longer related to the producing states but put under federal control. They were to be used to develop oil-associated industries such as refining and petro-chemicals and to establish basic industries such as cement works, fertilizer plant, pulp and paper mills and iron and steel plant using the lean Kabba ore. This basic industrial development was considered necessary because, hitherto, Nigeria's manufacturing had consisted mainly of the assembling and processing of imported commodities for the domestic consumer goods market. The aim was to establish a broad industrial base with vertical and horizontal linkages and convert Nigeria into a secure self-sustaining industrial nation rather than one which, at great cost, was importing the appearance of modernization rather than creating the reality. While oil was exported refined oil products had to be imported because Nigeria's oil refinery capacity was insufficient to supply the nation's demand. Cement was imported and so too were fertilizers and iron and steel. Yet agriculture remained organizationally and technically backward though it employed 64 per cent of the country's labour force. It too was allocated investments including the implementation of major irrigation schemes. In other respects farming received but token attention with heavily subsidized fertilisers and insecticides and tractor-hire facilities made available when the rural economy in reality required a radical reshaping. The large and growing population placed demands on educational, medical and other social services. The Third National Plan encompassed all. In terms of its funding and range of objectives, it was the most ambitious plan ever to be launched in an African country and it was to be financed in its entirety by Nigerian resources and that meant oil.

The emphasis on basic infrastructural investments, necessary though they were, was characterized by high ICORs and slow returns so the impact could not be immediate. Meanwhile Nigeria continued to import manufactured consumer goods, components for assembly industries, raw materials and even food. Significantly her exports were of primary products rather than manufactures. The structure of her economy had not fundamentally changed despite the increase in manufacturing. Inflation rates rose from an annual average of 4 per cent from 1960–70 to one of 14.2 per cent in the following decade. It was an inflation created not only by home demand but also imported as the spiralling oil prices of the early 1970s increased the cost of goods from the industrial nations.

Muhammad had come to power amidst chaos, congested ports, corruption and a roaring inflation. The Third National Plan was intended to provide for a better organized and more productive future and, as Muhammad promised, for a return to an elected civilian government. But the tiger struck again and Muhammad was assassinated in 1976. His successor, General Obasanjo had the task of implementing the plan, the vulnerability of which soon became evident when a drop of oil prices in 1977–78 reduced Nigeria's earnings. A balance of payments crisis emerged and Obasanjo began to cut back the plan's investment programme. It was a warning but oil prices resumed their upward movement. In the election of 1979 a civilian government was returned to power with President Shagari at its head. But the questions still remained. Could investment and entrepreneurial skills create a stable self-sustaining economy before oil revenues ran out? Could the pull and influence of the major industrial centres, of which Lagos was by far the most important, be counter-balanced? Could the new regional capitals and federal capital disseminate development into the untouched stagnant hinterlands? Could these towns be given positive growth functions, functions which can be put to use, or would the capitals become mere bureaucratic replications? Could Nigeria manufacture industrial goods rather than import them in such large quantities and could she export manufactures? Could she reduce her great reliance on oil revenue? Could agriculture and rural life be given the stimulus to an acceptable change? Nigeria had the resources to feed her population and at a higher level of nutrition; could this be done in systems which would allow the farmer a fair return and enable him to participate in the new Nigeria and cease to be a poor follower-on? The second civilian government had as daunting a task as the first. In sum it was the problem of the efficient use of the great but finite oil wealth.

Under Shagari the building of Abuja was started and the twenty new states began functioning but the pressures which had led to their existence were still at work. Distinctive groups within each state wanted their own separate territory and representation believing that other groups dominated them, wanting a greater say in federal decision-making and, importantly, thinking that by separate status they would gain a bigger share of federal funds. The further sub-division of Nigeria would, however, produce such a fragmentation as to imperil the unity of the country and a still further replication of buildings and officials would be a woeful drain on resources. The country has proved to be far from healed of its war wounds and its spatial administration is still unsatisfactory.

Equally significant is the failure of Nigerian governments effectively to use oil revenue to restructure the economy. It was true of Gowon's and Muhammad's administrations despite the Third Plan and it was to be true of Shagari's. Oil which had accounted for 3 per cent of Government revenue in 1963 represented 80 per cent in 1982 and 90 per cent of the value of all Nigeria's exports. The role of this wealth in funding large scale imports under Gowon and Muhammad has been discussed. Shagari inherited the Third Plan and its aims but he also was heir to the financial and technical inefficiencies which had impeded the best laid of plans, the lack of adequate data to monitor allocations and progress, and the continuing inflow of imports while the infrastructural and basic investments took slow effect.

THE FOURTH NATIONAL PLAN AND THE GLUT OF OIL

In 1981 the fourth of Nigeria's national plans was announced. It was based on the assumption that oil would continue to fund the country's economic transformation and, like its predecessor, was ambitious. An annual growth rate of GDP of 7.2 per cent per year was predicted in which manufacturing, communications, electricity supply, water and other public utilities were to be the fastest growing components. Agriculture, having experienced a negative growth for so long, was planned for an increase in output of 4 per cent per year and, after transport, received the second highest allocation of funds in the public sector. In the private sector, manufacturing and construction were the lead components accounting for almost 50 per cent of investment while agriculture was put at 15.6 per cent. The plan did refer to the 'volatility of the international oil market' which might require a reassessment of investment priorities. In the event the slump in oil prices beginning in 1980 and falling, in real terms, to below those pertaining in 1970, threw Nigeria's fourth plan out of balance giving little prospects for its targets to be met and leaving unobtained fundamental objectives in her structural transformation. It appears unlikely that Abuja will be built on the scale originally envisaged. The high level of governmental infrastructural expenditure could only be sustained by those same high oil prices which had adversely affected so many developing countries. Nigeria began to borrow on the international market and her debt commitments rose significantly. The investment programme was cut back and this resulted in unemployment. Infrastructural programmes which had been completed such as roads, schools, universities, transmission lines and power stations all required maintenance and staffing. Major projects which made good, long-term economic sense had to be abandoned or at least indefinitely postponed. This situation can best be exemplified by the aborted project for natural gas.

Natural gas is a valuable source of energy but presents problems in its transport. Some 87 per cent of the world's natural gas is consumed in the country of its origin. Nigeria produces natural gas unavoidably with the oil she raises but has an insufficient industrial capacity to make use of it. The gas is flared off and a valuable resource wasted. In addition, substantial gas-only fields exist in the oil field area and remain unexploited because of the lack of a local market and the difficulty of transporting the gas to the industrial markets of Europe and north America. Encouraged by the upturn in oil prices in 1979 Nigeria established a consortium to build a plant for the liquification of natural gas so that it could be transported by refrigerated tanker. The plant was to be the largest in the world and costing US $10 billion required foreign participation. It would have enhanced Nigeria's resource wealth appreciably. The fall in oil prices subsequent to the consortium's establishment led to Nigeria withdrawing its financial support and the dissolution of the consortium in 1982. For Africa's largest country and one of the world's major oil producers the scheme was too costly. Moneys were, however, allocated for a pipeline system to carry previously flared gas to a new gas-fired electricity station. In 1983 Shagari's government was overthrown by yet another military coup.

Nigeria's development dream has yet to materialize. There have been gains in the twenty-five years since independence but many have been the products of the buying power of oil wealth. An efficient restructured economy has not emerged. Agriculture is in a sorry state. Whereas in 1960 the small farmer earned the bulk of Nigeria's exchange earnings and fed the country, some twenty years later the import of agricultural commodities had increased fourfold, agriculture has remained stagnant and the young and virile have increasingly migrated to the towns leaving the countryside with an ageing workforce. Between 1978 and 1981 the volume of agricultural production fell by 14 per cent. The output of palm-oil was down and Nigeria, once the second producer of cocoa in the world, now tails behind Ghana, Cote d'Ivoire and Brazil. Not only agriculture but the rural economy, as is so often the case, had been left neither understood nor cared for. In manufacturing there is as yet insufficient linkage between Nigeria's raw materials, basic industries, and intermediate and consumer goods manufactures. The emphasis is on textiles, soft drinks, soap, tobacco and servicing. There has been no significant development of manufacture for export even though manufacturing has increased at some 12 per cent per year since the mid 1970s.

Nigeria has not effectively broadened her production base, has grossly neglected her agriculture and has placed too much dependence on the one commodity of oil. She has yet to solve the issue of regional development and urban drift. There is a need to increase efficiency markedly at all levels and, if the new regime is to be believed, to stem the haemorrhage of bribery and corruption. It is a sad example of the difference between finance and productive capital.

Nigeria's development is yet to come and must come for it is a great country, a country with people undisciplined but throbbing with vitality, a violent society and yet one with a precious and living culture rather than one which is an anthropological relic. Nigeria still has abundant oil wealth even though it is diminished by current prices. She holds the prospects for take-off but has demonstrated the difficulties of developing quickly enough a capacity to absorb investment. The first twenty-five years of independent development have been uncertain, the next are crucial.

13 Zambia

'Given a period of peaceful development, Zambia has excellent prospects for economic growth, better than those of almost any other country in tropical Africa'

A T Grove
Africa South of the Sahara 1967

Zambia, the former Northern Rhodesia, became independent in 1964. Like Nigeria she had experienced over half a century of colonial rule but both the acquisition of the territory now Zambia and the nature of her colonial experience were different. Unlike Nigeria, Zambia without a coast is a land-locked state in the interior of central Africa and this location meant she remained one of the 'unknown' regions for a longer period. Explored by missionaries, notably Livingstone, there appeared little at first to attract economic exploitation and Britain was hesitant to embark upon an expensive venture with little prospect of reward. Indeed at one stage it appeared likely that the area would pass into the hands of the Portuguese. In the event it was the striding ambition of Cecil Rhodes to see the British present on African soil from the Cape to the Mediterranean which initiated a complex and often unsavoury, chain of events which led to much of what is now Zambia becoming part of the British Central African Protectorate (Hall 1965).

Having amassed a fortune in the diamond mines in Kimberley and augmented it by his involvement in the development of the gold deposits on the Witwatersrand, Rhodes who was Prime Minister of Cape Colony from 1890–96, obtained in 1888, a royal charter for the British South Africa Company which he founded. In effect this chartered company began to administer a sizeable proportion of south central Africa on behalf of the British Government. Rhodes, a complex man, was spurred on by a political ambition and a desire for wealth and saw his company as an instrument for the development of the riches he thought lay in this lightly populated and little known interior. He was to do this by extending the railway from the Cape Colony into what became Southern Rhodesia then named Southern Zambezia (Fig. 32A). He hoped to discover other gold deposits and to establish white settlers on suitable agricultural land. In the first he was disappointed, in the second he succeeded. The Company was permitted in 1891 to extend its activities north of the Zambezi into what is now Zambia. The frontiers of the territory had been drawn up in Europe as the King of the Belgians received the Congo, Portugal Angola and Mozambique and

Plates 31 and ***32*** **Decentralized development: manufacturing in the rural economy.**
A rural tractor factory in China; the process and the product.

Plates 33 and **34** **The newly-industrialised nations.**
The Jurong industrial estate, Singapore (below). Flatted factories in Hong Kong
(opposite).

Plates 35 and **36** **Dimensions of trade.**
The international dimension, the container terminal, Singapore (above). The domestic dimension, a periodic street market in a rural town, China. (below).

Plates 37 and **38** **Urban attraction.**
A main street in Singapore (above). A main street in Nuku'alofa, Tonga (below).

Plates 39 and **40 Townscapes in the Developing World.**
Vernacular domestic architecture, Zaria, northern Nigeria (above). Colonial
institutional architecture, Kuala Lumpur, Malaysia (below).

Plates 41 and **42 Educational contrasts.**
A traditional Hausa school, Zaria, northern Nigeria (above). Ahmadu Bello
University, Zaria, northern Nigeria (below).

Plates 43 and **44** **Natural beauty: the intangible but fragile resource.**
The river Kuei in the limestone country of Kwangsi Chuang province, South China
(above). Fijian shores: the peace of the South Pacific (below).

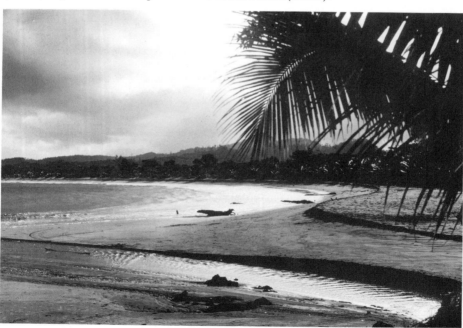

Germany Tanganika. Rhodes took the railway northwards. In 1902 lead and zinc deposits were discovered at Broken Hill (Kabwe) and the railway was taken to them in 1906. By 1909 it had reached Katanga in the Congo pedical where extensive copper ore-bodies had been discovered. Coal from the Wankie mine in Southern Rhodesia and mining equipment reached these Belgian Congo mines via the Rhodes railway from South Africa and the concentrated copper was brought out by the same means to Salisbury and then by rail to Beira. A major modern transport artery bisected Northern Zambezia from south to north and gathered its traffic almost entirely from outside the territory. But the area eventually to become Zambia was now connected to the outside world and this connection was to the south, to the lands south of the Zambezi increasingly being settled by European farmers, traders and mine-owners.

Lean copper oxide deposits had been worked sporadically in Northern Rhodesia in the early-twentieth century but proved uneconomic. In 1923 a major, rich, copper oxide ore-body was discovered at Nchanga near the Congo border. Deeper sulphide ores were identified in 1925 and by 1930 the copper potential of Northern Rhodesia was realized. This led to capital investment in mines and infrastructure on a large scale. Towns were built to house the workers drawn from an otherwise agricultural community. It was a development to have a lasting effect upon the space economy of the country which is now Zambia. The capital invested was foreign, so too was the ownership and management of the mining companies. The earnings of the mines financed the necessary social and physical infrastructure to support them, while those of the miners created a local market for food and consumer goods, but these impacts were highly focused. There was little development of associated industries and the copper, once refined, was exported out of the country to European and North American markets.

Later augmented by road, the railway from Livingstone in the south to the Katanga border was now busy with Rhodesian copper traffic. It became an axis of accessibility and development and was, and is, referred to as 'the line of rail' (Fig. 32B). The greater involvement of European interests from South Africa and Southern Rhodesia encouraged European settlement north of the Zambezi. Using African labour, European-owned farms were established on the better land and with access to the line of rail. The farms were large-scale commercial units producing crops for sale. There was now present not only European science and technology applied to the mining of copper at depths and on a scale unknown to the local population, but also Europeans in agriculture practising an implanted system which was both different and dominant and associated with a wealthier alien group. Digging for copper was one thing, farming African land was another. Since the majority of European settlers had moved in from Southern Rhodesia and South Africa, they brought with them attitudes to agricultural developments and local labour which had grown up to the South. The words of J. F. Hone written in 1909 illustrate these attitudes.

Figure 32 Zambia

It is generally recognized by those who have studied the difficulties which arise between black and white races, that the differences in character, temperament, intellect and humanity itself, are so well marked, so clearly defined, that never will it be possible for the two to blend and amalgamate into one . . . It must, however, be recognized that in industry, commerce, manual and domestic labour, white and black races will be indispensable to each other, the former as employers . . . the latter as labourers

(Hone 1909).

The British South Africa Company's charter ended in 1923. In a referendum taken in 1922 the white population of Southern Rhodesia had chosen not to become part of the Union of South Africa and the country was made a self-governing colony. Northern Rhodesia was administered by the Colonial Office in London through a Governor and Legislative Council (Hellen 1968). Between 1955 and 1965 Northern Rhodesia formed part of the Central African Federation of which the other members were Southern Rhodesia and Nyasaland, a liaison which came to an end when the latter country withdrew and became independent Malawi. It was a further episode in Zambia's history which has left its mark on her post-independence development. Not only were Zambian attitudes to Europeans coloured by their experience of European settlement but the status of the country was felt to have been relegated to that of up-country poor relation in the Federation. Under colonial rule the people of Northern Rhodesia were required to pay taxes to help in the administration of their country. This gave them an incentive to enter the cash economy. For farmers in the more remote areas this was difficult to achieve and increasing numbers sought work in the mines and in the towns and on European farms along the line of rail. All these developments heightened the contrast between the towns, importantly those of the copper belt and their economies, and the countryside with its villages and their economies. Development had been highly focused on the mining and export of copper, on the copper towns and the line of rail. Apart from the European commercial farms, the rest of this large country had hardly been touched by the twentieth century save where men had been lost to the mines.

THE BEGINNINGS OF DEVELOPMENT PLANNING

In the year following the collapse of the Confederation, Northern Rhodesia became independent, changed its name to Zambia and declared itself a republic. Within two years of independence the First National Development Plan was published to embrace the years from 1966–70 (Zambia 1966). In his foreword to the plan, President Kaunda clearly states his country's main goals and outlines his assessment of Zambia's colonial legacy.

We in Zambia are fortunate in that the problems of famine and disease are not present in the manner they appear in some over-populated countries. However, this does not mean that the problems of growth are in any way less urgent for us by comparison with the rest of the world, for Zambia, faced by the barrier erected by European domination south of the Zambezi, is in the front-line of independent African countries. So it behoves us to demonstrate, in no uncertain manner, our determination and ability to provide standards of living for our peoples which will bear comparison anywhere in the world. The structure which we inherited from the colonial era resulted in many situations which we have to put right: an education system which was so far below requirements that at the time of independence only a handful of people had anything like sufficient training to enable them to take their place in the service of Government; a transport system which is linked in a situation of subservience to Southern Africa and which has led to all the inconvenience and frustrating difficulties which have since been provoked by the unilateral declaration of independence of Rhodesia; a system whereby all our supplies of petrol and oil come to us by the southern route as did coal for our mining industry; our dependence on the jointly-owned Kariba Dam for our electricity; and trade so organized that we seem irrevocably linked to supply from Southern Africa not only for raw materials but for the ordinary consumer goods of everyday life. So it is that, by opening a frontal attack on these inherited structures – themselves a major factor in holding back the level of economic development in Zambia – the First National Development Plan lays the foundation not only of true economic independence but also of growing prosperity

(Zambia 1966).

This was clearly to be a development plan with a difference. Not only was it to lay foundations for a more productive nation it was also intended to secure the nation in a strategic sense. It highlights the vulnerability of a land-locked nation dependent for outside access upon lines of communication which traversed, and were therefore in the control of, other nations which, in Kaunda's view, were hostile not only to Zambia but to the peoples of Black Africa. The situation was made more dramatic by the declaration of unilateral independence by Rhodesia which was regarded as a further attempt at white domination of an African people and hence Kaunda's view of Zambia as a nation in the front-line. It is impossible to understand fully Zambia's approach to development unless the political-economic situation surrounding her emergence as an independent nation is appreciated.

President Kaunda chose to make special mention of several of the plan's proposals. First, he referred to the plans to increase both secondary school and university enrolment. Second, he mentioned the intention to complete a new rail and road link to Tanzania which would give access to the port of Dar-es-Salaam (Fig. 32). Third, he described the need to secure Zambia's supplies of energy. He stated that this was to be achieved by constructing an oil pipeline to Dar-es-Salaam, by developing Zambia's coal resources and by constructing a hydro-electric plant on the Kafue river. Both the transport and energy proposals represented large infrastructural investments and the President wrote of using both foreign loans and locally generated capital. Fourth, he made particular reference to the regional differentials and the urban-rural dichotomy in standards of living. The regionalization of economic activity with its social and economic implications is present in Zambia as in Nigeria and likewise it is a consequence of the period of colonial economic development and is manifest in the focus on the 'line of rail'. Kaunda put the regional development problem succinctly stating:

> a constant preoccupation of my Government is the disparity in the standard of living between the rural masses and the comparatively limited urban and industrial sector. Throughout this plan an effort has been made to localize investment and to increase to a maximum, consistent with their capacity of absorption, investment in the less-favoured provinces of the country. This does not mean we have neglected the growing industrial and urban centres of prosperity. A close examination of this plan will show that investment levels in the urban centres still outweigh those in their rural counterparts; for, while we must attempt to redress imbalance, we must at the same time invest in growth and it would be foolish to exclude the areas of prosperity which will themselves contribute directly or indirectly to raising the prosperity of neighbouring provinces.

Similar views were expressed in Nigeria's second development plan and point to the need to ensure a maximum return on investments in favoured localities in order to generate capital to fund the disadvantaged.

President Kaunda's identification of the central components in the Plan is important. It reveals his view, the view of an able and powerful leader, of the development situation as he sees it, with his emphasis and his interpretation of the mechanics of the plan. The plan itself spells out in great detail its many proposals and the allocation of sectoral investment. It identifies Zambia's resources and refers specifically to seven features — a stable government, a foreign exchange resource in the copper industry, the country's agricultural potential, the potential resources of hydro-electric power and the basic, though incomplete, transport network. Two human resources are mentioned, first the stable industrial and labour relations and second the people of Zambia themselves, 'desirous for self-improvement and hard work'. The unfavourable legacies to which Kaunda referred are discussed further in the plan. In particular it stresses the way in which the functioning of the Central Africa Federation was to Zambia's disadvantage. It states the copper revenues were used to fund developments in Southern

Rhodesia and that the Federation led not only to a greater extension of European settlement in Zambia but also to the European community and economy receiving first and favoured treatment with African development regarded as an associated ancillary development. For example, it claims that the quality of education services was higher for the Europeans and that the agricultural extension services provided for European farmers were funded by the Federation whereas the Africans received only locally-funded services. The organization of the railway network was centralised on Southern Rhodesia as were air services. In the joint venture of harnessing the Zambezi to generate electricity for the Federation, the power station at Kariba had been built on the Southern Rhodesian bank. To it was connected an extensive transmission grid supplying electricity to the Zambian copper belt and to the major urban centres of Southern Rhodesia. During the short life of the Federation this integrated development made sound economic sense. After Zambia's independence and with the unilateral declaration of independence in Southern Rhodesia under a white-dominated government, the location of the Kariba power station posed a potential threat to the power supply for Zambia's copper mines (Williams 1977). Power supplies were not interrupted but the need to secure them was regarded as a priority in the plan. A further legacy of the Federation was to be found in Zambia's limited manufacturing sector; most of the plants were branch plants of Southern Rhodesian establishments rather than independent or parent firms. The European farmers, some 700 in number, accounted for a £7.7 million production of cash crops, chiefly tobacco and maize, and of cattle, while 450,000 African farmers sold produce worth only £3.2 million. The European output was a positive contribution to Zambia's economy and was a reflection of the scale, modernity and organization of their farms and of their access to transport via the line of rail. It was, however, a situation which highlighted the low productivity of African farmers and the plan included measures designed to involve them more fully in the cash economy and to spread this involvement more widely throughout Zambia.

All these considerations of resources, legacy and regionalism were incorporated into the plan. Schemes to provide alternative connections between Zambia and the coast, to diversify the industrial sector and modernize the agriculture, to secure a wider and more varied raw material base and to develop energy supplies, were all presented in detail. It was felt that in her land-locked position Zambia must develop as far as possible a self-reliance and establish its own basic industries such as iron and steel, cement and fertilizer production upon which other developments could be founded. It was a philosophy of import-substitution within broad front-planning with the establishment of vertical and horizontal linkages. It was a first plan and like those of most other countries, it was ambitious and, perhaps, over optimistic. In its four year span it set itself the objective of increasing employment by 100,000 and of raising per capita output by over 50 per cent which, taking into account the increase in population, would require an increase in the GDP of 11 per cent per annum over the plan period. Two-thirds of investment was to be in the public sector which ranged across the whole field of economic, social and administrative activities and included very substantial infrastructural investments. Copper mining was left essentially funded by private finance.

In agriculture the intention was to reduce imports of food and move into a situation where agricultural products could be exported. A detailed specification of the extent to which self-sufficiency would be reached by the terminal stage of the plan in 1970 was constructed with a further five years allowed for the attainment of full self-sufficiency. By 1970 it was planned that supplies of maize, eggs and sugar should be adequate to meet home demand with occasional surpluses for export and that cotton should be at parity with demand. The biggest shortfalls despite developments within the Plan period were anticipated to be in livestock products, fruit and vegetables. In the rural and agricultural sector investment was to be made in roads, water supply and land conservation with a focus on land of high potential. Resettlement schemes were planned to move people from the overpopulated line of rail area into tsetse consolidation areas where the fly, which inhibits both settlement and cattle-keeping over wide areas of Zambia, had been eliminated. The resettlement of 12,000 families was envisaged. Additionally the establishment of co-operative farms, the provision of credit and the introduction of subsidies and grants were developments which it was hoped would both increase agricultural production and revitalize rural areas. It is significant that these agrarian proposals involved a considerable degree of state participation. There were to be state co-operatives, state dairy farms and beef ranches and state farms concentrating on crops with an export potential such as tobacco, citrus fruits, coffee, tea and sugar. Tractor mechanization schemes likewise signalled a centralized state involvement. In concert these proposals were expected to raise total agricultural production from K15 million in 1964 to K35 million in 1970. In addition to manufacturing and agricultural proposals, the plan paid some attention to tourism as a means of diversifying the resource base and earning exchange revenue essentially by building more hotel accommodation. The prospects for tourism were, however, limited. Though there are game parks with the attraction of African wild animals, the fauna is not as rich and varied as in Kenya and Tanzania. Over much of Zambia the natural landscape lacks the beauty of neighbouring Malawi. The major scenic attraction, and it is indeed one of the greatest natural spectacles in the world, is that of the Victoria Falls on the southern border with Zimbabwe. Here a new hotel was built to augment the old rest-house. The major activity by far in terms of the generation of revenue was, of course, copper mining. From this was to come much of the money to finance other developments. In this venture the government did not wish to interfere save to ensure that it was able fully to monitor the marketing and pricing policies of the mining companies. A special expert governmental unit was established for this purpose.

In the event many of the targets of this first development plan were not achieved and its terminal period was extended for a further year. Importantly it had effected little in the diminution of the imbalance between the central corridor, from the copper belt through the capital, Lusaka, to Livingstone in the south, and the rest of the country. Indeed, in a mere four years any shift could only have been small but the imbalance had actually increased. Of the total national investment, 69 per cent had been allocated to the central area because, as President Kaunda had stated, it was there that investment was most likely to be productive. In practice, however, this area had absorbed 82 per cent of investment with only 18 per cent entering developments spread throughout the rest of the country. In 1969 this central corridor contained 98 per cent of all manufacturing establishments. The legacy of colonial development was still deeply etched upon the economic geography of Zambia.

The regional imbalance remained, and still remains, to be resolved. Here, as in Nigeria, there is the regional issue of the built-in momentum of a more developed axis with, on the one hand, its economic advantages and investment rationale and on the other, the problems of disparate development leaving problem regions with tribal affinities. Greater infrastructural investment in these areas might link them into the developing economy but would inevitably give a slower return and in consequence retard the development of overall national progress in a directly economic sense.

During the plan's life the average annual growth in GDP was at 10.6 per cent per annum very near the planned level of 11.7 per cent but it was an average derived from marked oscillations which were essentially related to copper prices. So important is copper in the Zambian economy that Zambia was, and still is, almost a hostage to world copper prices. In 1969 world prices were high; in 1970 a mine disaster in Zambia cut back her production and GDP sank by a negative 3.1 per cent. Wage employment increased by 77,000 a considerable shortfall in the planned 100,000. Investment as a proportion of GDP increased and reached 28 per cent in 1970.

The poorest performance was on the agricultural front. Targets for crops were rarely met and output was often very low and income disparities between town and country increased. Only 79 per cent of the planned investment in agriculture was achieved. Farmers did not appear to respond, the co-operatives were unsuccessful, agencies such as the Marketing Boards performed badly, investment schemes were not fully implemented. In all explanations of this unsatisfactory situation the reason given has been the lack of trained manpower. A reading of the assessment of performance between 1966 and 1971 which is made in the Second National Plan, reveals the failure in agriculture and, indeed, in forestry. Energy, initiative and drive does not appear to have been stimulated by the government's efforts amongst the 70 per cent of Zambia's population who are agriculturalists.

In manufacturing, excluding copper mining and refining, although employment targets were not met, a number of significant new industrial units were established but the majority were in the copper belt of the north where a brick and tile factory, a lorry assembly plant, a tyre factory and a cement works were built. A brewery in Lusaka, the Zambian Sugar Corporation refinery, and the two large establishments at Kafue, a textile works and a fertilizer plant, were the other major installations overwhelmingly reinforcing the line of rail axis.

The achievement in infrastructural investment was considerable. Here were enterprises laying foundations for future development and increasing the country's economic security. The construction of the 600 MW hydro plant at Kafue was begun, with the first stage completed in 1972, and in 1969, the decision was taken to build a power station on the Zambian side of the Kariba dam (Williams 1977). The railway from Kapiri Mposhi in Zambia to Dar-es-Salaam was begun, financed by an interest-free loan from the Peoples Republic of China and built by 10,000 Chinese and 30,000 Zambian and Tanzanian labourers. It was completed in 1975. The oil pipeline through Tanzania was operative by 1968.

THE SECOND NATIONAL PLAN AND SUBSEQUENT DEVELOPMENTS

With the experience derived from the first plan its successor came to terms with economic reality and, in particular, attempted to address the problems created by the unreliability of copper earnings. By making cautious estimates of copper revenue and allowing for the inflation of the prices of imports, the plan assessed the likely limits on investment. The growth in population of 2.9 per cent per annum set the lower limits on developmental achievement if it were to solve the employment problem which, with the movement in to the line-of-rail axis with its towns, was becoming serious. The plan stated 'a simultaneous development of industry and agriculture is a basic pre-requisite for achieving optimal results in employment and a rise in living standards' (Zambia 1972).

In its broad objectives the plan gave agricultural production the highest priority again expressing the hope that it would achieve self-sufficiency, reduce imports, provide exports and produce raw materials for industry. The aim was to concentrate on the traditional farming community and convert it into one of commercial farming. Again the stated intent was to focus on areas of greatest potential. Manufacturing industry was to be further diversified and in the case of the giant copper industry, its processing functions were to be enlarged so as to increase value-added revenue. The so-called Tan-Zam railway was to be completed and feeder roads built to open up the countryside while new administrative and economic organisations were specifically instituted to stimulate rural development. The plan was thus much as before but characterized by a greater

217

realism. Throughout its life this plan's intent was beset by the problems south of the Zambezi and increasing hostility between Zambia and the new Rhodesia. Zambia became a base for thousands of freedom-fighters whom she had to support and her routeways to the south became increasingly vulnerable.

By the termination of the second planning period, much outlined in the first plan had still to be attained and the following plan carrying the period up until 1981, had to contend with the same issues of regional imbalance, of an inadequate and little changed agriculture, of not only a dependency upon copper revenue but of an inability to invest it effectively to stimulate a true development process. The inadequacies of rural opportunities and the illusion of the city continued to promote an influx into the towns notably the capital, Lusaka, which is now surrounded with wide areas of squatter settlement.

The plan continued the programme of rural road-building, agricultural marketing, credit and advisory work but in addition identified two particular initiatives. First there were to be set up specific agricultural projects which included tea plantations, a sugar scheme, a wheat project with Canadian aid and an irrigation project with German support. These were large-scale commercial schemes rather than developments involving the traditional farmer and in a sense could be regarded as State replications of the large-scale European-operated holdings. Secondly, a rural reconstruction programme was inaugurated. This aimed to give compulsory training in new agricultural techniques to a captive workforce namely the National Service Units of the Zambian army in which 42,000 could be trained each year. Both these initiatives represented a further direct involvement by central government in the economy but were not the only instances of the process. All land in Zambia was nationalized so that all farmers became tenants of the government. This included the large commercial farms operated by Europeans, a group which produced 70 per cent of all the beef, fruit, vegetables, milk and poultry sold in Zambia, as well as all the seed for maize improvement. In industry, the state-owned Industrial Development Corporation, INDECO, now dominated. The state also participated to a much greater extent in commerce and mining. The Zambia Industrial and Mining Corporation, ZIMCO, is the main holding company of many industries including all insurance companies, all building societies and all mining activities with the control of the two major copper mining companies in the hands of a subsidiary of ZIMCO. Newspapers and all cinemas have been nationalized and there are national energy, transport and hotels corporations. In part the movement to the overwhelming state dominance of the economy must be a product of the war-footing upon which Zambia was placed through the long years from Rhodesia's unilateral declaration of independence until the emergence of Zimbabwe but not wholly so. It must be seen by the government of President Kaunda as a means to solving Zambia's considerable development problems. It is a policy that can be questioned since it puts so great a burden upon limited administrative, economic and technical skills within the government's agencies and it tends to stifle and indeed prohibit, individual initiative.

Faced with increasing energy costs and higher prices of imported manufactures following the OPEC instituted increase in oil prices, Zambia's economic problems have been exacerbated and foreign indebtedness grown. In this situation, overseas aid has risen dramatically in importance. Between 1975 and 1980 it increased by 400 per cent (Wood and Smith 1984). A large proportion of this aid has gone to the funding of agricultural projects and has been augmented by overseas technical assistance. As Wood and Smith indicate, much of the location and direction of these aid projects is in the hands of the donors because Zambia is still deficient in appropriate provincial manpower and has no provincial planning centres. Although an Integrated Rural Development Programme (IRDP) has been established the donor countries tend to allocate their aid according to their perception of Zambia's needs. While the Swedes and Dutch act in accord with the IRDP and locate their projects so as to spread developments into the less developed areas and so reduce the rural-urban differentials, both the World Bank and EEC authorities advocate a concentration upon areas of highest and quickest returns with the goal as the maximisation of national output (Wood and Smith 1984). The latter approach is that adopted by Zambia in the early years of planning. The two approaches present the dilemma facing all regional development issues. They occur in countries as small as Fiji, as large as Nigeria and indeed, as will be discussed, underlie development issues in China, the world's largest nation. In Zambia the inadequacy of indigenous professional manpower to implement the IRDP and the opposing views taken by donor nations, means that an integrated, well-considered plan for rural development has yet to emerge. It is an issue central to the development dilemma and will be returned to in the concluding chapter of this book.

Zambia has, therefore, still to energize her agriculture and create a meaningful rural economy. It can be argued that unless she can do this, she cannot sustain an efficient industrial sector. Zambia's economy remains fragile, for all her copper wealth, and wealth it is despite the difficulties created by declining prices. As in Nigeria, Zambia's skewed economy raises the issues of precipitate urbanization, the neglect of the rural economy and the difficulties of investing productively. Between 1970 and 1980 Zambia's annual growth rate in her GDP averaged only 0.4 per cent. The average rate for the world's lower middle-income economies of which she is a member was 5.6 per cent. The solutions are not easy and throughout most of Zambia's independent history have been made more difficult by events beyond her borders. As yet her development process is still in its initial stages.

14 Sri Lanka

'. . . it is possible that – precisely because of popular awareness of economic problems – exaggerated or unreasonably hopeful expectations could be placed in the efficacy of planning in general, as well as in a particular planning exercise – such as the Five Year Plan – as the panacea for Sri Lanka's prevailing ills'

L A Wickremeratne
Sri Lanka (K M de Silva ed) 1977

Lanka, the Sinhalese name for the island so long referred to as Ceylon, the Taprobane of Ptolemy and 'the utmost Indian isle' of Milton, is a country of plantations and indigenous agriculture, yet a country which finds itself importing food. Being an island it was able spectacularly to eliminate the malarial mosquito which, in considerable measure, led to a massive increase in its population. It is a former colony. It is a country, therefore, with many of the ingredients of the Developing World and for this reason its development path is worthy of examination. But there are other features which make this Asian nation a significant case study of the realities of development planning in practice. One is the lasting imprint of its early history upon its human dimension. Another is the persistence of a parliamentary democracy which in so many former colonies has not survived the rigours of independent politics.

Three-quarters of Sri Lanka lies below 150 metres. Its northern half is lowland broken up by north-south ridges separating the drainage basins. The whole of this lowland surface is covered by a mantle of deeply weathered rock called *kabouk* which conceals much of the underlying solid rock so that its nature is imperfectly known. It would appear to be largely of ancient metamorphosed material and of low mineral-endowment. There is neither coal nor oil and little indication of any metalliferous or non-metalliferous deposits of consequence with but one exception. Rich deposits of gem-bearing gravels yielding rubies, sapphires, garnets, amethysts and opals have been worked over the centuries in the hills of the south-west around Ratnapura. Out of this lowland of hills and valleys rises abruptly a central core of mountains with plateaux of from 900 to 1400 metres and peaks rising from 2000 to 2400 metres. This area accounts for less than 10 per cent of Sri Lanka's area but it is an important tenth since it carries the tea plantations. The increase in altitude reduces the temperatures from the 27 °C which prevails throughout most of the year on the coast to a range of between 15 and 20 °C in the mountains and favours not only the growth of tea but also some temperate crops. Sri Lanka experiences both a south-west and a north-east monsoon with the former being the most significant of the two bringing heavy rains to the mountains and the south-west where everywhere precipitation exceeds 1300 mm and wide areas experience more than 2500 mm. To the north and east of the central highlands the south-west monsoon yields less than 500 mm and most of the rain comes from the weaker north-east monsoon from November to February. This area is referred to as the Dry Zone because of its high evapo-transpiration losses and the greater variability of the rains even though its rainfall exceeds 1300 mm. The Dry Zone extends over two thirds of Sri Lanka and is a significant physical component in development planning. The wet south-west and the central highlands are green throughout the year and, as the focus of commercial cropping, have the greatest density of road and rail networks and support the bulk of the population (Figs. 33, 34).

Upon independence Sri Lanka was a country with a marked internal contrast in environment and level of economic development and with a resource base which was almost entirely agricultural. There was another significant division and that was in ethnic composition. It too has had a bearing upon social and economic progress.

THE PEOPLES OF SRI LANKA

The aboriginal people of Sri Lanka, the Veddahs, may still survive in small numbers. Originally collectors and hunters they pre-date the other peoples of the island. In 1770 the Abbé Raquel described them thus: — 'The Bedas who were settled in the northern part of Ceylon . . . go almost naked and upon the whole their manners and government are the same with that of the Highlanders of Scotland'. By 1945 they had been reduced to a few thousand in the eastern dry zone. The great majority of Sri Lanka's population are of Aryan and Dravidian stock from the Indian sub-continent. It is necessary to review their early history since the consequences in population distribution and attitudes is so strongly present today. Prior to the fifth century BC there were Dravidians in Sri Lanka identical with those of South India. Towards the end of that century peoples of the Aryan stock characteristic of northern India, entered Sri Lanka intermarried with the Dravidians and became the forebears of the ethnic group described as Sinhalese. This race occupied the northern part of the island. They were a civilized, cultured people of high material and intellectual attainment, skilled in architecture, irrigation and agriculture. From the fifth to the third centuries BC a sophisticated civilization flourished in what is now the Dry Zone based on an intricate irrigation system. The Wet Zone with its rain forest was regarded as inhospitable peripheral territory. Buddhism was introduced around 300 BC and adopted by the Sinhalese, 90 per cent of whom are

221

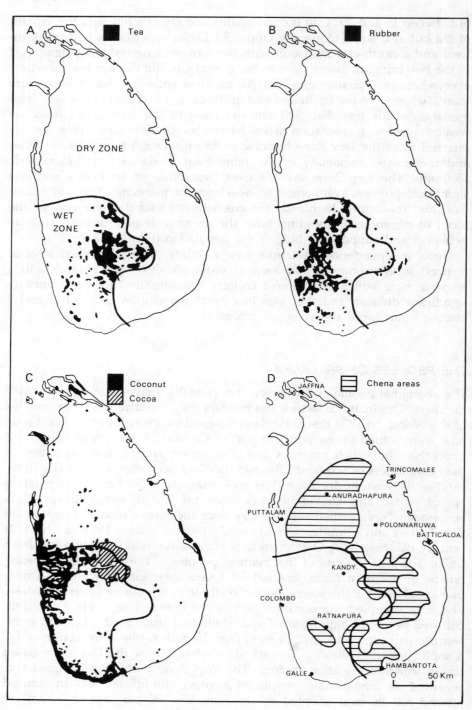

Buddhists to this day. Shortly after the advent of Buddhism, Dravidians from South India began to invade the island. They were referred to as Tamils because of their language and were Hindus of the Saivite cult. Religious, linguistic and cultural differences kept the two races apart and armed conflict followed. The civilization of the Sinhalese withstood these early assaults but from 300 AD to 1100 AD the history of Sri Lanka is one of repeated Tamil invasions. By the twelfth century AD the Sinhalese kingdoms were broken, their irrigation works abandoned and the Sinhalese retreated to the hills and forests of the South West. Jungle grew over the ruined cities of both Anaradhapura and Polannaruwa, destroyed in Tamil invasions, water stagnated in abandoned *tanks* and canals and malaria became rife. The Dry Zone which had once cradled the elegant Sinhalese kingdoms became known as *Wanni* — the wasteland. In the fifteenth century a strong Sinhalese king defeated the Tamils of the north and united Sri Lanka. In 1505 the Portuguese landed at the site of the present capital Columbo and the period of colonial interest and interference had begun.

THE COLONIAL PERIOD

The Portuguese interest was in spices, especially cinnamon, since Sri Lanka produced most of the world's supply. They were followed by the Dutch with their East India Company which had a similar interest in the spice trade. Having allied themselves with the Sinhalese, the Dutch fought the Portuguese and had displaced them by 1658. They introduced a legal system, organized the spice trade and built a series of forts to protect the ports; that at Galle survives almost intact. These early colonial exploits were essentially coastal and extractive. Their impact on Lanka its peoples and economy was slight. The British were to play a role of much greater and lasting consequence. They had two interests. First the British East India Company, like the Portuguese and Dutch, had an interest in the spice trade but secondly the British Government coveted Trincomalee Bay as a valuable naval base on the Bay of Bengal. The conflict in Europe between the Dutch and British in the eighteenth century gave Britain the excuse to fight and displace the Dutch in Ceylon. In 1796 the Dutch were ejected and the British established themselves securely in the coastal lowlands only to find themselves opposed by the King of Kandy in the central hills. He was defeated and deposed in 1815 though revolts continued into the mid-century. The British occupation was no longer simply a matter of spice trading ports. A governor was installed and a road network commenced. Between 1820 and 1834 Governor Barnes built some 650 kilometres of road producing a network which not only allowed the inland areas and central highlands to be controlled and subdued but also, importantly, to be opened up to eco-

Figure 33 Sri Lanka: cash crops; chena cultivation

nomic developments in a manner previously not possible. Colonialism as an economic system was being implemented.

Cinnamon, at first the only important export commodity, was cultivated on British-managed estates in the hot, wet south-west. The British monopoly was destroyed by competition from cinnamon exports originating in China, India and Java and the investors looked for other crops. Now accessible because of Barnes's roads, the central highlands provided both climatic and edaphic conditions suitable for coffee. Plantations grew apace until 1865 when the market collapsed. The surviving plantations emerged with better organisation and techniques so that by 1878 101,000 hectares were under coffee, a railway had reached into the interior mountains and Ceylon had 4800 kilometres of road. A colonial infrastructure was developing but unlike the situation in Nigeria it was characterized by a plantation economy in which the British were owners and managers. Ceylon became in international terms a one-crop export country. A rust disease began to attack the coffee plant in 1868 and by 1880 all plantations were infected and coffee was abandoned. The colony's chief resource of revenue had gone; coffee had provided the money for roads, railways, harbours and for the repair of old irrigation works. With coffee had also gone the livelihood of thousands of plantation workers. The solution was found in tea plantations. Previously less profitable than coffee, tea was planted extensively from 1884 and it was found that Ceylon's environment was ideal. It became a highly organized and scientifically based agricultural system with an associated curing industry exporting almost all its production to the United Kingdom and its Dominions and to the USA. Tea emerged as the most important single commercial activity in the country and by 1945 with 227,000 hectares under tea, about 17 per cent of the cultivated area, Ceylon produced 30 per cent of the world's tea. A highland wet zone crop, with 90 per cent grown at altitudes of over 600 metres, production became increasingly based on large estates as plantation ownership passed into the hands of the big tea companies which also operated the tea factories. Labour costs represented two-thirds of production costs. Both the Sinhalese and the Ceylon Tamils, who were peasant peoples working their own land, were uninterested in employment as hired plantation labourers so the labour force was recruited almost entirely from southern India. The Indian Tamils were regarded as quite distinct from the long-established Ceylon Tamils of the colony. Not all tea production was in European hands. Some estates were owned by Sinhalese and 12 per cent of tea was produced on small holdings but a classic plantation economy with foreign-owned and managed estates dominated Ceylon. Profits went to Britain though some revenue was retained to support the colonial administration of Ceylon and maintain the physical and social infrastructure.

Figure 34 Sri Lanka: population characteristics; relief

The growth of tea was augmented by other agricultural commercial ventures (Fig. 33). Rubber was introduced, and as the market for it grew in the twentieth century, extensive areas in the lowlands of the wet south west were planted with rubber, the area totalling 265,000 hectares by 1950. This lowland crop, unlike tea, came to occupy land used in shifting cultivation and again, unlike tea, was much more a crop of the Sinhalese with 50 per cent owned and managed by them. Cocoa was a further, but minor, export crop with similar environmental requirements to rubber but important only in that it offered a further diversification of cash cropping. Coconuts were more important in terms of area and Ceylonese involvement with less than 25 per cent being grown on European estates. Furthermore, they constituted an important subsistence crop providing food, oils, timber, fibre and alcohol with two-thirds of the product consumed in Ceylon. The cash economy for agricultural export was therefore one in which the Sinhalese and Ceylon Tamils were little involved either as owners or workers. The tea plantations were worked by temporary, imported hired labour. In other export crops the Ceylonese were essentially part-cash and part-subsistence farmers.

As an Asian hot and wet country, Ceylon is a land where rice is the staple of the diet. Paddy, or wet rice, is characteristic of the south west where two crops per year can be grown. A crop of the lowland and alluvial valley bottoms, it is also grown in impressive irrigation terraces on the western hill slopes. In the Dry Zone paddy was grown in large compact blocks of irrigated land where the ancient tanks or reservoirs had been restored and in a myriad of tiny plots near small more recent tanks. Malaria was rife and the population small and Dry Zone yields were characteristically low but throughout Ceylon inadequate manuring, poor seed, an absence of transplanting and a fragmentation of holdings were the hallmarks of a poor and undeveloped peasant agriculture. Ceylon imported half its rice needs. In addition to the permanent farming of paddy rice, throughout the Dry Zone and in the forested areas of the Wet Zone, shifting cultivation, *chena*, was practiced (Fig. 33). This extensive form of farming could persist because of the low population densities in the Dry Zone and made use of land which could not otherwise be used since it could not be irrigated with existing tank systems. The crops grown were hill rice, maize, millets and a range of minor crops without irrigation. As in other countries, the Government looked at the possibilities of improving *chena* systems by, for example, introducing rotation and by incorporating cash crops. More importantly, however, the Colonial Government in the 1930s implemented plans to regularize the settlement, the so-called colonization of these Dry Zone areas, giving tenure to settlers and financial grants in return for a requirement continuously to cultivate the land (Farmer 1950, 1957).

In an overwhelmingly agricultural colonial economy, manufacturing was hardly developed. The country had no significant raw materials other than the products of agriculture so its industrial plant consisted of tea-curing factories, rubber mills processing latex, and coconut-oil mills. Domestic consumer goods such as cloth and clothing were manufactured on a very small scale as were foodstuffs and beverages. The countryside was a place of small handicraft industries. In 1950 manufacturing accounted for four per cent of the Gross Domestic Product.

DEMOCRATIC INDEPENDENCE AND DEVELOPMENT PLANNING

When colonial rule came to an end in 1948, Ceylon possessed an economy the die for which had been cast in the colonial period. It lacked balance and diversification. Earning exchange revenue from a few primary products it was at risk from world price fluctuations. Its people were poor and their agriculture far from productive. Manufacturing was almost non-existent. A population, regarded as alien, of nearly one million Indians working the tea plantations had been brought in by the British. These were features which could be seen but the explosion of population had only just begun and was hardly appreciated let alone built into projections. The imprint, far older than British colonialism, of duality of race, religion and language was still clear; it too was to have a bearing on the shape of Ceylon's political economy.

The party which formed the first government was the moderate United National Party (UNP). It had at first little idea of structural planning. The view that there should be state control of basic industries was mooted, reflecting, perhaps, feelings that after the experience of colonialism it was necessary to be in control of the nation's destiny and that private enterprise was associated with foreign domination. The colonization of the Dry Zone initiated by the British was examined and plans were made for new major irrigation projects to further this aim particularly since malaria was in the process of eradication there. Like so many new governments of the period that of Ceylon had little previous experience to draw upon in identifying the problems and potentials of development or of techniques in resolving the one and developing the other. In 1952 the International Bank for Reconstruction and Development, the World Bank, sent a mission to Ceylon which made an analysis of the economic situation on behalf of the government (World Bank 1953). In 1954, drawing upon the findings of this report, the Government issued a six-year programme of investment (Ceylon Planning Secretariat 1955).

The World Bank's mission stated that the resource of agriculture must form the basis of development. It argued that Ceylon had the capital, derived from buoyant exports and external assets which had accrued during the Second World War and the Korean War, to fund a major development programme. Investment could be made in hydro-electric-irrigation projects on major rivers associated with peasant colonization (Farmer 1957). The World Bank viewed manufacturing as a means of diversifying the economy, of providing employment and of replacing imports by home-manufactures

227

but stressed that industrialization itself would not be able to solve the country's problems. The resource base was too weak and development was unlikely to take place at a rate which would provide sufficient employment. The Bank recommended that private enterprise be given every incentive to develop the manufacturing sector. Taking up these points the United National Party in its Six Year Programme laid emphasis upon agriculture and advocated a higher input into the land and improved methods of cultivation in the case of the export crops of tea, rubber and coconuts. It thus advocated a greater production without an extension of the cultivated area. In most cases, it was advice little needed and in the case of tea, the industry was already highly efficient and organized. In the case of food production, the programme aimed at reducing the large imports by increasing yields of rice from the paddy fields of the Wet Zone and by extending the area under paddy rice in the Dry Zone. This was to be achieved by restoring old irrigation tank systems and, as the World Bank had recommended, by constructing entirely new large scale irrigation schemes. It had been estimated that of the 243,000 hectares in the Dry Zone which were capable of being irrigated, half was not yet irrigated. The largest single scheme to emerge from this programme was the Gal Oya multi-purpose scheme though its beginnings pre-dated both the World Bank's report and the Six Year Programme. Designed to control floods on the Kala Oya, energize a 10 MW power station and irrigate 48,565 hectares, it involved a massive investment. It was calculated that it would be farmed by 125-150,000 persons which together with supporting services might total a population of 250,000. To settle such numbers was a big achievement but it is put in a truer development perspective when placed against a population expansion of 200,000 per year. In the case of manufacturing, the programme outlined plans of the development of small-scale private enterprises to operate import-substitute industries and larger scale schemes for the production of tyres and fertilizers. It was not envisaged that the state would operate large-scale industries at least as a permanent feature of the economy.

This first planning programme was imprecise and uncertain. It was formulated at a time when the prices for Ceylon's export products were high. When these dropped markedly in 1956 they reduced the income available for development and exposed the vulnerability of Ceylon's economy, dependent as it was upon the export of a few primary commodities. It was an experience shared by many developing countries. The situation was made more difficult by the increasing evidence of population expansion. An ever-growing mismatch between employment demand and employment opportunities was one manifestation. A second was the growing gap between food production and food need. The Government held rice prices low by subsidy but this itself drained away government resources. The population explosion hit hard at a goal, which to their great credit, has been held dear by all the governments of independent Sri Lanka no matter their political complexion. To the fore has always been put the provision of health and education facilities. It has undoubtedly contributed to the subsequent reduction in birth rates which make Sri Lanka anomalous in its income group (Ch. 4) but in its initiation its increasing costs, so directly related to population size, became a growing call upon central finances (Wickreme-ratne 1977). A leisurely patrician attitude could no longer be taken to national economic problems; they had become urgent and immediate.

In the second general election of 1952 the United National Party had been returned to power. In that of 1956 it was defeated and the Sri Lanka Freedom Party (SLFP), a left-of-centre party, came to power in a coalition which included a Marxist faction. Mr Bandaranaika, its leader, had courted the Sinhalese rural vote by stressing that the Sinhalese language and the Buddhist religion were the strength of the nation of Ceylon. The first UNP Government had enacted legislation determining citizenship which effectively removed it from almost all the Indian Tamils. As B. H. Farmer has described, throughout the post-independence period both Indian and Ceylon Tamils had experienced political and psychological pressure from the Sinhalese majority. The colonization of the Dry Zone had settled Sinhalese in areas which had previously been dominantly Tamil (Farmer 1963b). Matters were brought to a head when in April 1956 the newly-elected government introduced legislation which declared Sinhala to be the only national language. Not only did the Tamils see this as an attack on their culture and religion but also an exclusion from the economy if fluency in Sinhala was necessary. Rioting with a considerable loss of life occurred. A second violent outbreak took place in 1958 and a state of emergency declared. The ancient racial division was becoming manifest.

In 1959 the SLFP leader was assassinated and in the ensuing elections his widow Mrs Bandaranaika took over its leadership and led the party to a second victory in 1960. The Bandaranaika governments had come to power at a time of economic crisis and had as their goals the creation of a socialist society. A planning council had been set up in 1956 and a Ten Year Plan was published in 1959. It involved a massive investment by the state with an increasing control of basic resources. Government expenditure was to be cut over a wide range and taxation was to be increased. The aim was to increase production, become more self-reliant and reduce unemployment.

The Ten Year Plan was faced with one problem which no amount of political rhetoric could disperse. Ceylon's rapidly growing population was increasing the size of the development task as each year went by. The plan stated;

a sizeable proportion of the resources for investment have to be devoted to meeting the social needs of the rising population in the way of school buildings, houses, sanitation systems and so on. Investment in these fields compete with investments in directly productive spheres and result in an allocation of resources unsuited to the needs of

229

maximum growth. Such a maldistribution of resources would itself have a cumulative depressing effect on the level of future investment. Ceylon is clearly facing problems of this sort. Not only does the consumption need of a growing population tend to depress the rate of investment but the social services, education, health and housing themselves make increasing claims on investment resources

(Ceylon Planning Secretariat 1959).

The Government must have been sorely tempted to reduce this social provision and indeed contemplated it.

Over its ten year span 41 per cent of the total investment was to be devoted to the manufacturing sector compared with only 22.9 per cent to agriculture. It was a radical change from the less precisely defined UNP views with their agricultural emphasis. Sri Lanka was to be put on a new course. The plan was as costly as it was ambitious. It was hoped that foreign investment would facilitate this structural transformation of the economy into one with a much stronger manufacturing sector. The economic situation continued to deteriorate and in 1962 a Short Term Implementation Scheme was introduced. It had the same goals but was less ambitious and characterized by a realism sharpened by the lack of funds.

It could be questioned whether it was wise to put this elaborate industrial cart, constructed by the state, before an undernourished and infirm agricultural horse. Sri Lanka is but one of many countries to do so. The arguments underlying the proposed industrialization seemed reasonable. The vulnerability on the primary export market had been demonstrated; there was an obvious need to diversify the economy; there was a need to reduce the costs of imports which could be made at home; crucially there was an urgent need to provide employment. Industrialization seemed the answer but the real question was one of timing and balance. Despite the vagaries of the export market the earnings of tea, rubber and coconut products were essential to any investment programme and Mrs Bandaranaika's government was aware of this. It was, however, critical of the large-scale colonisation schemes of its predecessor with their high ICOR's and high costs of social provision. It felt that, instead, more attention should be focused upon the individual peasant farmer since much lower ICORs would pertain and results would be quicker. The industrial emphasis was to remain because of all its perceived virtues and its likewise quick returns. This experiment of Sri Lanka's first socialist government failed. As the situation deteriorated, massive import restrictions were imposed as import costs went up and as, in the face of a rising population, per capita GNP declined. Between 1960 and 1965 despite the emphasis given to it, the contribution of maufacturing to GNP rose by only 0.9 per cent. In the general election of 1965 the government was defeated.

The party to return to power was the centrist UNP which established a Ministry of Planning and Economic Affairs but was wary, in the light of its predecessor's experience, of over-ambitious plans and long-term planning proposals. Indeed, the new government was coming to power in conditions of economic crisis some seventeen years after independence when Ceylon's development plans appeared to have achieved little and her enlarged population was enjoying no improvement in their economic and social conditions. It was felt appropriate to institute a recovery programme to establish a securer basis upon which longer term programmes could be founded. This programme set itself a target of an annual growth in the economy of 5 per cent which would encompass the expansion in population and allow a slight increase in the per capita GNP. In establishing foundations it laid emphasis upon the agricultural sector in an attempt to improve the condition of the mass of the peasantry and to make more secure what was seen as the central strength of the economy, the export crops. Measures were taken to improve the output from the traditional paddy farms and irrigation schemes constructed to extend the area devoted to paddy rice. In addition encouragement was given to a diversification in food crops grown, such as potatoes and onions and other vegetable and fruit crops, not only for consumption on the farm but as cash crops for the urban markets. In the central hills and highlands, slopes on non-tea land were terraced to produce food crops favoured by the more temperate conditions. These steps served to reduce Ceylon's dependence upon food imports and together with the securing of the export crops were designed as a necessary prerequisite for subsequent industrial developments. The plan incorporated industrial funding but to an extent only two-thirds of that devoted to agriculture. The agricultural effort was repaid by increases in paddy rice production which rose by 16.5 per cent between 1965 and 1970 and by the successful establishment of intensive vegetable farming. Growth in per capita GNP more than offset the population increase and allowed a sizeable proportion of the population to experience an increase in real income. This progress was set back by events external to Ceylon. Prices for her exports of tea and rubber fell and, as the decade ended, the price of imported goods increased, a trend to be further accelerated in the early 1970s as oil prices escalated. Ceylon had no overseas assets with which to pay for her imports and had to resort to borrowing.

Both the SLFP and the UNP had followed policies which stressed Sinhalese paramountcy rather than a national unity and the feeling of isolation remained among the Tamils. It was not, however, this issue which brought down the UNP Government in the election of 1970 but the government's decision to reduce the ration of subsidized rice (Jeyaratnan Wilson 1977). Expenditure on social services had expanded to such an extent that it accounted for 35 per cent of government expenditure by 1963. The state had taken over the running of all schools in 1960 and added to its financial commitments. Since rice subsidies were the biggest call upon resources the Government, in the face of a deteriorating economy, cut the subsidy and lost the election. The new government, once again led by the SLFP with

Marxist support and calling itself the United Front Party, found itself in a further insurrection unrelated to the Tamil disputes. An extreme left wing group the Janatha Vimukthi Peramuna, or People's Liberation Front, drawing on the discontent of the educated unemployed, often of middle-class groups, attempted to install by force what they regarded as a true socialist society. Eventually crushed by the army, the insurrection damaged the prospects for economic development and delayed the development initiatives of the UFP.

A Five Year Plan was produced at the end of 1971 and set out the proposals for a socialist society and the involvement of the people in planning and the country's name was changed to Sri Lanka. In reality the plan was little different from that of the displaced UNP party. Again there were proposals to increase the output of the peasant farmer, extend the amount of irrigated land and to widen the agricultural export-base by extending it to pineapples, passion fruit and other crops including the revival of cocoa exports. As before the goal was to reduce export vulnerability and make Sri Lanka more self-sufficient in rice. Importantly, the Government turned its attention to land holding. As an ideological tenet it intended both to redistribute land-ownership more widely and to extend the degree of state ownership and control. Evidence existed which indicated that land tenure systems in Sri Lanka inhibited the increase in the productivity of peasant holdings of foods for home consumption. Tenurial forms, though several, were essentially variations in forms of share-cropping referred to in Sri Lanka as the *ande* system. The land-owners provided seed, draught animals, usually water-buffalo, and other inputs; the tenant provided the labour and turned over between 50 and 75 per cent of his harvest to the owner. Many land-owners had moved out of agriculture into other occupations but had retained their land as a source both of income and security. A symbiotic traditional relationship between landlord and tenant was common in many rural communities. Nor was it all bad. The Paddy Lands Act of the socialist government in 1958 had addressed the issue and converted shares into rents. It was unsuccessful. Rents were equated with half-shares of cropping and what had been a far from rigid relationship involving friendship and often kinship, became a commercial transaction.

In its Land Reform Act of 1972 the government did little to change the status of the peasant working the paddy land with its share-cropping systems since the Act did not apply to holdings of less than 10 hectares. Most paddy holdings were smaller. Private individuals were not allowed to own more than 20 hectares and any excess was to be redistributed. The holdings of public companies were exempt. In the event under this Act the state acquired waste and uncultivated land and land growing tea, rubber and coconuts. Of the order of 72 per cent of the tea area and 34 per cent of rubber was removed from private ownership. It was a drastic change but it did not lead to land redistribution since the government was aware of the dangers of fragmenting the large plantations; instead they became state plantations. Thus very little land was redistributed. It went to co-operatives, district authorities and the state while a further act set production norms on private land with the threat of confiscation if they were not met.

In its industrial section the plan laid emphasis on the provision of employment with a stress on labour-intensive methods to secure this goal. It was a policy with much to recommend it in the field of small-scale import-substitution industries but could not be implemented in industries such as steel, chemicals and cement if modern large-scale methods were to be used. The policy was that such industries would be state-owned and operated. In all these policies the issue of unemployment was ever present. Its political ideology put the government in difficulties. On the one hand it believed the state should own and administer as wide a section of the economy as possible. On the other, it was aware of its own inefficiencies and inabilities to do this effectively and that it therefore required the energy and initiative of private enterprise. Its policies had done much to stifle this enterprise. The plans of the United Front Government, whether wise or unwise, were not able to prove themselves. Buffetted by the rising prices of all imports subsequent to the OPEC rise in oil prices, Sri Lanka's economy became further burdened with indebtedness. With but one or two exceptions Sri Lanka had experienced an adverse balance of payments every year since 1957 and in some years before that. Import costs had gone up as prices had inflated. Import levels had increased both to service Sri Lanka's development proposals and supply her increasing population. Her educated population had developed an increasing awareness of higher levels of material well-being and its level of expectations increased accordingly. The UFP did not survive the next election nor indeed subsequent ones as the middle-of-the-road UNP party led by K. R. Jayewardene has proved itself more acceptable to the electorate.

Under Jayewardene the government has moved away from the restrictive, command economy of its socialist predecessor and endeavoured both to open up the country and broaden the basis of its economy. This had been attempted earlier but there were now three further dimensions of economic consequence. First, tourism has been encouraged on a scale far greater than ever before and with Sri Lanka able to offer much of attraction with its climate, dramatic scenery, ancient cities and modern temples, it has been a development of success earning extra exchange revenue. Second, there has developed a considerable temporary migration of Sri Lanka's workers to the Middle East and Singapore chiefly into the industrial and construction sectors in countries where wage-levels are much higher than in Sri Lanka. The remittances home are economically significant and the pressure of unemployment is eased a little. Third, and perhaps most significantly, the government of Mr Jayewardene has established an Industrial Export Zone north of Colombo. Foreign capital and expertise uses Sri Lanka's labour-producing goods not for the home market but for export. The zone is a significant source of industrial employment and has to-date been successful.

Throughout her post-colonial history Sri Lanka has maintained a parliamentary democracy. It has survived considerable oscillations in ideology, economic policy and economic depression. It has given a voice to the people of the nation and undoubtedly allowed the release of political tensions but its very oscillations have made the development path a far from straight one. So climacteric have been political events that it has been questioned in Sri Lanka itself as to whether democracy could survive. Resort has been made on several occasions to rule by decree in periods of disturbance and the issue of Tamil separatism which caught fire in the disturbances of 1983 is far from resolved. It alone could prejudice the recent and successful venture into tourism, and, indeed, has far wider consequences. The two communities have not yet been welded into one nation.

Progress there has been but it has been slow and meagre. Great achievements have been made in social provision with Sri Lanka's population as well educated as almost any country in Asia, and with her death rates and birth rates now commendably low. Though the economic situation in the mid-1980s is better than in the preceding thirty years, a self-sustaining economic development has, however, yet to emerge. The mesh of reality has proved an exacting filter of development ideas.

15 India

'There just does not seem to be any one panacea for India's vast socio-economic problems; the most to be hoped for is to be able to suggest means to ameliorate major areas of difficulty'

T Scarlett Epstein
South India, Yesterday, Today and Tomorrow 1973

By virtue of her size, the second most populous nation in the world, her history, the diversity of her environment and her rich and complex cultural heritage, India selects herself as a case study of development issues. The focus of this exemplification will be, however, upon the dimension of population. In Sri Lanka both the increase in population, its distribution and its ethnic plurality have been seen to be central to her development. So too it is in the case of her giant neighbour.

Not only is India the second largest nation with a population estimated as 690.2 millions in 1981, she is, if measured in per capita terms, one of the poorest. In 1981 the GNP per capita stood at US $260 putting India in the bottom half of the World Bank's category of low income countries. Amongst the industrial nations of the world in 1981 Switzerland topped the list with a per capita GNP of US$17,450. India's GDP rose by 3.4 per cent per annum between 1960 and 1970 and by 3.6 per cent per annum between 1970 and 1980. Her population increased at a rate of 2.3 per cent and 2.1 per cent in these same decades. The net result has been that over the years from 1960–81 the average annual rate of increase in per capita GDP has been only 1.4 per cent. This is a measure of the very slow rate of improvement of conditions for the Indian people. It would be low enough if it were equally distributed amongst them but it is not.

The burden of population growth discussed in earlier chapters is vividly exemplified in India and it is a growth which has two dimensions; the first is the rate of growth and its relationship to the rate of the expansion of production, and the second is the absolute size of the increase. On India's large population base small percentage increases yield very large numbers. In 1981 her population was 17 million larger than in 1980. Conversely a small percentage increase in per capita GDP applied to a low income base produces miniscule improvements in absolute terms. Most of this large population, 69 per cent in 1980, are agriculturalists. Only 13 per cent work in industry and the rest in the service occupations. By these basic parameters, India is a large, poor, agricultural country though these are generalisations which conceal both sophisticated industrial developments and more affluent sections of the population. Within any reasonably conceivable demographic trends, one dimension is certain, namely that India's population will continue to increase very considerably beyond its present size. In a speculative but reasoned projection, the World Bank estimates that India's population will reach 994 million by the end of the century, attain unity in the reproduction rate by 2020 AD, that is its fertility will be at replacement level, and that a stationary population may not be reached until 2115 AD when its size will be 1694 million. This latter figure is hypothetical but it gives some indication of the development problem faced by India. While in terms of plans for development this ultimate figure is of little significance since it is so far in the future, present plans and objectives have to be conceived and implemented in the context of population increases which are inevitable and large. The demographic transition in India is at the stage of maximum population increase. Death rates have fallen steeply from 22 per thousand in 1960 to 13 in 1981. Crude birth rates though falling from 44 in 1960 to 35 per cent in 1981 must fall much further before the transition is completed. The years between 1961 and 1981 added 251 million to India's population. India is thus having to cope with a population which has expanded by more than the total population of the United States (227.7 million) in a mere twenty years. The majority of this population is rural with only 22 per cent classified as living in towns in 1980, despite the existence of 36 cities of over half a million in size, and it is unevenly distributed. The greatest densities of population occur in the wide valleys of the Ganges and Bhramaputra rivers and on the coastal plains and deltas of peninsular India.

INDIA'S DEVELOPMENT PLANNING

Economic development involves raising the productivity of a country by more fully and efficiently utilizing its resources so that this eventually leads to a transformation in the economy with an associated and large increase in production. In the case of India this would involve transforming the economy from that of a mainly pre-industrial society, prior to independence, into an industrialized society in which further growth was self-sustaining, and from a situation of many localized economies into one of macro-regional economies within that of the nation. It could be argued that this increased material wealth would allow for social developments as this wealth was distributed, as it funded health, education and other social services, and as it raised the opportunities of a fuller life for all.

The independent India of 1947 set about planning for precisely such a social and economic development though the tragic upheavals of communal rioting and massacres which marked the separation of Hindu and Muslim communities set back the institution of formal plans. The first development plan appeared in 1951. It encapsulated, as have all subsequent plans, four

major goals, by the attainment of which it has been felt, a true and continuing development can be engendered. These objectives are, first, a high rate
of national growth to create material wealth for distribution and productive
reinvestment; second, to achieve over as wide a front as possible national
self-sufficiency and self-reliance so as to be free of any foreign dependency;
third, to provide employment for all and fourth, to reduce economic inequalities in the population, both being measures towards the attainment of
economic security, a fuller life and human dignity by India's millions. Many
development ideals would wish as much. The attainment of these goals has
been marked by difficulties, uncertainties, by qualified successes and
unqualified failures.

The plan of 1951 was followed by subsequent five-year plans. In none of
the plan periods has the planned growth been achieved. Most aimed at an
annual growth rate of at least 5 per cent. As has been noted, throughout
the 1960s and 70s the average rate was less than 3.6 per cent. When coupled
with the increase in population this rate of growth has been insufficient to
improve significantly standards of living. For many they have not improved
at all in the almost forty years since independence. Industrialization has
neither produced the wealth to distribute, nor generated sufficient employment to provide an adequate alternative to farming. Despite the Green
Revolution and other undoubted improvements in agricultural productivity
which led to average annual increases in production of 1.9 per cent between
1960 and 1970 and 2.6 per cent in the following decade, the increase in agricultural output was below that of population in the 1960s and but little
above it in the 1970s when the population increase averaged 2 per cent. Per
capita output has barely increased over the whole period. Certainly by the
early years of the 1980s, India had not achieved a self-sustaining and
vigorous economy.

During the long years of the British Raj, India's resources had been
developed for export and commodities such as tea and jute were shipped
to the European market. But India was a large country with a population,
even in the nineteenth century, much larger than that of any other British
colonial territory. It represented a large internal market in a country rich in
craft skills and traditional marketing systems. It was Indian initiative, and
not British, which led to the establishment of the first large-scale cotton
textile mills in India. The great Indian industrial entrepreneur Janshedjee
Tata set up India's first modern iron and steel plant at Jamshedpur in 1911.
Both the textile and steel industries catered for the home market and were,
in effect, import-substitution activities. The country remained, however,
overwhelmingly agricultural with three-quarters of its work force on the
land and a manufacturing base of craft and cottage industries rather than
one of blast furnaces and steam-driven looms and this situation pertained
after independence. Furthermore, the nature of Indian society, the beliefs,
customs and attitudes of the vast majority of its population were
unchanged. The caste system, associated as it is not only with status, but

the kind of work in which the members of a caste can participate, was strong and led to a social and economic inflexibility less conducive to change than in a less-codified society. Both before and after independence India was a country of contrasting variety. Large cities stood in a teeming countryside of peasant farmers. Industrial plant using sophisticated science-based techniques were at work alongside ancient crafts drawing upon inherited skills. Despite the changes of the last three to four decades much of this contrast remains and so too do the old values and beliefs. This mix makes it difficult to generalize about the Indian situation. Despite the modern industrial centres, the existence of the greater part of the population is little changed. It is rural, poor and under-nourished. The urban centres too are thronged with the poor after thirty years and more of economic forecasts and plans.

PLANS FOR DEVELOPMENT

In striving for self reliance India has followed the Soviet model of industrialization. She has placed, quite deliberately, an emphasis upon the basic capital goods industries and on the range of industries producing intermediate goods which represent a processing of the output of the basic industries and which in turn become the components and raw materials of end-product industries. Structures for vertical linkage were thus established. The process began in the first national plan covering 1951 to 1956. This plan was the least definitive and detailed of all India's plans almost as though it was to serve as a breathing space before coming to firm decisions. Its balanced projections were overthrown by the harvest failure of 1955–56 which raised food prices, led to food imports and upset the balance of payments. The insecurity of the agricultural base was thus early made apparent. In the second plan, with much more ambitious schemes for development, came definite proposals and here the Soviet model, emphasizing investments in basic heavy industries, began to emerge more strongly with state involvement more conspicuous. The emphasis on laying foundations for self-sufficiency meant that investment goods received priority over consumer goods and so the consumption of the general population was purposefully held in check. In the Draft Outline of the Fourth Five-Year Plan this industrial policy is described:

> A special feature of industrial development, especially since the commencement of the Second Plan in 1956–57 has been the growth of capacities in steel, aluminium, engineering, chemicals, fertilizers and petroleum products.
> Apart from these, large investments have been made in industries producing heavy electrical equipment, heavy foundry forge, heavy engineering machinery, heavy plates and vessels etc – all of which will become available in increasing quantities from now on
>
> (Indian Planning Comm ion 1966).

Within the industrial sector, investment allocations to these industries were 70 per cent in the Second Plan and 80 per cent in the Third Plan. In the Second Plan overall there was a shift away from agricultural investment. The Indian economists Bhagwati and Desai stated that this shift was vigorously debated at the time and in the event has proved to have retarded the country's economic development (Bhagwati and Desai 1970). The heavy industrial sector is not labour-intensive and the Second Plan looked to labour-intensive cottage industries both to meet consumer-goods needs and to provide employment. Neither it nor the subsequent Third Plan specifically addressed the issue of unemployment which was rising rapidly with the growth in population. The Second Plan's ambitious growth targets proved unrealistic and were not attained since the resources to carry out the proposals did not exist. Poor harvests again underlined the fragility of an economy which could not secure the food supply for its growing population. Food imports contributed to an adverse balance of trade and to foreign exchange problems. The planning period, beginning so optimistically with large projected investments, saw its close characterized by low levels of investment.

The Third Plan gave greater emphasis upon agricultural developments. It too was buffeted by unforeseen events. The wars with China on the Himalayan frontier, and with Pakistan in 1965, both diverted resources. The harvest failure of 1965–66, due to drought, was on a major scale requiring international aid. The balance of payments situation deteriorated still further and the rupee was devalued. A further bad harvest put millions of Indians at risk and they were only saved by international efforts. The Achilles heel of India's situation was once again dramatically revealed. All her investments, many not directed to agriculture, were not reducing this vulnerability to harvest failure which, when it occurred, not only faced millions with death and starvation but made nonsense of the careful calculations of India's development plans. Resources were not being harnessed to secure, even at a basic level, a large proportion of a population growing by the size of Australia each year. The chaos of the mid 1960s delayed the inauguration of the Fourth Plan until 1969. It was little different from its predecessors though it did enunciate a concern with social change and in the more equitable distribution of wealth.

R. H. Cassen, in his penetrating analysis of the travails of India's economic development, attributes the unsatisfactory situation which prevailed throughout the 1950s, 60s and 70s and which was characterized by slow industrial development and even slower agricultural process, to a number of interrelated factors (Cassen 1978). First, he argues that the emphasis upon heavy industry in the early plans produced an unbalanced industrial structure. To utilize heavy industrial products there must obviously be a demand for them on a scale to allow them to operate efficiently. This demand could only be generated if there were investments, sustained and continuing, in other sections of industry not only of the intermediary goods type but also the tertiary industries. The heavy industries producing boilers, generating equipment and machines for making tools, required lighter manufacturing activities to use them yet these other industries were deliberately subdued in early plans and so vertical integration was truncated. Secondly, the level of productivity in agriculture, since it produced not only food but industrial raw materials such as cotton, jute, sugar and oil seeds, had an important bearing upon the production levels of a range of significant industries. When agricultural output fell not only had food to be imported but also raw materials for industry or industrial capacity had to be left under-utilized and capital diverted from productive investment to an emergency deployment to stave off starvation. The goal of self-sufficiency meant that no manufactured consumer goods were imported so the main imported commodities were raw materials, oil, fertilizers and food. Cassen argues that the cost of these imports and the difficulties of ensuring a secure and regular supply, were increased by the bureaucratic inefficiencies of exchange and import controls. To these problems Cassen adds those of technical failures in electricity-transmission systems, of inefficiencies in the transport network so that goods arrived late and damaged, and the unreliability of power supplies because of hydro-electric shortfalls during drought. This dismal ensemble of lack of demand, foreign exchange shortages, technical unreliability and administrative inefficiency, together with labour problems in part associated with India's vibrant political scene, makes it small wonder that India's industrial expansion has been slow. Indeed, it is an even greater wonder that so much has been achieved. The lack of a balanced, broad-front and integrated approach which accords true importance to agriculture would seem to have limited India's development prospects.

The Fifth Plan designed to cover the period from 1976–81 played down the goal of self-sufficiency. Oil-field exploration and development within India had yielded sufficient production to ease the economic difficulties created by oil imports. Remittances from Indians overseas again made a minor but significant contribution. But in many ways, the fifth of India's plans was not a major diversion from the path marked by its predecessors and like them it did not address in any direct way the major problem, the size and growth of her population. As Cassen points out, some thirty years of investing in heavy, capital-intensive industry does not make provision for the employment of the many millions entering the labour market.

THE CASSEN ANALYSIS

The social and economic development of India since its independence has, despite many achievements, been diminished by the interrelated issues of population and agricultural production. They are not issues peculiar to India, indeed it can, and will, be contended that they are the most significant among the development issues facing developing countries. India has not achieved her third and fourth development aims of providing employment and reducing economic inequalities amongst her population.

R. H. Cassen has examined the interplay of population dynamics and economic development in India and this analysis will now be considered (Cassen 1978). The demographic transition referred to in Chapter 3 leads, in its second phase, to a marked increase in population as death rates fall while birth rates remain high. India's position is shown in Figs. 9A and 11B. Not only does the population increase but so too does the dependency ratio as more children survive and as old people live longer and so form a large proportion of the population which consumes but does not produce. Consumption thus goes up but not production and investments decrease as savings are diverted to support dependents. It takes place not only at family level but also at national level. A larger share of national investment has to be directed to providing social and health services and educational facilities for this enlarging dependent sector rather than be placed in productive investment. These processes can retard economic growth, though it could be that their effects are of too small a dimension in the overall economy to be of any significance. It could also be that, for some reason, population growth had the effect of stimulating the economy. Cassen refers to the work of Coale and Hoover who examined precisely this last issue in the Indian context and modelled alternative fertility situations (Coale and Hoover 1958). One postulated alternative compared a situation in which fertility rates fell by 50 per cent over a period of fifteen years with one in which they remained static. The analysis suggested that with the falling fertility rates GNP would be 17 per cent higher than in the alternative with static rates. In another projection, the number of consumers after fifty-five years of high fertility rates was calculated at twice that where fertility rates were lower while the output per consumer had halved leaving the GNP the same. Even when altering the model to allow for higher rates of productivity of capital and labour so that GNP grew faster with a bigger population, it was never enough to compensate for the growth in population. The evidence of Coale and Hoover, and indeed of other similar analyses, is that population growth does not stimulate an economy sufficiently to accommodate the growth.

Cassen argues that the Coale–Hoover calculation does depend upon the effect which the dependency burden has upon savings and investments. He points out that a large proportion of India's population simply do not have any savings to divert away from investment in order to support their children. It is only the better off who have savings to invest and they are the group characterized by smaller families and who are not contributing to high fertility rates. India's poorer families simply consume less per head as their families grow. There can be no diversion of savings which are non-existent. Secondly, Cassen comments that social investments in health and education are not wholly unproductive. In time, as was noted in Chapter 8, these can contribute to increases in production when circumstances are favourable. In

India's case they formed a relatively small item in total national investment so again it can be argued that increases in them are not of major significance. So while these twin ideas of the increasing dependency ratio drawing upon both private and public resources and diverting them from productive investment do play a part, Cassen's opinion is that things are not of the magnitude to change economic performance dramatically. Instead he argues that underlying India's problems is what he describes as the changing composition of the resource costs of producing basic consumption goods. By this he means changes in the relative significance of the resources which are used to produce a basic consumption good. The way in which the failures of the agricultural sector have affected the whole economy have been described. It is the agricultural sector to which Cassen is referring.

From independence into the early 1960s agricultural output was increased by both bringing more land into cultivation and by increasing, to some extent, output per hectare. Both activities demanded greater inputs of labour and were in large measure due to increases in labour intensity though use was made of fertilizers, better seeds, an extension of irrigation and improved techniques. The Green Revolution of the 1960s and early 1970s increased output considerably and was almost entirely due to yield rather than area increases. As was discussed in Chapter 5, the increased yields were consequent upon higher yielding seed varieties, the greater use of fertilizers and pump irrigation with pump engines for tube-wells. This agrarian development did absorb more labour but much more significantly it required capital. To be fully effective, fertilizer, irrigation equipment, pumps and bore-holes were essential in many areas. This involved investment in fertilizer factories and engineering plant. It involved the import of chemical raw materials to make the fertilizers, and indeed fertilizers themselves, and the purchase of foreign equipment. All these imports utilized exchange revenue. These developments saw agriculture becoming more dependent, more of a drain upon capital resources.

The sequence of events described represents a transformation of the input needs of agriculture. Initially output is increased by a greater input of labour, derived from the growing population, applied to the finite resource of land. This is subject to diminishing returns unless the effectiveness of the labour input and the responsive quality of the land base can be improved. To achieve this, technical innovations requiring more capital are needed. Cassen argues that this stage of a change-over in the kind of inputs required was reached in India in the 1960s. Investment which could have been productively invested elsewhere went into the agricultural sector and this was made necessary because the population was growing so rapidly and so much in absolute numbers. A slower growing population would have made this level of investment in agriculture less necessary and would have delayed the change-over from the labour-based to a technological-based input for a little longer. In economic terms the marginal cost of increasing food output had gone up. It is of course possible to postulate a situation where the ability to produce lifts the production curve above that of population (Chapter 8). The more rapid the increase in population in absolute and relative terms, the more difficult is the task of raising that curve. Cassen thus ties agricultural performance to population growth and demonstrates that the growing population by placing increasing demands on agriculture is causing investments to be diverted. It is not that investments should not be made in agriculture, indeed the evidence is, and this will be debated later, that insufficient investment and attention is paid to the rural sector, but that the primary, physiological needs of a vastly growing population prevent adequate attention to other developments. It is not therefore simply a matter of 'unproductive' investment going into schools, hospitals and social provisions on a larger scale than would be necessary with a smaller population, but of a restriction of the range of 'productive' investments by the need to cover the basic essential of food production. A Malthusian element is thus present in the Indian situation. The pressure on food supplies has meant pressure on the land which in turn has led to soil erosion and river siltation with an increased risk of flooding so that the very resource base itself is being diminished. There is a mismatch between India's population and resources she has harnessed to sustain it. As Sartaj Aziz has pointed out, the minimum size of land holding which is economically viable in India is between 3 and 5 hectares. If all the available land were redistributed on this basis, with owners who can afford a pair of bullocks to work the land with a few basic implements, there would still be 20 million rural families in India with no land whatsoever (Aziz 1978).

In India population growth and size appear to be retarding social and economic progress. In western Europe population increases during the demographic transition were never of the order experienced by India and furthermore took place at a time when manufacturing industry was much more labour intensive. India has been striving to reduce the size of families by widespread and rigorous family planning campaigns. Crude birth rates have decreased though at 35 in 1981, it is still high reflecting the absence of social and economic conditions conducive to smaller family sizes among the millions of her poor. She has not been able effectively to utilize her growing population, and hence growing labour force, in furthering the productive capacity of the nation. There is chronic overmanning as jobs are spread thinly amongst increasing numbers so that both income and living levels remain low. Savings are at too low a level to generate investment and new employment at rates commensurate with the ever-increasing labour pool. The millions on the land cannot move into other sectors where diminishing returns are less evident so that despite substantial developments in India's manufacturing sector, the proportion of the working population employed in agriculture has diminished very little since independence.

Even the relationship between education, values, economic priorities and family size which were discussed in Chapters 3 and 4, appear to be weak in India. Nor has education markedly influenced skills and productivity.

Cassen again attributes this to the sheer weight of numbers. The mass of young people has diluted the investment in education so that low standards are characteristic of education at all levels while the absence of employment opportunities for the educated have meant that the relationship of education and family size is barely discernible. Indeed millions of poor parents in India often withdraw their children from school in order to put them on to the jobs market. When poverty is severe and bellies empty, the rice bowl takes precedence over the blackboard.

THE CENTRAL IMPORTANCE OF THE RURAL SECTOR

For the reasons cited by Cassen, India's population size and growth appears to have placed limitations on her development progress which may explain her less than satisfactory attainment of the goals contained in her development plans. The distinguished Indian economist Raj Krishna while admitting the poor overall growth rate defends the industrialization emphasis and its stress upon the basic sectors and on import-substitution (Krishna 1980). He comments, however, that this policy has been much criticised in India and elsewhere because of its neglect of rural development and the supply of consumer goods and admits that, so far, the goals of full employment and an equitable distribution of income are far from being obtained. Indeed the effects of limitations on growth fall far from evenly on India's population. Percentage increases in average per capita GNP represent averages around large variations in India and in real terms small percentage increase on tiny incomes can mean very little. Unemployment and under-employment, both difficult to measure in India, appear on all the evidence available to be very substantial and that means poverty. It would seem that the condition of the poor in India has improved little if at all over the past three decades. The wealthier minority may have benefited from the aggregate growth in production which has taken place in India. Most other classes have benefited less while the growing agricultural population has continued to sub-divide land holdings and jobs as pressure increases on the precious land resource (Epstein 1973).

This rural scene, and this is not forgetting the poverty of the urban poor, is central to the whole problem of India's development. It must be when 69 per cent work on the land, when a vast population has to be fed and when food imports use capital and foreign exchange needed for other purposes. The national output of the major food grains has kept pace with total population increase but output per head shows no strong upward trend. It is therefore an output essentially based on labour input rather than radical changes in agricultural organization and methods. The latter have taken place only in restricted localities and are submerged in the immensity of peasant subsistence agriculture. It is not, however, solely a matter of national grain output. By itself this does not solve the problems of nutrition and poverty. Not only is food needed but the money to buy it. Raj Krishna refers to grain surpluses because of the lack of purchasing power of the poor (Krishna 1980). The landless of the rural areas, the jobless of the cities of India may be too poor to buy the food available.

Agriculture and the rural community requires a special focus of development initiatives in India. It is easy to recommend but difficult to implement in any circumstance. In India much effort has gone into programmes such as those characterizing the Green Revolution where, as was discussed in Chapter 5, the need for investment meant that the richer were differentiated from the poorer in their degree of participation in, and benefit from, the programme. Can a momentum for the improvement of agricultural production, rural-based industry and services, and rural infrastructures, be established and maintained in such a fashion as to benefit most and not a few? Can the quality of rural life be so improved that the socio-economic mechanisms which seem to lead to family planning come into play and begin to stem the flood of rural births and allow the emergence of wider horizons of a better life? A substantial increase in food output of 4 per cent per annum would achieve much though beyond its initial stages it would require technical injections. Associated with this would be the essential requirement to spread participation and benefits equitably so that increases in per capita incomes were not skewed. Secondly, in the non-agricultural sector an industrialization policy less focused on basic heavy industries and using appropriate labour-intensive techniques, would afford more employment, create demand for basic and intermediate products and so use their capacity more fully. It could not only substitute for imports but importantly enter the export market. The task is forbidding with 170 million or so new extra jobs being required by the end of the century. Additionally, manufacturing employment could be more rurally diffused in small towns to help provide employment for the rural landless and limit the further subdivision of holdings.

Without providing employment and alleviating poverty, India's movement through the demographic transition will be all the slower. It is a condition which increases the need for carefully organized family-planning programmes to be pursued rigorously but humanely but it also requires the creation of circumstances in which smaller families appear desirable. A way forward may be a greater focus upon policies designed to ensure a more secure and productive agricultural base, to create a more cohesive rural structure in which manufacturing as well as farming is incorporated, and which places the enlargement of employment opportunity as the pre-eminent goal.

India's problems in their magnitude represent some of the gravest in the Developing World. The country is large, is internally divided by many features in a complex of tongues, cultures and faiths. It is an amalgam which makes neither for easy government nor easy planning. Like Sri Lanka, India has retained a parliamentary democracy, a vessel which has not yet foundered despite the most testing of storms. Her Asian neighbour, China, has chosen another vehicle of government and a contrasted approach to economic and social development for a population which is even larger. This approach will be considered next.

16 China

'The mansions of princes and nobles all have new lords
And another generation wears the caps and robes of office'

Li Po (699–762 AD)
Autumn Meditation

The development path chosen by China has a significance beyond that of any other country in the Developing World. Her size alone with her 992 million representing 22 per cent of the total world population, contributes to that distinction. Of even greater significance is the uniqueness of her approach to development problems. It is an approach which had sought to transform not only her economy but the whole structure of her society. From a country which has suffered the occupation of an aggressive and destructive foreign power, Japan, and had been torn by a bitter civil war, from a country characterized by corruption, chaos and poverty, China has converted herself into an orderly, organized nation of pride and purpose. Her development path has not been a straight one, nor has her progress been smooth and uninterrupted. China remains a poor country, yet her achievements have been great. It could be argued that they are without equal in the Developing World. But it has been a success dearly bought. The price has been the near total loss of freedom by the people of China for three decades.

In the complex interaction of China's planning strategies, one aspect stands out, it is the attention paid to the countryside with its farms, villages and country towns. It has been a concern which has not only embraced agricultural production but the whole rural economy and with it the issue of the industrial-agricultural relationship, the urban-rural dichotomy and the rural to urban drift. It is precisely in this ensemble of issues that least success has been achieved in most developing countries. The failure to maintain adequate agricultural productivity, to give a self-sustaining vitality to rural areas, to stem the flood of cityward migrants, has underlain the problems of so many developing countries. While the Chinese have held to this concern, their approach to it has evolved from experimentation. Alternative strategies have been tried and the final solution, successful though it has been in terms of its own objectives, is proving itself to be but a stage in an unending process of social and economic evolution.

Central to all developments from the founding of the People's Republic in 1949 until his death in 1976, was Mao Tse Tung. The reputation of Mao and the esteem in which he was held stood above the internal intrigues and strife of the new republic. A dominant personality and a great thinker, in Mao were combined the role of spiritual leader and political philosopher. Though he created a totalitarian state he felt strongly that the state must not be an entity separated from the people. He saw an increase in national production as a central task but not as one designed solely to create revenue for the state. In part this was, no doubt, a reaction against the policies whereby the state throughout China's long imperial history, had kept alive its political and administrative functions and huge bureaucracy by heavy taxation. If people were the state then, in Mao's view, the benefits of increased production should go to them. Equity was another, and obvious, goal of his new People's Republic. Sustained by a Marxist-Leninist ideology he none the less considered entrepreneurship to be important but the entrepreneurial roles were to be taken by groups rather than individuals. He believed that China could achieve the material levels of well-being experienced by the Industrialized World and that this could be attained quickly. Within his ideological pronouncements were often strong pragmatic undertones.

The new China, heir to one of the richest and oldest cultures in the world, was as complex and paradoxical a society as any which had preceded it. In it were contained both spiritual and ideological components; it aimed for equity yet it was characterized by a party elite and personality leadership; it had grown out of revolution but required stability; it despised the bureaucracy of the Mandarins yet created one of its own; it required expertize yet denied the existence of the expert; it clung to the anchorage of an alien ideology from which its indigenous pragmatism was continually trying to free it. The enormous and forbidding reality with which it was faced was that of providing over 500 million people with food, shelter, health, employment and, most importantly, hope. Politics were indeed tempered by pragmatism.

In facing this challenge one of the most striking features of China's approach has been her recognition of the importance of psychological conditioning. By a combination of devices both loud and brash, muted and subtle, the thoughts and energies of the Chinese people have been harnessed to the radical transformation of China's society and economy. The manifestations of religious beliefs, competitors with the new ideology for hearts and minds, have been suppressed and temples turned into museums, factories and grain stores. The reception of external radio transmissions was prevented and the availability of foreign literature restricted. Travel outside China became impossible. Levels of expectations could thus be confined to circumstances within China and the population kept ignorant of alternative systems and their levels of attainment. The bad conditions of pre-revolutionary China were kept alive in the minds of the young who had never known them, by displays of photographs, models and artefacts in museums on housing estates even twenty five years after the Revolution. It was seen as essential that the young should have some measure of the progress which had been made if the revolutionary fervour was to be kept alive. Commercial advertisements were totally absent; in their place were quotations from Marx, Lenin and Engels, exhortations to work and sustain the Revolution and, everywhere, the picture of Chairman Mao. The great aesthetic legacies of China's past, amongst the finest artistic achievements in the world, were not rejected but took their place in the new order. They gave to it a sense of belonging and continuity and nourished a feeling of national pride in the great civilization to which the people of China are heirs. This astute awareness of the need to control minds if events were to be controlled, produced a disciplined, patriotic, enthusiastic and largely compliant populace.

THE EMERGENCE OF MODELS OF DEVELOPMENT

In 1948 China was a wide expanse of agricultural peasantry. The distribution of the population was in large measure topographic and climatic, densely packed in river valleys and on the coastal plains, thinly spaced in the mountains of this mountainous country and sparse to almost non-existent in the high arid interior of central Asia. Modern industrial installations were located in a few large, and mainly coastal, cities. Many had been established in the 'treaty ports' set up by European powers in the nineteenth century. Private land-ownership, with landlord and tenant systems, characterized a countryside in which craft industries were scattered throughout villages and the rural towns. A complex system of indigenous marketing at local and regional scale had developed over the centuries to handle internal trade. China's foreign trade had never been very large but that which had grown up in the nineteenth century was very much in foreign hands. The Chinese Communist Party realized that only a massive reorganization of the whole country could transform it into the socialist society of the People's Republic. It began by transferring to the state all means of production. In the industrial sector, the state requisition of the large, relatively modern manufacturing units seemed obvious and simple. Agriculture and the countryside with its millions of small landowners and peasants presented an entirely different and more difficult problem. Clearly both major sectors were essential to China's development aspirations, both needed to be encompassed within the socialist beliefs of state ownership and management and the goal of equity, and both needed revitalization and development if the dreams of enough for all were to be realized. The problem was urgent since China's population was growing apace and the momentum of the revolution could be lost.

The only model of development which was at hand in a Marxist state in 1949 was that of the Soviet Union. Ideologically the two nations appeared to have much in common. The Soviet Union had not entered the war against Japan but had been an ally of those who had. Mao's rejection of the old society and his endeavour to create a socialist state in China led him to base his initial experiment in development upon the Soviet model. In the USSR the economy had been developed on the basis of a concentration on heavy industry on the one hand and the collectivisation of agriculture on the other. A policy of rapid incremental growth especially in capital-intensive industry had taken precedence over agricultural investment. Mao's China followed suit.

The first Chinese planning period from 1953–57 attempted to organize the structures necessary for subsequent economic development and the inevitable socialist bureaucracies were constructed. The Soviet balance between agriculture and industry was, it could be argued, less suitable for China's socialism and its advocacy of heavy-industry investment questioned, but Soviet policies were adopted and heavy industrial plant from Russia were transported to China and set up with the help of Soviet technicians. These large units were established in the major cities and functioned at a scale which their scale-economies required. They thus reinforced the pre-existing concentration of manufacturing and they made large demands on available capital.

In assuming control of the land, the Government encouraged the formation of mutual aid teams which were groupings of six to ten families to work the land jointly. By 1952 the process had incorporated approximately 40 per cent of rural households. It was the initial and elementary way of accommodating the transfer from private to public land ownership but the teams were essentially private rather than state enterprises. Out of these simple groupings co-operatives were established. These in turn were reassembled into large more elaborate co-operatives where the individual was subordinate to collective action and where the co-operative produced to meet targets set by the state. By 1957, it has been estimated, 95 per cent of Chinese peasants were working on these large co-operatives. This sequence of events, briefly stated, marked the transition from private ownership, individual enterprise and hired labour in a market economy to a collective organisation in a command economy. These agricultural developments were, in part, a corollary of those in manufacturing. The state controlled all forms of agricultural production. Since manufacturing was to receive the major emphasis in investment because it could more effectively use it, the reorganisation of agriculture had to be carried out in such a way as to minimize its capital requirements. Since the state controlled the cost of all inputs and the price of products, it could manipulate the agricultural economy so as to extract a 'surplus', a revenue, from it which could then be reinvested wherever the state chose and not necessarily in agriculture.

The confiscation of land and the dispossession of landlords, the rupture of market relationships and the reorganization of agrarian labour and production, all made for deliberate and drastic changes in social and economic systems which had evolved over the centuries. The past was to be broken, agrarian conservatism shaken and, with the aid of the cadres, salaried party officials drafted into the countryside, the world of the Chinese peasant opened to new developments. This initial reorganization of agriculture did increase production and at first led to a rise in the income of agricultural workers. This latter improvement was, however, the product of the more equitable distribution of income rather than as a result of increased output. As the state continued to manipulate the agricultural economy, increasingly its surplus was siphoned off to fund industry and the prospects of greater affluence for the peasants receded. The huge central bureaucracy attempting to manage the co-operatives on a national scale was far too big, too remote, too inexpert in agronomics to be able to articulate policies sensitive to the wide range of environmental conditions which are present in China. The contact with the land was too insulated from reality. It was a manifestation of the now familiar problem of over-centralized state control. These agrarian developments did achieve a widespread parity in agrarian incomes and they did not result in agricultural disaster such as that which the Soviet Union had experienced in its enforced collectivisation in the late 1920s but they were not a satisfactory solution to China's agricultural problems.

The large industrial units proved more easy to co-ordinate and manage and industrial production of basic products rose appreciably. During this first Five Year Plan with manufacturing growing more rapidly than agriculture and with industrial investment being city-based, the contrast between countryside and town was being heightened as growing industrialization was accompanied by growing urbanization. The familiar pattern of over-industrial emphasis, of core and periphery, of backward agriculture and forward industry, of change in the town and stagnation in the countryside, was beginning to appear in China. This was taking place despite the agricultural reorganization. As China's population continued to increase rapidly and become more urban-based so the pressure of demand on food production grew. In China in the mid-1950s the situation which has been described in India began to emerge. Agriculture was not producing enough raw materials for industry and retarded its growth; food supplies for the towns began to fall. The mismatch between the two sectors became apparent and the Soviet model was called into question. As Mao Tse Tung stated in 1958 'Since we didn't understand these things and had absolutely no experience, all we could do in our ignorance was to import foreign methods' (Schram 1974). The Chinese began to reexamine their development problems themselves.

THE DEVELOPMENT OF THE PEOPLES' COMMUNES

Mao introduced the idea of the Peoples' Communes in 1958. They represented a significant shift away from the Soviet view of state-managed agriculture and were a distinctively Chinese creation. Larger than the co-operatives which they replaced, they covered a much wider range of activities which they managed themselves as discrete administrative and economic entities. Mao claimed 'the agricultural policy of the Soviet Union has always been wrong in that it drains the pond to catch the fish and is divorced from the masses' (Gray 1969). In stating this he rejected the pre-existing Chinese collective system with its inbuilt disincentives to enterprise and productivity. By the autumn of 1958, 26,000 communes had been formed out of 740,000 co-operatives. It was a development which marked also a move away from the heavy industry-led development of Soviet strategy.

The commune covered a large area of land and its boundaries were generally those of pre-revolutionary administrative areas. Within it there was occasionally an old market town and a number of villages. The size of communes has varied with time and place. In 1962 the 26,000 communes were subdivided to make 74,000. The more fertile areas have the smaller communes. In 1977 the range in size quoted by Sartej Aziz in a sample of 42 communes was from 800 to 4000 hectares though some are known to be 8000 hectares in extent. Populations ranged from as low as 1000 to 80,000 with the majority in the range 10,000 to 40,000 (Aziz 1978).

Each farming family lived in a village often in its own house. Each had a small plot of land for the family's use growing crops for themselves or for sale but with restrictions on the sale of staple food grains. The members of the family worked for a wage in a production team with the wages based on sex, age and amount of work. The wages formed by far the greater part of incomes. The production team was the working unit. It managed its own budget and administered its own work programme but all its work tasks and production targets were set by a decision body at a higher level in the commune of which it was a part. The commune provided the necessary working equipment. Production teams were organized into production brigades composed of a dozen or so teams with a similar number of brigades forming the commune. Norms of working and production and the marketing of crops were determined at commune level by the Workers Revolutionary Committee, the management committee, and were passed down via the brigade to the production teams. Thus at each level of activity the participants were involved and each level was integrated with the next above it in the hierarchy. Not only were agricultural functions thus planned and managed but also social services. For example, primary schools and first-aid stations were operated at brigade level while secondary schools and hospitals were operated at commune level. One of the most notable deficiencies in the developing countries has been the lack of provision of adequate health services for their populations and particularly their rural populations. Commonly doctors and hospitals are urban-focused and in many cases they are not free. The poor and the rural areas remain beyond the reach of medical care. In China the training of 'bare-foot' doctors, essentially medical orderlies operating at brigade level, and the provision of fully-trained physicians in commune hospitals, has made medical care available to everyone. With the characteristic appreciation of the psychological factor, both traditional herbal medicines and modern drugs are utilized. In a hierarchical arrangement of facilities the Chinese peasant can receive treatment for minor ailments in his local clinic or undergo major surgery in the nearest large town. To accommodate a thousand million people in such a health service is an achievement of which any nation would be proud.

The commune was, itself, part of the organisation of the state and as such had cadres upon the committee. It received high-level decisions from regional and central government and passed them down to its constituent parts. In return it could forward ideas, initiatives and responses to the higher levels of government. It was a system which thus gave an intimacy of contact and allowed individual communes to develop their own initiatives but it co-ordinated this into a national agrarian effort. The commune system thus grew into a remarkably successful way of managing the world's largest population in a system which was highly structured and yet allowed individual or group ingenuity to nourish it. It is, perhaps, the most original and significant of development initiatives in the Developing World, harnessing the abilities, resourcefulness and energies of whole communities in endeavours which they could see as of direct benefit to themselves and not solely for some distant government. It gave to the Chinese peasant the opportunity for pride in his achievement, a justifiable pride which is apparent to any visitor to China.

THE GREAT LEAP FORWARD

Initially the commune system was introduced as part of the strategy to increase agricultural output through a labour-intensive effort achieved by injecting the whole community with an urge and zeal for greater efforts and ultra-efficiency in what were essentially traditional methods of husbandry. A simple concept but an enormous psychological task, it was destined to fade in time. The strategy recognized the possibility of running the economy in two discrete sections each with a distinctive mode of operation, technology and development-objective. On the one hand the modernization of large-scale industry could take place using large investments of capital in modern plant with the resulting production being re-invested in further production and, to some extent, in the production of exports. Its activities were to be largely unrelated to the 80 per cent of Chinese population who lived in the countryside. On the other hand the communal system of agricultural production using little capital, deriving little from the industrial sector but gaining its energy from millions of peasants could feed the country and supply its agricultural raw materials. Mao spoke of 'walking on two legs'. He was referring to the need for balancing the two sectors of the economy and the possibility of utilizing, at one and the same time, two levels of technology. It was, perhaps, an unconscious adoption of Nurkse's views on the substitution of labour for capital but it involved much more (Nurkse 1953). This phase in China's development was promoted as 'The Great Leap Forward'. The development of appropriate technologies and the emergence of industry within the countryside were also associated with the ripening of the commune concept. They came to have a special significance when the impetus of the Great Leap was fading and when the issue of population became pressingly evident.

THE DIMENSION OF POPULATION

There was clearly a limit to what could be done in the agricultural sector by exhortation to greater effort and by ideological fervour and zeal applied to a labour-intensive input without concomitant technological advances. Output fell off and by 1962, coupled with bad harvests, the situation was such that resort had to be made to food imports. The Great Leap Forward had not secured the basis of the nation's food supply nor agricultural raw materials for industry. The situation which has been described in the case of India was present also in China and, as in India, the dimension of population was a major factor.

In 1955 China's population was estimated by the Chinese as 615 million; in 1977 it was 934 million. Investment in China during the Great Leap Forward was at such a low level that full, effective use could not be made of the nation's labour force. China had, and still has, a population surplus to the means of fully using it. Labour was substituted for capital but it is an input to which the law of diminishing returns applies rigorously unless other steps are taken to increase per capita output. The situation in India, discussed in the previous chapter, applies to China also. An over-large population can retard development. In the early 1950s China had adopted a policy of family planning but by the time of the Great Leap Forward this had been dropped. Mao claimed in a classical Marxist manner, that the answer to the problem of population was production and that, therefore, there was no population problem; the problem was one of production. These two items are, of course, interrelated in all development issues. There is a problem created by a rapidly expanding population and this can be compounded by large, absolute resultant numbers. Both features applied in China's case, as in India. It was not a problem which could be dispelled by rhetoric. China came to realize that production was not enough and that some control of population growth was necessary. Family planning became official policy again in the early 1960s since when it has never been dropped. Propaganda and persuasion has raised the age of marriage; young mothers are urged to the point of coercion to restrict the size of their families; from time to time punitive measures on the one hand and privileges on the other have been used to reduce the birth rate. Birth control advice and appliances are readily available as are abortions. China has, as a result, achieved the demographic transition in thirty years. Even so its population base is so large that each year in the early 1980s it is increasing almost by 14 million.

INDUSTRY IN THE COUNTRYSIDE: DISPERSED DEVELOPMENTS

By 1962 the population issue was clearly recognized and with the stagnation of agricultural production a new phase of planning was introduced which laid stress upon the need to increase agricultural output and to relate, in some measure, industrial developments to it. But during the Great Leap Forward developments were also taking place in the communes which enhanced their contribution to the process of development and helped cushion the impact of population growth. These developments were a part of Mao's wider concept of the commune and were spread by the advocacy of Premier Chou En Lai who toured throughout the country. The concepts involved self-reliance and self-sufficiency and the creation of innovations from within Chinese society and by its people. Clearly labour input by itself was insufficient; it required technical support. Mao saw mechanization as more meaningful if it grew up within the community which was to use it than if it were brought in as an alien thing, little understood. The centralized tractor-stations of the Soviet Union seemed an imposed factory system unsuitable for the rural society of China. Chemical fertilizers and machines were needed but these could be produced in small factories in the countryside within the communes, run by the communes and for the communes. Rural workers would be involved in their design and production and by doing so would understand how machines work and how to repair and modify them. It was a development which could draw upon the inventiveness of the people and was a further example of Mao's shrewd awareness of the role of psychology. The significance of this view is apparent to all who have witnessed in so many developing countries, imported machines and vehicles lying idle because they have not been understood by their users who, as a result, were unable to repair them.

The creation of small industries in rural areas which began in the Great Leap Forward and has continued since, had other consequences. By the early 1970s the increase in population meant that between 10 and 15 million Chinese were entering the job market each year. The cities would absorb less than a million of this increase so any drift to them would only lead to the problems experienced in many developing countries. Chinese policy has been to restrict that drift and until recent years neither a free movement of population was allowed nor any freedom in the choice of employment. Industrial developments in the countryside could provide employment, increase industrial productivity and give technical support to agriculture. Mao's communes came to incorporate these features and an integrated development of the rural economy characterized by a disaggregated pattern of production began to emerge.

Carl Riskin has pointed out that while local rural industry was not promoted in China's first development plan, by the end of the period the need was appreciated and designs for small-scale plants to be set up in rural areas, worked by rural people and utilizing local raw materials, were being produced (Riskin 1979). This development became a special feature in the Great Leap Forward and many thousands of small manufacturing units were set up at brigade and commune level. By the mid-1960s 60,000 were operating at the *Hsien* or county level and 200,000 in the communes. They produced iron and some steel, agricultural machinery, the walking or two-wheel tractor, chemical fertilizers, some non-ferrous metals, coal, bricks and engineering production materials. In addition and very importantly, electricity was produced in these rural areas for their own consumption. Civil engineering works were completed almost entirely by manual labour as dams were built for irrigation and hydro-electrical power, canals dug and roads constructed. The rural infrastructure to support both agriculture and the new small industrial enterprises was thus consolidated. Many things went wrong and many mistakes were made. Resources were not deployed efficiently, products were sub-standard, craft production suffered, but these problems were tackled and the industrial plants which survived became more efficient and more attuned to the reality of local economic needs and resources. Furthermore, the peasant had gained experience from the involvement. As may be imagined, the central bureaucracy with its nationalization mentality saw this proliferation of small producing units as chaotic, unorganized, untidy, unplanned and unmanageable. It did not appear to be part of the grand design for the new China and yet it was. Those who understood saw it as utilizing local resources often too small to be worthwhile to any large industrial enterprise but with the virtue of proximity; they saw it as developing local initiative, and creating self-reliance, and as participation in true development rather than external imposed growth.

The virtues of a dispersed rural development became more obvious as it became more effective. It was a feature which survived the otherwise disastrous Cultural Revolution which put itself above economic reality and humanitarian concern and in doing so brought about its own eclipse. In so many respects the Cultural Revolution retarded China's development quite apart from the human suffering and thousands of deaths which accompanied it. Its ideological vanguard, the Red Guards, in searching for revisionist tendencies so utilized transport in their countryside movements that the transport of essential raw materials could not take place. Factories were closed or run only part-time, disputes and struggle further interrupted production and national output fell. Ironically one manifestation reinforced the development of the disaggregated rural economy. The leaders of the Cultural Revolution not only stemmed the movement to the cities but reversed it by their policy of rustication, the *Hsia Fang* or back-to-the-countryside policy. It is estimated that between 1968 and 1975, 15 million were transferred from the cities to the rural areas.

By the mid-1960s the virtues of local production and self-reliance had been appreciated and were preached. Rural raw materials supplied rural factories which made products needed in the countryside. Cement for water-management works, small hydro-electric generators, diesel engines, water pumps, insecticide sprayers, chemical fertilizers are examples of the involvement. By 1971 local rural fertilizer factories accounted for 60 per cent of China's total production. The product, ammonium bicarbonate, was typical of the approach. As Riskin points out, ammonium bicarbonate is a poor fertilizer being very low in nitrogen and losing much of its ammonia if stored or transported. It is not an apt product, therefore, for large modern fertilizer plant and indeed is not used outside China. To the Chinese it had, however, great virtues. It involved a simple technology, could use local deposits of coal, lignite, methane or other sources of hydrogen, and could produce a solid fertilizer for local use so that neither transport nor long storage were necessary. It was produced locally, from local materials for local use cheaply and with a technology and labour force the countryside could muster (Riskin 1979). Local iron and steel furnaces using methods and working on a scale more reminiscent of early eighteenth-century England, were in 1971 producing 20 per cent of China's pig-iron. While the early furnaces in the 1950s had been less than successful, their more efficient successors came into their own as they became vertically integrated into engineering concerns producing agricultural machinery. Many rural factories concerned with processing agricultural products on a small scale were likewise dispersed throughout the countryside. The electrification of rural areas which has been mentioned, taking inanimate power into places which had never before experienced it, was brought about by local initiatives and did not come from the tapping of a huge national grid. Some came from small local thermal stations but most from tiny hydro-installations 35,000 of which accounted in 1972 for 16 per cent of the total hydro-power capacity installed in China.

By the early 1970s an integrated rural economy had emerged in the Chinese countryside. Small-scale, locally-based industrial units integrated horizontally and vertically and operating for the most part at *Hsien* or county level, had become part of the commune concept. As such these units could seek expert advice, and indeed obtain more sophisticated equipment, from a higher level in China's hierarchies while at the same time they could relate to local needs. It was not a development evenly distributed throughout the whole of China. The economically-backward areas developed more slowly.

As may be imagined, though many were ingenious, these self-developed technologies were unsophisticated. They represented the so-called intermediate technologies which have attracted much attention. Their significance lies, however, not in their being an *intermediate* technology but being an *appropriate* technology and this is the lesson they have for the rest of the Developing World. They represented a crucial stage in development, a stage omitted by almost all other Third World nations, a stage which has so appropriately bridged the development gap between the agricultural peasant and the skilled industrial worker and brought the countryside with all its vast population into the development process. It has been a truly remarkable development.

Two cautionary and explanatory points need to be made. First the scales and technologies of industrial and power production used were not in absolute and clinically abstract terms, economically efficient. They did not make the most efficient use of resources in the sense of minimizing factor costs. It was therefore essential that this dispersed local production should not compete with modern large-scale and efficient industrial units for resources either of capital, raw materials or energy. In China it did not. It made use of resources which would otherwise not have been deployed. It was not, nor ever had been, the intention of the Chinese government to neglect the development of large manufacturing plant using the most modern methods. This development could, and did, run parallel to that in the countryside. The 'walking on two legs' doctrine of Mao implied that the two should operate in harness. It is this combination in which the countryside is not abandoned to neglect and stagnation which makes the Chinese experiment so remarkable and so significant a pointer for other countries. It was a strategy which made use of a whole range of resources including those too small and, in the case of labour, too untrained, for modern large-scale technology. Scattered low-grade mineral resources could be drawn on and used, power sites capable of generating only small amounts of electricity could be given a local significance. People were given the chance to use their initiative and the opportunity for everyone to participate in the development process was provided. The second point to note is that the industrial developments in the countryside did not play a major role in providing alternative employment to farming. The new rural industries, unsophisticated though they were, none the less were more efficient in the use of labour than the craft industries or farm and family methods of material and food processing. They released labour to agriculture rather than drawing labour from it. Even at peak harvest times the rural industries processing agricultural products used only around 5 per cent of the rural labour force (Riskin 1979). The new local industries did play an exceedingly important role in the agricultural sector. Their activities and products not only increased agricultural production but also enabled a greater input of labour to be used more effectively and so counteracted the diminishing returns on labour input. The rustic industrial development played a part in diminishing the size of China's 'surplus' population.

There were other benefits resulting from the development of the rural economy. One was to minimize the movement of raw materials and products in a country which, for its size, was, and is, poorly endowed with transport facilities. As Leung has commented, China's transport policies since the revolution have been much concerned with connecting the peripheral, border areas with the main focus of population and industry on the coastal plains (Leung 1979, 1980, Leung and Comtois 1983). The main trunk roads were constructed by the state while the local road system was in the hands of communes as a part of the policy of self-reliance. Much development has taken place, though the Cultural Revolution effectively put a stop to road improvements for four or five years, but the carrying capacity of many roads and the absence of bridges still inhibits large-scale, long-distance movement. In such circumstances, localized developments eased the pressure on the road system. These advantages, the minimizing of transport costs which compensated for sub-optima production costs and the retardation of rural-urban drift were, therefore, further attributes of the development of a dispersed, but integrated, rural economy. It should, however, be appreciated that it was not conceived of as a static achievement. As industries in the countryside grew and matured they could move out of the stage of intermediate technology into another more appropriate technology larger in scale, more demanding of capital and much more sophisticated in technique. As they developed they would become a more directly integrated part of the national economy requiring national levels of research and development and major national resources. The new developments would more efficiently meet national needs. It would therefore be a development in which the distinction between the rural self-help economy and the modern world progressively disappeared. This remarkable Chinese manifestation must therefore be thought of as a stage in the development of the world's largest nation. It is one which has meant that the countryside has become something more than a mere adjunct to the town, that towns have not been the only centres of change and modernization, that the contrast between core and periphery has been diminished, that a form of integrated development of rural areas and societies has come into being. For the Developing World, essentially a rural world, it has been a development of great significance and achievement. Since it involved men and not the gods it has been a flawed development but it laid foundations for future progress and the building of the new China. As such it must be seen.

A NEW PHASE IN DEVELOPMENT: CHINA AFTER MAO TSE TUNG

After the death of Chairman Mao in 1976 and the subsequent and rapid eclipse of the 'Gang of Four' who had led the Cultural Revolution, China entered an entirely new phase of development. It was not simply a cry of 'The king is dead long live the king'. The China which has emerged is a country considerably different in its approach both to development problems and to the outside world. The achievements of Mao's China had been great. It was still a poor country but one which had made provision for the essentials of life for all. Few other countries in the Developing World could claim as much and in none had the size of the task been greater. Some would suggest that progress would have been quicker and more substantial by taking another route but there is no means of testing the proposition.

The new regime in China made a close and searching scrutiny of what had gone before and identified its many imperfections. They have opened up China to the outside world and given the Chinese people a much greater freedom, indeed it is this freedom which is the striking contrast with the China of Chairman Mao. He had built foundations; it is to be hoped that they are strong enough to carry the weight of freedom because a free society is much more difficult to manage and direct. The new China is engaging in trade to a greater extent and in doing so is becoming less self-reliant. From its use of intermediate technology it is moving rapidly into a phase of modernization and is attempting to acquire not only new means of production but also of management. The transitional phase of the 1980s is a crucial one.

THE RURAL ECONOMY

It was in the rural sector where Mao's China had made such a distinctive contribution and here there have been changes. What has changed, indeed, some would claim that it has broken down, is the rigidity of the three-tiered structure of the communes. Workers within each tier had been responsible to its leader who in turn was responsible to those above him. The Cultural Revolution, with its radical extreme Marxist ideology, had made this system much more inflexible and bureaucratic. As J. and M. Gray report, there has emerged not one system but several with every indication of a state of flux out of which Chinese experimentation may produce a new development model (Gray and Gray 1983). The reappraisal of agrarian and rural policies has identified their strengths and weaknesses. Output of the staple grains had been increased though the Cultural Revolution saw a fall in the rate of growth. The production of cotton, sugar-cane, the edible oils, tea and the most important meat in China, pork, fell to an even greater extent as the policies of the ultra-left faction in power stressed the need to concentration on the basic food grains. The new government of China saw this action as stifling rather than stimulating agrarian production. Even when the Red Guards enforced rustication and put more workers on the land, production had declined. Clearly the food grains were of basic importance in securing the nation's food supply but it is now felt that this could be achieved by positive incentives rather than by the enforcements of the Cultural Revolution which clearly blunted them. Families had been prevented from earning an income by growing crops for local sale additional to the cereal targets. During the Cultural Revolution a party member described to the author these individual plots for private production as undesirable residues of capitalism. Profits which could have come from the sale of vegetables, cotton and other crops could have been invested to further agricultural production, and, as the Grays state, the concentration on grains meant a selected depletion of soil nutrients which could have been avoided (Gray and Gray 1983). The Cultural Revolution starkly demonstrated the inadequacies of a political direction of technological matters. The cadres had neither the ability nor training to direct the complexities of a mixed-husbandry agrarian economy. These weaknesses were clearly a product of inadequacies in the management and direction of commune activities rather than of the commune system itself.

The new government of Deng Xiaping is taking a fresh and less political view more rooted in economic than political science. The goal of a secure grain harvest is viewed in the light not only of the physical basis of agriculture but also its significance in terms of comparative advantage and regional specialization. Rather than vast areas being required to grow their quota of strategic grains, those which are best suited will specialize in them while others, using the same evaluation of opportunity cost, will grow a wider range. This approach will encourage agricultural diversity within the nation and will allow returns on investment to be maximized by acknowledging the spatial variations in the productive environment. It is a policy which can both raise the output of the staple grains and of a variety of other crops of nutritive and industrial importance.

The communes, it will be recalled, were defined by old administrative boundaries. In a purely administrative sense and in ease of demarcation this was convenient. In terms of managing an environment, more particularly its water supply for irrigation, it was clearly most unsatisfactory since river basins and stream systems do not acknowledge lines on commune maps. Thus while water and other resources had been integrated within communes, this did not necessarily correspond with their most effective use. A reorganization of boundaries could remove many of these inadequacies. At all levels the management of the communes was shown to have been inefficient. There were two obvious causes which in the climate of the Cultural Revolution and indeed before, could not be cited with impunity. One was the role of the political cadre placed in a position of power to execute decisions about matters beyond his competence; this was the dead hand of bureaucracy. The second was an inevitable product of the 'do-it-yourself' basis of commune activity. The refusal to accept the existence of expertize, at least openly, meant that unnecessary trial and error retarded both development and efficiency. According to the Grays many cadres had little idea of how to formulate and execute development plans and often kept no accounts whereby programmes could be monitored and controlled; nor had they a knowledge of the scientific basis of farming (Gray and Gray 1983). The cadres were civil service bureaucrats who were neither agriculturalists nor entrepreneurs.

The commune system, brilliant in its concept, required for its successful operation a level of competence, a mixture of skills, and an amount of capital investment rarely available to it. It is reported that a very large proportion of the communes' revenues was absorbed in their administration rather than deployed in production. Peasant workers in the production teams saw, in consequence, a low return on their efforts and their incentive to work was progressively diminished. In the command economy of China, in which prices and market conditions were fixed by the state in a state monopoly, the energy of input was again made remote from the benefit of return. The deficiencies identified by the new government of China all pointed to the cloying and stifling containment of an overweight bureaucratic system which tried to manage too much in too great a detail. The personal initiatives and participation which Mao had put to the fore were dimmed by the self-defeating mechanism of their implementation. The inability to design and implement a scheme which fairly recompensed, by a scheme of work points, a worker for his efforts is but one example of the problems of attempting to engineer a whole society down to its last nut and bolt. To break down the management of millions of peasants into the discrete unit of the commune had been a concept of genius. The truly impressive commune system, ensuring as it did a steady rise in agricultural output, the emergence of industry within the countryside and a wide distribution of participation, had been frustrated in its full flowering by its sheer size and complexity and by the ideological frosts of the Cultural Revolution. The state had set itself a task of management which it was unable to accomplish. It too had begun to drain the pond to catch the fish. Despite three and more decades of political indoctrination the incentive of service to a remote state had not replaced that of personal interest. Much had been achieved and pride in the new China was widespread and real but the removal of opportunities of self-improvement, other than that of political advancement, seems to have had a deadening effect. The task of Mao's successors was to inject a new vitality into the system.

The systems which are emerging do not involve the replacement of socialist ideals by capitalism but they certainly draw upon capitalist ideas of free enterprise and attempt to put them to use within the socialist state of China. On the commune, contracts have replaced labour tasks on the part of the individual and quota production by the tiers of the commune. Contracts may refer to production or the supply of a skill or to the completion of a particular project in what are known as 'production responsibility systems'. In areas with difficult environments and hence low levels of production, communes in the past found that the standardized costs of administration took almost all of the revenue leaving little for the commune members. In such areas almost all the means of production have been handed back to the production team or even the individual family so that administrative overheads have been reduced to a minimum. The situation thus becomes very like that of a rented farm. More commonly the commune or brigade remains intact and within it work-teams or groups of families contract with the brigade or commune to produce a stated quantity of crops or perform a particular task. The significant development is that the group involved becomes responsible for the task involved and directly reaps the reward for its efforts. The incentive of personal gain, either directly or through participation in a group, has been restored.

Contractual arrangements vary widely both in scope and in terms of participants. Clearly China is experimenting in ways of using the input of labour to meet her society's needs. A new model systematizing the relationship may emerge or a system less structured and doctrinaire may result. A distinction remains, however, between activities related to the production of staple food grains and the growth of other crops and livestock. As has been mentioned, China is very aware of the need to secure the nation's food supply but this is now to be more in the hands of specialist grain producers in the most environmentally favoured areas. In a sense regional self-sufficiency is being replaced by national self-sufficiency. The individual producer has greater freedom. He can, for example, choose to specialize in vegetable or tobacco growing or, as some in South China have chosen, in the production of mulberry leaves for silk-worms and hence silk, fish-farming and sugar-cane growing, all integrated in a balanced ecological cycle. The new policy encourages agricultural diversity and allows specialization both by the producing unit, be it the individual, a work team, brigade or commune, and by localities. The activities can include manufacturing as well as farming. Since a degree of regional specialization will result as economic concepts of comparative advantage and opportunity costs come into play, so local self-sufficiency will decline and a greater inter-regional movement of goods will occur. This will increase the pressure on transport facilities so that a concomitant development, which is taking place, is the improvement of the transport infrastructure. It is hoped, and this is the intention, that the contract system will stimulate initiatives by offering the possibility of pursuing independent self-interest which at the same time contributes to the national good. The initial results of the system have been satisfactory. The peasant has enjoyed higher prices for his produce which he has been able to produce at lower cost. His additional cash income has created a market for consumer goods which in turn has stimulated industry.

Despite the many large cities, (Fig. 35), the peasantry of China form such a large proportion of her population that an improvement in their well-being is an improvement in that of the nation. Mao Tse Tung had long regarded the harnessing of the resources of the countryside as a way to drive the engine of social and economic development. Rural development encompassing not only agriculture but also manufacturing and services remain important in China even though the production effort is less structured and more disaggregated than in the commune system.

THE MANUFACTURING SECTOR

Similar changes have been taking place, though perhaps more slowly, in the large-scale manufacturing sector. Plant managers have expressed a wish for a greater freedom of action in making decisions and in the exercise of their entrepreneurship in a sector where the central planning bodies of the state had imposed quotas and targets. As on the communes, it represents a reaction to inefficient state-run bureaucracy. The enterprising manager working within the highly-structured and vertically-integrated manufacturing sector is frustrated at all points by the super-imposition of state plans. He is not able to evaluate the cost-effectiveness of any particular process since both prices and costs are artificially controlled, nor is he able to attempt any market analysis. The industry of the new China of the post-Mao period contained many of the structures and philosophies evolved during Mao's lifetime. The self-sufficiency approach was still practised even in large installations in which as many products as possible were made to result from one industrial activity. For example, the author has visited a large sugar mill in which not only were sugar, molasses and spirits produced but also paper from the bagasse, building bricks from the cinders and a range of pharmaceutical products from the several materials used in the refining process. None of these activities other than that of producing raw sugar and spirits could be justified in purely economic terms. Such schemes made full use of all inputs and by-products but the opportunity cost of using these inputs and deploying capital and labour to do so, were not evaluated. As in agriculture the self-sufficiency approach meant that specialization, with associated technical development, was inhibited and comparative advantage could not be maximized. It was a system which made developmental and political sense in the initial stage of harnessing China's people and resources in isolation from the rest of the world. It has made less sense as this stage has passed. Specialization has begun and again, as in agriculture, this involves the inter-regional movements of both raw materials and products and makes necessary better transport facilities. It is also a development which suggests a much greater participation in international trade.

The egg of containment has been cracked and the new China which is emerging is encountering new experiences, new challenges and new problems, the majority of which are those of transformation. State-management, self-sufficiency, appropriate technologies were all understandable, highly relevant and successful stages in the process of development of the Socialist People's Republic. The question is now one of how to build upon that which has been achieved. The changes necessary in industry may prove even more difficult and slower than those in agriculture. It is a sector which has experienced little participation in decision-making since it was much more centrally planned than agriculture with its disaggregated commune system. Few industrial managers in China have any experience of seeking and developing markets, of international trade, of industrial planning and resource management. They have been merely executants of policy made by others. China wishes to modernize both agriculture and industry, indeed, the slogan of the government coined in 1977 referred to the 'Four Modernisation's of agriculture, industry, defence and education. The Chinese planning system particularly that of manufacturing may make modernization difficult. China is demonstrating the problem of over-centralization which all socialist command-economics have encountered.

THE GROWTH OF INTERNATIONAL INVOLVEMENT

In both agriculture and industry and in town and country greater managerial initiative is now being allowed. To be effective, this requires training in and experience of, modern management techniques. The advanced technology which China wishes to use, whether it is imported or designed and developed within China, needs a scientific work-force of managers and technicians. This in turn requires education to be more selective in its intake and more specialized in its focus. Both these features were an anathema in the Cultural Revolution. They are developments which demand an international dimension. China needs to buy in the new technology both in ready-made machines or in plant to fabricate high-technology goods and needs to acquire scientific and technological 'know-how'. Isolation, long characteristic of the People's Republic and at the most absolute during the Cultural Revolution when all scientific intercourse with other nations ceased, is incompatible with the goals of modernization.

Trading relationships between China and foreign powers were, of course, established before the death of Mao Tse Tung. A trade treaty was made with the old enemy, Japan, as early as 1963 and the Shanghai Communique of 1972 had, at long last, restored normal relationships between China and the USA. China had, of course, used Hong Kong as a trading outlet for many years. After Mao's death and the eclipse of the Gang of Four, the new government took much more positive steps to develop international contacts which involved not only trade but foreign investment on Chinese soil. The internal changes which have been taking place in the organization of labour with the development of specialized skills, the emergence of the money incentive, the growth of the managerial responsibility and initiative, have all brought China closer to the outside and largely non-socialist world. Her internal changes enable her more readily and efficiently to incorporate innovations, to engage in trade and to participate jointly in foreign investment in China. The great industrial cities of the nineteenth century in which European nations had invested and developed industries and which were interlinked by the Chinese rail network, once again have become recipients of foreign capital so that the older involvement has influenced the spatial pattern of the new. Direct investment of foreign capital is not characteristic of foreign involvement over much of China. Sub-contracting, licensing agreements, joint enterprises are more common. Agreements on the transfer of technology are also a feature of China's policy of modernization.

THE SPECIAL ECONOMIC ZONES

The most overt manifestation of China's change in its relationship to the

world of international capital and of its new policy of economic development
are the Special Economic Zones (SEZ) the first of which were established
in 1979 in the two southerly provinces of Guangdong (Kwantung) and
Fujian (Fukien). Two of these zones are located in Guangdong; one Shenzen
is across the border from Hong Kong and the other Zhuhai is situated a
short distance north of Macao. The Shantou (Swatow) and Xieman Zones
in Fujian province are on the Chinese coast opposite Taiwan (Fig. 35). In
these zones there are few restrictions on the investment of foreign capital.
Independent capitalist enterprises can be set up as well as joint ventures
with Chinese state organizations. The zones are primarily concerned with
manufacturing not for the Chinese home market but for export. The land
is Chinese, the labour is Chinese and both have the virtue of being cheap,
indeed very cheap when compared with Hong Kong, Singapore, Taiwan or
South Korea. The design of the products, the expertise involved, both technical and commercial, is foreign as indeed are many of the components
assembled and materials processed. The machines installed will almost
invariably be foreign. No restrictions are placed in the way of foreign investors and manufacturers but they are required to pay Chinese taxes. Chinese
joint ventures are likewise free of state interference. Exchange revenue from

Figure 35 China: cities over one million

exports when Chinese companies are involved, taxes from all businesses in the zones and labour opportunities for China's growing labour force are obvious, if limited, benefits of this venture. Of greater significance is the opportunity they offer for the acquisition of modern industrial skills by the work-force and the experience of the latest business-management procedures by the Chinese managers in joint schemes. At both workshop and management level the Chinese are becoming more familiar with modern technology. Capitalism has been implanted in China but it is controlled. It functions within the demarcated zones guided by regulations which, though loose, can be tightened. Developers are allowed in, many coming from Hong Kong, to lease land but only on twenty-five year leases. The factory buildings constructed by the developers can then be sub-let by them to manufacturers. Not only have factories been erected but also hotels and even residential accommodation to be bought by the 'overseas Chinese' who can now return to the country of their birth to retire.

The connections between the SEZ and Hong Kong are very strong, especially so in the case of the Shenzen and Zhuhai Zones and it is deliberate. The Chinese have long been involved in Hong Kong; they see its skills, expertise and success. Guangzhou (Canton) is connected by rail to Hong Kong's modern port facilities and much of what is produced in the SEZ goes to Hong Kong for shipping or final processing. Most of the development of the SEZ has been in the hands of Hong Kong property tycoons.

The advantages of this particular facet of China's modernization are, of course, debatable. It can be questioned whether the SEZ do facilitate the transfer of technological and business knowledge and skills. They provide employment in China but may draw in too many of the skilled and enterprising from surrounding areas in the same way in which urban opportunities commonly do. If, instead, they do achieve a spread effect by the circulation of labour and management through the zones, then their creation can have positive and beneficial effects. Without this circulation they will become isolated enclaves detached from the rest of the Chinese economy.

The SEZ systems and the general opening-up of China to outside contacts does remove the protective shield from her pure socialist ideals. The market place is there to behold and its development, or more accurately its re-development, is taking place throughout China and not only in the SEZ. It is especially noticeable in the southern provinces for these are the areas from which the 'overseas Chinese', now found throughout the world, have come over the centuries. They and their descendants have often retained contact. Now they can visit their ancestral areas and in doing so become a window on the outside world.

The many various involvements with foreign firms, foreign investment and joint ventures both within and without the Special Zones are part and parcel of China's programme of modernization and of her intent to restructure her economy and participate in world trade to a greater extent than ever before. In all her characteristics, save population dynamics, China is a nation of the Developing World albeit a very distinctive one. Her huge population presents to the world a very large market diminished, of course, by its limited purchasing power but none the less very significant since China wishes to import development. This same population represents also the world's largest labour force. Its cheapness, its present skills together with the new skills it may acquire in the modernization process, represent a great productive resource which can form the basis of competitive Chinese exports. The modernization process may well result in a shift away from basic heavy industries to lighter consumer-goods production particularly in the deployment of labour and there is evidence that this is taking place. Care must be taken that the greater influx of imported manufactures do not cause sectors of Chinese manufacturing to atrophy. The attractiveness and size which the Chinese market offers can be seen in the streets where large numbers of Japanese vans and lorries are replacing the home-produced vehicle and where Maoist posters with their Victorian moral postures and political exhortations, have made room for advertisements of Mitsubishi and Nissan products. Vehicles and machinery which China herself could produce are being imported. There could be no stronger contrast with the days of self-sufficiency and the Great Leap Forward. The balance between basic manufactures and capital goods on the one hand and consumer goods on the other has shifted. It is not necessarily a retrograde step as the experience of India demonstrates. It may indeed be a desirable readjustment of balance.

China is thus undergoing a radical transformation and one which requires careful management and control. If ill-managed it will not foster the development of a secure industrial base for future developments, it will weaken her industrial linkage potential and it could lead to the balance of payments problems so often encountered in developing countries if too much is imported before an ability to produce counterbalancing exports is developed.

Since 1979 China's trade has continued to increase markedly, an increase in which light industrial exports from China have figured prominently. With the growth in imports from the outside world have come exotic tastes and increased expectations in what constitutes the 'good life'. Whether this is viewed as a taint or an enlightenment it is none the less happening, certainly in the south-western provinces and in the big cities. The high-rise flats and houses built for the returning 'overseas Chinese' are in size and quality far superior to those inhabited by the Chinese peasant. Other life styles are being implanted. The equity is being disturbed.

It is, of course, wrong and unrealistic to imagine that the People's Republic can be fossilized and held in a stage where everyone is equal but is poor, where low level technology is seen as a virtue when the real issue is one of *appropriate* technology, where isolation from the rest of the world may have been a necessary prerequisite for the laying of foundations but can hardly represent an eternal condition. Development implies change and what the example of China shows, as indeed do other case studies examined, is that change does not take the form of an overnight metamorphosis from the eighteenth-century world of China as it was in 1948, 1968 or indeed 1978, into one of the high-technology and overweight society of the Western World. What is discernible, and China's recent history has marked it out clearly, is a ladder of development up which countries climb, some falteringly, some overtaken and some replacing those at the top. China is climbing by every rung to make safe her ascent; too many developing countries have tried to leap to the top. It is this sequential development involving all aspects of society which, slow though it may have seemed, provides an instructive model for the nations of the Developing World.

China's entry into world trade is of considerable international significance. She is rich in raw materials and energy resources which are, as yet, little developed. She has the world's largest supply of labour with every indication that it can be trained in machine-production techniques. Resources and cheap skilled labour will give China a powerful comparative advantage. Just as the attributes of labour in Hong Kong, Singapore, Taiwan, the Philippines, Malaysia and South Korea have had a dramatic impact on labour-intensive industries in Europe and North America, so the increasingly export-orientated manufacturing of China will affect them in turn. Indeed China's labour-led industrialization will have an impact throughout the world both of the developing and the industrialized nations. Third World countries attempting to industrialize by labour-intensive methods will face the competition of China. Industrialized nations will increasingly move into high-technology capital-intensive industries in a process of structural transformation in part responsive to Third World development. As China develops more sophisticated technologies she will eventually emerge as one of the industrial giants of the world. The transformation so modestly begun behind closed frontiers will be of a truly international dimension.

The change now taking place within the socialist People's Republic of China presents her with formidable economic, managerial and indeed ideological problems. It is not an inevitable change nor can it be an easy one. For her sake, and indeed in the interests of the rest of the world, it must be hoped that she can accomplish the change satisfactorily, if not without difficulty, so that the truly laudable achievements in the first three decades of the People's Republic can be seen as foundations to be built upon rather than destroyed.

17 Taiwan

'In 1953 in Taiwan the average per family income of the top twenty per cent was fifteen times that of the bottom twenty per cent; by 1979 this ratio had been reduced to 4.2 times. This equalisation of incomes constitutes a distribution revolution greater than any achieved under socialist or communist auspices and was one of the main policies that fueled high-speed growth'

Chalmers Johnson
The Taiwan Model 1981

'Taiwan has a good claim to be ranked as the most successful of the developing countries'

Ian M D Little
An Economic Reconnaissance 1979

In the light of the evidence presented in the case of China it might be thought that Maoist-socialism is the only way to secure a sound and equitable development. However, one has only to look across the straits which separate it from the People's Republic to the island called Taiwan to see another. There in a free-enterprise society equally impressive achievements in the equitable development of a formerly rural and colonial society are to be seen. There is an alternative way. As the People's Republic has much to teach other countries in the Developing World, so too has Taiwan. Her development path provides a marked contrast with those of other former colonial territories which have been discussed such as, for example, Sri Lanka and Zambia. The work of a number of economists, notably J. C. H. Fei, S. P. S. Ho, A. Y. C. Koo, S. W. Y. Kuo, S. Kuznets, G. Ranis and E. Thorbecke, has made it possible not only to trace and evaluate Taiwan's approach to development but also to relate it to the basic issues of development found throughout the Developing World.

Taiwan is an island of some 35,988 square kilometres. In the mountains which cover half the island, altitude and steepness of slope inhibit agricultural development though the forests which clothe them are inhabited by aboriginal tribes who practise shifting cultivation. The environment in the lowlands favours agriculture. A wide range of minerals occur but few are of any significance and there is no iron. Small amounts of oil and natural gas have been raised but coal is of greater importance though even this resource is modest; the recoverable reserves are put as low as 210 million tonnes (Rhynsburger 1956; Chen 1963). Clearly richness in natural endowment is not the explanation of Taiwan's success in the development stakes to which Little refers (Little 1979).

FROM ABORIGINAL ISLAND TO COLONY

The island now known as Taiwan lying off the coast of China but originally neither part of it nor inhabited by Chinese, was referred to by the Chinese as Pakkau-tao or Hsiao Liu-ch'iu. When Europeans first saw the island in the sixteenth century they called it Ilha Formosa, the beautiful island. According to Kerr, it was at this time a 'formidable wilderness' inhabited mainly by aborigines who did not speak Chinese, did not regard their island as part of a China they had never seen and did not trade with China (Kerr 1974). There had been, however, a long history of sporadic Chinese settlements and when the Dutch set up a trading base on Pakkau-tao in 1624 there was already a small Chinese settlement. The first Dutch fort was built on an islet called T'aiwan, a name the Dutch subsequently applied to the whole island, and from it they began to conquer and organize the tribes of the western lowlands and to engage in farming. During the period of the Dutch settlement substantial numbers of Chinese crossed from the mainland to settle in Taiwan and by 1650 numbered at least 100,000 (Ho 1978). Dutch rule came to an end in 1662, when they were defeated by a Chinese army led by the Ming general Koxsinga. His army seized all Dutch lands and, together with the thousands of Chinese civilians which accompanied it, settled and farmed the accessible lowlands. In 1683 when the ancient Ming dynasty of China was replaced by the Manchu Ch'ing dynasty, Taiwan became a prefecture of Fukien Province and so, for the first time, was formally incorporated into the administration of Imperial China (Ho 1978). Further substantial migrations of Chinese enlarged Taiwan's population, which reached two million by 1827. In 1887 Taiwan was raised to the status of a Chinese province administered by its own governor. Within a few years, however, following her defeat in the first Sino-Japanese war, China had ceded Taiwan to the Japanese and the island, reverting to its earlier non-Chinese name of Formosa, became a colony of Japan and was developed as such from 1895 until 1945.

As Ho points out, in the two centuries of its government of Taiwan, the Ch'ing Dynasty of China had done little to enhance the economic development of the island (Ho 1978). The Japanese attitude was in marked contrast; Taiwan, as a colony, was to be actively developed to supply Japan with agricultural produce, notably rice and sugar. The subsistence agricultural community was transformed into a society of commercial farmers and as such became a market for Japanese manufacturers. It was a classic example of the colonial model. Japan saw her own interests best served by taking control of the Taiwanese economy and making its agricultural sector as efficient and productive as possible. In order to secure her claim to the new colony, she deliberately kept Taiwan and the Taiwanese isolated from China. In consequence during the fifty years of colonial rule, the Taiwanese people though remaining Chinese in culture, came to have a distinctive identity of their own. On the other hand their economy, as part of a colonial system, was changed from one discrete and internally-focused into one linked to an external source of capital and initiative and to an external market. This transformation served as a great stimulus to agricultural output as capital, new technology, and new economic systems were applied to Taiwan's resources of land and labour.

The Japanese participated directly and actively in the economic development of Taiwan. As Ho reports 'Because of both its economic size and autocratic nature, the colonial government was the paramount force in the economy' (Ho 1978). Unlike many other colonial governments who confined their investments to infrastructural developments and their administrative functions, over 40 per cent of expenditure by the Japanese colonial government was commonly devoted to productive investment in agriculture. It was for Japan a cheap way of securing a food supply for her own large population without having to buy it with industrial exports. Taiwan became, in effect, an extension of Japan's agricultural area. The value of food imports from Taiwan greatly exceeded that of industrial exports to the island. Infrastructural investments were designed to support agricultural production. A road network was established in the agricultural lowlands and a railway was built to connect the northern port of Keelung to the southern port of Kaosiung. The government was directly responsible for a number of major irrigation schemes and in addition financed many others promoted by the Irrigation Association, itself a body whose initiatives required its approval. Between 1900 and 1940 the area under irrigation was doubled and by 1942 accounted for 64 per cent of all cultivated land. Research stations and advisory services were established further to modernize agriculture while the quality of the workforce was improved by investment in education and health facilities. The package of investment, research endeavour and advisory services had the effect of greatly increasing agricultural production while at the same time providing additional employment on the land for the rapidly growing population (Ho 1978; Thorbecke 1979). The dissemination of new ideas, techniques, seed varieties and other innovations brought in and demonstrated by Japanese agronomists, was greatly facilitated by the formation of the *nokai*, the Farmers' Associations which had their beginnings in 1900 near Taipei. The original initiative came from a group of wealthy farmers and land owners but the Japanese seized upon it not only as a vehicle for the dissemination of agricultural innovations but also as a means of controlling agricultural development. Farmers' Associations were, therefore, set up throughout Taiwan but with Japanese officials and scientists in control. Membership was compulsory. In effect the Farmers' Associations became a means of managing the agricultural economy in a disaggregated way but with a central overall control. In this respect, despite many other differences, it was not dissimilar to the commune system of Mao Tse Tung. Unlike the commune model, that of the *nokai* was not one of self-help. Experts, both scientists and administrators, were brought in from Japan and speeded up the transformation of agriculture from a largely subsistence peasant economy into a reorganized, commercial system capable of continually generating new developments. As the Green Revolution in India many years later was to show, one innovation or technical development requires the support of other changes if it is to be effective. The Japanese package ensured the changes taking place in concert. Neither the distribution of land ownership nor the tenurial system were altered in any radical way.

The development of a modern manufacturing sector in the colonial period was much slower. Most industrial units were small, scattered throughout the countryside and concerned with processing agricultural products or in servicing agriculture with fertilizer and tools. In 1930 food processing accounted for three-quarters by value of manufacturing production (Ho 1978). By far the most important industry was sugar refining followed by the chemical industries, chiefly producing fertilizer, and the non-metallic manufacturing industries. Factories averaged only ten workers each and six large firms, five of them sugar refiners, accounted for 80 per cent of capital investment in industry. Many industrial products were imported and though in her preparations for war Japan sought to reduce her industrial exports to Taiwan by diversifying industrial activity on the island, by 1941 Taiwan's industrial sector was still small and overwhelmingly concerned with agriculture. Japan throughout her colonial rule exerted an almost complete control over manufacturing. Over 90 per cent of the invested capital was Japanese and many Japanese immigrants, who settled in Taiwan between 1920 and 1940, took up employment in manufacturing as well as in mining and transport operations. In addition to this Japanese-dominated sector of corporate industries, many long-established, small-scale craft industries owned and operated by Taiwanese still persisted. In all respects they differed from those in the modern sector (Ho 1978).

THE POST-WAR TRANSITION

When the Second World War came to an end the United States ensured that Taiwan was returned to China once again to become one of her provinces. This move was complicated by the continuation of the civil war in China. When the Communists emerged victorious the Nationalist Government fled to Taiwan and established an alternative government with the intention of using the island as a base for a reconquest of the mainland. They were joined by many thousands of refugees. By 1950 a million mainland Chinese had settled in Taiwan and its population had increased from 5.87 million in 1940 to 7.54 millions in 1950. The people of Taiwan who had regarded themselves as Taiwanese rather than Chinese were now ruled by yet another government which came from outside rather than within. The colonial power had gone and with it the whole raison d'être of the colonial economy. Taiwan had to face an economic future destined to be entirely different from the preceding half century.

The new Taiwan, which called itself the Republic of China, was largely agricultural, had a rapidly growing population augmented by a million refugees from the mainland and was cut off from both China and Japan. It had suffered extensively from war damage and possessed an economy unable, at first, to absorb the influx of people but it acquired assets in two ways. The immigrants from the mainland included many capitalists, entrepreneurs and professionals possessing both skills and resources. Even some industrial plant was transferred to the island. As in Hong Kong which similarly received refugees, the injection of this human resource proved to be important. In Taiwan's case it was especially significant since the industrial sector had been almost entirely in the hands of the now vanquished Japanese. Secondly, for political reasons, the Nationalist Government of Taiwan began to receive development aid from the United States. These two elements were catalytic in Taiwan's development process rather than its sole cause. In other respects Taiwan's position was like that of so many newly independent and former colonial territories. She was faced with an entirely new situation and an uncertain future, with her former markets gone, a larger population than she could effectively employ and few significant natural resources. Her agriculture was, however, better organized, more commercial and more scientifically based than in many developing countries of the day and it was upon this resource that the restructuring of the Taiwanese economy began. In this enterprise the Joint Commission on Rural Reconstruction (JCRR), an American-Taiwanese organisation, played an important role (Ho 1978; Thorbecke 1979).

Prior to 1945 almost all the economically viable land in Taiwan had been brought under cultivation. The greatly increased population therefore increased pressure upon a limited resource and future development could only be ensured by increasing agricultural output per capita and per unit area and by developing alternative employment. The new government, in part no doubt because it was in one sense alien and with no political ties to local invested-interests, introduced early and radical reforms in land holding. First, agricultural rents were reduced by law. Second, state-owned or public land was sold, not to speculative land-owners, but to practising farmers and third, privately owned land was redistributed by compulsory sale to farmers. These successive actions, completed by 1953, represented a significant redistribution of land holdings, some 25 per cent of all cultivated land being affected. A land-owning small-farmer class was securely established. By 1953 owner-occupiers accounted for 55 per cent of all farm holdings in Taiwan and the proportion continued to increase so that by 1970 nearly 80 per cent of farmers owned the land they farmed (Ho 1978; Tang and Hsieh 1961; Lin 1981; Wei 1981). These early government actions did much to ensure a wide measure of equity in the agricultural sector in terms of both income and ownership of the major factor of production. Upon this secure base increased agricultural productivity resulting from a greater intensity of use of land and labour took place. It took place in what can be described as a labour-surplus economy, a type commented upon in the context of both India and China, in which it is essential for developments to occur which enable the more effective use of labour either by increasing the marginal returns upon it in agriculture or by providing alternative employment or by doing both (Fei and Ranis 1975; Ho 1978; Fei, Ranis and Kuo 1979). Taiwan both reorganized her agriculture and developed a manufacturing sector initially supported by agriculture.

Two organizational structures assisted in this post-war development of Taiwan's agriculture. One was the American sponsored JCRR which administered American aid. Not only did it handle monetary aid it also provided much scientific and administrative help, was responsible for many innovations and identified new overseas markets for Taiwanese crops. It replaced the former Japanese role by one which was even more supportive and free, of course, of the colonial framework. The other organization was created by the Taiwanese government out of the former Farmers' Associations. They were converted into true farmers' institutions representing and serving the common interests of their members. They gave co-operative strength to the multitude of small-holders and further strengthened the agricultural sector and the rural economy. The results were impressive. Agricultural production rose by 42.8 per cent and output of crop production per worker by 96.1 per cent between 1950 and 1960. This alone was not enough to accommodate the problem of population pressure, nor was the redistribution of land in itself sufficient to promote growth and retain equity. The agricultural population rose by 33 per cent between 1952 and 1964 and pressure on the land increased accordingly (Fei, Ranis and Kuo 1979).

People left the countryside for the cities but in the rural areas themselves three developments were significant. One related to changes in the crops grown as higher value crops began increasingly to replace longer established staples. Asparagus and mushroom-growing are examples of innovations which helped retain higher incomes on smaller holdings. A second related to the technologies used in farming. As Ranis has pointed out, technological innovations in agriculture can be put into two groups, the engineering which involve the greater use of machines and which are more appropriate on large scale enterprises where labour surplus is not a problem, and the biological which relate to improved varieties of seed and livestock, improved techniques of husbandry, and more effective use of fertilizers (Ranis 1979). This second type is able to use more effectively increases in supplies of labour and is, therefore, more suited to labour-surplus conditions such as that in Taiwan. This use of appropriate technologies enabled Taiwan to absorb more people on the land and at the same time increase productivity per worker. Together with the activities of the Farmers' Association, the provision of rural credit and the work of the JCRR, this application of appropriate technology to the extensive and well-engineered irrigation systems established in colonial times, meant that agricultural income levels remained buoyant and helped to reduce the differential between farm and industrial wages. The third development was that of the location of industries in the countryside. In part this was an inheritance of the widespread Japanese agriculturally-related industries. They provided alternative full-time or part-time employment in rural areas and their expansion was necessary to absorb labour and to prevent the rural economy becoming a mere adjunct to the growing cities as in so many countries. The sum total of these developments was the maintenance of an equitable distribution of incomes and a diffusion of growth points in the economy in this first phase of independent development.

Developments in the industrial sector were likewise significant. There was no inbuilt industrial power group in Taiwanese society since manufacturing in terms of both capital investment and managerial skills had been in the hands of the Japanese. The influx of refugees from the mainland provided entrepreneurial and technical skills, some capital and industrial labour and, of course, it provided the government. This new government identified the industrial gap and set about building up this sector. It did so, not by separating industry from agriculture, but by working the two in harness. Agricultural exports provided revenue for industrial investment and the processing of agricultural products provided a basis for industry. The strategy adopted was that of import-substitution, the policy followed by so many developing nations. Taiwan's industries developed rapidly as both consumer goods and intermediate products previously imported, were produced at home. As in agriculture, in Taiwan's labour-surplus society this expansion was based upon labour intensive methods allowing a greater take-up of the unemployed and under-employed. Import-substitution, as has been discussed in Chapter 7, can be a self-containing policy, particularly in small countries if it persists too long. In Taiwan it was a phase which was used effectively. The traditional agricultural exports together with some new higher-value ones had earned exchange revenue, while import-substitution had reduced its subsequent loss. More savings were available for investment and much of this went into capital goods. A larger and experienced industrial labour force was created. By the end of the 1950s this phase had run its course. It was important not to become entrapped by it but to build upon it.

EXPORT-LED INDUSTRIALIZATION

In the early 1960s the Taiwanese government moved the economy into a second phase of development. Import-substitution of consumer goods was to be replaced by the development of export-led manufacturing. Agricultural exports were not to be diminished but instead of being almost the sole export earners they were to be augmented and then surpassed in a relative sense by industrial export. The over-valued Taiwanese dollar which had limited export opportunities and made quota-restriction against imports necessary, was gradually devalued in the late 1950s and early 1960s. Incentives were given to foreign investors and industrialists to set up factories in Taiwan and a number of Export Processing Zones were established, the first being in the southern port of Kaohsiung in 1966. The protection of home consumer industries by quota restrictions on imports was gradually removed, the tax system was modified to encourage exports and a number of further measures were introduced by the government to stimulate the growth of export-orientated industries. All these initiatives were taking place at the beginning of a decade in which the world economy was booming and the world market was reaching dimensions never before experienced. This second phase of export-led industrialization proved to be singularly successful. Industrial output rose by an annual average of 20.1 per cent between 1963 and 1973 and, using labour-intensive methods, Taiwanese exports of manufacturers were able to secure a place in the international market. By the early 1970s Taiwan was experiencing trade surpluses. This phase of a dramatic industrialization of the economy made full use of the labour surplus in Taiwan and changed the balance of employment to one in which, by 1971, equal numbers were employed in agriculture, 35.1 per cent, and industry, 35.6 per cent, including mining, construction, energy and transport (Galenson 1979). So great was the capacity to absorb labour of these new economic developments that by 1970 the labour surplus had disappeared and labour shortages emerged. Unemployment levels which were 4.3 per cent of the labour force in 1964 were down to 1.7 per cent in 1970 and stood at 1.3 per cent in 1979 (Wu 1981). By the 1970s Taiwan's manufacturing sector had overtaken agriculture as the major contributor to exports and its needs accounted for an increasing proportion of imports.

THE ISSUES OF EQUITY

Taiwan has emerged as a newly industrialized country, as have Hong Kong and Singapore discussed in a later chapter. Unlike them she has a substantial and efficient agricultural sector in her economy and, indeed, used it to fuel her initial economic acceleration. What is remarkable about her development is the equitable distribution of incomes which she has been able to maintain throughout this process. It is an achievement which runs counter to the experience of almost every other country where increasing disparities in incomes throughout the population have been so commonplace as to suggest to many scholars that this is an inevitable phase in development.

This inevitability, it is argued, explains why incomes are more markedly unequally distributed in developing countries than in the mature-economies of the industrialized world. Many economists have held to the view that some sectors of the economy must inevitably develop more quickly than others, and with them the incomes of their participants, in order to maximize growth opportunities. It will be recalled that these issues are implicit in the discussions of balanced and unbalanced growth strategies. To attempt to achieve equity, it was felt, might dramatically retard the total growth of the economy. Some would argue that the People's Republic of China could have advanced its total industrial and agricultural productivity more quickly if less attention had been paid to equity. The tendency has been to stress increase in production as the first goal with a fairer distribution of rewards taking place later when there was something substantial to redistribute. In this model inequality would increase as production went up, reach a maximum at some stage in the modernisation process, level off and then decline as society matured and the nation became more affluent (Kuznets 1955; Paukert 1973; Ahluwalia 1974). In Taiwan this has not happened and it is this feature which has attracted the attention of John Fei, Shirley Kuo and Gustav Ranis (Fei and Ranis 1975; Fei, Ranis, Kuo 1979; Kuo, Ranis, Fei 1981).

As in all case studies it could be argued that Taiwan's situation is unique and in some respects this must be so. On the other hand, her former colonial status, her agricultural based economy, her rapidly expanding population and low levels of income placed her very much in the Developing World. The peculiar historical circumstances which left her as an independent territory in 1949 also burdened her with a need to maintain a large army. Her mineral resources were poorer than those of many less successful developing nations. She did possess advantages deriving from the particular nature of the Japanese occupation and, as it transpired, from acquiring an alien government. Crucially important was the way in which the Taiwanese government identified and used to good purpose the advantages and recognized and overcame the disadvantages. Government policies did play a significant part in the achievement of equity and may, therefore, have a wider applicability outside Taiwan. Kuo, Ranis and Fei argue that equity in levels of income can be achieved by the kind of economic growth that is created. In Taiwan's creation of the appropriate kind of growth several significant factors can be identified. First there was a well-established agricultural infrastructure. This consisted of the irrigation works set up by the Japanese and the road and rail networks they constructed. Second, the rent control and land re-allocation legislation of the Nationalist Taiwan Government distributed the resources of agriculture production widely and essentially equitably throughout the countryside. Thirdly, initial manufacturing was associated with agriculture and was again dispersed throughout the countryside. Subsequent manufacturing enterprises were likewise widely distributed throughout the villages, rural towns and regional centres as well as in the cities. Urban primacy, a characteristic legacy of colonization, was not present in Taiwan. The urban hierarchy is much more rank-size in its character and its distribution favours the spatial dissemination of economic activities (Pannell 1973).

In 1951 Taipei and its semi-urban prefectures accounted for 22.1 per cent of all industrial establishments; in 1971 the proportion was 26.1 per cent. For the same years the proportions in rural areas were 21.5 per cent and 23.9 per cent. The proportion of industrial establishments in the five largest cities remained essentially unchanged throughout the period of rapid industrialization and the proportion of persons employed in them actually declined from 43 to 37 per cent between 1956 and 1966 (Ranis 1979). This dispersion of non-farm activities enabled the rural areas to participate in the growth and prosperity of industrialization. In a labour surplus economy industrial wages did not rise dramatically above agricultural, particularly since labour-intensive techniques were used in all factories both large and small. Likewise on the land, labour-intensive techniques were associated with the more intensive use of the land characterized by double-cropping. The returns to labour did not diminish and the growing of high-value crops sustained agricultural income levels. The net result of all these factors was a close association of manufacturing and agriculture in both a spatial and, at least initially, in an industrial-linkage sense. Importantly, distinctions between an urban-industrial sector and a rural-agriculture sector were far less clear and significant than in most countries. Ranis quotes average annual growth rates in real wages for agricultural labour as 2.5 per cent between 1952 and 1960 and 5.1 per cent from 1960–69. For the same two periods the industrial wage rates rose by 5.6 and 5.9 per cent respectively (Ranis 1974). Although agricultural exports were used to fuel the economy and finance industrialization in its early stages, agriculture was not drained of resources for changes and development nor neglected as a backward underpaid sector. In the Developing World this is exceptional. The re-allocation of land and the improvements to agricultural infrastructures were indications of government support and gave strength to the sector. Crucially the import-substitution phase was not allowed to persist overlong and lead to economic stagnation.

The export-led phase of industrialization was also characterised by features which promoted an equitable distribution of incomes. Taiwan's comparative advantage lay in her abundant cheap labour. Using this but also drawing upon American capital for the bigger industrial projects, the industrial upsurge of this phase took up even more surplus labour and allowed agriculture to stave off further the point of diminishing returns on labour and a fall in wage rates. Labour-intensive techniques in both agriculture and industry were, of course, associated with lower levels of investment in capital equipment. This linked the returns on labour much more closely to increases in production so that labour benefitted directly from economic growth. Also manufacturing in Taiwan has been characterised by a large number of small to medium-sized businesses rather than a few giant firms. This has meant that a greater number of entrepreneurial, supervisory and senior skilled posts have been available; the opportunities for advancement are more widely available and this in itself promotes a more equitable distribution of income. Furthermore, the indigenous ownership of firms has meant that industrial wage levels have not been distorted by international companies, and foreign enclaves with foreign wage levels do not exist. Taiwanese society has emerged as one characterized by economic and social mobility with more freedom and opportunity to move between income classes than in almost any other developing country. The wide availability of uniformly high-standard educational facilities has done much to promote this mobility and economic and cultural equity.

In the period since the 1960s Taiwan's labour surplus has disappeared and increasing equity has been the product of higher wage levels in a situation where differentials in wage rates between skilled and unskilled workers have been diminished due to labour shortages. This is a phenomenon experienced in mature industrialized nations. Prior to 1970, however, Taiwan's history of growth and equity is exceptional. The transition from a land-based agricultural society into a labour-based industrial society has been achieved in a free-enterprise context. Comparative wage rates have been manipulated neither by trade unions nor by the government. The government has, however, been a strong one. Its control of the economy through land reforms, fiscal policy and monetary reforms, though indirect rather than direct, has none the less been a major force guiding Taiwan along its path of development. Alongside Hong Kong and Singapore, Taiwan has joined the industrial nations of the world and with them is readjusting to the evolving situation as high technology begins to dominate the lead sectors in manufacturing and new countries enter the phase through which Taiwan has recently passed. But the Taiwanese experience raises again the question of equity in both its spatial and societary dimensions in economic development planning and the issue of the purposeful planning of an integrated rural economy. Together with the People's Republic, Taiwan gives much food for thought. A return will be made to these issues in the concluding chapter.

18 Brazil

'Why did the United States industrialize in the nineteenth century, keeping pace with the nations of Europe, while Brazil in the nineteenth century evolved in the direction of transforming itself into a large underdeveloped region?'

Celso Furtado
The Economic Growth of Brazil 1959

'Brazil ranks among the few nations of the world which have potential for the achievement of major power status within the next century'

J Saunders
Modern Brazil 1971

One of the nations of Latin America whose colonial history began over four centuries ago, Brazil's independence was achieved in 1822 long before many of the former colonies of the Developing World had become colonies. The chronological sequence of her first settlement by Europeans, her colonial development and her final emergence as an independent sovereign state is not greatly different from that of the United States but, as Furtado suggests, while the United States followed the industrial road of Europe, Brazil did not (Furtado 1959). Though one of its more affluent members with a per capita GNP which places her securely in the upper middle-income group of the World Bank's classification, Brazil is still today in the Developing World. This position in the continuum of the development spectrum selects Brazil as a case study but she possesses other characteristics which call for special comment.

Brazil is one of the giant nations of the world. Her area is exceeded only by that of the USSR, Canada, China and the USA. Her present population ranks her as the sixth most populous nation in the world. Second, it will be recalled Brazil exhibits a highly skewed distribution of income (Ch. 4). The top 20 per cent of family incomes groups accounts for two-thirds of the national total of family incomes. This feature is itself a product of a third characteristic, the existence of a strongly marked dual-economy. It is this which allocates Brazil to her middle-income classification since the productivity of one sector is diluted by that of the other. It is a feature which has resulted both from Brazil's history and the development path she has followed. Her transitional position between the Developing World and that of the industrial market economies in no small measure is the product of this characteristic. It is thus possible to visit Rio de Janeiro and form the impression that Brazil is a modern affluent nation little different from that of the United States. Even its backstreets and shanty town areas, the *favela*, give no clear indication of Brazil's less developed status; New York and Chicago have their not dissimilar areas of deprivation. To visit the dry but populated lands of Brazil's north-east is, however, to see a different world and an economy which puts the stamp of the Developing World upon Brazil. Those features are all associated with that spatial characteristic of Brazil which results, in part, from her great size. After nearly five centuries of European involvement, the settlement of Brazil is still essentially peripheral. Most of the population remains concentrated along the Atlantic coast. Three hundred kilometres inland the population density falls sharply; beyond 650 kilometres the terrain is barely populated (Fig. 37B). This means that the greater part of the nation is devoid of towns and huge areas, notably in Amazonas, contain no people. Other parallels come to mind. Australia's population has a similar distribution but it is very much smaller and more urbanized than that of Brazil and the Australian interior presents environmental difficulties which are more daunting. Brazil's present position is suggestive of that in the United States one hundred and fifty years ago when her population was eastern and coastal in its disposition and the 'West' was a vast and almost untouched interior. This issue of the interior adds a distinctive spatial dimension to Brazil's development problem. It becomes one not only of transforming an economy but also of involving and integrating a large and little-touched area. The former colony has become a colonizer and the geographical periphery an economic core.

THE IBERIAN LEGACY

The Portuguese first made contact with Brazil in the opening years of the sixteenth century and a scattering of tiny coastal settlements resulted. In 1530 the Portuguese Crown began to formalize the organization of settlements under the *capitanias* system. Large land grants were made which, in effect, established a landed aristocracy in Brazil. In the first emergence of a plantation system, sugar and tobacco were early amongst crops grown for export. Initially the labour input was supplied by Portuguese peasants and South American Indians but by the middle of the sixteenth century African slaves were being shipped into Brazil in increasing numbers to work the land. By the seventeenth century Brazil, though it was then neither a defined territory nor an economic entity, had become the world's major source of cane sugar with Bahia as the most important producing area. Further inland in what was then the 'interior' similarly large land grants were formed into cattle ranches with hides as the main export. Brazilian

Figure 36 Brazil

A

RORAIMA

AMAPA

N O R T H

NORTH EAST

AMAZONAS

PARA

MARANHAO

CEARA

RIO GRANDE DO NORTE

PIAUI

PARAIBA

PERNAMBUCO

ACRE

RONDONIA

CENTRE WEST

ALAGOAS

SERGIPE

MATO GROSSO

BAHIA

GOIAS

DISTRITO FEDERAL

MATO GROSSO DO SUL

MINAS GERAIS

SAO PAULO

ESPIRITO SANTO

RIO DE JANEIRO

—— Regional Boundary

- - - State Boundary

● Regional Growth Poles

• Rural Incorporation Centres
  suggested by Babarovic

PARANA

SOUTH EAST

SOUTH

SANTA CATARINA

RIO GRANDE DO SUL

0   800 Km

B

Equator

❘❘ Equatorial Rain Forest

Height in Metres

■ >800

▨ 200–800

□ <200

Tropic of Capricorn

0   800 Km

sugar output subsequently declined in the face of competition from more efficiently run plantations which British and Dutch interests established in the Caribbean. In 1650 the non-Indian population of Brazil was put at 74,000 Europeans and 110,000 African slaves (Vianna 1961–62).

In 1694 the discovery of gold in what is now the province of Minas Gerais helped to compensate for the decline in sugar output. It also led to a shift in economic emphasis from the declining sugar areas of the north-east to the central and southern coastal provinces. Sugar planters and their slaves abandoned their plantations and settled as prospectors in the gold areas. In 1729 the attraction of Minas Gerais was enhanced by the discovery of diamonds and these together with the gold, sugar and tobacco came to characterize the colony's exports together with cotton, rice, cocoa and some coffee. The colonial capital was transferred to Rio de Janeiro in 1763. By the eighteenth century Britain was in the throes of the industrial revolution which in Portugal had barely begun. Anxious to protect her home manufactures from possible competition from her own colony, Portugal, in 1785, passed a law prohibiting the establishment of manufacturing in Brazil designed to serve the Portuguese market (Cardozo 1969).

IMPERIAL BRAZIL 1833–89

To escape from the invading armies of Napoleon, the King of Portugal and his whole court fled from Portugal in 1808 and set up a government in exile in Brazil giving the trans-Atlantic colony an additional tier of administration to support. This presence which lasted until 1822, served to centralize the administration of Brazil and give it an individual identity. When the King returned to Portugal, his son whom he had left behind, declared Brazil to be independent and set himself up as Emperor. The political ties with Portugal were effectively severed but Portuguese influence was pervasive and lasting.

Both land and labour were cheap in Brazil, the one because it was abundant and the other because it was slave labour brought in, as required, from Africa. Where these two factors of production were of such low cost it was almost inevitable that they were used extravagantly. Since the owners of these two factors were made wealthy by the sheer size of their possessions, there was little incentive for intensity in their use or their careful husbandry. The Brazilian economy was essentially agrarian but it had two parts. One was concerned with producing for export focusing on the crops which have been mentioned but with sugar, still chiefly in the north-east province, and coffee, initially in the province of Rio de Janeiro, as the outstanding items (Galloway 1968). Both crops were produced on large estates worked by slaves. The other sector was very much larger and involved the greater part of the population. Its concern was with feeding Brazilian bellies. In part it was made up of subsistence farmers working small holdings, the *minifun-*

dios, and in part by farmers producing crops for sale in Brazil. This latter group was characterized by large land-owning units, the *latifundios*, but not by slaves nor exclusively by large producing units. Most farmers were tenant farmers of one sort or another. Maize, manioc and beans were typical products. Wage rates for labourers were low because labour was in abundance. Share-croppers were poor and in no position to improve their lot. On the frontier of settlement in the interior, systems of shifting cultivation were common and, of course, did nothing to improve the land. This sector, made up of subsistence and cash-croppers for the domestic market, accounted for by far the greatest part of Brazil's agricultural economy and it remained the most important throughout the nineteenth century. By its very nature in terms of land tenure, technology, systems of husbandry and in the absence of market stimulus, it remained backward and non-progressive.

The Government, the merchants and the more enterprising land-owners concerned themselves with the commercial export sector. It yielded foreign exchange revenue and was more readily taxable but it too was technically backward, leisurely and inefficient. While sugar continued to decline in importance, that of coffee increased. By 1850 the main focus of coffee growing was in the Paraibo valley betwen Rio and Sao Paulo with easy access to the coast for export and Brazil had become the world's leading exporter of coffee. Increasingly the slave labour which once had been applied to sugar was diverted to coffee estates. It has been estimated that between 1800 and 1852, when the British navy put a stop to the shipment of slaves into Brazil, over 1.5 million slaves had been brought in from Africa (Curtin 1969; Bethell 1970; Leff 1982). In 1888 the number still in a condition of slavery in Brazil was half a million. In that year, slavery in Brazil was abolished and in the political turmoil which followed, the Emperor abdicated and in 1889 Brazil was declared a republic.

THE REPUBLIC OF BRAZIL

During the Empire the population had grown from 4.6 million to 13.9 million largely by natural increase but also augmented by the shipments of slaves from Africa and immigrants from European countries. The Brazil of the new republic, in the last decade of the nineteenth century, was little different in terms of economic development from fifty years earlier. Exports were still made up of primary products of farm, forest and mine. Much of the economy and most of the population were concerned with the domestic market and subsistence and most of the country remained unsettled. The territory of the new republic was still a vast and largely empty expanse devoid of an integrating network of modern forms of transport. In 1884 there were only 6300 kilometres of railway in the whole country and most was in the vicinity of Sao Paulo and Rio and associated with the coffee exporting area. The road network was similarly rudimentary. The physical means to integrate Brazil's vast spaces into a cohesive whole did not exist. Importantly also, as Leff points out, these transport inadequacies had the effect of raising the costs of products arising in the interior, and not simply the deep interior, and in consequence restricted export opportunities to the accessible and essentially coastal areas (Leff 1982).

Cheap labour had been a characteristic of the Empire. Its costs were kept low by the system of land tenure and the use of slaves. When slavery was abolished both the landowners and the republic's government, which was drawn from their ranks, made every effort to maintain the supply of labour and keep its costs low. Migrants had come in from Europe throughout the Empire but in relatively small numbers. The new republic began to subsidize the passages of migrants and the average annual inflow more than doubled. This new labour was used mainly on the land and in the mines but there was no significant redistribution of land holdings and they remained as wage labourers (Hutchinson 1961). Increasingly the growth points in the economy came to be associated with the south-east states leaving the sugar and ranching areas of the north-east province even more deprived and backward.

Up until the First World War Brazil's economy remained dominated by agriculture both in terms of the proportion employed in farming and in its contribution to the Gross National Product. Manufacturing did emerge and grow but only slowly at first and it too was characterized by technical backwardness and a slowness in adopting innovations. The industrial labour force like that in agriculture was, for the most part, poorly paid and badly educated. Little government investment had been applied to the social infrastructure and illiteracy was widespread. It will be recalled that Portugal had restricted manufacturing in Brazil but this is not a convincing explanation of the slow growth after independence. Neither is Brazil's lack of large coal deposits significant, though coal was important in the age of steam and coke iron making. Other coal-less countries industrialized more quickly. Industry which did develop was directed towards import-substitution and most of it was concerned with processing agriculture products so that cotton textiles and food products were the main manufactures. They were made behind protective tariff barriers for the home market and Brazil's exports remained dominated by primary products.

Much of the lethargy in the Brazilian economy of this period can be related to her agriculture. It had developed in a situation of abundant low-cost land and labour. The subsidization of immigration when slavery came to an end and lack of any reforms of land-holding ensured that this situation remained. As a result the majority of the population was poor, landless and wage labouring and this condition persisted throughout the nineteenth century. Brazil's internal market was thus too small, because it was so poor, to generate a large demand for consumer goods and the market stimulus of manufacturing remained weak. This impoverished mass was unable to accumulate savings for investment; nor did it represent a major taxable resource from which the Government could extract revenue for investment. The Government derived revenue from export taxes and it taxed land but the abundance of land and its low value together with the political influence of the large landowners, kept taxation levels low. The agricultural export sector was not a sufficiently large component of the national economy to fuel the engine of economic development and generate enough investment capital. In the years 1911–13 agricultural exports represented only 16 per cent of the GDP. Had a much greater part of the land and the agricultural population been energized into effective production the impetus to move forward would have been greater. As it was the inertia of the dead weight of an unreformed agriculture and rural poverty held back economic progress. Infrastructural developments which the government should have financed were slow in coming because of its meagre resources. Transport in particular was neglected even allowing for the difficulties of terrain and the distances involved in Brazil. In consequence many resources could not be adequately harnessed. It was not until the government of the republic began to borrow on the overseas money market in the last decade of the nineteenth century that railway building on a large scale began. Railway construction did stimulate settlement and promote other initiatives but the focus was mainly in the province of the south-east leaving the North East region once more disadvantaged (Fig. 37A). Towards the end of the century, Brazil began to import industrial capital goods. Her small market hedged around by tariff barriers was not a great attraction to external suppliers of consumer goods. Apologists for Brazil's development cannot therefore attribute blame to this form of mercantile imperialism; indeed the country's balance of payments remained consistently healthy.

Brazil enacted no legislation to facilitate land settlements and achieve a more equitable distribution of land holding and resources comparable with the Homestead Act and other similar land acts which in the United States in the nineteenth century achieved these ends. She adopted a policy enforcing low returns to labour. Her policy led to the fossilization of much of Brazil's agriculture and created a burden which all the development initiatives of the nineteenth century could not lift. Increased borrowing from overseas to fund investments for development did occur before 1914 and foreign industrialists did begin to invest in Brazil and, as a result, manufacturing began to grow apace. The late nineteenth-century initiatives in railway building, continuing into the twentieth, undoubtedly further facilitated these developments. They survived the collapse of the rubber export trade which along with coffee had been a leading export commodity. As British and Dutch rubber plantations came into production and destroyed the market for wild rubber from the Amazon, Brazil's rubber exports fell from holding 90 per cent of the world market in 1910 to 10 per cent in 1920 (Bergsman 1970). Furthermore, the cutting off of industrial imports into Brazil during the First World War still further stimulated Brazil's manufac-

A

Belém

Manaus

Fortaleza

Trans- Amazonica Highway

Recife

Brasilia

Salvador

Railway

Highway

Sao Paulo

Rio de Janeiro

0   800 Km

Port Alegre

B

Population Density
per sq. Km. 1970

>25

5–25

<5

0   800 Km

turing sector which had grown up to serve the home market in an essentially import-substituting role. Between 1914 and 1922 industrial output rose by 150 per cent (Furtado 1976). None the less, in 1920 no less than 68 per cent of Brazil's labour force was still employed in agriculture. Coffee remained a successful export crop and the industrialization thrust weakened. It had been associated with the three main components of food products, textiles and iron goods together with the construction industry. Between 1922 and 1929 industrial output grew hardly at all. In 1929 came the world economic slump bringing coffee exports down with it. The contribution of the industrial sector to the GDP in that year was 11.7 per cent (Furtado 1976). Brazil's political scene was thrown into ferment and in a political coup the presidential link with the vested interests of the landowners of the coffee region was broken. The new president, Getulio Vargas, saw Brazil's future as one best served by a more broadly-based economy and, for the first time, the government of Brazil began actively to stimulate industrial developments.

The fall in the world coffee prices was dramatic and its effects far-reaching. It reduced Brazil's ability to service her debts and led to a devaluation for her currency. In turn these events made imports into Brazil more costly and at the same time rendered coffee a less attractive investment proposition. The price of coffee was subsidized so that its production did not collapse and the home market remained more buoyant than it would otherwise have been. Brazil's import-substituting industries, because imports were made more expensive by the devaluation of the currency, could expand rather than contract. Investments were diverted from coffee planting into manufacturing industries. The economic collapse of the industrialized world made used industrial plant cheap and available and this was brought into Brazil to help manufacture investment goods and intermediate products too expensive to buy in. Encouraged by President Vargas, the process of industrialization was resumed.

AN IMPORT-SUBSTITUTION POLICY OF INDUSTRIALIZATION

It has been remarked earlier that import-substitution has been a commonly adopted approach to industrialization. It was the road Brazil had embarked upon in the nineteenth century and it was this road which Vargas and his successors were to follow for over thirty years. In Brazil's case it was not, however, concerned solely with the production of consumer goods for the retail market, it went to the foundations of industrialism. Under a cover of protectionism, all sectors of the manufacturing spectrum were involved. Energy resources were developed notably that of hydro-electricity but also that of the meagre non-coking coal deposits in the state of Santa Caterina.

Figure 37 Brazil

Oil exploration was begun and production, though in very small quantities, had commenced by 1940. The rich iron ore deposits near Belo Horizonte in Minas Gerais, together with Brazil's manganese ores were further developed and bauxite mining and aluminium production began on an increasing scale. A whole series of regional cement plants were set up and transport facilities, particularly roads, were improved. While some of these activities did yield exports, their raison d'être was to secure the bases of industries for the home markets. Until 1946 almost all Brazil's increasing output of iron was produced almost entirely with the use of charcoal. In that year a new large iron and steel plant at Volta Redonda, which itself enlarged Brazil's iron and steel making capacity by 25 per cent, was brought into operation using specially processed Brazilian coal in its blast furnaces. By 1964 there were ten large steel-producing companies in the Itabira-Belo Horizonte area. This laying of foundations allowed the establishment of vertically and horizontally-linked industries. Steel rolling mills, engineering plant, aluminium fabricating units and, eventually in the late 1950s, motor vehicle plant, all came into operation. Chemical production and the long-established manufacture of textiles were increased.

Such was the progress of this industrial expansion that home production came to meet almost all the needs of the domestic market across the whole spectrum of industry. In 1949, 65 per cent of capital goods had been imported; by 1959 it was 33 per cent and by 1964, 10 per cent. Intermediate goods were likewise produced almost entirely in Brazil and her reliance on imports fell from 27 per cent in 1949 to 7 per cent in 1964. The import of consumer durables fell dramatically from 65 per cent in 1949 to 10 per cent as early as 1955, falling further to 2 per cent in 1964. Non-durable consumer goods had long been produced almost entirely in Brazil but even in this sector imports were halved (Bergsman 1970). This process of rapid industrialization involved both the state and foreign firms. Strict protective measures effectively excluded the import of goods manufactured abroad. The import of motor vehicles, for example, was prohibited but foreign motor vehicle manufacturers were encouraged to set up plant in Brazil and produce within her borders. The funding of this expansion came from taxes on the export of primary products, notably those from agriculture, from borrowing on the international money market and from the investments in Brazil of foreigners. The three components referred to in Chapter 9 as sources of development revenue were all utilized in Brazil but agricultural exports were the most significant source.

Vargas was finally replaced as President in 1954. His successors maintained the policy of industrialization via import-substitution which was so wide-reaching that it was tantamount to a policy of self-sufficiency but one which accepted and used foreign capital and expertise. Manufacturing was essentially a matter of replacing imports so that even as late as 1960, 97 per cent of Brazil's merchandise exports were made up of primary commodities. By extending industrial developments into all strata of industry, initially with the use of revenue derived from agriculture and hence dependent upon agriculture, by the mid-1960s a broadly based and much more fully integrated industrial structure had been created. This structure was much less dependent upon agricultural exports but in creating it, Brazil had become much more dependent upon international capital.

Import-substitution has its own self-limiting features. It caters for the home market and in doing so is limited by the size of that home market. It is necessary, therefore, for that market to grow either by population increase or by becoming more affluent or by both. This issue of an expanding work force creating itself an expanding market was discussed in Chapter 8. The process of industrial integration which characterized Brazilian development itself, of course, helped to ensure a market for intermediate and other goods which are not consumer end-products. This is in contrast to the situation in India where the focus on the basic industries to the exclusion of industries which processed their products, effectively curtailed the industrial market and led to unused capacity.

Brazil's market difficulties lay in the distinctive nature of her internal market. In the mid 1960s industrial output in Brazil began to fall in part, no doubt, because of the socio-economic disturbance associated with the period just before and after the military coup of 1964 which overthrew the presidency. However, as Furtado points out, while industrial production declined a larger proportion of its output was exported, indicating that it was the home market which placed limits on output (Furtado 1976). The character of Brazil's internal market is a product of her long history of abundant labour. This keeps wages low in the industrial sector and confines demand to a limited range of consumer goods. The agricultural population is itself poor with limited disposable incomes and movement into industrial employment does not raise incomes significantly. As industry has become more sophisticated it has tended to become more capital-intensive so that its level of output is less tied to labour input. In a situation of import-substitution, these features effectively retard the growth of the domestic market and a mismatch occurs between productive capability and demand. The more affluent sector of society (the top 10 per cent of families by income level account for 50.6 per cent of the total of family incomes in Brazil) represent a significant and different market which grows as greater incomes, the product of commercial and technological advances, accrue to this sector. Its tastes are more specialized and for the individual groups of goods within its demand spectrum the demand is small and inhibits economies of scale in their production. Unused capacity in Brazil has developed in this situation which restricts the level of returns on investment and holds back industrial dynamism (Furtado 1976). The nature of Brazil's domestic market has a significance which is detrimental to economic development based on import-substitution. Its second feature is as much of social as of economic significance. It is the persistence of economic inequalities on a large scale. On the one hand it was produced by the systems of land-holding and agriculture going back to the days of the Portuguese conquest and the use of slaves and on the other it was allowed to develop in the manufacturing sector in the nineteenth century and has persisted into the second half of the twentieth.

The lowest 30 per cent of total household incomes groups account for only 16.4 per cent of total household incomes. Both social injustices and a limitation of the full opportunity of economic expansion are features of this situation. In this respect it would not be inaccurate to say that Brazil has grown but not developed.

MANUFACTURING FOR EXPORT

In the late 1960s the Government attempted to reduce surplus industrial capacity by enlarging the market for Brazil's manufactured goods in two ways. First, following Brazil's long-established practice, the Government stimulated those industries which served the small affluent sector of Brazil's domestic market. Second, and much more significantly, the Government adopted a policy of promoting the export of manufactures. It was hoped that the market enlarged by these endeavours would not only absorb surplus capacity, but also permit economies of scale to be achieved while at the same time allowing a degree of specialization in those items where Brazil might have comparative advantage. In 1960 manufactured goods had accounted for only 3 per cent of Brazil's exports. By 1977 the proportion had grown to 26 per cent and in 1980 reached 39 per cent. Some 55 per cent of these manufactured goods went to other developing countries. Though still a primary exporter, Brazil has moved strongly into the industrial-export field. In doing so she has broken free of the limitations which an import-substitution policy imposes even in a country as large as Brazil.

It can be argued that Brazil retarded the structural transformation of her economy and her economic development by unduly delaying entry into the international market for industrial exports in those commodities where she was competitive. It can also be argued that the maintenance of a low-wage economy was not only socially suppressive but likewise held back the industrial dynamism which Brazil undoubtedly possesses. None the less, in the period between 1950 and 1980 manufacturing in Brazil has grown steadily and rapidly with average annual industrial growth averaging 10 per cent while that of the GNP was 7 per cent. Average per capita incomes have increased greatly in real terms from around US $600 in 1950 to over US $2000 in 1981 with both levels measured at 1980 values.

Brazil's industrial boom was in some measure coincident with the world-wide upsurge in industry and trade. Both the dramatic rise in oil prices and the resulting world economic depression which terminated the good years, seriously affected Brazil. Once again she resorted to import-substitution where it was possible, but she had, of course, acquired a capacity geared to the external dimensions of the market. To sustain her growth, Brazil needed to borrow on the external money market. The need for capital was all the greater because of the size of her industrial sector. By 1979 Brazil had the highest level of indebtedness to commercial banks of any country in the Developing World. Her commitment in terms of public borrowing in 1981 was second only to that of Mexico which, unlike Brazil, is a major oil producer. The issue of debt servicing, referred to in Chapter 9 has, in Brazil's case, come to the fore requiring an expansion of exports, a cut-back in domestic expenditure and a greater and exacting efficiency in the management of her resources. In 1981 Brazil's debt service was the equivalent of 31.9 per cent of the value of her exports. Only Peru demonstrated a higher ratio.

Brazil's great development which has raised her into the higher-middle income group of the world's nations, ranked by per capita GNP, has made her a significant industrial nation. In terms of total value-added her manufacturing exceeds that of any other nation in the Developing World, though data for China are not available. In part this is a function of her giant size, in part it is the result of the measures taken towards industrialization which have been taken by successive governments. That her economy is far from secure is indicated by the state of her indebtedness in the mid 1980s. That her society is as yet immature is shown in the inequitable distribution of incomes. Brazil possesses a society and economy which is clearly dualistic. A small affluent community participates in, and has access to the benefits of, her sophisticated industrial and service sector. At the same time the majority of the population is still comparatively poorly paid. Thirty per cent still work in agriculture and this group is the most separate and deprived. The remainder work in the industrial and service sectors. The equity which is so noticeably present both in socialist China and capitalist Taiwan is equally noticeable by its absence in Brazil. The work of Kuznets, Paukert and Ahluwadia, referred to in the discussion of Taiwan, would seem to be more applicable in the case of Brazil (Kuznets 1955; Paukert 1973; Ahluwadia 1974). It remains to be seen whether the present stage of Brazil's development will be followed by one of more equal opportunity and spread of benefits.

In this Brazilian metamorphosis little mention has been made of governmental development plans. Prior to the Second World War, they did not exist. Governments in Brazil have played a major role in economic development but it has had a distinctive flavour imparted to it by the patrician attitudes of its leaders, by the paternalistic views of the ruling aristocracy and, in recent years, by an abhorrence of socialism and with it the concept of a planned command economy. Plans there have been with the first series running through until 1960 with subsequent plans covering the 1960s, 1970s and into the first half of the 1980s. These National Plans have become more comprehensive and sophisticated as they have evolved, but they have been formulated in an atmosphere of capitalism and free enterprise even though some enterprises are totally state-owned while in others state participation is considerable. Planning has been pragmatic and consultative rather than rigid and ideological. Consultations have been essentially between industrialists and investors, both Brazilian and foreign, and the departments of Government. Government policies which, as has been seen, have significantly influenced Brazil's development, have often taken the form of import controls, of tariff and exchange rate manipulation and of investment subsidies, all of which have often determined the allocation of resources.

THE SPATIAL DIVIDE: BRAZIL THE COLONIZER

Prior to the late 1950s, the governments of Brazil paid little attention to where the economic activities which they were encouraging or suppressing were taking place. Developments which took place before 1914 had tended to be concentrated in the central and southern coastal areas and the nearer interior valleys, setting up a regional bias which has persisted. The successive governments in the republic pursued a centralized form of administration in part, perhaps, in an attempt to stress national unity in such an extensive but unintegrated territory. It may well have been a policy running counter to the maximization of economic development. Though it is debatable, greater regional autonomy could, possibly, have more effectively promoted the development of still unused resources. The risk was, of course, political separatism. As it is, in the last years of the twentieth century Brazil is still divided spatially between the economic core on the geographical periphery and the economic periphery in the geographical core. The focus of population and economic activity still leaves much of Brazil little integrated into the body of the political economy. As Dickenson has put it, 'In contrast to the Turnerian frontier in North America, the Brazilian frontier has not been a continuous, advancing sweep but instead piecemeal and hesitant and is still active' (Dickenson 1982).

President Vargas had been disturbed by the neglect of the greater part of Brazil and had attempted, by reducing the powers of regional governments, to bring the nation into a more cohesive and integrated state. During the periods of office of his successors, planning bodies for the main regions were established. The Superintendency for the Development of the North East, SUDENE, was set up in 1959 and that of Amazonia, SUDAM, in 1966. A similar body, SUDESUL, for the densely-populated and economically vigorous core area in the south-east was also established. The presidency of Kubitschek (1956–61) also saw two much-publicized developments which could be taken as tokens of governmental recognition of the issues of regional development. Brasilia, the new purpose-built capital referred to in Chapter 10, was inaugurated in 1960 with a design size of 500,000. Located in an area of low population density over 900 kilometres from Rio, it represented a step into the interior by national government and national interests. Though still peripheral to much of the country in many respects, it none the less represents a significant frontier gesture and in its appearance symbolizes the emergence of the new modern Brazil. In a more practical sense its impact on Brazil's economic periphery is limited. In Katsman's view, Brasilia will not contribute much to the industrialization of the state of Goiás, though it will stimulate agricultural developments by the very presence of a large urban market. The interior areas have long suffered from their remoteness from the markets along the coast (Katzman 1977). The second development was the commencement of the Brasilia-Belem Highway as part of a plan to connect the new capital to the rest of the country. Begun in 1958 as an unsurfaced road, it was completed as a surfaced all-weather road in 1973. Katzman calculates that between 1960 and 1970 the Brasilia-Belem Highway by stimulating settlement accounted for between one-third and one-half of the growth of the population in Goiás (Katzman 1977). A more ambitious project has been the construction of the Transamazonica Highway reaching westwards from the arid lands of north-eastern Brazil across the rain forest of Amazonia to the Peruvian border (Figs. 36B and 37A).

Sufficient time has not yet elapsed for the full impact of the work of the regional development agencies to be felt nor yet that of Brasilia and the Transamazonica Highway, but the development of most of Brazil's interior is still in its most early stages. In part this is a result of the great size of the territory to be settled. The distribution of population and the penetration of the railway network shown in Fig. 37A indicates how little, or how much, has as yet been achieved. There is little indication of either a transport network or hierarchy of urban centres which would integrate this vast territory into a cohesive space economy. Brazil indeed raises all the issues discussed in Chapter 10.

Ivo Babarović in his penetrating statistical analysis of the regionalisation of Brazil's economy makes the point that while regional problems exist within regions themselves they raise issues which can only be addressed at national level (Babarović 1978). He states that regional imbalances, as was indicated in Chapter 10, are common in developing countries which have reached the stage in which Brazil finds herself and stresses that the resulting undesirable effects cannot be left to some speculative restoration of spatial equilibrium by natural processes. He lists in Brazil's case the catalogue of adverse consequences so often associated with spatial skewness and its linked social and economic inequalities. First the urban agglomerations exceed optimum size and produce diseconomies which retard natural growth. Second, regional concentration of growth, the mushrooming of the core, means the periphery is neglected, which is so clearly the case in Brazil. This neglect in turn leads to an impoverished group whose market stimulus to the economy is, as has been seen, thus enfeebled. Third, Babarović refers to the moral and social injustices which are inherent in spatial inequalities in welfare and, fourth, he points out that too great a discrepancy in regional levels of economic activity, social and income benefits and participation in the nation's progress, can lead to social and political conflict and put at risk both the political and territorial integrity of Brazil. This is no small risk in a country so large as Brazil in which its distant borders are so tenuously connected with its centre of economic and political gravity. Brazil shares her border with no less than ten other countries and with most of it more than 1600 kilometres from Brasilia. Babarović holds to the view that the near or 'frontier' regions of Brazil's periphery should be settled and encompassed into the national economy, while regions further out, but none the less settled, should also be linked into the national economy so as to enhance the domestic market for industrial growth. Conversely, he feels some attempt must be made to inhibit the growth of the big urban complexes. His solution is a greater degree of spatial deconcentration of economic activities, a theme which has been referred to in many of the case studies in this book and which will be developed further in the concluding chapter.

Babarović makes the point that while growth-pole strategies have been adopted as a means of achieving regional development they have often resulted in the same spread/backwash situation associated with primate cities and become enclaves of modernization such as have been referred to in Chapter 10. Instead he recommends the now more favoured view of a greater number for more widely spread development centres of differing orders. Babarović's solution for Brazil is essentially the creation of a more integrated urban hierarchy with an accompanying reorganization and modernization of agriculture in the tributary peripheries. In Brazil's case with her long-established and archaic land-holding systems, this is no easy solution. The statistical analysis which Babarović makes is designed to assess the geo-economic potential for interaction in terms of accessibility in spatial units and results in an identification of centres for development in such a scheme. The large regional poles so identified together with those stimulating rural incorporation have been plotted on Fig. 36A.

Brazil's problems of her dual economy, dual society and disaggregated spatial development remain unsolved, but a beginning has been made. It is not a process which necessarily involves Brazil in an attempt to settle and urbanize the forests of Amazonia, clearing them for some commercialized form of agriculture. Indeed there are those outside Brazil who urge upon her the preservation of the last great tract of tropical forest left in the world. It is a process which needs to achieve, and achieve quickly, the integration of Babarović's 'frontier' areas which are already settled, if but lightly, and it is one which urgently must address the problem of social and economic inequalities. If the status of a major world power is within Brazil's grasp as Saunders claims, it is a problem which requires an early settlement.

19 Peru

'From the time of the Spanish Conquest, foreigners have displayed
energy, skill and daring in their attempts to open up the country and
carry away its riches, and in rendering up its wealth, first to the
enterprise of capital investors, Peru has suffered a fate analogous to that
of the oyster, which it, too, is 'opened up' for its riches'

R J Owens
Peru 1963

Peru shares with Brazil many of her characteristic Latin American features,
though in Peru they are more dramatically drawn and neither Peru's present
level of attainment nor her future prospects compare favourably with those
of Brazil. Peru's people are poor. In 1981 the average per capita GNP was
US $1170, the lowest in South America after Bolivia and Guyana. Further-
more, this average conceals, as it does in Brazil, a markedly skewed distribution of income. In 1972 the poorest 20 per cent of Peruvian families
accounted for only 1.9 per cent of the national total of family incomes;
indeed the bottom 60 per cent of household income groups represented only
18 per cent of the national total. It was estimated that 31 per cent of Peru's
population 'lived under conditions of absolute poverty, i.e. earning incomes
that did not permit them to consume what is considered an adequate
volume of food and non-food items' (Thumm 1981). Peru's development
history has produced a most inequitable distribution of the material benefits
of development. Nor is this situation improving. By 1979 the real incomes
of the lowest group had fallen by 18 per cent and of the middle-income
group by between 10 and 17 per cent, while that of the top income group
rose by over 10 per cent (Thumm 1981). Poverty is thus extreme and widespread. This is the country of the Incas. Its present situation has its beginnings in the destruction of their empire.

THE SPANISH CONQUEST

Between 1530 and 1533 the Spaniard Francisco Pizarro destroyed the
political and military power of the Incas and disrupted the socio-economic
system they had established. In 1544 the Spanish Crown established the
Vice-royalty of Peru, covering a territory much larger than that of the

present Peru, and attempted to exert an absolute control over its lands and people. Though some negro slaves were imported from Africa, their numbers were very small partly because of Peru's location and partly because of the greater size of the indigenous Indian population compared with the situation in Brazil. Instead the people of the Inca Empire were made virtual slaves in their own country. The new colony was administered in systems which gave the appointed Spaniards, the *encomenderos*, total control over the local people in their charge. Their labour could be directed at will. Land was taken from Indian use and redistributed to the Spanish officials or sold to Spaniards.

The extent to which this occupation took place varied within the contrasted physique of this large territory. Along Peru's entire coast is a long stretch of desert lowland (Fig. 38). Inland, foothills rise into the cordillera of the high Andes where peaks reach to 6000 metres in a series of ranges and high plateaux separated by deep valleys. To the east of the Andes the land drops down to the hot wet lands of Amazonia, the Selva. At the time of the conquest the main focus of Peruvian population was in the valleys of the Sierra and it was in this area that Spanish interest was focused since it possessed resources of gold, silver and mercury.

For the next two centuries Spain extracted large amounts of silver and significant amounts of gold from the Andean Sierra of Peru. Neither the deserts of the Costa nor the rain forests of the Selva were of much interest to them. The colonial economy was extractive and the colonists made rich by their exports had little cause to develop agriculture and manufacturing of goods which could be imported from the home country. Gradually, however, the descendants of the original Spanish settlers began increasingly to organize their estates, the *haciendas*, and produce a range of crops both for local consumption and, in the case of sugar, cotton and tobacco, for export. Likewise manufacturing for local needs developed despite Spanish laws to the contrary.

By the beginning of the nineteenth century, Peru, along with other Spanish colonies in Latin America, had grown to be largely independent of Spain. The revolutions led by Simon Bolivar and José de San Martin, and beginning in 1810, resulted eventually in many countries achieving their independence. The process in Peru's case was an involved one and included participation in a confederation of Peru and Bolivia, which was dissolved in 1839. Peru had grown out of armed revolution, her final independence involved the warring of generals and her first civilian government did not come into existence until 1872, fifty-one years after San Martin had taken Lima and declared Peru free of Spain. It was not an auspicious beginning, nor was the subsequent history of military rule, punctuated by revolutions, a period conducive to an ordered economic and social development let alone development planning. The foundations of a long period of a prodigal misuse of resources, of inefficiency and injustices were laid.

SILVER AND SUGAR, COTTON, COPPER AND BIRD DROPPINGS

Independent Peru was little different from the colony out of which it emerged. A series of laws were enacted which would, in theory, have given back rights to land to the Indians who had never known individual land ownership, as well as distributing land more widely among the descendents of the settlers. In practice this legislation facilitated the assemblage of large land-ownership units on the better land upon which the Indians worked mainly as share-croppers. These *haciendas* were located in the broader valleys of the Sierra and on the coastal plain, the Costa, where land could be reclaimed by irrigation. In the more difficult high Sierras and in the Selva, land was farmed in systems little different from those of pre-Conquest days. In mining the Indians continued to provide labour for the dangerous and difficult work of silver and mercury extraction. The Indian remained as the bottom layer of society in all these activities and the Peruvian economy, like that of Brazil, was characterized by an abundance of cheap labour.

In 1841 the discovery that the guano, the bird droppings which accumulated in the huge colonies of sea birds along the arid coastline of Peru, was a valuable sources of nitrogen, invested Peru with a new and valuable resource. The guano could be, and was, used as a rich nitrogenous fertilizer on Peru's cotton and sugar estates. The extractive mentality in which the exploitation of Peru's mineral resources had first developed soon identified guano as a potentially valuable export. Using Indian labour it was mined on a massive scale in an uncontrolled exploitation. Bird droppings came to exceed the value of silver exports, guano mining was declared a state monopoly and its export revenue did much to sustain the Peruvian economy. In the southern-most coastal areas of Peru, the arid climate had given rise to another valuable mineral fertilizer, the nitrate deposits at Tarapaca. These too were exploited as a state monopoly. The contractors associated with the extraction of guano and nitrate deposits came to be a rich and politically powerful group known as the *guaneros*.

Peru's economy was seriously affected by her participation in two wars in the second half of the nineteenth century. In the first, Peru and her neighbours fought off an attempt by Spain to re-exert her authority over her former colonies. In the second, Peru was herself in conflict with both Bolivia and Chile over the nitrate deposits in the desert lands on her border with Chile. Peru was defeated and lost her valuable nitrate fields to Chile. Peru entered the twentieth century with an insecure, disorganized economy. The capital for her infrastructural developments and the exploitation of her mineral resources had come largely from Europe and North America. Political power lay in the hands of a small group of landowners and mineral developers. In the periods between the succession of military coups when elected governments were returned, the Indian majority in the country were effectively disenfranchised since literacy was a prerequisite. Exports of sugar, cotton, guano, silver, copper and other minerals had sustained Peru in the nineteenth century. Both exports and imports were taxed and such manufacturing as there was produced only for the small home market.

Peru was essentially an exporter of primary products and though not a political colony bore all the marks of a colonial form of economy. She is fortunate in that the mineral resources she possesses are not only large but varied. The orogenic belt of the Andes yields substantial amounts of zinc, lead and copper and in addition manganese, antimony, silver, tungsten, bismuth, cadmium, tin and gold are also mined. Even today the mineral exploration of the Sierras is far from complete. As the exploitation of these resources progressed, the small-scale mining companies were replaced by large and mainly foreign companies which could raise the capital and provide the technology. Mining became increasingly capital-intensive so that while mineral exports formed a large part of material exports, mining sustained only a small labour force. Sugar and cotton were both important export items. The increasing concentration of land-ownership in the late-nineteenth century which has been mentioned, meant that the production of these two leading agricultural exports was in the hands of a few. The result of these developments was that the growth in Peru's economy associated with increased exports spilled over little to the benefit of the majority of the population. The greater part of Peru's population and economy was detached from these export developments. There was growth, therefore, without development in its true sense. As has been discussed in earlier chapters this colonial type of export economy was characterized by infra-structural developments specific to it, by the import of technology and equipment for its particular use, and by its relative insulation from other industries. The bulk of Peru's population because they did not benefit remained poor. This limited the size of the domestic market and so inhibited the development of import-substitution industries financed by export earnings. Too little of these earnings were retained in Peru and those which were entered too few pockets. Since labour was abundant in Peru, the wages of even those participating in the export economy remained low.

While the variety of her exports gave Peru a degree of protection against the market fluctuations in any one particular commodity, her mineral exports in particular were geared to the needs of the industrialized countries of Europe and North America so that when the economy of these countries collapsed in the great recession of the late 1920s and early 1930s so too did the markets for most of Peru's exports. The capital for her mining was from these same areas and it too diminished with the markets. In Peru this world-wide recession did not result in a vigorous drive for industrialization since much of the economy was untouched by it. Only gradually did Peru begin to develop some import-substitution industries and even in this activity was disadvantaged by the world trends referred to in Chapter 9, in which the relative value and demand for manufactured goods, including production machinery, compared with primary products changed to the detriment of the latter. Peru's politically and financially powerful minority had long been associated with land-owning and mining rather than industrial expertise and entrepreneurship. Her population had very little experience of factory production. As a result when the world economic crisis faded away Peru maintained her primary export economy and this persisted through and after the Second World War. In the 1950s when many former colonies achieved their independence and were characterized by colonially initiated primary export economies, Peru, which had achieved independence some 130 years earlier, was still in that same category. Changes were to come but they came slowly.

THE ECONOMIC SITUATION IN THE MID-TWENTIETH CENTURY

Peru entered the second half of the twentieth century with a government and business community which still viewed the development of the economy as a process of expanding the export of raw materials both in volume and variety. The important foreign investors obviously saw their business as one of extracting primary products for use by the industrial nations. The developments which took place after 1950 continued to reflect these attitudes so that while Peru experienced a period of rapid growth in production it was, in the main, concerned with this characteristically insulated export activity.

Oil had been discovered in Peru in the nineteenth century and output from the Brea-Parinas field on the coast near Ecuador's border reached two million barrels per day by 1914. In the 1950s, however, oil exploration was actively encouraged. New oil leases were granted in 1952 with the Peruvian Government participating in 50 per cent of the profits. By 1960 oil output reached 20 million barrels and Peru became a net oil exporter. Exploration was extended east of the Andes and in 1962 the Mobil Oil Company tapped natural gas in the Aguayita region. Oil is now produced near Ganso Azul on the Pachitca river. The output of copper, long a significant Peruvian export was greatly increased when the newly-discovered deposit in the coastal ranges of the Andes at Toquepala was brought into production. The first exports from this field took place in 1959 through the former fishing port of Ilo developed specifically to export the ore and carried to it by a railway built to connect the mines. The ore body is large, some 400 million tonnes, and its development made copper Peru's most important export in 1960, overtaking cotton which had long held the premier position. In this copper development the companies involved were American. Iron ore which had not figured prominantly in Peruvian mining took on a new significance when in 1955 the Marcona Mine, 560 kilometres south of Lima, began producing a very rich iron ore which, with a 60 per cent iron content, was readily exportable. The high grade component in the ore body was estimated at 70 million tonnes with the lower grade at eight times that amount. By 1960 the output from Marcona reached 3 million tonnes, most of it being shipped to North America (Owens 1963). Other iron ore bodies were developed in the 1950s by American companies as in the case of Marcona.

In the agricultural sector the export of primary products was further increased throughout the 1950s as the acreage under cotton and sugar was enlarged and yield increased. Production was on large estates and both Peruvian and foreign capital was involved in both the agricultural and manufacturing aspects. Coffee production also grew sufficiently to allow it to meet home demand and become an export commodity.

Fisheries resources were developed for the first time in Peru during this period. For centuries fish had been regarded of little importance. When the guano deposits came to be worked it was realized that inshore fish shoals were supporting the dense bird colonies which produced the guano. Because of the great importance of guano as an export in the nineteenth century, the influential guaneros were fearful, with some justification, that fishing might deplete the bird population and with it the source of guano. The importance of guano mining declined as alternative fertilizers became available and in the 1940s a small fishing industry, canning bonitos, was established. Peru came gradually to realise that she possessed one of the world's richest fishing grounds off her shores. Expansion in the 1950s was rapid and involved not only the canning and freezing of the big fish, notably bonito and tuna, but also the harvesting of the huge shoals of oil-rich anchovies which became, by far, the most important component in Peru's fishing industry. Pressed for oil in coastal oil-extraction plants, the residue of the anchovies becomes fish meal which is a very high-protein livestock feedstuff. By 1963 there were 138 fishmeal factories along Peru's coast. Fish exports which had totalled 21,500 tonnes in 1950 reached 592,000 tonnes by 1960 and by 1970 the amount was 2.25 million tonnes and formed an important new export commodity. The industry began as an essentially Peruvian venture with 70 per cent of the invested capital in 1960 being Peruvian (Owens 1963). Despite an awareness of the risk of over-fishing, this important new development began to run into difficulties as the inshore shoals were depleted resulting in an increase in fishing costs. At this stage foreign companies began to take over more of the industry since they could supply the needed capital (Furtado 1976).

The pattern of development in the 1950s and 60s was thus clear. It was very much the situation as before. Much of it came from external stimulus and much involved foreign capital and expertise and it was largely a development in which the value added to Peru's raw materials took palce outside Peru. It is true, of course, that the smelters for refining the ores such as copper, zinc and lead were set up in Peru by the mining companies but their products were for export. Expansion did, however, take place in Peru's iron and steel-making capacity with the inauguration in 1957 of the integrated iron and steel works at Chimbote powered by a hydro-electric station and

Figure 38 Peru

with an associated steel rolling mill. (Fig. 38). A government-owned concern, the small plant proved a loss-maker even though it was supplied with iron ore from the Marcona mines at a low cost. In 1960 the Government initiated plans for a considerable enlargement of the plant with a Swiss firm responsible for its operation. It was a move into the phase of import-substitution. The plant continued to lose money while its products were protected by high tariff barriers. The Chimbote plant produces solely for the home market but cannot meet its total demand, while its products cost more than imports. Utilising Chimbote's output together with imported semi-processed products, metal-working and engineering industries grew significantly in the 1950s and 60s. The most important manufacturing industries were, however, those concerned with processing agricultural products, the food and textile industries characteristic of early developments in industrialization.

The result of this ensemble of developments was a marked increase in

Peru's GDP. Between 1950 and 1960 the annual growth rate of GDP averaged 5.3 per cent. Much of this growth can be attributed to foreign investments and most, though not all, was concerned with the exports of primary products. The multiplier effect of these developments was limited and a large part of the population was not involved. In consequence, the ability of Peru's economy to absorb and make use of the retained earnings of her export activities was much diminished. The essential corollary of absorptive home developments, particularly in the manufacturing sector but also in essential infrastructural developments, was missing. Export-led growth was not leading to a full and self-sustaining development. As has been seen, the situation was not entirely negative. Industrialization was beginning to accelerate, social and physical infrastructural investments were taking place and even schemes to ameliorate the worst features of the traditional landholding structure were attempted. All these were changes which had been unduly delayed and all were insufficient in both the scale and rigour of their implementation to lift Peru's population to any significant extent up the ladder of social and economic development. In 1960 primary products still accounted for 99 per cent of exports. Of the work force 53 per cent were employed in agriculture and 19 per cent in mining and manufacturing (World Bank 1980a). Significantly Peru's import coefficient, that is the value of imports as a percentage of the GDP, grew throughout the 1950s from 11.9 per cent in 1950 to 21.1 per cent in 1960 (Furtado 1976).

Peru's population was growing rapidly. In the 1950s annual growth appreciably exceeded 2.5 per cent and between 1960 and 1970 average annual growth was 2.8 per cent. Her backward agricultural systems farming difficult terrain were unable to meet the demand for food. It should be remembered that only 25 per cent of Peru is suitable for agricultural use without major modifications and much of this area is devoted to grazing. A very large proportion of the country is mountain in the Sierra, much of the Costa is desert, unusable without investment in irrigation, and only the Selva possesses much untapped land potential though beyond its fringes it presents all the problems discussed in Chapter 5. The demand for non-durable consumer goods by Peru's poor population was small and met largely by home production. Peru's export activities did, however, require imports, so too did her small affluent sector, while the beginnings of industrialization further increased the import coefficient. Peru was earning revenue from export but her problem, and in some respects it is not dissimilar from that of Nigeria, was in developing her internal economy in such a way as to be able effectively to broaden her economic base, modify her economic structure and provide employment for her growing population. As in Brazil, Peru's dual economy was not only inequitable but was retarding development. The average annual growth in GDP which had reached 6.1 per cent between 1960 and 1965 fell to 3.4 per cent in the next five years. The import coefficient rose to 26.1 in 1965 and was still 25.6 in 1970.

The nature of land-holding both impeded agricultural efficiency and denied many rural dwellers the opportunity of sharing the benefits of economic growth. The small size and immature nature of the manufacturing sector, much of it located in and around Lima, was a further index of Peru's unbalanced development. Both were features which required urgent attention. Restricted opportunities in the countryside stimulated an increasing rural to urban migration to towns ill-prepared to receive the influx. Between 1960 and 1980 Peru's urban population rose from 46 per cent of the total population to 67 per cent. Action had been taken by successive governments in an attempt to address these problems but with little enthusiasm. The situation changed in 1968 when the army seized power and set about the implementation of a radical reform of Peruvian society and economy. It was a policy socialist in its approach with a greater equity in society as its goal and nationalization of wide sections of the economy as its method. In retrospect it would seem to have been more concerned with the reorganization of ownership and control rather than with improving productivity and efficiency and its actions transferred more power to the state than to the people. The Military Government's initial policies were incorporated in the Peruvian Agrarian Reform Law of 1969. Here the new government faced up squarely to the seemingly intractable issue of land ownership and initiated radical changes. In the Costa region much of the land was farmed in large estates growing chiefly sugar and cotton with the associated processing industries located on them; most were foreign owned. These estates and factories were nationalized and the process began of converting them into co-operatives. Second, the Military Government addressed the problem of the *minifundios*, the tiny holdings which accounted in 1960 for 88 per cent of all farms but only 7.4 per cent of farmed land. To make more viable units the Government sought to amalgamate groups of small farmers into collectives organized and operated by their members in their common interests. The hold of the *latifundio* owners was to be weakened by placing an upper limit on the size of holding which an individual could own. The precise limits varied according to the region of the country and as to whether the land was irrigated and, indeed, according to the level of wages paid to farm workers. *Latifundios* had covered 82.4 per cent of agricultural land while accounting for only 1.1 per cent of farm units. This process of land distribution was carefully and methodically implemented throughout the country. In practice most of the land was reallocated to various types of co-operative or collective holdings and very little to individuals. The socialisation of agriculture appeared to be the intent. Furtado writing in 1973 believed that this drastic agrarian reform did not appear to have resulted in a fall in agricultural production as is so often the case (Furtado 1976). Later evidence, however, as will be seen, shows Peru to have been no exception and agricultural output fell considerably. Agrarian reform was essential. The form it took appears not to have achieved either the equity or improvement it presumably intended. The military government of Peru in the 1970s could have learned much from either China or Taiwan.

The government also took decisive action in the fishing industry and in 1970 created state marketing authorities for all fish products and three years later set up PESCAPERU, a government organisation which took complete charge of all fishing and the fish processing industries. Public utilities, transport, communications and energy production likewise were taken into the control of the State. In manufacturing, state control was to some extent extended and private enterprise hedged around with restrictions, but more significantly the developments in industry were characterized by an increasing move towards capital-intensive activities and the state borrowed extensively to fund developments. This phase of import-substitution development suffered from all problems which Griffin, Enos and others have identified and which were discussed in Chapter 7. The measures enacted by the military government failed to improve the quality of life of the majority of Peru's population, did not put the country's economy on a secure footing and in 1977–78 brought the country near to economic collapse. In 1980 the military government gave way to elected civilian rule and a new democratic government took over power in 1981.

PERU IN 1980: THE REPORT OF THE ECONOMIC MISSION

In 1980 during the period of transition from military to civilian rule, an economic mission led by Ulrich Thumm visited Peru and made a report on its economy for the World Bank (Thumm 1981). It is a report which reveals the many weaknesses in the Peruvian economy but puts forward recommendations for development action.

In the case of agriculture, the mission points out that while the military government had focused upon tenurial reform and other institutional changes, it failed to raise agricultural production. It had devoted most of the trained personnel of the Agricultural Ministry to the agrarian reform and had totally neglected its advisory services. These were of vital importance to the small farmers who suffered in consequence. In the establishment of the co-operatives the same problems referred to in Chapter 6 were identified by the mission. They mention that the newly erected co-operative enterprises required to be operated in a co-operative spirit. This was something new to the farmers of Peru and it was not cultivated as an essential component of radical reform as it had been in China. The same lack of adequately trained staff which bedevilled Zambia's ventures with state farms impeded progress in Peru. On the sugar estates disputes between the new co-operative members and the management and technical staff led to resignations of the latter, leaving the estates without the leadership and technical skills they required. The state could not engender the requisite capital nor provide the necessary skills to operate the agricultural economy as a branch of government. The marketing system was, according to the mission:

> heavily burdened by a large number of intermediaries and excessive government regulation as well as direct government involvement. During the past decade, the Government relied heavily upon controls (price controls, subsidies on food imports, prohibition of farm storage, control of inter-regional movements of agricultural products) to achieve its goal of reasonable prices for both producers and consumers. Virtually nothing was done, however, to make marketing through private channels more efficient and less costly. In practice, all government policies had a strong bias towards the urban consumer and penalized the producer through inadequate prices, thus contributing to the stagnation of agricultural production
>
> (Thumm 1981).

The mission is equally critical of the Military Government's industrial policy stating:

> Weak performance and present structure of industry are the results of the strategy begun in the early 1960s and vigorously pursued during 1969–75. Abundant credit at subsidised interest rates, cheap imports of capital and intermediate goods through an over-valued exchange rate and low tariffs, high protection for finished products, subsidised power rates and fuel prices, and relatively high labour costs created a highly capital-intensive, inefficient and inward-looking modern industrial sector. Although the traditional industries (food, beverages, textiles, garments) continued to be important, industrialization during the 1970s moved strongly towards the processing of natural resources and was heavily concentrated in chemicals, basic metals, metal products, and non-metal minerals . . . industries that are all relatively capital-intensive and, therefore, contributed to an increase in the sectors, overall capital intensity . . . by at least 50 per cent in real terms during 1971–78. Increasing capital intensity has not been a matter of 'appropriate technology', but rather a matter of shifting the industrial structure towards industries that are not best adapted to the country's resource endowment which, besides minerals and some agricultural raw materials, fundamentally consists of abundant labour
>
> (Thumm 1981).

The mission was similarly critical of the inadequacies of investment in the physical infrastructure, particularly transport, in the development of energy resources, notably hydro-electric power, in public utilities such as water supplies and sewerage facilities and comments on the low levels of efficiency manifest over a whole range of activities.

The mission's analysis presents a dismal picture resulting from years of mismanagement. It lists the problems which it regards as acute such as the persistent high inflation (60 per cent in 1980) the high public sector deficits, the high levels of unemployment and under-employment which reach 50 per cent in the urban labour force. It refers to stagnating agricultural production 'as a result of ill-conceived agricultural policies during the past decade and exacerbated by drought' and speaks of the further deterioration in income distributions, of increased poverty and malnutrition, especially in the towns. It points out that Peru's primary goods export pattern makes the balance of payments situation a precarious one. In speaking of deeper-seated and longer-term problems the mission's report points to widespread poverty, to the problems created by the rapid increase in population placing as it does burdens on the social and economic infrastructure, and to the increasing magnitude of unemployment. These features all contribute to the high incidence of disease and infant mortality rates which characterize Peru in the 1980s.

The full integration of the country in a regional or spatial sense is still far from complete as the transport network is quite inadequate and, as a result, its resources are neither fully nor rationally utilized. The mission's recommendations attempt to ameliorate the impact of these problems while recognizing that tackling short-term problems must not be regarded as solving the fundamental basic problems. Central to them is the need to increase production. This is basic to the provision of jobs and so must be achieved by methods which make full use of the resource of labour. It is also the means whereby measures to improve health and nutrition can be implemented. In both agricultural and industrial sectors the mission recommends a decontrol of activities and a liberalization of trade and marketing and decentralizing of the management of private enterprises away from the state. It is a proposal spelt out in some detail but in general terms it favours private enterprise and the creation of incentives which will allow all to participate in the developments. It is the pursuit of a middle-road between the capitalist exploitive and laissez-faire approach of decades of Peruvian governments and the extreme, negative and enforcing regime of the military government of the 1970s which, in purporting to put people first, froze them into a mould of regulations set firm by inefficiency. As Furtado has stated '. . . to a greater extent in Latin America than in any other important area, obstacles to development are mainly of an institutional nature' (Furtado 1976).

20 Hong Kong and Singapore

'For other Third world countries, the developing market economies of East Asia may be seen as providing a powerful "demonstration effect" though the outward orientation of their economic policies, their reliance on market signals, the stability and predictability of their macroeconomic policies, and their avoidance of confrontation between government and business'

Parvez Hasan
Adjustment to external shocks 1984

If the countries of the world form a continuum of development in the way in which Berry's analysis has suggested, and if their relative position is not fixed, some countries must currently occupy that indeterminate transitional borderland between the less developed and the more developed (Berry 1960). Hong Kong and Singapore are in such a position and for this reason have been selected as case studies. In many respects they can be regarded as having achieved development goals and status indistinguishable from the industrialized nations of Europe. In terms of per capita GNP they are ahead of all countries in Africa, South America and Asia save Japan; in Europe the figure exceeds that of Portugal, Yugoslavia and Greece. Both have passed through the demographic transition and exhibit vital statistics characteristic of western Europe. Both are industrialized and belong to that small group of newly industrialized countries of which Taiwan and South Korea are also members. It is, perhaps, significant that three of these four countries are peopled by persons of Chinese origin; indeed Hong Kong and Taiwan are regarded by the People's Republic as part of China. But not only are Hong Kong and Singapore industrialized, they are among the world's leading exporters of manufactured goods. It is salutary to remind Europeans, who may think of Hong Kong as a country of squatter huts and plastic-flower makers, that the value of her industrial exports is exceeded nowhere in the world outside Europe, North America and Japan and that in 1980 she was the eleventh largest exporter of manufactured goods in the world if the Soviet Union for which data are not available is excluded. Singapore at fifteenth is not far behind. Both Hong Kong and Singapore are city states in which urban and national functions are coincident. Though so alike in many ways they are significantly different in others.

HONG KONG

The colony of Hong Kong extends over a mere 1062 square kilometres. It comprises the small island of Hong Kong taken by the British in 1841 and 75 square kilometres in area, the Kowloon peninsula on the Chinese mainland ceded to the British in 1860, and a much larger area of over 900 square kilometres made up of islands in the Hong Kong archipelago and a portion of the Chinese mainland which were leased to the British as from July 1898 for 99 years. This leased area is known as the New Territories. The distinctions are significant. Without renewal of the lease, the New Territories were due to be returned to China in 1997. The Treaty of Nanking which ceded Hong Kong island and the Convention of Peking of 1860 which ceded the Kowloon peninsula to Britain were treaties in which Britain insisted on diplomatic equality and ensured it by force. The Chinese regarded the treaties as 'unequal' and this view, maintained by all successive Chinese governments, has meant that they have seen little distinction between the territory leased in perpetuity and that leased for 99 years whereas the British Government has held a different view. It could be argued that this difference of opinion and the uncertainty it created has had a bearing upon economic development in this colonial territory. As the title of one book on Hong Kong (Hughes 1970) has it 'Borrowed Place, Borrowed Time'.

A sprinkle of islands and sliver of China Hong Kong may be, but it has a very distinctive character of its own which is a product of its separate existence. Between Hong Kong island, Lantau island to the west and the mainland to the north, lies a deep and sheltered stretch of the sea which forms a large and secure natural harbour. Like other European powers Britain was seeking, by establishing a secure base, to further her trading opportunities along the Chinese coast. It was this harbour rather than the island itself, which Palmerston had described as 'a barren island with hardly a tree on it', which was a major asset. This barren island was to become the centre of the Colony of Hong Kong which some 140 years later contained a population of over 5 million and where land values in its central business district exceeded those of central London.

For over a century after the acquisition, Hong Kong functioned as a Far Eastern entrepôt port. As trade links widened, as colonialism brought more areas into international trade and as improvements in ships and shipping facilitated long distance movement, so the reach and complexity of Hong Kong's trading relationships grew. The original military settlement on Hong Kong island grew into the town of Victoria. Across the harbour, Kowloon was transformed from a small walled Chinese town into a growing commercial community. The population of the colony grew from 35,000 in 1851 to 841,000 in 1931. Much of this increase was due to immigration. With the collapse of the Manchu dynasty many had fled from China into Hong Kong. As the Japanese, who invaded China in the 1930s, penetrated further into the country refugees poured in their thousands into the colony. By 1941 when the Japanese invaded Hong Kong itself, the population had reached 1.6 million. Hong Kong had become what essentially she is today, a society composed of refugees and the descendants of refugees. During the Japanese occupation many fled Hong Kong seeking to avoid Japanese oppression in the parts of China less securely under their control. When the British returned in 1945 the population was some 600,000. The years immediately following witnessed a flood of refugees the like of which Hong Kong had not experienced before. They came in from China both during the civil war between the Communist and Kuomintang armies and after the establishment of the People's Republic. In 1950 the population stood at 2.3 millions. Until the early 1970s refugees from China continued to augment Hong Kong's natural increase in population. The population in 1981 was estimated at 5.2 millions. This small territory with no material resources, an accented mountainous topography, a population which has increased by over 760 per cent in 36 years, a refugee society of town dwellers, where urban population densities are the highest in the world, has somehow transformed itself into a major industrial nation. Hong Kong has done this with but two assets, its people and its fine natural harbour in a strategic location. It is a development of interest and significance.

Hong Kong began as a trading centre; it was her prime function until the Second World War. She was geared to the handling of ships and their maintenance, to storage and transhipment of goods and to the financial transactions associated with trade. She was outward looking, since there was nothing to look in upon, and she was very much concerned with Chinese trade. Merchants of Chinese, European and American origin settled and traded there. Many of the great Hongs, or business houses, of Hong Kong today can trace their origins back into the nineteenth century. Hong Kong's position on the Chinese coast had been her beginning and raison d'être. The revolution which created the People's Republic in China did much to change this situation. The United Nations placed an embargo upon trade with the People's Republic, an embargo to which Britain was a party, and the long-established link was severed. Out of China had come more than a million refugees who needed accommodation and employment. Amongst them were Chinese entrepreneurs and shrewd businessmen from Shanghai and other industrial centres skilled in management, with knowledge of production techniques and experienced in commercial dealings with the industrial nations. Though Hong Kong's trade and entrepôt activities continued they were restricted by the United Nations embargo and there was an urgent need to develop other aspects of the economy both to maintain it and to provide employment. Agricultural developments on any large scale, even though many of the refugees came from rural peasant backgrounds, was made impossible by Hong Kong's small size and the nature of her terrain. People were the resource, not land, and the harnessing of their abilities and productive capacity has been the colony's remarkable achievement and the basis of its transformation. It was a productive capacity

311

which had to be used in a special way. The territory had no raw material or power resources of any significance. It had a work-force, a harbour with a potential for considerable development and a commercially strategic location and it had a history of experience in international trade. The genius of Hong Kong was in bringing these attributes together in such a way as to mark out a meaningful path of development. The path was that of manufacturing for export, using imported raw materials and energy supplies. The ships, the port, the trading experience and connections were fully utilized to facilitate this inward and outward movement. The entrepôt trade had played a similar role in the movement of goods; now the significant difference was that Hong Kong was a manufacturing, value-added, intermediary so that which went out was quite different from that which came in. There was no question of import-substitution policies, none of indigenous growth, no issue of core and periphery imbalances except on a town-planning micro-scale. The policy was simple and clear, to manufacture goods to sell abroad.

To generate this activity and sustain it, there was a need for capital and labour. Hong Kong's growing population proved to be a most efficient hard working and adaptable labour force and was seen as a positive asset which attracted capital. The capital came from the long-established Hongs, from Chinese capitalists who had left China, and importantly from Britain, other European countries and North America. It was an economy as vulnerable to the vicissitudes of world trade as any other yet it has remained a success. Success tends to breed success and Hong Kong's achievements have received an increasing flow of international capital. The keys to that success have been first, and importantly, Hong Kong's flexibility in enterprise and labour. With no subsidy or protection her industrialists have had to demonstrate an ability to identify changing conditions in both market and methods of production and adjust both what they made and how they made it to these changes. The industrial ear in Hong Kong has been finely tuned to detect such changes. Secondly, this industrial endeavour has not taken place in an isolated-outpost sense solely concerned with manufacturing. Rather it has developed within the commercial context in which it was born so that the one has nourished and stimulated the other and it has taken place alongside the continuing development of Hong Kong's port facilities and trading connections. Expertise in, and facilities for, financial transactions have so developed that Hong Kong has become the third largest banking and financial centre in the world. Her container terminal is also the world's third largest while her airport is one of the busiest in the Far East. The service sector accounts for 60 per cent of GDP. This ensemble of developments has both nurtured and been nurtured by Hong Kong's transformation into an industrial nation.

The approach to economic development could hardly provide a greater contrast with that of the equally successful People's Republic of China. On the one hand the world's giant is transforming its society while on the other the world's midget is transforming its economy. The one is experimenting with perhaps the most interesting and original planning programmes for economic development in the Developing World, the other not even contemplating economic planning. Hong Kong represents free enterprise capitalism in perhaps its most classic form. The port is a 'free port' with neither import nor export duties. No restriction is placed on the movement of the world's currencies. Manufacturing and commerce is wholly in the hands of private enterprise as are such public utilities as bus and ferry services and fuel and power supplies. The Colonial Government does play a major role in providing social services and exerts overall control over urban planning developments. It has built a large part of the accommodation needed to house the growing population though, despite its great achievements, the influx of people has meant that it has never been enough. There are, however, no state industrial or commercial activities nor is there a state bank issuing currency. This is done by three private banks. The Colonial Government does not set out an economic development policy for the Colony. Its role is one of active non-participation.

Hong Kong's entrepreneurial resources applied to a labour force which is hardworking, adaptable, eager to acquire new skills and both psychologically and socially receptive of factory-machine techniques, has generated capital for further development and attracted it from overseas. But entrepreneurial skills and an excellent labour force cannot maximise their opportunities in a country the size of Hong Kong without an external dimension. Capital is one, markets are another. To sustain her level of activity Hong Kong requires access to world markets, an access sometimes impeded by tariffs, quotas and other devices. To enter these markets the sensitivity to changes in them, to which reference has been made, is vital; so too is competitiveness. Hong Kong's industrialists do not devote capital to the research and development of new techniques. Instead they take in the very latest in techniques and products from the outside world and use and produce them. Only by remaining at the forefront of development can they remain competitive. This is another aspect of Hong Kong's flexibility and clearly it can most effectively apply to the lighter high-technology industries rather than heavy basic manufactures. By utilizing the latest techniques in textile manufacturing, in engineering and electronics from Japan, the United States and Europe, she draws upon the development resources of the industrialized world. The factors involved thus become mutually reinforcing ones as indigenous enterprise, adaptable labour force, excellent infrastructure, international technology, international capital and international trade, interact. Hong Kong has striven to become, and is, a window where the world can look in, invest and buy. She sustains a large tourist traffic not only to derive revenue but also to facilitate contact and encourage international involvements. In the late 1970s, of foreign investments in Hong Kong, 46 per cent were American, 20 per cent Japanese and 7.5 per cent British. The remainder were a mix of Asian and European investors. These foreign investments were made in electronics (26 per cent of the total),

313

textiles (15.8 per cent), chemical products (12 per cent), electrical goods (10 per cent), printing and publishing (7 per cent) and toys (3 per cent).

In an investigation carried out at the time by members of the Chinese University of Hong Kong, the most influential factors determining foreign investment in the colony were revealed (Lin et al 1979). American investors ranked these factors in the following order: peaceful industrial relations; efficient labour force; the stability of the Hong Kong Government; freedom to repatriate earnings; freedom to transfer capital assets; low tax-ceiling; easy to serve export markets. The British order of factors was: low taxation; freedom of capital transfer; freedom to repatriate earnings; local market potential; peaceful industrial relations; efficient labour; easy to serve export markets; the existence of supporting industries. In Japan's case, the most important inducement by far was the low tax-ceiling. In all three cases lower wages were considered less significant than the factors listed. Though prevailing wages were much lower than those of Japan, the USA or Britain, those in Korea, Philippines, Taiwan and Singapore were even lower than in Hong Kong.

Production for export has meant two things. First, a vulnerability to market changes whether these were the result of recessions and taste changes, of free market forces or protective tariffs. The response to this has been the adaptability which has been mentioned. Secondly, it has meant that Hong Kong producers have continually to identify comparative advantage and minimize their opportunity costs. This in turn requires them to specialize in a narrow range of industrial activities and while this allows them to enjoy scale economies it does require a special alertness and an awareness of changing events.

The transformation of the Hong Kong economy has thus seen three phases. First the stage characterized by the entrepôt trade with associated activities such as ship-building and repairing, commercial developments and, as the years went by, the emergence of manufacturing concerned with textiles, engineering, electrical goods and sugar refining. The second phase emerged after 1945 with the China trade cut off and the influx of refugees encouraging a rapid restructuring of the manufacturing sector and massive increases in the production of textiles, clothing, plastics, toys, shoes, electrical goods and transistor radios. The emphasis was largely on cheap consumer goods produced by labour-intensive methods. During this period from the late 1940s to the late 1960s Hong Kong became known throughout the world for these commodities. What is commonly not realized is that this phase has been replaced by another. Hong Kong's industrial growth has continued but its nature has changed precisely because of changing market conditions and because her comparative advantage with respect to labour costs has altered. In her main market areas, restrictions on the import of the goods Hong Kong was making have meant that she has switched to different levels of products within the same section of manufacturing. Lower labour costs among her competitors and import restriction of her markets have moved Hong Kong firms into the manufacture of higher-value and more sophisticated products. More sophisticated forms of electronic and mechanical engineering products are now characteristic. In the textile-clothing sector there is a much greater emphasis upon high quality clothes rather than cheap cloth. The image of cheap low-quality plastic products is no longer accurate. Of the industrial labour force, 67 per cent are employed in the textiles, clothing, electronics, plastic products, toys, watches and clocks industries. This group of industries accounts for 72 per cent of Hong Kong's domestic exports, that is excluding re-exports. Textiles and clothing are the most important export and employment group with electronics second though Hong Kong is the world's largest supplier of toys. In recent years a polystyrene plant, an outboard engine factory, a steel rolling mill and a machine tool plant have been examples of further additions to Hong Kong's industrial spectrum.

The physical infrastructure of Hong Kong has continued to be improved and augmented unceasingly at a rapid rate. There is a developing urban motorway system with a cross-harbour road tunnel. A mass transit system, which is an underground-overground railway, is capable of carrying a million passengers each day and will place 40 per cent of homes and 50 per cent of work-places within ten minutes walk of its stations. The railway from Kowloon to the Chinese border has been double-tracked and a motorway to China was commenced in the early 1980s. All the paraphernalia of a large modern city exists in the heavily built-up areas which fringe the harbour. The growth in population has been so large, however, that the Hong Kong Government has planned, and is building, new towns out in the mainland New Territories, towns with populations of a million or so each, towns which will be completed by the 1990s. These infrastructural and economic developments raise, of course, the issue of Hong Kong's relationship with China.

The former insecure settlement on a barren island has become a large densely-populated city state. It has demonstrated a successful expanding economy which has weathered the post-war strains and sustained itself throughout the world economic recession. It is legally and politically a colony yet it is the most peculiar of colonies. It was never a populated area whose people were exploited in a colonialist fashion. Its population is made up of people who chose to come in. If conditions were not good, they were none the less preferred alternatives. The activities which it has practised have benefited local workers and manufacturers as well as foreign capitalists. The benefits have not been equitably distributed but the distribution of income is not as skewed as some would have it. The top 20 per cent of households accounted for 47 per cent of household incomes and the bottom 20 per cent for 5.4 per cent. The equivalent figures for France are, for example, 45.8 per cent and 5.3 per cent. It is a territory whose economic development is totally free of any influence from the colonial power; even its currency is not related to the pound sterling. It is self-governing and

315

being essentially a collection of contiguous cities this is carried out by elected city councils but its supreme government, the Colonial Government, is not elected. In such circumstances, the relationship between the Colonial Government and the people of the Colony is a complex and subtle one (Kuan 1979). It is one in which the role of China, the motherland of Hong Kong's population and the cradle of their culture, is of fundamental importance and it is one which turns upon the past and the future of Hong Kong.

The British have regarded the Kowloon peninsula and Hong Kong island as their sovereign territory; in the development of Hong Kong, the leased New Territories and these sovereign areas have become inextricably linked. A severance of the two would be unthinkable in economic and social terms. The people of Hong Kong have increasingly expressed the natural wish for a greater say in their own affairs. On their part the British have not been averse to granting independence to their colonial possessions as the dismantling of the British Empire since 1945 has demonstrated. In Hong Kong's case an independent Hong Kong would, however, have been unacceptable to the government of Chairman Mao. It would have meant another Taiwan on China's shores, for the Chinese, not accepting the 'unequal treaties' of the nineteenth century, have regarded the Colony, in all its parts, as being sovereign Chinese territory. There was another dimension. Once the United Nations embargo on trade with China was lifted, trade with her resumed and cordial relationships prevailed between China and Britain. Far from being a capitalist sore on the socialist body, Hong Kong became China's window on the world and with her excellent harbour facilities, far superior to those of Canton on the shallow Pearl River, handled in the 1970s over 40 per cent of China's foreign trade. China invested in factories and department stores in Hong Kong, operated a dry dock and established a banking system. The harbour of Hong Kong received many Chinese ships and the improvements to transport connections with Canton were further examples of the growing communication between the two areas. As has been described, the establishment in post-Mao China of Industrial Development Zones across the border from Hong Kong which replicate many of the features of foreign capitalist investment in Hong Kong, further stressed inter-connection rather than separation.

Prior to 1984 it was possible only to speculate on Hong Kong's future and with speculation came uncertainty as 1997 approached. The whole edifice of Hong Kong's commercial and industrial success was based, as it must be in a capitalist free-enterprise system, upon confidence. Once confidence in the future was gone, capital support would be withdrawn and the whole edifice would collapse leaving modern buildings and an elaborate infrastructure, inarticulate. This point was almost reached in early 1984. It was staved off by the agreement drawn up, after long negotiations, between the Chinese and British Governments over the future of Hong Kong. Its Chinese sovereignty has been recognized and a Chinese governmental presence will be established in Hong Kong, but the administration of the territory as part of China will be carried out by the Hong Kong people and will remain distinctive in its form and character from administrations in the People's Republic. Likewise its economy, for some fifty years after 1997, is to remain a free-enterprise capitalist economy. Clearly the future will depend upon future developments in China. The path taken by the post-Mao Government of China is more likely to make the twin developments of China and its tiny new territory one of greater accord than could have been conceived of in the recent past. Hong Kong may well play a significant role in the modernization of the People's Republic.

SINGAPORE

Singapore is a fascinating rejection of the long-held belief that the humid tropics plagued by climate and ravaged by disease and inhabited by peoples stunted in intellectual and physical development by the environment, could never be part of the modern world. Singapore, near the equator, experiencing high rainfalls with continuously high temperatures, with a natural vegetation of tropical rainforest and mangrove swamps on her coasts, has been transformed into a large modern city which, to an even greater extent than Hong Kong, lays claim, in appearance at least, to be more a part of the modern world than Manchester, Marseilles or Milan.

Singapore's history is longer that that of Hong Kong. Singapore Island at the tip of the Malay peninsula has always held a strategic position in a zone where the great cultures of the Indian sub-continent and China have mingled in Malaya and the East Indies. In the late-eighteenth century the British identified its strategic importance to their East Indian and Chinese trade but it was the Dutch who came to dominate the East Indian trade and to control the Straits of Malacca and the Sunda Straits. Under the aegis of the Governor General of India, Sir Stamford Raffles explored the area for possible bases for British trade and ships. He landed on Singapore Island in January 1819 and, after treaties were signed with the Sultan who owned the island, Britain secured a trading base and began to develop her commercial interests. Subsequently these interests spread to the peninsula where Britain displaced the Dutch from Malacca and Singapore became the seat of an administration which ruled Malacca, Penang and Singapore as the Straits Settlement. This administration was managed by the British East India Company until 1867 when the Colonial Office took over. After the Second World War the Straits Settlement was abolished, Singapore became a separate colony in 1946 with the rest of the Settlement joining the Malayan Union. In 1959 Singapore became an independent country. However, in 1961 it was proposed by Malaya that a new nation be created composed of Malaya, Sarawak, North Borneo, Brunei and Singapore. This new state, named Malaysia, was created in 1963, though Brunei chose not to join it. After some difficulties within Malaysia, Singapore herself became a separate country in 1965.

Independent Singapore is a small country made up of one island, 616 square kilometres in extent, and a few islets measured in hectares rather than square kilometres. Her population in 1981 was 2.4 million of whom 77 per cent were ethnically Chinese, 15 per cent Malay and 6 per cent Indian. The population density is over 4000 per square kilometre (4900 ps km in Hong Kong).

Like Hong Kong, Singapore has no natural resources of consequence. Her population is well-educated with schools at all levels, polytechnics and a university. It is a population which was growing at 1.5 per cent per annum from 1970 to 1981, though this rate is being lowered by immigration control, family planning services and by fiscal measures to encourage small families. Its strategic trading location and its well-trained and disciplined labour force again suggest comparisons with Hong Kong but there are differences. First, Singapore is independent and, second, in its foreseeable future it is not envisaged that it will be absorbed into some other nation. Third, both its economy and society is much more strictly controlled than that of colonial Hong Kong. Indeed it is this organized, detailed and ultra-efficient planning of so many aspects of life in Singapore which its critics have focused upon. Yet the achievements have been substantial and impressive (Ooi and Chiang 1969).

From an economy still very much tied to its port activities at the time of its emergence as a separate nation in 1965, Singapore has become much more involved in manufacturing, though the port activities have not been neglected and facilities have been markedly expanded and modernized. Singapore today is one of the world's busiest ports with a substantial entrepôt trade in South East Asia and a large modern container terminal. The British maintained a military base on Singapore Island which provided employment for 40,000 persons, a very large number in the Singapore context. When the base closed in 1968 these workers, including highly-trained and skilled personnel, were added to the already high number of unemployed and the economy of this new country appeared at risk. The decision was taken to embark upon a vigorous policy of industrialization; there was indeed little alternative. To be successful it required not only labour but investments, a high level of export activity and the establishment of a range of diverse export markets. The political party in power, the People's Action Party, saw its role in this economic endeavour as an involved, positive-planning role giving not only political stability but direction, with its plans to be carried out with a clinical efficiency. The contrast with the laissez-faire approach to economic developments in Hong Kong could hardly have been greater. Singapore is a democracy with its government elected in free elections, yet no party other than the People's Action Party has been returned to power and opposition parties are virtually non-existent. In practice, Singapore has become a one-party state. Led by Prime Minister Lee Kwan Yew, the government has become a vigorous, planning and enforcing administration reaching out into all aspects of life. It has proved to be efficient and successful and Singaporeans enjoy the benefits of this success, though critics of the regime would say that equity has not been to the forefront of the government's goals.

In 1968 an industrial estate was set up at Jurong, which is now run, together with twenty other smaller estates covering 6300 hectares, by the Jurong Town Corporation (JTC) (Chiang 1969). Some 100,000 workers in 1099 factories are employed on the main Jurong estate with a further 98,000 on the smaller estates. These estates have planned development schedules extending to 1990 which take into account population projections and the overall distribution of population in the development of the industrial estates and their supporting industries. The Jurong Town Corporation designs and builds factory buildings as well as providing factory sites. It operates a port which handles raw materials for the estate and it has a marine base which serves as a central distribution point for South East Asia for a range of oilfield equipment and services, including exploration. It operates repair yards and provides a spare parts service. JTC is an example of the integrated, planned approach to industrial development which consolidates foreign enterprises within the country's plans. The Singapore Government has signed investment guarantees with Canada, France, West Germany, the Netherlands, Switzerland, the United States, the United Kingdom, Belgium, Luxemburg and Sri Lanka. This foreign investment is largely characterized by multi-national companies which account for over half of Singapore's industrial employment. The external dimension is very much present in Singapore's economy as it is in Hong Kong.

To retain an ability to react quickly to changing technological demands and market circumstances, a Skills Development Fund has been established to promote training and retraining in skills to facilitate the restructuring of the economy. An Economic Development Board, a government agency, is active in attracting high-technology, skill-intensive industries to the country, of which micro-wave links, pneumatic controls, precision optical instruments and computers are examples.

Between 1960 and 1970 the average annual growth in manufacturing was 13 per cent. Between 1970 and 1981, despite the world recession, it was 9.7 per cent and in 1981–82 reached 12 per cent and employment went up by 7 per cent. Labour has been brought in from other countries, such as Sri Lanka for example, to work in the industrial sector. Manufacturing contributed 28 per cent to the GDP compared with 12 per cent in 1960 which had included work in the military base. Not all industries have made progress but as in Hong Kong, the electronics and electrical sectors have made particular advances. Singapore now has the world's third largest oil refinery complex and the functions of this investment are clearly related to the interaction between oil prices and the level of world industrial activity. Tourism with the attractions of modern hotels and duty free goods as in Hong Kong, is buoyant and brings the world to see Singapore's achievements for despite the recession of the 1970s and 1980s Singapore is demonstrating health, strength and flexibility.

The great city supported by this economy is modern, well-planned and growing. Great attention is paid to preserving open space and greenery and in creating amenities in what is very densely populated area. Over 70 per cent of the population live in government-built housing, mostly high-rise flats. They represent a great improvement in material living conditions though there are those who say that Singapore's urban renewal is designed to remove the core of the radical proleteriat. There are also those who point out, quite accurately, that the years which saw the transformation of Singapore's economy were the boom years of the 1960s and early 1970s when world production, trade and demand were at a level never exceeded before and when the contribution of the new Singapore could only be welcomed. There are those who say that in a world recession Singapore's position is revealed as weak and vulnerable. She has, of course, to compete in a diminishing market and her small size, like that of Hong Kong, means she has to depend upon external markets whether they be for tourism or manufactured products. Her port functions, her financial services all depend upon the level of trade. All this is true yet the evidence shows how well Singapore, like Hong Kong, has survived these adverse circumstances and in real terms both GDP and per capita incomes have grown significantly (Geiger 1976; Goh 1977; Wang and Tan 1981).

An evaluation of the society which has been created as part of Singapore's development process depends upon priorities, values and, to some extent, political stance. It is very much a state-run society. The main physical and social infrastructure is in government hands. Contributions to the Central Provident Fund at the rate of 45 per cent of earned income, are taken from all individuals and used to support national economic development projects. The rate of saving for investment, so central to early development theories, is determined by the Government. The Government's record is one of sound investment and as yet it has not had to borrow from overseas to fund its own industrial development projects, which involve shipyards, shipping and airlines and smaller companies. The foreign companies operating in Singapore tend to be wholly foreign-owned and capitalized and joint schemes and licensing agreements are few.

Lee Kuan Yew's model republic remains in good heart and is envied, if not emulated, by neighbouring states. With Hong Kong it has moved along the development conveyor belt into the league of industrial nations, there to compete with the other NICs, such as Taiwan, South Korea and now the Philippines. All the NICs will experience competition not only from the established industrial nations but also increasingly from other developing countries which, as they modernize, retain initially their low labour costs.

These lower costs will erode one feature of the NICs comparative advantage. Among these new competitors will be the giant of them all, China, the cold wind of whose competition will be felt not only in the flowered avenues of Singapore and the flatted factories of Hong Kong but throughout the nations of the world, developed and less-developed alike.

21 Retrospective and Prospective Views

'Ah! What avails the classic bent
And What the cultured word,
Against the undoctored incident
That actually occurred?'

Rudyard Kipling 1865–1936
The Benefactor

'The Golden Rule is that there are no golden rules'

Bernard Shaw 1856–1950
Maxims for Revolutionists

The experience over three and more decades of the formulation of development theories and the implementation of development policies has allowed their evaluation and called into question their efficacy. They were characterized by a concern with production rather than distribution, an emphasis on national output rather than per capita income. It was presumed that the growth of a national economy would improve the conditions of all, that many would gain from direct involvement and the rest from a trickle down of benefits. It can be seen that, with but a few exceptions, this has not been so. Growth is not coincident with development and in many countries growth itself has not been substantial. The process of development and the transformation of societies and economies is a slower process than the confident years of the 1950s and 1960s would have had us believe.

The evidence presented in the case studies has demonstrated this situation and the schemes for the initiation and guidance of development discussed in earlier chapters require a re-examination. Indeed it will be recalled that their consideration was left not in a state of complacency but in one of questioning. These grand schemes and elegant models were implemented in the belief that a society and economy could be engineered and managed as smoothly as a machine. It was a view integrated into the practice of Marxist societies but it was also espoused by those who, while believing in the market economy, also thought that development models could be designed which would embrace all significant aspects of the development process and ensure its speedy progress. Rostow wrote of a process of transformation which involved a space of two or three decades (Rostow

1956). Developments have taken place, growth has been experienced as has been exemplified in the countries discussed in this book; industrialization has occurred as Chenery and others have shown; per capita GNP has in most cases risen. Self-sustaining growth, which Rostow and his contemporaries identified as the attainment of development, has however, proved elusive in all but a few cases. That it is attainable has been demonstrated in Hong Kong, Singapore and Taiwan and it appears to be within the grasp of Brazil but it is everywhere evident that growth alone does not constitute development. There are other dimensions. As the twentieth century, the century in which the Developing World was conceived, approaches its end, the salutary and often bitter experience in that world has revealed the holes, the gaps, the missing pieces in the grand designs. The questioning had indeed began before the end of the 1960s (Bruton 1965; Myrdal 1968; Healey 1972; Killick 1978).

The general theories like those of Rostow have been largely rejected, at least as simple, unqualified statements in the manner in which they were often quoted and used. The 'big push' and 'critical minimum effort' ideas, referred to in Chapter 8 as a means of escaping from the low-level equilibrium trap have been brought into question. The injection of capital, vital though capital investments are, has not by itself solved problems. Its impact has been conditioned, not only by the nature of the investment, but also by the socio-economic environment in which it has been implanted. The difficulties in achieving effective investment have been widely encountered; they were demonstrated in the case studies of India, Nigeria, Peru and Zambia. Rostow warned of the necessary prerequisites without which the launch into his stages of growth could not take place. This is the crux of the matter. Too often the outward appearances of development have been bought in and mistaken for its substance.

This disillusionment with development theories does not imply that the analysis and planning of sectoral investments has been rejected; far from it. Nor does it imply that pricing systems, quota and tariff protection, rates of exchange and other forms of financial manipulation are not significant tools in the useful management of an economy. Nor yet does it reject classical economics. Over-confidence amongst development economists may have gone, there may not exist a consensus of opinion among theorists, but development initiatives have not been dissipated, nor have all the old ideas and techniques needed to be rejected. Importantly, the areas of failure have been identified and with this have come new definitions of development giving a new focus to development thrusts.

THE MOVE FROM THE GENERAL TO THE PARTICULAR

There are thus two aspects in the changing attitude to the problems of the Developing World. First there has been a rejection of solution by the grand design, the all-embracing panacea. The models and theories were too abstracted from reality, too clean of people. Their implementation did not anticipate the practical difficulties of the real world, rich in all its variety. Three development economists have put it thus: 'In the real world the process (policy formation) is higgledy-piggledy with changes in government, changing circumstances resulting from the impact of development itself, a changing environment, and events such as bad monsoons or the discovery of new mineral resources that lead to changes in objectives and hence in policy instruments required' (Cody, Hughes and Wall 1980). The variety and complexity of the problems faced by individual countries cannot be addressed by macro-theories. This is not to say that groups of countries within the wide span of the Developing World do not possess similar problems or potentials, clearly they do, but rather that common problems may require uncommon solutions. In this context it is of interest again to read the views of Cody, Hughes and Wall, writing of the issues of industrialization:

> It is doubtful whether any meaningful generalizations can be made about industrial strategies. Individual countries have to devise policies which fit particular conditions and social and economic objectives. Efficiency is clearly important to industrial growth, but has little meaning beyond such generalities as the need for higher productivity of capital or labour, appropriate utilization of the factors of production and price competitiveness. What is efficient for one country may be inefficient for another. The principal lesson of the past is that policy-makers have to be alert to changing circumstances and opportunities.
>
> (Cody, Hughes and Wall 1980).

It should be said that there are still those who hold to a world-wide solution. The Marxist view, with its deterministic concept of evolution, is that the world economy must be radically changed by an inevitable revolution. To use the astronomical analogy it is the 'Big Bang' solution but like most terrestrial explosions is likely to be more destructive than constructive.

THE REDEFINITION OF DEVELOPMENT GOALS

The second aspect of changing attitudes to the problems of developing countries is the redefinition of development goals. The failures of development policies have been identified but it is not a question solely of repairing holes in the bucket of development but of asking what the bucket is for. Joan Robinson writing in 1979 stated: 'It is a very remarkable fact that there is no discussion at all in orthodox economics of what form of investment is desirable from the point of view of society' (Robinson J 1979). But this issue has been considered and is being considered, by economists, sociologists, geographers and political scientists. The world of reality is not composed of rational economic man invaluable though a construct of the normative situation may be in order to measure the costs of deviation from it. An awareness of the undesirable by-products of economic growth has become evident in the redefinition of development. Increasingly proposals for development have as their premise the well-being of people rather than the size of the national economy. It represents a major change in emphasis and is the product of three decades of experience.

It is important to stress that the concern with the sharing of benefits and equity in participation cannot be divorced from the need to increase production and material wealth. The two approaches must work in harness and the work of the orthodox economist cannot be rejected. Concern itself is not enough. As one team of scholars who have been examining the process of combining growth with equity have expressed it: 'Researchers run the risks of having to navigate a narrow course between accusations of sloppy humanitarianism and those of esoteric irrelevance' (Fei, Ranis and Kuo 1979).

HOLES IN THE BUCKET

An examination of the case studies in this book, and indeed of the many other developing nations not considered, reveals the difficulties encountered in development. Increases in production tended to be associated with some sectors of the economy rather than all. It was an unbalanced growth which had two results. First it meant that the benefits of increased growth were unevenly distributed. It produced divisions in society. It identified growth sectors with which were associated employment opportunities, increases in income and often access to amenities and welfare. Other sectors were neglected and sectoral lags, notably in agriculture, were characterized by deficiencies in the benefits of growth. As was discussed in the context of Taiwan in Chapter 17, to such an extent were these features evident that theories were formulated which explained the process of growth as involving an inevitable disequilibrium in the economy and with it an inequitable participation in the proceeds of growth. It was presumed that this stage in the development transition would be followed by one of greater equity (Kuznets 1955; Paukert 1973). That this sequence of development is not inevitable, common though it may be, is shown by the experience of both communist China and capitalist Taiwan, both of whom, as has been seen, have combined growth with equity. This suggests that the sequence of development depends upon how it is managed.

The second consequence of uneven sectoral growth has often meant that the designated lead sector, almost invariably manufacturing, has in the event been held back by a failure to develop other sectors, notably agriculture. This neglect has been illustrated with reference to India, Nigeria and

Zambia; it is characteristic of many other countries. In China and Taiwan the successful implementation of complementary developments is an instructive example for all.

These manifestations of unbalanced sectoral growth, with all their social consequences, are evident also in the spatial context as was discussed at length in Chapter 10. Industrial and commercial growth have been associated with urban areas and, coupled with the neglect of agriculture, has marked out a geographical pattern of inequitable development. The consequences of the disregard of the regional dimension are dramatically evident in Nigeria but comment on it is pertinent in countries as different in size and resource as Fiji and Brazil. As in the case of uneven sectoral development, regional problems are the product of the transition from one state of near-equilibrium to another.

The sectoral and spatial issues are crucially important and they present problems frequently compounded by inappropriate policies such as those which led to the misuse of resources in Peru or the undue delay of an industrial export initiative as in Brazil. Many developing countries have suffered from their own administrative inefficiencies, a product both of their stage of development and the poverty or inappropriateness of their educational systems. It is an example of a deficiency in an essential prerequisite. Zambia, it will be recalled, has attributed much of its failure in the agricultural sector to the lack of suitably trained personnel. Commonly it is not a matter of a shortage of university trained manpower but of intermediate and artisan personnel in the technical sector. As the author has put it '. . . too many PhDs and not enough plumbers' (Simpson 1971a). The net results of these inadequacies, flaws and imperfections has been sectoral, regional and income distortion, and growth has failed to provide adequate employment. To all this is linked the dimension of population. In those countries which have failed to contain it, the growth of population has made the goals of development the more difficult to attain. In turn the absence of a significant improvement in socio-economic circumstances makes the conditions conducive to the formation of small families the less likely to emerge.

These symptoms are common. The developing countries still contain large numbers of people who are in a condition of poverty and who can see little prospect of improvement in their futures. It is a condition which cannot await the dubious benefits of the big bang of Marxist revolution. Nor can the people of the Developing World patiently await the emergence of a world like that which the first Brandt Report envisages, a world which recognizes common interests. The Report states: 'We believe that nations, even on the grounds of self-interest, can join in the common task of ensuring survival, to make the world more peaceful and less uncertain. A fundamental change in relations between the North and South as well as East and West is crucial to this change' (Brandt Report 1980). It is a viewpoint with which all persons with a concern for humanity and in particular for the world's poor, must agree, but clearly alongside whatever international changes take place, the less developed countries must continue their individual efforts. Indeed the Brandt Report itself says: 'The governments and the people of the South have the primary responsibility for solving many of their own problems, they will have to continue to generate most of their resources by their own efforts, and to plan and manage their own economies' (Brandt Report 1980).

NEW PATHS TO NEW GOALS: A STAGE OF DEVELOPMENT APPROACH

Paul Streeten in 1973 set out a definition of development which has received wide acceptance. It may appear to state the obvious. He is, however, listing many of the desirable goals which the development plans of most developing nations have failed to attain. He writes:

> The purpose of development is to raise the standard of living of the masses of the poor countries as rapidly as is feasible, to provide secure jobs, adequate nutrition and health, clean water at hand, cheap transport, education for children. The test of any (development) strategy is the extent to which it helps or hinders in meeting the basic needs of the majority of people
>
> (Streeten 1973).

The question is whether there is some means to achieve these goals. The answer is that it can be done. Hong Kong and Singapore have achieved them though in the special context of the city state. But so too has the People's Republic of China, even though its people are still poor in terms of per capita incomes, and Taiwan, which is now in the upper-middle income category. Each, with their contrasted approaches, has in large measure passed the Streeten test of success. They have lessons to teach. Out of the evidence which is now available, there may emerge a programme of development, or at least an approach to development, which can incorporate measures which will give some prospect of providing for the basic needs of which Streeten speaks.

Such an approach must incorporate the spatial dimension and the issues of sectoral imbalance in the context of a space economy. In doing so it must make special provision for the lagging sectors and areas, the forgotten people. It must accommodate the problem of developing dispersed activities rather than solely urban agglomerated functions. It must achieve these goals without foregoing opportunities for modernization and structural change. Importantly, and this is the key to the approach, it must recognize that differing stages of development exist not only between countries but *within* countries and this makes essential what can be called a stages of development approach.

The countries of the Developing World are still strung out along a spectrum of development like that identified by Berry and discussed in the introduction to this book. This situation raises fundamental issues. Is it a situation which is inevitable and permanent or is there a ladder of development up which all nations can climb to reach the top? Will some countries inevitably take longer to make the climb? Are there stages of development through which all must pass or can some be omitted? Are there technologies and economies appropriate for each of the several stages which at those stages will ensure that the basic needs for all are met and facilitate the transition to the next? The evidence from China appears to support this case. It is an approach which begins with the provision of basic needs but lays foundations for the future. Too many developmental edifices have been built on insecure foundations or indeed none at all. It would appear a preferable alternative to approaches which confuse the appearance of modernisation for the achievement of true development.

While such an approach can be called 'a stages of development approach', it is greatly different from that of Rostow. It cannot be a rigid model since this would be to replace one abstract panacea by another. It must be a flexible approach with the nature of its application varying with the circumstances, indeed with the level of development. It must be an approach which integrates the many components in development planning which have remained disconnected. Crucially, it must involve the active participation of the people whose condition it hopes to improve. Again, all the evidence points to the continuing failure of imposed solutions. The aim must be to combine greater productivity and a modernization of the economy with economic and social equity. This does not imply a regimented uniformity and on the contrary must allow the incentive of personal and community advancement to energize the process. The Chinese experience has revealed this need. This reach for greater production must therefore be achieved without the gross sectoral lag which perpetuates poverty and inequity. This means the rural sector must receive special attention since, as has been demonstrated, it is commonly the backward sector and is at the root of many development problems. Where the rural economy has been secured, as in China and Taiwan, other parallel developments can take place without the emergence of a dual economy. As Chenery and Hughes have stated and as was cited in Chapters 7 and 8, the rapid transformation of economies and the ascent of the ladder of development has been associated with industrialization *provided* that other sectors have not been neglected (Chenery 1979; Cody, Hughes and Wall 1980). It is for this reason that it is necessary to stress the need for development in the *rural* sector and not solely in agriculture. It is this need for 'walking on two legs' which takes the argument into the spatial dimension.

THE SPATIAL DIMENSION: DECENTRALIZED DEVELOPMENT

In a situation where technological developments are emphasising central places, agriculture the lavish user of space, whose work-force is the very fabric of rural society and often the keeper of traditional values, requires a positive development stimulus not in an isolated, singular way, but in conjunction with other developments in the countryside. The rural sector cannot be left stranded to accommodate change and development as best it can. This has happened in Nigeria and many other countries. It did not happen in Taiwan partly because of historical accident and partly because of intent. In China it was avoided by the planning of the rural economy. It is the main cause of the failure to attain the development goals which Streeten cites. It plays a major role in the rural-urban migration and with it the many consequent problems which have been discussed. The need is for an integrated rural economy which embraces not only a healthy and maturing agriculture but also industrial centres, energy generation, servicing centres with health and education facilities, and a marketing arrangement which further welds rural regions into cohesive space economies. Manufacturing can range not only over the obvious processing of agricultural products and the provision of agricultural needs such as fertilizer and implements, but also include more sophisticated manufactures not sensitive to scale restrictions or dispersed locations. Industrial development is a means of both increasing the level of employment and the marginal productivity of agricultural labour. Such a rural economy cannot be an instant creation and its nature and composition will vary with the stage of development.

What is envisaged is the articulation of an urban hierarchy in which rural towns function as centres of development interrelated with the surrounding rural areas in an economic and social sense. As has been discussed, the urban hierarchy in most developing countries is imperfect and attempts to complete and activate it have often failed because the towns remained outposts of the metropolitan centres rather than becoming embedded in the surrounding economy. The case is, therefore, for truly integrated functional cities. It is a scheme incorporated into the development plans in Fiji and is the substance of Babarović's proposals for Brazil. Its need is widely evident in countries of the Developing World. Only in this way can the poverty which is the product of sectoral lag be eliminated and the drainage of the periphery restrained. It could do much to create an integrated space economy. It puts the fabric over the frame of the umbrella.

Clearly, in many countries such developments will require a radical reorganization of land tenure in order to allow changes in the agrarian economy. The land tenure situation present in most Latin American countries is, for example, incompatible with the developments suggested. The reorganization of land can take many forms. In China, though the State acquired the ownership of land, the genius of the commune concept lay in the degree of local management and involvement it allowed and in the disaggregation of development. The answer would not appear to lie in the establishment of state farms. All the evidence of the past three decades runs counter to this. In Taiwan the key to rural success was the redistribution of land, including state land, among the working farmers. The experience of Tanzania is instructive. There an attempt was made to reorganize the rural economy and redistribute the rural population in a bold experiment incorporating villagization within its *ujamma* concept. It has met with but limited success and has failed to eliminate rural poverty. In so much as it did not incorporate industrial developments and envisage an integrated spatial economy it was an incomplete if well-intentioned project (Briggs 1980; Hyden 1980).

APPROPRIATE TECHNOLOGIES

To achieve the implementation of integrated rural development in conditions of labour surplus and capital scarcity requires the use of labour-intensive methods which are widely available as alternatives in most economic processes. The stages of development concept requires the use of appropriate technologies, technologies appropriate to the stage of development, to the skills and resources which can be used and appropriate to the particular sector; a rural manufacturing enterprise could use a technology different from that used contemporaneously in a large urban centre. The virtues of this approach have been demonstrated in China but it is widely applicable. Since countries vary in their stages of development, as sectors of economies likewise differ, appropriateness is the crucial concept. Without it terms like intermediate or elementary or primitive creep into use. It is not a concept which sees virtues in the home-made, the small-scale, the unsophisticated for their own sake, nor is it one rooted in some nostalgia for the pre-technical past. It is concerned with techniques which make possible a greater productivity from resources which are too small to justify large capital investments, from people who have not received a technical training, and for purposes which are meaningful to the communities which engender them. The last point is important. Properly conceived and implemented, the use of appropriate technologies draws upon the inventiveness and initiative of the people involved and produces things which they see as useful. The answers must come in the involvement of local populations from the beginning with their identification of priorities and in the light of their awareness of social and economic implications. Inappropriate technologies and outside impositions have little chance of success (Robinson A 1979; Barnett et al 1982; World Bank 1975, 1980b and 1980c).

The stages of development approach conceives of using technologies appropriate for each stage in terms of achieving the development objectives of that stage and as one stage passes into another so the technologies will change. It is a dynamic concept. These technologies can bring energy, raw material extraction and manufacturing into the countryside and are compatible with a dispersion of economic development. It has been done and China is again the model. The creation of an integrated rural economy allows the absorption of appropriate levels of technology at appropriate phases in the development process. Without it, industrialization, vital though it is to the structural transformation of developing economies, will take place only in the great urban nucleations leaving the populous periphery in a condition of atrophy. The over-reach for industrialization without first securing agriculture, without developing an integrated rural economy, without therefore providing for basic needs, produces the very problems which bedevil so many countries in the Developing World.

These developments, the establishment of an integrated rural economy and the use of appropriate technology interlink with other dimensions of development. If successful they will ensure a greater degree of self-sufficiency for a larger proportion of the population and by doing so reduce the vulnerability of the national economy to fluctuations in external market conditions for its exports. Greater self-sufficiency would have assisted the primary product exporters such as Nigeria and Zambia. Second, the policies described can, and must, incorporate the dimension of appropriate educational and health services in the small rural towns. An example from medical care will suffice to illustrate the point. Reference was made in Chapter 4 to the situation in most developing countries in which medical provision is confined to the large cities and is not free. What is required is a much wider access to medical services of a less sophisticated kind by the urban poor and the vast and scattered rural populations. China has achieved this with remarkable success; so too has Sri Lanka, Cuba and Fiji. By this focus upon the appropriate form of health service and by attending to prophylactic measures such as the provision of pure water supplies and sewage disposal, a wider attainment of good health can be experienced at lower costs. In turn this more appropriate medical care and its wider dissemination, together with the securing of the nation's food supply achieved by agricultural developments, will create conditions in which family planning facilities are more easily provided and, importantly, more readily accepted. Again the proof is evident in those countries which have passed more completely through the demographic transition. It will be apparent also that all these components in a decentralized development will tend to counter the rural-urban migration and its attendant problems.

The stages of development approach applies within countries with the achievements of one stage acting as the foundation for the next. It also applies to the whole range of nations in the Developing World which exhibit a wide range of developments. Not all hold out the prospect of reaching the top of the development ladder. It is vital to see that in such cases this does not mean either stagnation or the perpetuation of poverty. The stages of development approach can ensure not only the provision of basic needs, and this would be a major achievement in many countries, but also the attainment of a fuller life and the greater likelihood of the survival of cultural values. It offers the opportunity for the populations of both the countryside and the towns to be more fully involved in the planning of their own futures, and is therefore more likely to incorporate indigenous values and priorities. It thus can achieve some degree of compatibility between modernization and tradition. In countries short in capital but rich in people it gives some reality to the prospect of achievement and with it the self-respect essential for human dignity.

This approach, this emphasis upon the appropriate and the attainable, does not reject economic evaluation indeed it incorporates it. It does not reject industrialization and modernization. It does not relegate developing countries to permanently truncated development but it does reject the idea of instant development which can be achieved quickly and automatically as though it were an issue of a single causal factor being accommodated by a single solution. Industrialization in large-scale modern units located in the major urban agglomerations is not incompatible with the developments in the rural economy which have been outlined. Higher technologies and modernization must and will come but these initiatives must be incorporated into the structure of autochthonous development rather than used as a veneer masquerading as development.

In so much as it deviates from the established and superficially more attractive development programmes which concentrate upon the implant of large-scale, high-technology industries in the large and ever-growing cities with the assistance in many cases of multi-national companies, the decentralized stages of development approach is open to misunderstanding. Even if adopted it can, like any other programme, be the casualty of misconception, inefficiency and bureaucratic suffocation. If fully understood and sensitively and efficiently implemented, it is adaptable to a wide range of conditions, can meet the basic physiological and social requirements of all and can harness the energies of the population in their own social and economic development. Its great strength is its flexibility and adaptability. The rigid boxes of earlier development models could not contain the multitude of shapes and sizes which constitute the variety of the Developing World of reality. Its success depends upon the nature of government. Perhaps there are forms of government which themselves vary in their appropriateness for stages of development. This raises a further retrospective and prospective issue.

MATTERS OF POLITICAL ECONOMY

It will be apparent from the case studies which have been considered that all economies are political economies and not entities separated from ideology and government. All development plans are, in essence, a government construct often implemented by the organs of government. In some countries of the Developing World the present system of government is the product of long years of independent evolution, as in Thailand. In others, notably in Latin America, it is a system, implanted by the original colonial settlement, which has persisted, though with modifications, over a century or more. In most, the former colonies which became independent after 1945, the translation to sovereign independence has required the rapid construction of a new political system and form of government. It is this very abruptness and recency which seems to underlie present difficulties.

The received political wisdom of many developing countries was derived, like their development concepts, from the industrialized world of Europe and North America. Whether it was the Marxist-Leninism of the Soviet Union, the parliamentary democracy of the United Kingdom or the presidential democracies of the USA and France, it may have proved less appropriate than its donors would have wished or its recipients imagined – and this applies across the political spectrum. Political colic as much as economic indigestion rumbles in the alimentary tract of the development process in the developing nations.

The demands on government systems are great. They need to incorporate the goals and aspirations of the people into a process of management which is both efficient and humane and which sets out policies to attain these goals which are clearly articulated and yet remain flexible. To the West European, a form of parliamentary democracy in which differing views can be expressed and discussed, in which governments can be changed at the wish of the people in a peaceful way, in which freedom of the individual within the law is put above all else, appears to be the best and indeed the only form of government. It was the model bequeathed to many former colonies but is it appropriate for developing countries? Clearly some have found it so as India and Sri Lanka exemplify but they also demonstrate that since it involves the possibility of changes in both governments and development policy, it makes long-term planning the more difficult; but it also, of course, reduces the risk of long-term mistakes. Many developing countries have adopted a form of democracy in which there is only one party, the party of government. In the uncertain early years of independence this is seen as a way of setting fixed goals and of defining a path to attain them with little chance of deviation from it. It is a system which appears to succeed when at its head are men of integrity, vision and statesmanship such as Kaunda, Nyerere and Banda in Africa. If the wrong person were at its head it could too easily slide into despotism. A third group of nations have espoused the non-democratic systems of totalitarian socialist government. When rigid, enforcing and doctrinaire, as for example in Kampuchea, they appear capable of reversing the development process. Where enlightened and tempered by pragmatism, as in China, they can achieve some of the most remarkable development transformations. Many nations of the Developing World are ruled by dictators or by military governments which have seized power by force. There is little evidence to show that these are effective forms of government in the promotion of development; nor do they afford stability since coups are contagious.

In the Developing World the forms of government are many. Parliamentary democracy is distinguished by its rarity, Marxist-socialism by its misapplication and dictatorship by its inhumanity. There appears to be no obviously applicable system. An uninformed, illiterate electorate, such as exists in many nations, cannot express its hopes and needs effectively and is easily manipulated. Economic peripheries become political peripheries and for similar reasons lack cohesion and strength. An educated population is both more able and ready to articulate its views and is less easy to contain other than by force. Its role becomes more significant as society and economy become more integrated. Is it, therefore, that the process of true development which involves all aspects of society and economy must also embrace the development of political systems and the political economy? Is it that what is appropriate at one stage of development may become, like technology, less appropriate at another? This may well be the case and this evolution of governmental systems may give rise to forms which are entirely new but apt and fitted to the countries which gave them birth. It is these systems which will more appropriately cradle the effective development initiatives of the future.

References

Abrams, C. (1964) *Man's Struggle for Shelter in an Urbanizing World*, Cambridge Mass., MIT Press.

Adelman, I. and **Morris, C. T.** (1973) *Economic Growth and Social Equity in Developing Countries*, Stanford California, Stanford University Press.

Agnew, C. T. (1982) 'Water availability in the development of rainfed agriculture in south west Niger, West Africa,' *Trans. Inst. Brit. Geog.*, **7**, No. 4, 419–57.

Ahluwalia, M. S. (1974) 'Income inequality: some dimensions of the problem' in Chenery *et al.*, 1974, 3–31.

Allan, W. (1965) *The African Husbandman*, London, Oliver and Boyd, New York, Barnes and Noble.

Allan, W. (1969) (2nd edn) *Studies in African Land Usage in Northern Rhodesia*, Rhodes-Livingstone Papers No. 15, Rhodesia, Rhodes-Livingstone Institute.

Alonso, W. (1968) 'Urban and regional imbalances in economic development', *Economic and Cultural Change* **17**, 1–13.

Amin, S. (1972) 'Underdevelopment and dependence in Black Africa', *J. of Modern African Studies* **10**, 503–24.

Amin, S. (ed.) (1974) *Modern Migrations in West Africa*, London, Oxford University Press.

Amin, S. (1974) *Accumulation on a World Scale: A critique of the theory of underdevelopment*, 2 vols, New York, Monthly Review Press.

Angier, F. R. *et al.* (1960) *The Making of the West Indies*, London, Longman.

Anthony, K. R. M. *et al.* (1979) *Agricultural Change in Tropical Africa*, New York, Cornell University Press.

Arnold, G. (1977) *Nigeria Today*, London, Longman.

Arnold, G. (1979) *Aid in Africa*, London, Kegan Paul.

Auer, P. (ed.) (1981) *Energy and the Developing Nations*, New York, Pergamon.

Aziz, S. (1978) *Rural Development: Learning from China*, London, Macmillan.

Babarović, I. (1978) 'Rural marginality and regional development policies in Brazil' in Kuklinski 1978, 189–319.

Bairoch, P. (1975) *The Economic Development of the Third World Since 1900*, London, Methuen.

Baklanoff, E. N. (ed.) (1969) *The Shaping of Modern Brazil*, Baton Rouge, Louisiana State University Press.

Baldwin, R. E. (1964) 'Patterns of development in newly settled regions' in Friedmann and Alonso 1964, 266–84.

Barber, W. J. (1961) *The Economy of British Central Africa*, London, Oxford University Press.

Barnett, A., Bell, M. and **Hoffman, K.** (1982) *Rural Energy and the Third World*, London, Pergamon.

Barraclough, S. L. and **Domike, A.** (1966) 'Agrarian structure in seven Latin American countries', *Land Economics*, **42**, 391–442.

Barraclough, S. L. (1976) 'Interactions between agrarian structures and public policies in Latin America' in Hunter, Bunting and Bottrall 1976, 93–105.

Basgupta, B. (1977) 'India's Green Revolution', *Econ. and Polit. Weekly*, Feb. 1977.

Beckfold, G. L. (1969 and 1973) 'The economics of agricultural resource use and development in plantation economies', *Social and Econ. Studies* **18**, 321–47. Reproduced in Bernstein 1973 as Ch. 6.

Beckford, G. L. (1972) *Persistent Poverty: Underdevelopment in plantation economies of the Third World*, Oxford, Oxford University Press.

Benneh, G. (1972) 'The response of farmers in northern Ghana to the introduction of mixed farming: a case study', *Geogr. Annaler*, 95–103.

Belshaw, C. S. (1964) *Under the Ivi Tree: Society and economic growth in rural Fiji*, London, Routledge and Kegan Paul.

Bergsman, J. (1970) *Brazil: Industrialisation and trade policies*, New York, London, Toronto, Oxford University Press.

Bernstein, H. (ed.) (1973) *Underdevelopment and Development*, London, Penguin.

Berry, B. J. L. (1960) 'An inductive approach to the regionalization of economic development' in Ginsburg 1960, 78–107.

Berry, B. J. L. (1961) 'Basic patterns of economic development', in Ginsburg 1961, 110–119.

Berry, B. J. L. (1972) 'Hierarchical diffusion: the basis of developmental filtering and spread in a system of growth centres' in Hansen 1972, 108–38.

Best, L. (1968) 'Outlines of a model of pure plantation economy', *Social and Econ. Studies*, Sept. 1968, 283–326.

Bethell, L. (1970) *The Abolition of the Brazilian Slave Trade*, Cambridge, Cambridge University Press.

Bhagwati, J. N. and **Desai, P.** (1970) *India: Planning for industrialisation*, London, New York, Bombay, Oxford University Press.

Blaikie, P. M. (1971) 'Spatial organisation of agriculture in some north Indian villages', Part I, *Trans Inst. Brit. Geog.*, **52**, 1–40, Part II, **53**, 15–30.

Bondstam, L. and **Bergstrom, S.** (eds.) (1980) *Poverty and Population Control,*, London, New York, Academic Press.

Boserup, E. (1965) *The Conditions of Agricultural Growth*, London, Allen and Unwin, Chicago, Aldine Publishing Co.

Boudeville, J. (1966) *Problems of Regional Economic Planning*, Edinburgh, University of Edinburgh Press.

Bradley, P. N., Raynaut, C. and **Torrealba, J.** (1977) *The Guidimaka Region of Mauretania*, London, War on Want.

Bradley, P. N. (1980) 'Agricultural development planning in the Senegal valley' in Simpson 1980, 41–58.

Brandt, W. (1980) *North-South: Report of the Independent Commission on International Development* (The Brandt Report), London, Pan Books.

Briggs, J. (1980) 'Rural policy in Tanzania since 1967: trends and issues' in Simpson 1980, 9–26.

Brookfield, H. C. (ed.) (1973) *The Pacific in Transition*, New York, St. Martins Press.

Brookfield, H. C. (1975) *Interdependent Development*, London, Methuen.

Brown, C. (1977) *China: 1949–76*, London, Heinneman Educational Books.

Brown, L. R. (1970) *Seeds of Change: The Green Revolution and development in the 1970s*, New York, Praeger.

Brunner, R. and **Brewer, G. D.** (eds.) (1975) *Political Development and Change*, New York, London, Macmillan.

Bruton, H. J. (1965) *Principles of Economic Development*, New Jersey, Prentice Hall.

Burns, Sir A. (1963) *Fiji*, London, H.M.S.O.

Campbell, G. (1972) *Brazil Struggles for Development*, London, Charles Knight.

Cardozo, M. (1969) 'The modernisation of Brazil 1500–1808' in Baklanoff (1969) 3–18.

Cassen, R. H. (1978) *India: Population, Economy and Society*, London, Macmillan.

Ceylon Planning Secretariat (1955) *Six Year Programme of Investment 1954–1959/60*, Colombo, Ceylon Planning Secretariat.

Ceylon Planning Secretariat (1959) *The Ten Year Plan*, Colombo, Ceylon Planning Secretariat.

Chakravarti, A. K. (1973) 'Green revolution in India', *Annals Ass. Am. Geog.*, **63**, No. 3, 319–30.

Chang, J. H. (1968) 'The agricultural potential of the humid tropics', *Geog. Rev.*, **58**, 333–61.

Chen, C. S. (1963) *Taiwan: an economic and social geography*, Taipei, Research Report, No. 96, Fu-Min Geographical Inst. of Econ. Development.

Chenery, H. B. (1960) 'Patterns of industrial growth', *Americ. Econ. Rev.*, **50**, 624–54.

Chenery, H. B. *et al.* (1974) *Redistribution with Growth*, London, New York, Oxford University Press.

Chenery, H. B. *et al.* (1979) *Structural Change and Development Policy*, New York, London, Oxford University Press.

Chenery, H. B. and **Syrquin, M.** (1975) *Patterns of Development 1950–70*, London, Oxford University Press.

Chenery, H. B. and **Taylor, L. J.** (1968) 'Development patterns among countries and over time', *Rev. of Econ. and Stats.*, **50**, 391–416.

Chiang, T. C. (1969) *The Jurong Industrial Estate: Present Pattern and Future Prospect*, Singapore, Nanyang University.

China, Republic of (1953) *First Four Year Plan for Economic development*, Economic Stabilisation Board, Taipei, Rep. of China.

Chiu, S. K. (ed.) (1979) *Modernisation in China*, Centre of Asian Studies Occasional Papers and Monographs No. 35, Hong Kong, Hong Kong University.

Clark, C. and **Haswell, M.** (1970) *The Economics of Subsistence Agriculture*, London, Macmillan.

Clarke, J. I. (1971) *Population Geography and Developing Countries*, Oxford, London, Pergamon.

Coale, H. J. and **Hoover, E. M.** (1958) *Population Growth and Economic Development in Low Income Countries*, Princeton, New Jersey, Princeton University Press.

Cody, J., Hughes, H. and **Wall, D.** (1980) *Policies for Industrial Progress in Developing Countries*, London, New York, Oxford University Press.

Colson, E. and **Gluckman, M.** (eds.) (1951) *Seven Tribes of British Central Africa)*, London, New York, Oxford University Press.

Conklin, H. C. (1954) 'An ethnoecological approach to shifting cultivation', *Trans. New York Acad. Sci.*, **17**.

Conklin, H. C. (1957) *Hanunoo agriculture: a report on an integral system of shifting* *cultivation in the Philippines*, Paper No. 12, **F.A.O.**, Forestry Dept., Rome, F.A.O.

Conklin, H. C. (1961–2) 'The study of shifting cultivation', *Current Anthropology*, 27–58.

Cook, E. K. (1953) *Ceylon: its Geography, its Resources and its People*, London, Macmillan.

Coppock, J. T. (1966) 'Agricultural developments in Nigeria', *Tropical Geog.*, **23**, 1–18.

Courtenay, P. P. (1965) *Plantation Agriculture*, New York, Praeger, London, Bell.

Cuca, R. (1979) *'Family planning programs: an evolution of experience,'* World Bank Staff Working Paper No. 345, Washington D.C. World Bank.

Curtin, P. D. (1969) *The Atlantic Slave Trade: A Census*, Madison, University of Wisconsin Press.

Dalby, D. and **Harrison-Church, R. J.** (eds.) (1973) *Drought in Africa*, SOAS, London, University of London.

Darwent, D. F. (1969) 'Growth poles and growth centers in regional planning – a review', *Environment and Planning* **1**, 5–32.

Dasgupta, A. K. (1974) *Economic Theory and the Developing Countries*, London, Macmillan.

Davies, H. R. J. (1966) 'Nomadism in the Sudan', Tijdschrift fur Economische Geo., Sep/Oct.

Davies, S. G. (1964) *Land Use and Mineral Deposits in Hong Kong*, Hong Kong, Hong Kong University Press.

Davy, E. G., Mattei, E. and **Solomon, J. I.** (1976) *'An evaluation of climate and water resources for development of agriculture in the Sudano-Sahelian zone of West Africa.'* Special environment Report 9, Geneva, W.M.O.

De, P. K. and **Mandal, L. N.** (1956) 'Fixation of nitrogen by algae in rice soils', *Soil Science*, **81**, 453–59.

Deleyne, J. (1973) *The Chinese Economy*, London, Andre Deutsch.

Derrick, R. A. (1959) 'Fiji's darkest hour: an account of the measles epidemic of 1875', *Trans and Proc. Fiji Society* 1959, **6**, 3–16, Suva, Fiji.

De Silva, K. M. (ed.) (1977) *Sri Lanka: a survey*, Institute of Asian Affairs Hamburg, London, C. Hurst and Co.

Dickenson, J. P. (1974) 'Imbalances in Brazil's industrialisation', in Hoyle 1974, 291–306.

Dickenson, J. P. (1982) *Brazil*, London, Longman.

Dixon, C. L. (1977) *The Agricultural Policy in Zambia 1964–71*, O'Dell memorial monograph No. 5, Dept. of Geog., Aberdeen, University of Aberdeen.

Domar, E. (1957) *Essays in the Theory of Economic Growth*, London, Oxford University Press.

Dos Santos, T. (1970) 'The structure of dependence', *Am. Econ. Rev.*, **60**, 289–90.

Dos Santos, T. (1978) 'Theory and the problem of dependence in Latin America' in Bernstein, 1978, 57–80.

Duckham, A. N. and **Masefield, G. B.** (1971) *Farming Systems of the World*, London, Chatto and Windus.

Dulles, J. W. F. (1969) 'The contribution of Getulio Vargas to the modernisation of Brazil' in Baklanoff 1969, 36–57.

Dumont, R. (1957) *Types of Rural Economy: studies in world agriculture*, trans. D. Magnin, London, Methuen.

Dunning, J. H. (ed.) (1971) *The Multinational Enterprise*, London, Allen and Unwin.

Eckstein, A. (1977) *China's Economic Revolution*, Cambridge, London, New York, Cambridge University Press.

Eden, M. J. (1978) 'Ecology and land development: the case of Amazonian rain forest, *Trans. Inst. Brit. Geog.*, **3**, No. 4, 444–63.

Eiches, C. K. and **Liedholme, C.** (1970) *Growth and Development of the Nigerian Economy*, Michigan, Michigan State University Press.

Emmanuel, A. (1972) *Unequal Exchange*, London, New Left Books.

Epstein, T. S. (1973) *South India: Yesterday, Today and Tomorrow*, London, Macmillan.

Evans, A. (1955) 'A study of crop production in relation to rainfall reliability'. *East African Agric. J.*, April, 263–67.

Fallen-Bailey, D. G. E. and **Byer, T. A.** (1979) *'Energy options and policy issues in developing countries,'* World Bank Staff Working Paper No. 350, Washington D.C., World Bank.

Farmer, B. H. (1950) 'Agriculture in Ceylon', *Geog. Rev.*, **40**, 42–66.

Farmer, B. H. (1957) *Pioneer Peasant Colonization in Ceylon: a study in Asian agrarian problems*, London, Oxford University Press.

Farmer, B. H. (1963a) 'Peasant and plantation in Ceylon', (Pacific Viewpoint, **4**, 9–16.

Farmer, B. H. (1963b) *Ceylon: a divided nation*, London, New York and Bombay, Oxford University Press.

Fei, J. C. H. and **Ranis, G.** (1975) 'A model of growth and employment' in the open dualistic economy', *J. of Develop. Studies* **2**, 32–63.

Fei, J. C. H., Ranis, G. and **Kuo, S. W. Y.** (1979) *Growth with Equity: the Taiwan case*, London, New York, Oxford University Press.

Feuchtwang, S. and **Hussain, A.** (eds.) (1983) *The Chinese Economic Reforms*, London, Croom Helm.

Fiefia, S. N. (1968) *Report of the Results of the 1966 Census, Tonga*, Nuku'alofa, Tonga, Govt. Press.

Fiji Education Commission (1970) *Report of the 1969 Fiji Education Commission*, Suva, Fiji, Govt. Printer.

Fiji Legislative Council (1966) *Fiji Development Plan 1966–70*, Development Plan Review, Legis. Council of Fiji, Coun. Paper No. 11 of 1966, Central Planning Office, Colony of Fiji, Suva, Fiji Govt. Printer.

Fiji, Parliament of (1970) *Fiji's Sixth Development Plan 1971–75*, Parliam. Paper No. 25 of 1970, Central Planning Office, Min. of Finance, Suva, Fiji, Govt. Printer.

Fiji, Parliament of (1975) *Fiji's Seventh Development Plan 1976–80*, Parliamentary Papers 1975, Central Planning Office, Suva, Fiji, Govt. Printer.

Fiji, Parliament of (1980/81) *Fiji's Eighth Development Plan 1981–85*, Parliam. of Fiji Papers 1980/81, 2 vols., Central Planning Office, Suva, Fiji, Govt. Printer.

Fisk, E. K. (1970) *The Political Economy of Independent Fiji*, Canberra, Australian National University Press.

Fleure, H. J. (1919) 'Human regions,' *Scot. Geog. Mag.*, **35**, 94–105.

Flinn, M. W. (1979) *British Population Growth 1700–1850*, London, Macmillan.

Food and Agricultural Organisation, F.A.O. (1982) *World Report: State of Food and Agriculture 1981*, Rome, F.A.O.

Forde, D. (1934) *Habitat, Economy and Society*, London, Methuen.

France, P. (1969) *The Charter of the Land: Custom and Colonization in Fiji*, London, Wellington, New York, Oxford University Press.

Frank A. G. (1967) *'Capitalism and Underdevelopment in Latin America'*, New York, Monthly Review Press. Historical Studies in Chile and Brazil Review, edition 1969.

Frank, A. G. (1969) *'Latin America, underdevelopment or revolution,'* New York, Modern Reader, Monthly Review Press.

Frankel, J. M. (1971) *India's Green Revolution: economic gains and political costs*, Princeton, New Jersey, Princeton University Press.

Frazer, F. R. (1952) 'Housing and planning in Singapore', *Town Planning Rev.*, **23**, 5–25.

Freeman, J. D. (1955) *Iban Agriculture*, Colonial Office Research Study No. 18, London, Colonial Office.

Friedmann, J. P. (1966) *Regional Development Policy: a case study of Venezuela*, MIT Press.

Friedmann, J. P. (1968) 'The strategy of deliberate urbanization', *J. Am. Inst. of Planning*, **34**, 364–73.

Friedmann, J. P. (1972) 'A general theory of polarized development' in Hansen 1972, 82–107.

Friedmann, J. P. and **Alonso, W.** (eds.) (1964) *Regional Development and Planning*, Cambridge, Mass., MIT Press.

Friedmann, J. P. and **Douglas, M.** (1978) 'Agropolitan Development: towards a new strategy for regional planning in Asia' in Lo and Salih 1978.

Friedmann, J. P. and **Weaver, W.** (1979) *Territory and Function*, London, Edward Arnold.

Friedmann, J. P. and **Wulff, R.** (1976) *The Urban Transition*, London, Edward Arnold.

Froehlick, W. (ed.) (1961) *Land tenure, Industrialisation and Social Stability*, Milwaukee, Marquette University Press.

Furtado, C. (1959; trans. 1963) *The Economic Growth of Brazil*, Berkeley, Cal., University of California Press.

Furtado, C. (1976), 2nd edn., *Economic Development of Latin America*, Cambridge, Cambridge University Press.

Gaitskell, A. (1959) *Gezira: a story of development in the Sudan*, London, Faber and Faber.

Galenson, W. (ed.) (1979) *Economic Growth and Structural Change in Taiwan*, Ithaca, New Jersey, Cornell University Press.

Galloway, J. H. (1968) 'The sugar industry of Pernambuco in the nineteenth century', *Annals Assoc. Am. Geogs.*, **58**, 285–303.

Gann, L. H. (1958) *The Birth of a Plural Society: the development of Northern Rhodesia under the British South Africa Company 1894–1914*, Manchester, Manchester University Press for the Rhodes-Livingstone Institute.

Gann, L. H. (1963) *A History of Northern Rhodesia*, London, Chatto and Windus.

Geertz, C. (1968) *Agricultural Involution*, Berkeley and Los Angeles, University of California Press.

Geiger, T. (1976) *The Development Progress of Hong Kong and Singapore*, Hong Kong, Macmillan.

Gilbert, A. G. (1975) 'A note on the incidence of development in the vicinity of a growth centre', *Regional Studies*, **9**, 325–33.

Gilbert, A. G. (ed.) (1976) *Development Planning and Spatial Structure*, New York, John Wiley.

Gilbert, A. G. and **Gugler, J.** (1981) *Cities, Poverty and Development*, London, Oxford University Press.

Ginsburg, N. S. (ed.) (1960) *Essays on Geography and Economic Development*, Chicago, University of Chicago Press.

Ginsburg, N. S. (1961) *Atlas of Economic Development*, University of Chicago Press.

Glass, D. V. and **Eversley, D. E. C.** (eds.) (1965) *Population in History: essays in historical demography*, London, Edward Arnold, Chicago, Aldine Pub. Co.

Gleave, M. B. (1980) 'Some further thoughts on population density and agricultural systems in West Africa' in Simpson 1980, 59–74.

Gleave, M. B. (ed.) (not yet published) *Tropical African Development: geographical perspectives*, London, Longman.

Goddard, A. D. *et al.* (1971) '*A socio-economic study of three villages in Sokoto close-settled zone*', Samaru Miscellaneous Papers No. 33, Samura, Nigeria, Ahmadu Bello University.

Goddard, A. D.. *et al* (1974) 'Population movements and land shortages in the Sokoto close-settled zone' in Amin 1974.

Goh, K. S. (1977) *The Practice of Economic Growth*, Singapore, Federal Publications.

Gottmann, J. (1983) 'Third World cities in perspective', *Area*, **15**, No. 4, 311–13.

Gould, P. R. (1970) 'Tanzania 1920–63: the spatial impress of the modernisation process', *World Politics* **22**, 149–70.

Gourou, P (1953) *The Tropical World*, London, Longman.

Gray, J. (1969) 'The economics of Maoism', *Bull. of Atomic Scientists* **25**, No. 2, 42–51. Also in Bernstein 1973.

Gray, J. and **Gray, M.** (1983) 'China's new agricultural revolution' in Feuchtwang and Hussain 1983, 151–84.

Gray, R. H. (1974) 'The doctrine of mortality in Ceylon and the demographic effects of malaria control', *Population Studies* **28**, 205–29.

Greaves, I. (1959) 'Plantations in the world economy' in Pan. American Union 1959.

Greenwood, M. (1936) 'English Death Rates, Past, Present and Future', *J. of Royal Stat. Soc.* **99**.

Griffin, K. B. and **Enos, J. L.** (1970) *Planning Development*, Addison Wesley, (see also Bernstein 1973, 141–53).

Grist, D. H. (1975 5th ed.) *Rice*, New York and London, Longman.

Grove, A. T. (1967) *Africa South of the Sahara*, London, Oxford University Press.

Habakkuk, H. J. (1965) 'The economic history of modern Britain' in Glass and Eversley 1965, 147–58.

Habakkuk, H. J. (1971) *Population Growth and Development sincce 1750*, Leicester, Leicester University Press.

Hall, R. (1965) *Zambia*, London, Pall Mall Press.

Hansen, N. M. (ed.) (1972) *Growth Centres in Regional Economic Development*, New York, The Free Press.

Harris, B. (1971) 'The Green Revolution in Ludhiana District India', *Geog.*, **56**, 243–46.

Harrod, R. F. (1948) *Towards a Dynamic Economics*, London, Macmillan.

Hasan, P. (1984) 'Adjustment to external shocks', *Finance and Development*, **21** No. 4, Dec., 14–17, World Bank.

Hatcher, J. (1977) *Plague, Population and the English Economy 1348–1530*, London, New York, Macmillan.

Heady, E. O. (1952) *Economics of Plantation Production and Resource Use*, New Jersey, Prentice-Hall.

Healey, D. T. (1972) 'Development policy: new thinking about interpretation', *J. of Econ. Literature*, Sept. 1972.

Heathcote, D. (1972) 'Insight into a creative process: a rare collection of embroidery drawings from Kano', *Savanna*, Dec. 1972, **1**, 2, 165–74.

Hellen, J. A. (1968) *Rural Economic Development in Zambia 1890–1914*, Munchen, IFO-Inst. for Wintschaftsforschung, Munchen Afrika-Studienstelle.

Hendrix, W. E., Naive, J. J. and **Adams, W. E.** (1968) *Accelerating India's Food Grain Production 1967–68 to 1970–71*, Foreign Agricultural Economic Report No. 40, Dept. of Agric. USA, Econ. Research Service. Washington D.C., US Dept. Agric.

Hirschman, A. O. (1958) *The Strategy of Economic Development*, New Haven, Conn., Yale University Press.

Ho, R. (1964) 'Mixed farming and multiple cropping in Malaya' in Davies 1964.

Ho, R. (1967) *Farmers of Central Malaya*, Canberra, Australian National University Press.

Ho, S. P. S. (1978) *Economic development of Taiwan 1860–1970*, New Haven and London, Yale University Press.

Hone, P. F. (1909) *Southern Rhodesia*, London, Bell.

Hoyle, B. S. (ed.) (1974) *Spatial Aspects of Development*, London, Sydney and Toronto, John Wiley.

Hsiung, J. C. (ed.) (1981) *The Taiwan experience 1950–80*, New York, Praeger.

Hubback, E. M. (1947) *The Population of Britain*, London, Pelican.

Hughes, R. (1970) *Borrowed Place, Borrowed Time*, Hong Kong.

Hunter, G. (1969) *Modernizing Peasant Societies*, London, Oxford University Press.

Hunter, G., Bunting, A. H. and **Bottrall, A.** (eds.) (1976) *Policy and Practice in Rural Development*, London, Croom Helm.

Hutchinson, H. H. (1961) 'The transformation of Brazilian plantation society' *J. of Inter-American Studies*, **3**, 201–12.

Hyden, G. (1980) *Beyond Ujamaa in Tanzania*, London, Heinemann.

Ilich, I. (1969) 'Outwitting the "developed" countries', *New York Review of Books*, 6 Nov. 1969, 20–24. Reprinted in Bernstein 1978, 357–68.

Indian Planning Commission (1966) *Fourth Five Year Plan*, 10–11, New Delhi, Govt. of India.

Isard, W. (1951) 'Regional and interregional input-output analysis: a model of a space economy' *Rev. of Econ. and Stats.*, **33**, 318–28.

Isard, W. (1957) 'The value of the regional approach to some basic economic problems', *Regional income, studies in income and wealth* **2**, Princeton University Press.

Isard, W. (1956) *Location and Space Economy*, Boston: The Technology Press of MIT and John Wiley and Sons.

Isard, W. et al. (1960) *Methods of Regional Analysis: an introduction to regional science*, London, John Wiley and Sons.

Islam, N. (1967) *Tariff protection, comparative costs and industrialisation in Pakistan.* Pakistan Institute of Development Economics, Research Report 57.

Jakubowski, M. (1977) 'The theory of demographic transition and studies in the spatial differentiation of population dynamics', *Geographia Polonica*, **35**, 73–89.

Jeyaratnan Wilson, J. (1977) 'Politics and political development since 1948' in De Silva 1977.

Johnson, C. (1981) 'The Taiwan model' in Hsiung 1981, 9–10.

Johnson, E. H. J. (1970) *The Organisation of Space in Developing Countries*, Cambridge Mass., Harvard University Press.

Johnson, H. G. (1964) 'Tariffs and economic development', *J. Dev. Studies*, Oct. 1964.

Johnson, L. L. (1967) 'Problems of import-substitution: the Chilean automobile industry', *Econ. Develpt. and Cultural Change*, Jan. 1967.

Johnson, S. (1972) *The Green Revolution*, London, Harper and Row.

Jones, W. O. (1968) 'Plantations' in Sills 1968.

Jorgenson, D. W. (1967) 'Surplus agricultural labour and the development of dual economies', *Oxford Econ. Papers*, Nov. 1967.

Kadt, E. de (1980) *Tourism – Passport to Development?* London, New York, Oxford University Press.

Kamarck, A. M. (1976) *The Tropics and Economic Development*, Baltimore and London, Johns Hopkins University Press.

Katzman, M. T. (1977) *Cities and Frontiers in Brazil*, Cambridge Mass., and London, Harvard University Press.

Kay, G. (1967) *A Social Geography of Zambia*, London, University of London Press.

Kenworthy, J. M. and **Glover, J.** (1958) 'The reliability of the main rains in Kenya', *East African Agric. J.*, **23**, 267–71.

Kerr, G. H. (1974) *Formosa 1895–1945*, Honolulu, University Press of Hawaii.

Kessel, J. F. (1961) 'The ecology of filariasis' in May 1961.

Kilby, P. (1969) *Industrialisation in an Open Economy: Nigeria 1945–66*, Cambridge, London, Cambridge University Press.

Killick, T. (1978) *Development Economics in Action: a study of economic policies in Ghana*, London, Heinemann.

Knight, C. G. and **Newman, J. L.** (eds.) (1976) *Contemporary Africa: geography and change*, New Jersey, Prentice Hall.

Koo, A. Y. C. (1968) *The role of Land Reform in Economic Development: A case study of Taiwan*, New York, Praeger.

Kowal, J. J. and **Kassam, A. H.** (1978) *Agricultural Ecology of Savanna: a study of West Africa*, London, Oxford University Press.

Krishna, R. (1980) 'The economic development of India' in *Economic Development*, Scientific American 1980, 78–87.

Kuan, H. C. (1979) 'Political stability and change' in Lin et al., 1979.

Kuklinski, A. (ed.) (1978) *Regional Policies in Nigeria, India and Brazil*, U.N. Research Inst. for Social and Economic Planning, No. 9, The Hague, Paris, New York, Mouton.

Kuo, S. W. Y., Ranis, G. and **Fei, J. C. H.** (1981) *Rapid Growth with Improved Distribution in the Republic of China*, Boulder, Colorado, Westview Press and Praeger.

Kuo, S. W.Y., Ranis, G. and **Fei, J. C. H.** (1981) *The Taiwan Success Story*, Boulder, Colorado, Westview Press.

Kuznets, S. (1955) 'Economic growth and income inequality', *Am. Econ. Rev.*, **45**, 1–28.

Kuznets, S. (1979) 'Growth and Structural Shifts' in Galenson 1979.

Lall, S. and **Streeten, P.** (1977) *Foreign investment, Transnationals and Developing Countries*, New York, Macmillan.

Lange, O. (1960) *Essays on Economic Planning*, London, Asia Publishing House/Statistical Publishing Society.

Learmonth, A. T. A. (1957) 'Some contrasts in the regional geography of malaria in India and Pakistan', *Trans. Inst. Brit. Geog.*, **23**, 37–59.

Learmonth, A. T. A. (1978) *Patterns of Disease and Hunger*, London, Vancouver, David and Charles.

Lee, D. H. K. (1957) *Climate and Economic Development in the Tropics*, New York, Council on Foreign Relations.

Leff, N. H. (1982) *Underdevelopment and Development in Brazil*, Vol. 1 Economic Structure and change 1822–1947, Vol. 2 Reassessing the obstacles to economic growth, London, Boston, Sydney, Allen and Unwin.

Leibenstein, H. (1954) *A Theory of Economic-Demographic Development*, Princeton, New Jersey, Princeton University Press.

Leibenstein, H. (1957) *Economic Backwardness and Economic Growth*, New York, John Wiley.

Leung, C. K. (1979) 'Modernisation of railways' in Chiu 1979.

Leung, C. K. (1980) *China: Railway Patterns and National Goals*, Dept. of Geog., Research Papers No. 195, Chicago, University of Chicago Press.

Leung, C. K. and **Chiu, T. N.** (eds.) (1983) *China in Readjustment*, Centre of Asian Studies, Hong Kong, University of Hong Kong.

Leung, C. K. and **Comtois, C.** (1983) 'Transport reorientation towards the Eighties' in Leung and Chiu 1983.

Lewis, W. A. (1954) 'Economic development with unlimited supplies of labour', *Manchester School of Econ. and Soc. Sci.*, **22**, 139–91.

Lewis, W. A. (1955) *The Theory of Economic Growth*, London, Allen and Unwin.

Lin, C. Y. (1981) 'Agricultural and land reform' in Hsiung 1981, 140–43.

Lin, T. B., Lee, R. P. L. and **Simonis, U. E.** (1979) *Hong Kong: economic, social and political studies in development*, Institute of Asian Affairs Hamburg, M. E. Sharpe Inc. Dawson.

Little, I., Scitovsky, T. and **Scott, M.** (1970) *Industry and Trade in Some Developing Countries: a comparative study*, London, Oxford University Press.

Little, I. M. D. (1979) 'An Economic Reconnaissance' in Galenson 1979, 448–508.

Lo, F. C. and **Salih, K.** (eds.) (1978) *Growth Pole Strategy and Regional Development Policy*, Oxford, Pergamon Press.

Logan, M. I. (1972) 'The spatial system and planning strategies in developing countries', *Geog. Rev.*, **62**, No. 2, 229–44.

Long, N. (1977) *An Introduction to the Sociology of Rural Development*, London, Tavistock.

Mabogunje, A. L. (1965) 'The economic implications of the pattern of urbanisation in Nigeria', *Nigeria J. of Econ. and Soc. Studies* **7**, 9–30.

Mabogunje, A. L. (1968) *Urbanisation in Nigeria*, London University Press.

Mabogunje, A. L. (1978) 'Growth poles and growth centres in the regional development of Nigeria' in Kuklinski 1978.

Mabogunje, H. J. (1980) *The Development Process*, London, Hutchinson.

Mackinder, H. J. (1902) *Britain and the British Seas*, London, Heinemann.

Malthus, T. (1798) *Essay on the Principle of Population*, London.

Mansfield, J. E. *et al.* (1974) *Land resources of the Northern and Luapula Provinces Zambia*, Surbiton England, Land Resources Division.

Manshard, W. (1968) *Tropical Agriculture*, London, Longman.

Mathur, A. (1966) 'Balanced versus unbalanced growth: a view', *Oxford Econ. Papers*, **18**.

Maude, A. (1973) 'Land shortage and population pressure' in Brookfield 1973, 163–85.

May, J. M. (1958) *The Ecology of Human Disease*, New York, M.D. Publications.

May, J. M. (ed.) (1961) *Studies in Disease Ecology*, New York, Hefner.

McDonald, W. H. (1963) 'Disease in Fiji', *Trans. and Proc. Fiji Society*, 1963, **7**, 63–72, Suva, Fiji.

McGee, T. G. (1967) *The Southeast Asian City*, London, Bell.

McGee, T. G. (1971) *The Urbanisation Process in the Third World: explorations in search of a theory*, London, Bell.

McKeown, T. and **Brown, R. G.** (1965) 'Medical evidence related to English population changes in the Eighteenth Century' in Glass and Eversley 1965, 285–307.

Melamid, A. (1967) 'The geography of the Nigerian petroleum industry', *Econ. Geog.*, **43**, 51–56.

Mikesell, R. F. (1968) *The Economics of Foreign Aid*, Chicago, Aldine.

Miracle, M. P. (1957) *Agriculture in the Congo Basin*, Madison, Milwaukee, London, University of Wisconsin Press.

Mitchison, R. (1977) *British Population Change since 1860*, New York, London, Macmillan.

Mohammad, A. (1978) *The Situation of Agriculture Food and Nutrition in Rural India*.

Morgan, W. B. (1977) *Agriculture in the Third World: a spatial analysis*, London, Bell.

Morgan, W. T. W. (1963) 'The "White Highlands" of Kenya', *Geog. J. London*, **129**, 140–55.

Mortimore, M. J. and **Wilson, J.** (1965) '*Land and people in the Kano close-settled zone*', Dpt. of Geog., Occas. Paper No. 1, March 1965, Ahmadu Bello University, Zaria, Nigeria.

Mortimore, M. J. (1967) 'Land and population pressure in the Kano close-settled zone, northern Nigeria', *Adv. of Sci.*, **23**, 677–86.

Morton, K. and **Tulloch, P.** (1977) *Trade and Developing Countries*, London, Croom Helm.

Moses, L. (1955) 'Interregional input-output analysis', *Amer. Econ. Rev.*, **45**, Dec. 1955, 803–32.

Mountjoy, A. B. (ed.) (1971) *Developing the Underdeveloped Countries*, London, Macmillan.

Myint, H. (1964) *The Economics of the Developing Countries*, London, Hutchinson.

Myrdal, G. (1957) *Economic Theory and Underdeveloped Regions*, London, Duckworth.

Myrdal, G. (1968) *Asian Drama*, 3 vols., New York, Twenty Century Fund.

Needleman, L. (ed.) 1968 *Regional Analysis*, London, Penguin.

Nelson, R. R. (1956) 'A theory of the low-level equilibrium trap', *Americ. Econ. Rev.*, **46**, 894–908.

Newman, P. (1970) 'Malaria control and population growth', *J. of Dev. Studiess*, **6**, 133–58.

Nicholls, W. H. (1971) 'Agriculture and the economic development of Brazil' in Saunders 1971, 215–56.

Nigeria Federation of (1962) *National Development Plan 1962–68*, Lagos, Nigerian Government.

Nigeria Federal Republic of (1970) *Second National Development Plan 1970–74*, Lagos, Nigerian Government.

Nigeria Federal Republic of (1974) *Third National Development Plan 1974–80*, Lagos, Nigerian Government.

Nigeria Federal Republic of (1981) *Fourth National Development Plan 1981–85*, Lagos, Nigerian Government.

Nkrumah, K. (1965) *Neo-colonialism: the last stage of imperialism*, New York, International Publishers.

Norman, D. W. (1967 and 1972) *An Economic Study of Three Villages in Zaria Province*, Vol. 1 Land and labour relations, Vol. 2 Input-output Study, Rural Economy Research Unit, Ahmadu Bello University, Samaru, Ahmadu Bellow University.

Norman, D. W. *et al.* (1976) *A Socio-Economic Study of Three Villages in the Sokoto Close-settled Zone*, No. 64, Samaru Miscellaneous Papers, Samaru Nigeria, Ahmadu Bello University.

North, D. C. (1964) 'Location theory and economic growth' in Friedmann and Alonso 1964, 240–55.

Nulty, L. E. (1972) *The Green Revolution in West Pakistan*, New York, Praeger.

Nurkse, R. (1953) *Problems of Capital Formation in Underdeveloped Countries*, Oxford, Blackwell.

Nye, P. H. and **Greenland, D. J.** (1960) *The Soil Under Shifting Cultivation*, Bureau of Soils, Reading, Reading Commonwealth Bureau of Soils.

Odell, P. R. and **Preston, D. A.** (1973) *Economies and Societies in Latin America*, London, New York, Sydney, Toronto, John Wiley.

Odingo, R. S. (1971) *The Kenya Highlands: Land use and agricultural development*, Nairobi, East Africa Publishing House.

Onabamiro, S. D. (1953) *Food and Health*, Penguin West African Series, London, Penguin.

Ooi, J. B. and **Chiang, H. D.** (eds.) (1969) *Modern Singapore*, Singapore University Press.

Owens, R. J. (1963) *Peru*, London, Oxford University Press.

Pacione, M. (ed.) (1981) *Problems and Planning in Third World Cities*, London, Croom Helm.

Paige, J. M. (1975) *Agrarian Revolution*, New York, The Free Press, London, Macmillan.

Palma, G. (1978) 'Dependency: a Formal Theory of Underdevelopment or a Methodology for the analyses of concrete situations of underdevelopment?', *World Development.*, **6**.

Pan American Union (1959) *Plantation Systems of the World*, Washington Social Science Monographs No. VII, Washington, D.C., Pan American Union.

Pannell, C. W. (1973) 'T'ai- Chung, T'ai-Wan: structure and function,' Research paper No. 144, Dept. of Geography, University of Chicago, Chicago University Press.

Parr, J. B. (1973) 'Growth poles, regional development and central place theory', *Regional Sc. Assoc., Pages and Proceedings*, **31**, 173–212.

Paukert, F. (1973) 'Income distribution at different levels of development', *Internat. Labour Rev.*, **108**, 97–124.

Perloff, H. and **Wingo, L.** (1964) 'Natural resource endowment and regional economic growth' in Friedmann and Alonso 1964, 215–39.

Perroux, F. (1950) 'Economic space: theory and applications', *Quarterly J. of Econ.*, **64**, 89–104. Also in Friedmann and Alonso 1964, 21–36.

Peters, D. U. (1950) *'Land usage in Serenji district,'* Rhodes-Livingstone Paper No. 19, Rhodesia, Rhodes Livingstone Institute.

Phillips, J. (1961 and 1966) *The Development of Agriculture and Forestry in the Tropics*, London, Faber and Faber.

Prebisch, R. (1959) 'The role of commercial policies in underdeveloped countries', *Am. Econ. Rev., Papers and Proceedings*, May 1959.

Preston, D. A. (1965) 'Changes in the economic geography of banana production in Ecuador', *Trans. Inst. Brit. Geogs.*, **37**, 77–90.

Prothero, R. M. (1957) 'Land use at Soba: Zaria province Northern Nigeria', *Econ. Geog.*, **33**, 72–86.

Prothero, R. M. (1965) *Migrants and Malaria*, London, Longman.

Prothero, R. M., Zelinsky, W. and **Kosinski, L. A.** (eds.) (1970) *Geography and a Crowding World*, New York, Oxford University Press.

Radice, H. (1975) *International Firms and Modern Imperialism*, London, Harmondsworth, Penguin.

Ranis, G. (1974) 'Taiwan' in Chenery et al 1974, 285–90.

Ranis, G. (1979) 'Appropriate technology in the dual economy: reflections on Philippine and Taiwanese experience' in Robinson 1979, 140–59.

Ranis, P. (1971) *Five Latin American Nations*, London, Macmillan.

Rawski, T. G.; (1979) *Economic Growth and Employment in China*, London, Oxford University Press.

Reuber, G. L. (1973) *Private, Foreign Investment in Development*, London, Oxford University Press.

Rhynsburger, W. (1956) *Area and Resources Survey: Taiwan*, Taipei, International Cooperation, Administration and Mutual Security Mission to China.

Richards, A. I. (1958) 'A changing pattern of agriculture in East Africa: the Bemba of northern Rhodesia, *Geog J.*, **124**, No. 3, 302–14.

Richards, A. I. (1961) *Land, Labour and Diet in Northern Rhodesia*, International African Institute, London, Oxford, Oxford University Press.

Richards, A. I. (1968) 'The Bemba of north-eastern Rhodesia' in Colson and Gluckman 1968.

Riddell, J. B. (1970) *The Spatial Dynamics of Modernization in Sierra Leone*, Evanston, North-western University Press. Also in Knight and Newman 1976, 393–407.

Rios, J. A. (1971) 'The growth of cities and urban development' in Saunders 1971, 269–88.

Riskin, C. (1979) 'Intermediate technology in China's rural industries' in Robinson, 1979, 52–74.

Robequin, C. (1954) *Malaya, Indonesia, Borneo and the Philippines*, London, Longman.

Robinson, A. (ed.) (1979) *Appropriate technologies for Third World Development*, London, New York, Macmillan.

Robinson, D. A. (1964 reprint 1971) *Peru in Four Divisions*, Lima, American Studies, Detroit, Blain-Ethridge Books.

Robinson, G. and **Salih, K. B.** (1971) 'The spread of development around Kuala Lumpur', *Regional Studies*, **5**, 303–14.

Robinson, J. (1979) *Aspects of Development and Underdevelopment*, Cambridge, Cambridge University Press.

Rosen, G. (1975) *Peasant Society in a Changing Economy: comparative development in South-East Asia and London*, Urbana, University Press.

Rosen, G. (1975) *Peasant Society in a Changing Economy: comparative development in South East Asia and London*, Urban, University of Illinois Press.

Rostow, W. W. (1952) *The Process of Economic Growth*, New York, London, Oxford, Oxford University Press.

Rostow, W. W. (1956) 'The take-off into self- sustained growth', *Econ. J.*, Mar. 1956, 25–48.

Rostow, W. W. (1960) *The Stages of Economic Growth*, Cambridge, Cambridge University Press.

Rostow, W. W. (ed.) (1963) *The Economics of Take-off into Sustained Growth*, London, Macmillan.

Russett, B. M. (1967) *International Regions and the the International system*, Chicago, Rand McNally.

Ruthenberg, H. (1971) *Farming Systems in the Tropics*, Oxford, Clarendon Press.

Santos, M. (1979) *The Shared Space: the two circuits of the urban economy in underdeveloped countries*, London, New York, Methuen.

Saunders, J. (ed.) (1971) *Modern Brazil: new patterns and development*, Gainsville, Florida, University of University of Florida Press.

Scammell, W. M. (1980) *The International Economy since 1945*, London, Macmillan.

Schlippe, P. de (1956) *Shifting Cultivation in Africa*, London, Routledge.

Schram, S. R. (ed.) (1974) *Chairman Mao Talks to the People*, New York.

Schultz, J. (1974) *Explanatory study to the Land Use Map of Zambia*, Munich, Ministry of Rural Development, Zambia, Zambia Govt. of.

Schumpeter, J. A. (1911) (trans. R. Opie 1934) *The Theory of Economic Development: an enquiry*, Cambridge, Mass., Harvard University Press.

Scientific American (1980) *Economic Development* San Francisco USA., Oxford, Freeman and Co.

Shand, R. T. (1969) *Agricultural Development in Asia*, Canberra, Australian National University.

Shand, R. T. (ed.) (1979) *The New Strategy in India: agriculture in the first decade*, New Delhi.

Shonfield, A. (1960) *The Attack on World Poverty*, London.

Siddayao, C. M. (1978) *ASEAN and the Multinational Corporations*.

Sills, D. L. (ed.) (1968) *International Encyclopedia of the Social Sciences*, 12, UNESCO.

Simmons, A. B., Diaz-Briquets, S. and **Laquian, A. A.** (1977) *Social Change and Internal Migration: a review of research findings from Africa, Asia and Latin America*, Ottawa, International Research Centre, Ottawa.

Simon, J. L. (1977) *The Economics of Population Growth*, Princeton, New Jersey, Princeton University Press.

Simpson, E. S. (1969) 'Electricity production in Nigeria', *Econ. Geog.*, **45**, No. 3, 239–57.

Simpson, E. S. (1971a) 'Education, universities and geography in developing countries', Proceedings Sixth New Zealand Geog. Conference, **2** 118–24, N.Z. Geog. Soc. Conference Series No. 64, Christchurch, New Zealand, New Zealand Geog. Soc.

Simpson, E. S. (1971b) 'Northern Nigeria plans for peace', *Geog. Mag.*, **43**, No. 6, 3.

Simpson, E. S. (1972) 'Economic development in Fiji', *Perspective*, No. 9, Jan, 1972, 1–7.

Simpson, E. S. (ed.) (1980) *The Rural-Agricultural Sector*, Newcastle, Developing Areas Study Group. Inst. Brit. Geog.

Simpson, E. S. (1988) 'Energy Resources' in Gleave 1988.

Singer, H. (1950) 'The distribution of gains between investing and borrowing countries', *Am. Econ. Rev., Papers and Proceedings*, May 1950.

Singh. J. S. (1979) *World Population Policies*, U.N. Fund for Population Activities, New York, Praeger.

Smil, V. and **Knowland, W. E.** (eds.) (1980) *Energy in the Developing World*, Oxford, Oxford University Press.

Soja, E. W. (1968) *The Geography of Modernisation in Kenya*, Syracuse, University of Syracuse Press.

Soja, E. W. and **Tobin. R. J.** (1975) 'The geography of modernisation: paths, patterns and processes of spatial change in developing countries' in Brunner and Brewer 1975.

Soligo, R. and **Stern, J. J.** (1965) 'Tariff protection, import substitution and investment efficiency', *Pakistan Developt. Rev.*, Summer 1965.

Spate, O. H. K. (1959) *The Fijian People: economic prospects and problems*, Council Paper No. 13, Legislation Council of Fiji, Suva, Fiji, Government Press Fiji.

Spate, O. H. K. and **Learmonth, A. T. A.** (1967) *India and Pakistan*, London, Methuen.

Spencer, J. E. (1966) *Shifting Cultivation in south-eastern Asia*, Berkeley and Los Angeles,, University of California Press.

Stenning, D. J. (1959) *Savanna Nomads*, London, Oxford University Press.

Stevens, C. (1979) *Food Aid and the Developing World*, London, Croom Helm.

Stouse, P. A. D. (1970) 'Instability of tropical agriculture: the Atlantic lowlands of Costa Rica', *Econ. Geog.*, **60**, 78–97.

Streeten, P. (1972) *The Frontiers of Development Studies*, London, Macmillan.

Streeten, P. (ed.) (1973) *Trade Strategies for Development*, London, Macmillan.

Swami, K. (1973) *Moisture Conditions in the Savanna region of West Africa*, Montreal, Dpt. of Geog., Savanna Research Centre, McGill University.

Taaffe, E. J., Morill, R. L. and **Gould, P. R.** (1963) 'Transport expansion in underdeveloped countries', *Geog. Rev.*, Oct. 1963, **53**. 503–29.

Tang, H. S. and **Hsieh, S. C.** (1961) 'Land reform and agricultural development in Taiwan' in Froehlick 1961, 114–42.

Thorbecke, E. (1979) 'Agricultural Development' in Galenson 1979, 263–307.

Thorp, E. (1956) *The Ladder of Bones: the birth of modern Nigeria from 1853 to independence*, London, Jonathan Cape. Also 1966, Fontana Books.

Thumm, U. *et al*, (1981) *Peru: major development policy issues and recommendations*, Latin American and the Caribbean Regional Office, Washington, D.C., World Bank.

Tiebout, C. M. (1956) 'Exports and regional economic growth', *J. of Polit. Econ.*, **64**, April 1956, 160–65.

Tiebout, C. M. (1968) 'Regional and inter-regional input-output models: an appraisal' in Needleman 1968, Chp. 3.

Todaro, P. (1977) *Economic Development in the Third World*, London, Longman.

Tonga, Kingdom of, (1966) *Development Plan 1965–70*, Nuku'alofa, Tonga Government Printer.

Tonga, Kingdom of, (1970) *Development Plan 1970–75*, Nuku'Alofa, Tonga, Government Printer.

REFERENCES

Tosi, J. A. and **Voertmann, R. F.** (1964) 'Some environmental factors in the economic development of the Tropics', *Econ. Geog.*, **40**, No. 3, 189–205.

Tranter, W. (1973) *Population since the Industrial Revolution*, London, Croom Helm.

Tugendhat, C. (1973) *The Multinationals*, Harmondsworth, Penguin Books.

Twyford, I. T. and **Wright, A. C. S.** (1965) *The Soil Resources and Fiji Islands*, Suva, Fiji, Government Printer.

United Nations Organisation (1949) *Relative Prices of Exports and Imports of Under-developed Countries*, New York, UNO.

United Nations Organisation (1973) *Multinational Corporations in World Development*, New York, UNO.

United Nations Organisation (1978) *Transcontinental Corporations in World Development*, New York, UNO.

Venezian, E. L. and **Gamble, W.** (1969) *The Agricultural Development of Mexico: its structure and growth since 1950*, New York, Praeger.

Vernon, R. (ed.) (1968) *Multinational Enterprise in the 1960s*, London.

Vernon, R. (1977) *Storm over Multinationals: the real issues*, New York, Vail-Ballow Press.

Vianna, H. (1961/1962) *Historia do Brasil*, 2 vols., Sao Paulo, Melhoramentos de Sao Paulo.

Vieira, D. T. (1971) 'Industrial development in Brazil' in Saunders 1971, 156–89.

Wang, L. H. and **Tan T. H.** (1981) 'Singapore' in Pacione 1981, 218–49.

Ward, R. G. (1965) *Land Use and Population in Fiji*, London, H.M.S.O.

Webster, C. C. and **Wilson, P. N.** (1966 and 1980) *Agriculture in the Tropics*, London, Longman.

Wei, Y. (1981) 'Land reform and ownerships' in Hsiung 1981, 144.

Weinand, H. C. (1973) 'Some spatial aspects of development in Nigeria', *J. of Developing Areas*, **7**, 247–63.

Whyte, R. O., (1967) *Milk Production in Developing Countries*, London, Faber and Faber.

Wickizer, V. D. (1958a) 'The plantation system in the development of tropical economies', *J. Farm Econ.*, Feb. 1958.

Wickizer, V. D. (1958b) 'Plantation crops in tropical agriculture', *Tropic. Agric.*, July 1958.

Wickremeratne, A. L. (1977) 'Planning and economic development' in De Silva 1977, 144–71.

Wilkie, R. (1971) *San Miguel: a Mexican collective ejido*, Stanford Calif., Stanford University Press.

Wilkinson, R. C. (1983) 'Migration in Lesotho: some comparative aspects with particular reference to the role of women', *Geog.*, **6** 208–24.

Williams, G. J. (1977) 'Zambia balances Zambezi power', *Geog, Mag.*, **49**, 10, July, 611–14.

Windstrand, C. (ed.) (1975) *Multinational Firms in Africa*.

Wisseman, C. L. and **Sweet, B. J.** (1961) 'The ecology of dengue' in May 1961, 15–44.

Wolf, E. R. and **Mintz, S. W.** (1957) 'Haciendas and plantations in middle America and the Antilles', *Social and Econ. Studies*, Sept. 1957.

Wolf-Phillips, L. (1979) 'Why Third World?', *Third World Quarterly*, **1**, No. 1, 105–116.

Wood, A. P. and **Smith, W.** (1984) 'Zambia up for grabs? The regionalisation of agricultural aid', *Area*, **16**, No. 1, 3–8.

World Bank, The International Bank for Reconstruction and Development (1953) *The Economic Development of Ceylon*, Baltimore, World Bank.

World Bank, The International Bank for Reconstruction and Development (1955) The Economic Development of Nigeria, Baltimore, World Bank.

World Bank, The International Bank for Reconstruction and Development (1974a) *Population Policies and Economic Development*, Baltimore and Washington, D.C., Johns Hopkins University Press.

World Bank, The International Bank for Reconstruction and Development (1974b) *Country Economy Report: Nigeria options for long-term development*, Washington, D.C., World Bank.

World Bank, The International Bank for Reconstruction and Development (1975) *Rural Electrification*, Washington, D.C., World Bank.

World Bank, The International Bank for Reconstruction and Development (1979a) *World Development Report 1979*, New York, London, Oxford University Press.

World Bank, The International Bank for Reconstruction and Development (1979b) *Family Planning Programs: an evaluation of experience*, World Bank, Staff Working Paper No. 345, July 1979, Washington D.C., World Bank.

World Bank, The International Bank for Reconstruction and Development (1980a) *World Bank Development Report 1980*, New York, London, Oxford University Press.

World Bank, The International Bank for Reconstruction and Development (1980b) *Alcohol Production from Biomass in the Developing Countries*, Washington D.C., World Bank.

World Bank, The International Bank for Reconstruction and Development (1980c) *Energy in the Developing Countries*, Washington D.C., World Bank.

World Bank, The International Bank for Reconstruction and Development (1981) *World Bank Development Report 1981*, New York, London, Oxford University Press.

World Bank, The International Bank for Reconstruction and Development (1982) *World Bank Development Report 1982*, New York, London, Oxford University Press.

World Bank, The International Bank for Reconstruction and Development (1983) *World Bank Development Report 1983*, New York, London, Oxford University Press.

World Bank, The International Bank for Reconstruction and Development (1984) *World Bank Development Report 1984*, New York, London, Oxford University Press.

Wu, Y. L. (1981) 'The Taiwan experience in economic development' in Hsiung 1891, 119–29.

Yang, T. M. (1970) *Socio-Economic Results of Land Reform in Taiwan*, Honolulu, Hawaii, East West Centre Publication.

Zambia Republic (1966) *First National Development Plan 1966–70*, Lusaka, Zambia, Office of National Development and Planning.

Zambia, Republic (1972) *Second National Development Plan 1972–76*, Lusaka, Zambia, Office of National Development and Planning.

Index